GARDNER WEBB COLLEGE LIBRARY

W9-AVS-570

SIXTIES GOING ON SEVENTIES

SIXTIES
GOING ON
SEVENTIES

by Nora Sayre

ARBOR HOUSE

NEW YORK

Copyright © 1973 by Nora Sayre

All rights reserved, including the right of reproduction in whole or in part in any form. Published in the United States by Arbor House Publishing Co., Inc., New York, and simultaneously in Canada through Musson Book Co.

Library of Congress Catalog Card No. 72-87048

ISBN 0-87795-054-7

"Marching," "Black Panthers and White Radicals" and "Shooting Revolution" were first published in *Esquire* Magazine. "The John Birch Society" is reprinted by permission of *The Village Voice*. Copyright by The Village Voice, Inc., 1971. *The Progressive, The New Statesman* and *London Magazine* are thanked for permission to reprint the material that first appeared in its pages.

Manufactured in the United States of America

E
839.4
S29
1973

#8.46

B+T

10/8/75

To my father with love

SPECIAL THANKS

I'VE SPENT part of the last ten years fighting with the editors of various New York magazines, battling over style, opinions expressed, even vocabulary. Many of the fights were due to the notion of national circulation—which hinges on the idea that readers outside New York are idiots, hence you have to write down to their level. There's also the fear of offending advertisers. And some are still insisting on fidelity to their house-style, or to their own brand of packaging. So I owe a special debt to the *New Statesman,* and I particularly want to thank Paul Johnson—who was the Editor from 1965 to 1970—for an editorial freedom which was very scarce in New York, especially in the mid-Sixties. Any writer is fortunate when an editor and a periodical really turn him loose; Mr. Johnson and the *Statesman* did that for me.

And I'm extremely grateful to Mary Sheridan and Morris Rubin, the editors of *The Progressive;* their concern for writers is unique.

Also, I think that many would wish to join me in good memories of the late Alice Glaser of *Esquire.*

I would like to thank Donald Fine and Evelyn Gendel of Arbor House for letting me shape this book the way I wanted.

CONTENTS

9

PART III: NEW YORK FOR NATIVES

PART IV: THEATER AND MOVIES

PART V: CONTRADICTING THE CONVENTIONS

INTRODUCTION: ON REPORTING

JULY 1972

MANY KEEP remarking that a year now seems like a decade, or a decade like a century. And it seems that there's an acute hunger for quite recent history. A reporter is constantly asked about the past: to pull out facts and events from '67, or to go all the way back to '65. Few seem nostalgic about the Sixties, but many want to examine the chapters or details: to see how they did (or didn't) play into the present. Here I'm reminded of the famous computer which was given "Out of sight, out of mind." The answer was: "Invisible idiot." Perhaps some of us fear becoming invisible idiots—if we don't continually try to understand what's been occurring around us in the last few years. I also heard about a computer which was praised for recognizing ambiguities; it could tell the difference between "Time flies like an arrow" and "Fruit flies like a banana." Some of us are still working on that one.

And how did the Sixties turn into the Seventies? Surely the period has to be seen in chunks and slabs: pieces of a perennial process which disintegrates, congeals, dilates, collapses, and expands. Almost any evaluation is tinged by the flux and sludge we live in. What's true on Tuesday may be false on Friday—particularly if it's a question of conviction or belief. So this is a book of changes. I can vouch for what I've witnessed or listened to: that's how it was on February 6. An English friend of mine, a professor of philosophy, objected to the idea of "temporary truth"; he said, "But I always heard that truth was eternal." I found myself replying: not where I come from. So I also think of this book as my unquiet gravy. Also, so much of what's described was all going on at once—all over the country. Many themes are related, and others contradict each other.

Since about 1967, being a reporter has especially meant recording contradictions. Sometimes, the task is being clear about confusion. Or, when a movement is still very fluid—like the early New Left— you have to be careful not to freeze it prematurely, must stress that it's still altering.

I began as a cultural or feature reporter; by 1968, I found that I was feeling rather like a war correspondent, a sensation I could never have foreseen. As so many subjects became political or racial, the arts and some of the most casual conversations mirrored these themes. (An editor said, "You can't even talk about sex without ending up with Vietnam!") I was also intrigued by the first activist comic books. The Green Lantern, rescuing a well-dressed citizen from the assaults of a seedy young man, was shocked to find that an abused tenant was punishing a slumlord, and had to reverse his loyalties. Briefly defending himself against the rebukes of his colleague, the Green Arrow, the Lantern protested, "I have a job . . . I do it!" The Arrow retorted, "Seems to me I've heard that line before . . . at the Nazi war trials!" The newly enlightened Lantern soon shot off to battle other oppressors of the poor: "In the time it takes to draw a single breath. . . . The span of a heartbeat . . . a man looks into his own soul and his life changes."

□

I've especially wanted to portray the (very) American experience of recent years: people of different backgrounds discovering what each other's experiences were. I think that was the nature of the Sixties. Of course it was mainly the middle class which was educated. But a number of rather comfortable persons began to learn about the experiences of the black and the poor; some GIs learned what the Vietnamese were living through; older people realized what the young were feeling. Many on the left learned from and about the right: what Wallace's constituency was experiencing. And those who liked Viceroys or Kents began to learn a lot about heroin. A spell of heightened sensitivity? Of course much of what was absorbed was fairly soon forgotten—as after a cram course during a reading period. But, for a few years, quite a bit of experience was shared—when many were exposed to one another.

As a reporter, I've passed through so many people's lives, have seen them surface in such new incarnations. . . . For example, at the beginning of '66, I spent some time down at the Free University of New York (now defunct), where I met a few of the Weatherpersons of the future. FU was one of the first counter-universities; it aimed to provide "a substantial socialist education of high quality" while "combating mindless activism" and indeed there were some very good courses, ranging from "Rebellions That Failed" to "Revolution In Latin America." The main problem I heard the faculty discuss was the students' lack of preparation; in the seminars I attended, some seemed to have a lot of difficulty in understanding the concept of "spontaneity," and they were flummoxed by questions like, "What would you do if you were Poland in 1945?" One woman, a sober, reserved graduate student who taught a course in nineteenth-century Russian literature, later reappeared as one of the Crazies in '68; naked, she offered a pig's head to the fans of Humphrey and Muskie. In December 1970 she was arrested (and later convicted) as one of a group who were trying to firebomb a bank in my street. It was the anniversary of the murder of Panther Fred Hampton; the city detectives, pretending to be drunks, closed in and invited the technicians to a party while they were arranging their containers of gas and benzine outside the bank. . . . Others I've known in denim turn up in neckties and office jobs. Former progressives drone away about their real estate, or the down payments on rugs. And some people without politics discovered that they had plenty; sometimes an event, like Attica or Chicago, revealed their own views to them; others made the discovery gradually, as their surroundings seeped in on them. Others recoiled from those they were working with, finding that they couldn't accept the final product—whether it was supposed to be revolution or hairspray, a new business venture or a commune. Some have switched their sex. Lots have disappeared. A few are dead.

Again, I think that the period showed that one has no right to be surprised by the reincarnations. But, because the Sixties demanded such definite commitments, the reversals are more conspicuous than they might have been at other times.

Amid the problems of the left and the momentum of the right, the shattering of cities, utopias gone awry, revolts of blacks, women, and the very young, I've been obsessed with voices—in choruses or solos. Since I put all this material together, I see that the voices restate a loathing of institutions: even more so than I had realized at the time. And these voices—mounting and muttering and shouting and whooping and accusing and even agreeing—the voices yield the period. They were also a reporter's reward.

□

It appeared that the Sixties ended in about October 1970. But the largely conservative and cautious times that followed have been no less violent, no more secure, despite the gargle that public figures put out. Although urban riots decreased, it looks as though even more individuals are being killed, whether in New York or Vietnam. And as I allow the images of the Seventies to pile up and grab me, they're not soothing. On the eve of Nixon's departure to China, I read that the presidential plane was carrying lots of blood and champagne. There was "an adequate supply" of Nixon's blood type—in the likelihood of attempted assassination—and cases of American champagne, for toasting his hosts at a reciprocal banquet. (We never heard the menu for that one.) That vast jet, pounding through the skies full of blood and bubbly, stays with me as a symbol for peacekeeping in '72. The hijacker who dropped his ransom money while bailing out seems like a creature of the period, and so do all those demonstrators who have learned to wear their lawyers' names inked on their wrists. Also another hijacker whose bombs turned out to be a few large lemons wrapped in tinfoil. The *New York Post* provided some other imagery which distills 1972: "Did Wallace Toe Move?" (a rumor that paralysis might be abating), and "Edith's

Signature Doesn't Sell Art": an auction at the Chelsea Hotel which failed to raise much cash for Edith Irving's paintings—two hours after she had gone to jail. I do collect headlines, especially from the *Times,* and have a wallful of good ones: "War and People Called Hazards to Civilization"; "Touch of Humor in Science Urged"; "President Says His Mind Is Open"; "VD Upsurge Tied to Pace of Living"; "Slumming in Harlem Is Passé."

When you enter the Harvard Bureau of Study Counsel, the first thing you see is a huge gleaming tin box on the water cooler, labeled SURVIVAL RATION CRACKERS. Its metal flanks are dense with printed instructions, such as how many crackers a "Normal Adult" should eat. The thing appears to be a piece of fallout-shelter equipment from the early Sixties. A member of the bureau said that it had appeared at a white elephant gift party of some seven years ago. She added that it was puzzling that the box had never been opened or thrown away.

□

For several years, I've been hearing that reporting is the new art form. While that's beguiling, I feel that not enough has been said about how difficult it has become—as compared to '65, when you simply called people up, made appointments and interviewed them, and went home confident of your research.

Today, you struggle first with the facts which you know and cannot print—since you don't want to send certain people to jail, or to be subpoenaed for your confidential sources. Second, many are afraid to talk to you, fearing that they'll be quoted accurately—just as much as they fear misquotation. (Valid fears.) Third, although you deplore the established media's distortions, and feel that part of your job is to contradict or correct the straight press, honesty often demands that you report some bad news from your own side. (As a Panther said about a white revolutionary who wrote a complimentary account of a black conference which had ended poorly: "Now that really *is* paternalism.") While you're anxious about playing into the hands of the right, or about handing ammunition to the opposition, there's no choice but to give the full picture; otherwise, you'd share the establishment's guilt for fact-bending. The movement has been self-critical of late, but in the late Sixties reporters were pressured to praise whatever they saw or heard—which was impossible. You might share the ideas while worrying about the way they were being applied, and that double bind had to be recorded. Throughout this book, I've retained the dilemmas that many radicals had in common: about the uses of force.

Meanwhile, your own skepticism grows hairier: aside from those who lie to you, or pretend to be what they're not (as in '69, when both the Progressive Labor Party and the FBI were pretending to be members of SDS), or tell you four-fifths of the truth (when you happen to know the other fifth—which alters everything), or need days or weeks of acquaintance before they can trust you, by which time you don't trust them—aside from all these bear traps, there's sometimes a real problem in knowing what's definitely true, what actually occurred. (I doubt that we'll ever know much about the death of George Jackson in San Quentin.) So I dislike describing events where I haven't been present. You also meet people who don't even believe what they themselves are saying: I've especially encountered that in California. And even friendly sources may be deliberately misleading: one young peace activist said apologetically: "When you're dealing with the press you sometimes *have* to lie— just in order to get covered. So you say that your organization has three thousand members—instead of only seventy-five."

I find it hard to forgive those among my fellow reporters who invent a single quote or character. Let them write fiction. The groggy public no longer knows what to believe, and I think that the mistrust will last for at least a lifetime. But fact is also a victim of disbelief: ugly news which happens to be true becomes easier to reject or ignore.

Reporters have had to reconsider the whole problem of interviewing: how strangers can best talk to strangers. In my first years of reporting, I mainly interviewed people about their work; from judges to magicians or sanitation workers or dancers, they simply described what they did, or how they came to their profession. Now, I'm more concerned with what they believe—sometimes because or in spite of their jobs or their work. Much of the focus of reporting has shifted from what people do to what they feel or think. Naturally, the old styles of interviewing are dead: either that formality which used to put the subject more at ease (and now makes him rigid with apprehension), or the aggressive techniques that forced some to talk when they didn't want to (and now mean being told to get lost.) And silence doesn't work as it once did—in the days when A. J. Liebling used to unnerve his interviewees by staring at them but asking almost nothing, so that they began to babble, revealing far more than they'd intended. (Now, they'd leave it up to vibes—or simply leave.) Charming your victim to shreds has been outdated too. Today, the most fruitful interviews may be rap sessions with several people at once: while they argue or agree with one another. Meanwhile, the reporter has to show what he or she believes —in fact, may have to be interviewed. Yet it's still important to be unobtrusive, since it makes one less of a threat. Throughout, the matter of persona is getting trickier: what the reporter personifies while grilling an executive behind his desk or a Friend of the Foetus or an army narc. These days, a reporter needs more characters, more spontaneous selves. Yet if these selves are false, others are going to sense it and take alarm.

These are a few of the problems which plagued reporters as the mid-Sixties receded. But what I especially like about reporting is that it requires you to lead so many different lives in the course of one year or a few weeks or months—as you sink yourself as deeply as possible into the subjects or the ideas that you're writing about. I've found the experience almost as intense while I'm covering the Birchers as when I write about radical politics. But of course there are perils here too. At (MORE)'s Counter Convention of the press in April '72, Paul Jacobs described working on a farm in order to write about farm workers. But he emphasized the limits of everyone's understanding—since any reporter can afford to walk away from the situation, or go back to his own city. None of us can be experts in realms outside our own: we can only listen to others, and then make others listen to them. Also at the (MORE) Convention, I. F. Stone said that a friend of his compared muckraking to "peeing on a boulder. If you keep it up for a thousand years, you'll be surprised at the impact you'll leave."

☐

"Now that you don't work anymore, what do you do all day long?": some of my former colleagues in publishing do regard writing as a copout—they feel it's not a career, like editing. A writer who works at home is imagined to be lying half-dressed on a sofa or a hammock, eating chocolate, watching *Spellbound* or *It Started with a Kiss* on the tube, while somebody vacuums or mows the lawn around the recumbent body, or occasionally untabs a beer for wrists too weak to wrench it open. People phoning at noon ask kindly, "Did I wake you?" But perhaps my favorite question—which often comes on top of two deadlines for different publications which were met on the same day, or during the week when three articles happen to be published at once—is, "Are you still trying to write?"

While the public reads fewer and fewer magazines, but still seems to like books, I'm not quite sure why writing has ceased to be a respectable trade. Perhaps it came to be regarded as self-indulgent during the Sixties, when contempt for the past was paramount. Those of us who wanted to preserve the present—especially to study it as it quickly became the past—still believe rather stubbornly in history. Hence I've left the pieces in this book largely as they were written; I've merely cut what everyone knows now, or added details which there wasn't room for. I've left out some subjects I cherished—such as patterns of homicide in Manhattan, New York hospitals, children and racism, magazine editing, William Buckley's campaign for mayor, Head Start, Vietnam summer, the Job Corps, research on dreams and delinquency, a prestrike moratorium at Columbia in '68, more on addicts, New York's parks, congressional campaigns, high school dropouts and many others—simply because I had too little space the first time around, and I can't write them over again from scratch. But these enriched the subsoil for many other topics. In the "Hindsights," I wished to be rather informal: to talk with the reader about the past, or to simply relay new information—before hurtling into the next crisis or set of concepts. Throughout, I decided to take the reader back and forth in time—not only out of respect to *Slaughterhouse-Five,* but because the last eight years were divided by Chicago '68, and I think it's good exercise to keep reliving what happened before and after that summer.

Also at (MORE)'s lunch, Tom Wicker, referring to the established press, spoke of the deadening forms and "molds" imposed on writers:

"But every story dictates the *way* it ought to be told." I have tried to follow that dictation: the demands that every subject made on the narration. Researching each piece, I also valued the incongruities and complexities which couldn't be squeezed into any generalization, and it seemed very important to include them too. So the forms vary—because they had to. When I wrote about my own city, my priority was simply to make New York sound like New York. Some of these pieces are short documentaries, designed to give the tang of the time and the events, or the moment when we were first aware of a person or a new notion. Those who hate cities and those who like them often responded rather violently. Again, the reader's own experiences were involved. Because no one ever feels neutral about New York.

In fact, I don't seem to have found much neutral territory—maybe it's all evaporated, or disappeared, as some like to vow that New York will. But here is a series of way stations where many kinds of people spent their time; some of them were trying to make a different sort of history than what they'd already known. And the efforts of '65 or '67 or '69 are a reminder of how long it takes to change anything in this country.

PART I:
EXERCISES IN
UPHEAVAL

DEMOCRATIC DEATH-IN: CHICAGO
August 1968

SUCH BLOOD: released from bruised and broken veins, from fore-heads, scalps, and mouths, from eyesockets, shattered wrists, and skulls. Broad bloodstreaks on the pavements showed where bodies had been dragged. We all bleed inwardly from the particular atrocities we witnessed. I saw seven policemen beating one girl—long after she had fallen; a row of sitting singers whose heads were cracked open by a charge of running cops; a photographer's camera smashed thoroughly into his eyes. Each day, scores staggered bleeding through the streets and parks, reeling or dropping, their faces glistening with vaseline—for Mace. Gas rinses your lungs with the lash of iodine and vinegar: your own breath burns your throat.

Outside the Hilton, a little old lady patted a rebel on the chest, murmuring, "Knock the socks off them." I said to her, "Funny how the police seem rather powerless right now." Then she and I were suddenly hurled against the wall when some hundred policemen seized their blue wooden barricades to ram the crowd (mainly onlookers and press) against the building with such force that many next to me, including the old lady, were thrust through the hotel's plate glass windows. ("For no reason that could be immediately determined": *New York Times.*) The police then spilled through the smashed window and clubbed both those who'd gone through it and some of the drinkers at the bar. Outside, people sobbed with pain as their ribs snapped from being crushed against each other. (I still have ribs, thanks to an unknown man's magnificently fat, soft back. All praise to Fat Power.) Soon, a line of stick-whipping cops swung in on us. Voiceless from gas, I feebly waved my credentials, and the warrior who was about to hit me said, "Oops, press." He let me limp into the hotel, where people were being pummelled into the red carpet, while free Pepsi was timidly offered on the sidelines.

Since delegates, newsmen, and spectators were thrashed along with the demonstrators, many learned what blacks have always known: that the democracy of savagery makes no distinctions—everyone's guilty for his mere presence or existence. The Chicago cops taught us that we were rubble with no protection or defense. In future, we can understand the ghettos' rage: without uncoiling any imagination. Later, as I watched the beatings and gassings from a second-floor McCarthy room, twelve policemen surged in, slammed down the windows, drew the curtains, and told us to turn away and watch the TV set, where Humphrey was starting to speak—"And that's an order." The Chicago cops, whose trucks advise "Reach Out and Grab the Greatest Summer Ever," rarely speak, not even when asked for street directions, and they direct traffic as though they were flogging invisible bodies. Some of their faces do look like rejects from the hog bristle trade which used to thrive in Chicago. A veteran Chicago reporter said that the cops are extremely afraid of the local blacks. Hence they took a special revenge on the August marchers, primarily because the police failed to subdue the ghetto's April riots after Martin Luther King was killed. Yet even Humphrey has defended them—"I was targeted by an assassination team and supposedly to be taken care of. . . . We had intelligence information from the . . . police department and the FBI of planned assassination"—and a recent poll suggests that 71.4 percent of queried citizens thought the actions of the Chicago police were "justified."

Thus, it's difficult to determine what the protest accomplished. True, the world, the press, and all free minds throbbed with a communal concussion. But, as James Reston noted, the young, the poor, the black, and the intelligent "have the fewest votes," and the demonstrations were probably deplored by the voting majority. Still, "voting with bodies" wasn't bootless. Tom Hayden wrote, "We are coming to Chicago to vomit on 'the politics of joy'"—indeed they did, and the image was distilled by a stinkbomb at the Hilton, which smelled as though hundreds of gorges had risen. Rennie Davis said that the motto would be: "There can be no peace in the U.S. until there is peace in Vietnam"—and there won't be. At a Panther rally, young white revolutionaries vowed "to join the blacks—by putting ourselves in the same grists that blacks are in. We'll take the same risks. Cops who beat on them must beat on us." And perhaps a new collaboration is beginning—even though few whites seem able to realize that they can never fully share the black experience. A black militant replied, "The strongest weapon we have is all of us. United black-white opposition." It looked as though some new militants were created; some liberals became radicals; some dissenters began to talk about revolution. But the most moral point came from Dick Gregory: "Had there been a bunch of young people who challenged Hitler the way you challenged Mayor Daley, there might be a *whole* lot of Jews alive today."

After that statement, one's pride in the throng kept dilating. Many have observed that large groups often behave like the worst persons among them. But I felt that the Chicago crowd reflected its best members—who were also the majority. The aims are so simple: peace, liberation for blacks, an America where property is less valuable than human life. These goals must be constantly repeated, because the tactics confuse older—often sympathetic—people. (A seasoned, old-style liberal reporter, watching the mayhem from the Hilton, asked me in real bewilderment, "What do those people want?") But the movement seethes with such contradictions about method and leadership that, when Humphrey said it was "programmed," one only wished that he were right.

A few leaders were lavishly irresponsible: they excited the most naive—teen-agers and hippies—who didn't know that the mild term "personal risk" could mean getting killed or maimed. These gentle waifs, plus a few glittering hysterics, usually rushed to the front; at moments, one feared they would be used as fodder. Two young brothers—both tripping on acid and eager to tell me how their "really hip mother" had given them a hookah for Christmas, inscribed as "a *joint* present! Haw!"—were ecstatic when they misheard directions which came over the mike to go to the Limits Garage—to lend support to the striking black bus drivers. "He says we should *go the limits!*" one boy cried. Thinking that their heads were more vulnerable than some, I dragged them off to see Pigasus, the pig who was running for president on a platform of garbage. But they were ideal fodder.

SDS and the Mobilization Committee had had some disagreements about tactics before the convention. SDS—which decided that "mass confrontations don't effect constituencies"—didn't actually demonstrate; instead, it worked to organize and protect the marchers. One SDSer said, "We don't believe that a bop on the head is more educative than a pamphlet." But some MOBE workers generated a tension that split bones instead of hairs. Different leaders springing to the microphones instructed the crowd to be cool, to get hot, that they were helpless, that they were powerful, to go home, to gather, to disperse into small groups, to mass for a huge nonviolent march—in which other speakers warned that they'd be trapped. (And they were.) Many marchers were too inexperienced to choose clearly. Despite MOBE's love of spontaneity, the need for organization was as desperate as the ache for peace.

You come lurching out of these vast fleshpacks with a reeking dilemma about violence—which is now a suitcase word for assassinations, student protests, ghetto revolts, mugging, and nut crimes. For the right, these are indistinguishable. For some members of SDS, violence means wrecking Selective Service files or bombing a draft board—at night, when there's no one there to be hurt. One said, "We're *not* nonviolent; we'd like to take over the city. But we can't. So we'll use long-range political organization. We're ready to use force to achieve a political end. The question is whether it *does* achieve that end?" For others, "Revolution is a form of self-defense . . . since our society is already founded on force."

Meanwhile, for one who has never accepted violence and has

always believed in working through the political process, Dick Gregory's words kept echoing, underlining the realization that the threat of black violence has become a useful tool for black people. (A Watts militant told me: "Perhaps the *threat* of violence is even more important than violence itself.") And of course the cold war mentality has educated all of us about the international use of threats. Yet how do you draw a dotted line between street fights and killing, between "good" and "bad" violence? Any brand of violence is contagious, as this land of assassination knows. Moreover, since madness now seems to be the country's most pungent odor, more people may become violent merely to be heard: "Just to be taken seriously," as one calm man said. Many of us are wrestling with evaluations of the fact of force. If violence in the U.S. could result in peace in Vietnam, then I would support it—with a ravaging disgust at a society which forces anyone to make such a choice. I haven't the physical courage to fight in the streets, but in Chicago I had more and more respect for those who did. A white Chicago clergyman said he felt the same. He added that the church hadn't yet decided its own position: "Listen, we've been holding seminars on violence *ourselves*. Because we don't know what to say to our parishioners about it—we no longer feel able to tell them that they must be nonviolent. Because we know that no social change has ever occurred without violence." But the very new revolutionaries will never remold America on their own. And, at moments, some sound like the general who said he had to destroy a Vietnamese village in order to save it. But perhaps their momentary power could be a partial fuel for change—if a right-wing renaissance doesn't stifle us all. *That* possibility hums in every wire of the mind. Chicago taught us what law and order can mean. After all, these protestors were not violent. The streets were dangerous because of the police.

The images of Chicago come crowding in thicker now. The bravery of TV crews at night: their clumsy trucks lumber after the crowd that the cops have driven behind a screen of trees; their floodlights offer a little—but not much—protection. Two vast black men in Levi's, dancing lightly on their sneakered toes, almost waltzing in anticipation, who tell me: "The brothers are coming. It's going to be beautiful." But it doesn't happen—later that night, I see them both in different (daytime) clothes. Jean Genet's sweet pink smile in a dimpling Santa Claus face, as he tells the crowd that they're "very pretty and beautiful," but—pointing at the nearby policemen—"The ones I love most are those with the blue helmets who dress unconventionally also." Allen Ginsberg omming like a death rattle, his voice ravaged by the days of Hindu chants and gas. William Burroughs' incredibly white face beneath a gray fedora; although some students urge him not to march out front, he says that he and Genet must keep their promise to do so. The two rather sadly smell some bunches of flowers that were given them. A young man riding the statue of General John Logan, the Civil War hero, until the police drag him down and fracture his arm. At four and five o'clock each morning, as the hotel clerk gives me the key to my room, he cackles, "Hah! We really give it to them didn't we! Fix them dirty hippies! Wait until tomorrow!" An ice cream truck, weaving slowly through a frightened crowd, is cheered, and the driver's fingers split in the forked peace sign. Old reporters frozen on the sidewalks, goggling in disbelief at the clubbing, saying things like, "But this is *America!* This can't be hap—"

As the press stands ringed by National Guardsmen, an NBC cameraman points out that those who are supposed to be protecting us are aiming their rifles right at us and at the Hilton. One promptly drops his weapon. *"Jesus,* that's dangerous, he's *very* green." Before the convention, *Newsweek* said that Chicago's manhole covers were sealed up with tar, so that no one could hide beneath them. The only story that makes people smile: when some newsmen were picking up their credentials, they saw an old man in a baseball cap shouting, "But you *must* have press tags for me, I'm Walter Winchell! I'm Walter Winchell!" As a woman, wandering into the crowds each day, I'm nearly always joined by a couple of men: priests or blacks, students or photographers. One said, "I'm scared stiff, but would you like a little *psychological* protection?" I run whenever I want to, and usually find my bodyguards on my heels. With two doctors, I walk five blocks ahead of the group that Dick Gregory is leading to the Amphitheatre; we see the tank with the machine gun that awaits them. We turn back to tell them, discovering that the empty alleys —where we'd planned to disappear if necessary— are now crammed with police and Guardsmen. None who want to disperse will get away. One of the wounded says, "Now we know how the Vietnamese

must feel—we never knew we'd end by fighting our own people."
Peter and Mary sing "If I Had a Hammer," and a scowling
Chicagoan says, "They have the filthiest mouths." Angry cars in a
traffic jam honk like panic—then finally pound their horns to the
rhythm of "Hell-No, We-Won't-Go." Even an ice cream mixer in a
drugstore sounds like a siren. When the chairman of the New
Hampshire delegation, who was arrested, jailed, and accused of
biting a policeman, says on TV, "I swear that I have never bitten
anyone," a gathering of students whoops at the level to which the
convention has fallen. . . .

At LBJ's antibirthday party, which Ed Sanders of the Fugs said
was mainly inspired by Lewis Carroll, there was music by the Con-
quering Worm and the Holocaust. Dick Gregory mused about the
Prague citizens who had been pasting swastikas on the Russian tanks:
"Just you try that *here*." He added, "Can you believe, this country
is so insane that LBJ don't trust *you?*" And, "If you knew Daley's
record down through the years, you'd know that this week he is on
his best behavior." Finally, "If democracy is as good as we tell
you it is, why the hell do we have to go all over this world, ramming
it down people's throats with a gun." The audience cheered and
cheered when he read them part of the Declaration of Independence
—"Whenever black folks burn up and sack a town, I read this"—
concluding with, ". . . whenever any Form of Government becomes
destructive of these ends, it is the Right of the People to alter or
abolish it . . ."

Mixed media: leaving the gassy streets again, to watch from the
Hilton's twenty-third floor: Humphrey's voice chattering from the
haunted fish tank in the background: ". . . it is the special genius of
the Democratic party that it welcomes change . . ." Below, the police
slice savagely into the crowd, while, beside me, a man with a walkie-
talkie warns the crowd that fifty National Guard jeeps are arriving.
My notes are little newsreels: "bayonets fixed now . . . doctors try
to reach wounded . . . cops won't let them. . . . New marchers coming
. . . but they're trapped." *Walkie-talkie:* "You're about to be gassed
from the left." *Humphrey:* "We are and we must be one nation,
united by liberty and justice for all. . . ." *Crowd in Street:* "Pigs!
Pigs! Pigs! *Oink! Oink! Oink!*" (The frantic chorus bursts when
anyone's arrested.) McCarthy-workers to Humphrey delegates in

lobby, on *walkie-talkie:* "*You* killed the party! *You* killed the party!" Humphrey asks the young "to join us . . . Never were you needed so much . . ." The police are smashing heads more swiftly now. The crowd sings, "Where have all the flowers gone?" More have fallen who don't get up. Others shout, "Daley Sucks! Hump the Hump!" *Walkie-talkie:* "Look, I don't care if the Guard *has* brought bazookas inside the Hilton. They won't use them—it's a *very* impractical weapon for a hotel lobby. See, they need a long firing range, or they'll blow up everyone *behind* them." *Crowd:* "Peace . . . Now . . . Peace . . . Now." *Humphrey:* "I do not intend to appeal to frustration, but rather to your faith."

It all blows the mind farther than any discothèque hinged for destruction. Bombarded senses don't make succulent sense. Cosmic irony tinges many details; earlier, David Dellinger was interviewed by a TV network: as he said that technology was "looting the universe," both camera and sound kept breaking down. "Would you mind repeating that?" "Technology is . . ." "Oh dear. This isn't working again."

It's reported that the Hilton management is very angry because sheets were torn up to make bandages in the McCarthy headquarters.

Back in the street again. Speakers ask those who support them to blink lamps in the hotel's windows: the Hilton prickles with blurts of light. Rolls of toilet paper fall unwinding from above. The crowd's character has changed in five days: the hippies with flutes and recorders and finger cymbals have been joined by more conscious radicals, students, clergymen, numerous older people, girls with long earrings labeled EUGENE swinging from their pearly lobes, many costumes of propriety, plus all the bandaged heads. Many keep repeating that they used to be middle class, before they left the system. And the innocents are still there. Tête-à-tête: "We pool our money and buy one of those small independent islands in the Pacific, and have our own government." Sad reply: "But then won't Washington bomb us?" Tourists of violence prowl past, loving the nerve-splitting agony. The crowd shouts "Shaft the draft!" A few dance before the National Guard. "PEACE." A CBS man says that the police are outraged by the Guard's presence—they say it's hurt their pride. Crowd: "*Sieg heil! Sieg heil!*" Then they sing, "This land is made for you and me."

Hindsight: I spent my first evening home from Chicago in the Manhattan Criminal Court. My apartment had been broken into a few hours before I returned. But a neighbor called the cops and they found a young man with my typewriter in his hand. He was a pusher who had jumped bail several times, though he had no record as an addict. It's awkward meeting your own burglar—we traded defensive stares in court—but I didn't have to press charges, only to say that he wasn't an old friend who was free to remove my lock and my Smith-Corona.

Then the cops arrested my typewriter. They said they'd have to keep it for a couple of months as evidence for the trial. I had a ferocious deadline, it was Labor Day weekend, and it would be almost impossible to borrow anyone's machine. So I threw a fit, purposely blowing all the cool I'd tried to maintain in Chicago. I punished the New York cops as though they were responsible for the whole convention, insulting them as brutally as possible, while the very nice officer who'd nabbed the burglar pleaded with the D.A. to return "the tools of her trade—why, this is like taking a doctor's bag, or a taxi-driver's cab!" So I stopped hating all policemen, even though I didn't get the typer.

It did seem healthy that Chicago had served to shock so many spectators about the nature of their own country. But, like lots of others, I didn't sleep for weeks afterwards. I kept having documentaries instead of dreams. Each night was full of the same footage: people bleeding and weeping and running.

I kept playing Phil Ochs' song from '66, "Miranda." There was a verse which seemed to express the mounting lunacies around us:

> The sunburned skin is peeling
> On the doctors who are healing
> And the license-plates are laughing on the cars . . .

In a jolly voice, Ochs sang that "the dice of death are calling," and "the Howard Johnson food is made of fear." The rickytick accompaniment grows gayer: "The arguments are clashing/While commercial planes are crashing,/And the music of the evening is so sweet . . ."

Now, in '72, the sense-memories are just as alive as ever—the terrible creak of breaking glass as bodies burst through it, or the thick rim of the china cupful of bourbon which was offered as an antidote to gas—but some of the emotions seem a dozen years ago. Fright of course is easily relived. But that sense of confidence which came out of Chicago—that momentary hope that a number of people could possibly begin to change their society—feels remote. In '68, it would have seemed incredible that some could flee to Vermont to construct a life style that would take all their time: hours to bake the perfect loaf of health bread, days to build a bed, weeks to dig a well.

By the summer of '71, I'd had wailing calls from all over New England about carrots that didn't come up, or how sick a cow had become: the old comedy of intensely urban people expecting that farming would be easy. And some couples used rural settings to escape the whole issue of feminism: through a life which required *both* sexes to be home-makers all day long. But, in Chicago, many had seemed prepared to work for change. . . .

In '72, although we saw many young people working for McGovern, few of his supporters whom I knew were the radicals of the late Sixties. Many of those who were proud of revealing the hypocrisies of the Chicago convention have since been unable to back any candidate. The scar of Chicago may be cynicism, along with the curious exhilaration of a grim memory: indeed the ugliness of national power was exposed, and its institutions could never quite claim purity again. Of course others responded with the determination to strengthen those institutions, in hopes that those who marched in Chicago couldn't ever act so freely or so wildly in the future. The fact that they were reflecting their own society was incomprehensible to some—whose understanding will probably continue to diminish.

MARCHING
November 1969

FEAR CAN start in the scalp, which may sweat at the first soft splat of gas grenades, at the mere sight of nightsticks raised. The head may be suddenly wet before the knees or wrists dissolve, and the feet move. It's a reflex for many—since Chicago, marching or voting with bodies will never be quite the same: that old confidence in one's rights was punctured along with some lungs and kidneys and snapped ribs on Michigan Avenue. The fear can be unjustified, of course: in the dustups after the November 15 Moratorium in Washington the police were indeed controlled; marchers were gassed only for deciding to be in a certain place at a particular time: risk was choice. Still, while jittering with cold or apprehension, the memory of other demonstrations made one marvel at how easy it all used to be: before the symbols congealed, when the styles of conviction were unperilous. Free, in fact.

Today, a reporter needs several bodies at once—perhaps dozens— to experience and register the varieties within one fleshpack. You hardly know what to do with your only body, since it becomes a participant, a witness, a recording device, a piece of crowd: a range of schizophrenia is required.

Demonstrations have changed, both in style and purpose. It's no longer frivolous to weigh the behavior of protestors; if they act stupidly, the press and the opposition can ridicule their beliefs. Hence it's ironic that the (magnificent) character of the November mass left it curiously vulnerable afterward. The *Washington Post* described the event as an amiable binge for "youth culture": " a happening at which nothing happened." Many who scorn marches simply as a form of expression were especially caustic—"all those nice little people with candles"—as well as disgusted with those who were aggressive at Dupont Circle and at the Department of Justice. Now, if marchers are orderly, they're derided. And peacefulness in the cause of peace is patronized.

Of course, no single protest accomplishes its purpose; it's the accumulation of demonstrations that can finally slam a point home. Some think that the November Moratorium may be almost the last of the big tranquil marches. Having marched for ten years, I have fresh doubts about demos, yet see no alternative to intensifying them.

Aldermaston, Easter 1959: streaming in a vast, jubilant throng into Trafalgar Square, fighting with a brilliant ten-year-old boy (now a radical student) about the future of the Labour party, heaving with reluctant laughter at his jokes while struggling to maintain the dignity essential to one of eight Americans walking behind the U.S. sign. There were hoots from some Empire Loyalists, while the pigeons wheeled obligingly around Nelson, and everyone gleefully hailed their friends. In London, there are no strangers: all who tangle with politics or the arts are ghoulishly well acquainted, to the extent that one luminary groaned, "Oh God, isn't there *any*one on this march whom I don't know?" But the exhilaration was unique: for many, it was the first sense of strength in numbers. The initial intention was to force the Labour party to stop dithering about disarmament: it was an appeal to politicians from their own constituents. Naturally, it was also an attempt to put the squeeze on the Tory government. Before long, as a former CND activist recalls, "We were trumpeting to everyone who would listen—to the U.S. too—to try to educate them about a new horror." The movement very nearly converted the Labour party to unilateral nuclear disarmament, but Hugh Gaitskill finally fought it off. In the early Sixties, CND was shattered from within, and there's still a bomb to ban. However, CND alumnae feel that they helped to create the atmosphere of opinion which made the Test Ban Treaty possible: the revulsion at nuclear weapons which soon swam through so many bloodstreams, and could be no more easily shed than one's own bones.

After the tidal crowds from Aldermaston, it was odd to stroll slowly within the mild little cluster which picketed the White House on Easter 1960. While Ike played golf in Georgia, some of us carried signs protesting research on nerve gas and germ warfare (especially pneumonic plague), while students from Amherst, Williams, Trinity, and Wesleyan marched to support black sit-ins at southern lunch counters. A small unit called the Peacemakers vowed not to pay taxes for any kind of war, and one man hoisted a huge placard opposing Celestial Annexation. It was all very balmy and leafy, passive and pastoral—also very amusing for spectators. I shoved a cop's hat off with my clumsy sign, and we both apologized eagerly. I came away feeling that demonstrations were useless in this country: the effort was put down as a whimsical eccentricity; the impact was nil.

Before the March in Washington in 1963, the press was almost as alarmist as it was before the November Moratorium. (It's worth remembering that JFK didn't want the March, although he finally played at being a benefactor.) Editorials promised that "tomorrow may be a day of tragedy." A helpful friend said, "Holy shithead, you'll all be immolated. Be sure to crawl out quickly when the bus begins to burn." Buying Sara Lee pecan rings and hard cheese the night before (we'd been warned against liquids and runny foods), I did quail at the ravenish croaks from carking liberals. However, on CORE's bus, morale was restored by a *Newsweek* cover story on the March, which was dated September 2. It was read aloud on August 28th by those who hadn't yet marched. *Newsweek's* deadline crunched the event into the past tense: "Who were the marchers?" "Certainly, the ingredients of trouble were there . . ." Whoops and howls restored our queasy confidence.

Perhaps it was the only demonstration that ever made a lot of people happy—which was certainly its only accomplishment. (A derisive observer said, "It proved Negroes' ability to stand quietly and patiently on street corners, which I've known about for several hundred years.") How many remember that it was a march "for jobs and freedom?" (For something, not against—was that a mistake?) One black man, repeatedly jailed in Danville, Virginia, told me, "This isn't a protest. It's to show the numbers who agree about one thing. Also a ceremony of a sort. And—as the newspapers *don't* report—it's also a memorial for Medgar Evers and two others who were murdered."

Afterward, most of the press praised the acute degree of dignity and cheer as though it were a new brand of fudge ripple ice cream: sweet, soft, digestible—but hardly part of anyone's regular diet. (However, the fish-fry, *Green Pastures* theme stressed by many papers was a parody of logic: we'd been told to bring our lunches, and of course we sat upon the grass.) All that docility seems extra-ordinary from this distance, considering the mire and fury at Ole Miss in the fall of '62, plus the infinite cattle prods and dogs already used on nonviolent marchers in the South, and the punctual beatings and gassings (of blacks) which fired far less indignation than the clubbings (of whites) in Chicago '68. The line that still echoed from Ole Miss was a student's remark, widely quoted in the press, about James Meredith: "I'm a broad-minded individual, but he just isn't a good nigger."

Meanwhile, most northerners still refused to realize that their territory was as ugly as the South, in terms of that fingertip phrase of '63, "the racial problem." Only four I knew from New York went to Washington. The liberal response was remote, and marching wasn't yet fashionable. Some shrugged; whose problem? Others thought it hilarious. Others analyzed at length the recent self-discovery of prejudice (as it was called), for psychological reasons: an early spanking by a black maid, being beaten up on the way to school at the age of eight. Others jumped hard on culture: why was there no Negro Shakespeare, no black Mozart? But most hastily added that of course the educated Negro is just like anyone else. . . . A British visitor asked for a comparison between the class system in England and racism in America. I found myself saying, you don't kill people to keep them out of Eton. . . . Returning on the train from Washington, someone said, "It is *the* moral issue of this country." How simple that seems now—when a host of priorities have seized so many by the throat. And, in the months that followed, the March itself appeared as a betrayal: a substitute for any action at all.

In the next few years, we marched in Harlem and elsewhere to reinforce those who were marching in the South, went on sympathy marches for civil rights workers who were killed, or children bombed in churches, while the antiwar marches began. All those I took part in were calm and deeply serious: the style was still that of 1963, and the marchers were dressed for the office. However, a new angry response was erupting. Early in 1965, as a silent line of high school students and clergymen trickled down Lexington Avenue, carrying signs that merely read "Negotiate," I heard two bald men—clearly strangers—stirring themselves into frenzies on the curb. "If *I* had a boy in that group," one said, *"I'd* break his jaw for him, *I'd* make him crawl—" "So would I. I'd stop his allowance, I'd take his car . . ." And so on. They agreed that their sons would have to enlist—immediately. Finally, one growled, "Got any kids?" "No," snarled the other. "Huh. Neither have I." Suddenly awkward, they separated: two neat, embarrassed men, perhaps startled by their own ferocity as they waited for the traffic lights to change.

Styles of dissent had altered lavishly by April 15, 1967. Central Park blossomed with a giant be-in, a merry day for exchanging daffodils and pot and buttons saying "Puppies For Peace," parading new Day-glo ponchos and glistening jumpsuits, necking in the streets, body paint, rock bands, and chanting "Flow-er Pow-er." A counter-demonstrator's sign read, "Dr. Spock Smokes Bananas." Although the smoke from burning draft cards curled up through wet spring leaves, the big papier-mâché yellow submarine float was a more valid image for the day. A new arrival said, "There are sure to be some groovy people here, and I want to make the scene." I was angry at much of the crowd for being so blithe and careless: many seemed to have forgotten that Martin Luther King was waiting to speak outside the UN: to declare that the war was as destructive to the ghetto as to the Vietnamese. The idea was thought dreadfully controversial: the press rebuked him for daring to connect the war with poverty at home. However, editorials soon began to echo his convictions, tinged with the smugness of their own originality. But that April march was a fun fest: as on some other occasions, the participants disregarded the purpose of the demonstration, and the style contradicted the intentions.

A month later, an enormous pro-war parade—organized by a captain in the New York Fire Department, which contributed some engines—gathered in my street in the East Nineties for eight uproarious hours. PEACE was a large, loose-bellied doll, footless from being dragged behind the jeep to which it was tied: the cross-eyed face was painted to look insane. A young boy dressed as Uncle Sam nervously fingered his decomposing cotton beard as he slumped in the jeep's front seat. Signs read, "Eradicate RED CANCER," "Bong the Cong," "Death to Pink Finks." Two parachutists decked with flags landed in Central Park, and were arrested (it's illegal to jump on New York). Later, a spectator was beaten, tarred, and feathered by thirty marchers simply because of his sandals and long hair. The crowd alternated funeral dirges with Broadway tunes, yelling and stamping in and out of the battered Third Avenue bars, banging beer cans into the gutters. Less silent than in Nixon's dreams, they also seemed far more confident than many flights of doves.

Soon, desperation about the war exploded into more desperate shapes of protest. By late '67, the demonstrations began to resemble boils breaking out all over one vast sickened body. Wildness replaced the serene or celebratory styles: the word was "force," not yet "violence." At the Pentagon, many in the front ranks seemed to have brought their own very private neuroses to mingle with their loathing of the war. That was a far more bitter, much older crowd than the one at the November Moratorium. Heading for the Pentagon, many constantly disobeyed their own leaders, surging ahead when asked to wait for traffic. Screaming "Mother-fuckers!" at the stationary soldiers, some even pressed their chests close to the bayonets—as though on a dare—while others peed on the Pentagon. (Beforehand, when a human chain around the Pentagon was planned, some said that they were going to masturbate—but I couldn't see how, not if everyone was holding hands.) Many mouths were ringed with the white crusts of dried spit. Late in the afternoon, I became a marshal, one arm trussed up in baby-blue satin—the color that one now hideously associates with the Chicago police. The main assignment was to get slabs of the crowd along the rope ringing the Pentagon to sit down, so that those who wanted to walk across it and be arrested could make that choice, without forcing others to be shoved forward by the bodies behind them. Now and then, I was able to persuade about thirty to crouch down together; then one small man would leap to his feet, yelling "Only chickens sit, only chickens shit!" and the group would spring up again. So many appeared to feel that their personal courage was being tested or insulted. While some aspects of the grotesque were appropriate, those of us who didn't (quite?) believe in rioting for peace were slightly depressed. And many of us were losing faith in demos: it seemed as though the participants merely discharged their own energies and then felt virtuous. While the war went on.

By early '68, many were wrestling with notions of violence, kindled by the response to black revolts, plus the awareness that profound social change rarely occurs without violence. But the word "revolution" still sounded silly in Manhattan, especially tripping off the lips of editors and sociologists. Hence it was staggering to be in Paris in late May where, at the doors of the Odéon, students searched all purses and satchels for bombs, and then kissed those who carried none. (Among the wall posters, my favorite was *Attention! Attention! Les oreilles ont des murs.*) The elation of an uprising that nearly worked ebbed swiftly. Most radicals knew that the Communists certainly didn't want a revolution, and agreed that they themselves could achieve nothing without a party of their own. In early June, I joined a tremendous *manifestation* which strode from Montparnasse to the Gare d'Austerlitz. Those who firmly chanted, *"Ce n'est qu'un début/Continuons le combat!"* would then turn aside to explain that they knew they had lost, but that they must still turn out to show that their beliefs were as unshakable as ever, and that de Gaulle's claim to restored national unity was a lie. Workers and students greeted each other affectionately in the streets. Tricolors were torn in thirds to make red flags. Many praised Cohn-Bendit for his instructions on how to restrain violence, how to preserve lives. Then they would shout with the same sturdiness, *"Nous sommes plus en plus enragés!"* and *"Elections-trahison!"* Between slogans, they remained equally positive, practical, and sad: "It's all over now, we've had it—*Ce n'est qu'un début . . ."* That night, someone said that Russia would hate to see France go Communist, because the national frivolity and sensuality would set such a bad example for other Communist countries.

October 15, 1969: PEACE drifting down Manhattan avenues: sky writing. Once again, thousands used their bodies because others hadn't used their heads. During the large Wall Street rallies, a publisher said, "Businessmen used to pick up phones and punch out ticker tape when they wanted something done. Now they also take to the streets. . . . Maybe business isn't so big anymore in decision making. Perhaps it's become a submanagement of the new state management within the Department of Defense." No generation gap: at a high school students' rally, teen-age speakers urged seniors threatened with the draft to "talk to your parents—tell them to work legally against your going. Try to educate them if they don't yet understand." The participation of middle-class and professional people—many of whom had never demonstrated before—displeased some of the Left. There were jealous snorts about "co-optation," even an unwillingness to share a condemnation of the war. Jerry Rubin later complained in Washington, "It's like peace is becoming respectable." In the age of paradox, even the antiwar movement can lament its own success. Rubin himself came on like a camp counselor, leading chants, toasting the marshmallows of his thought. It seemed that many had bypassed him.

By November 1969, it was conspicuous that feelings against the war had flared in three distinct stages. In 1965, there was the response to the suffering of Vietnamese civilians, women or children maimed or dead. In 1967, Dr. King unleashed the consciousness of what the war was inflicting on the ghetto: suffering at home. By early 1969, there was a fresh burst of outrage at the killing of soldiers on both sides—such sympathy for the U.S. military had hardly existed before. When protesters in Washington walked across Arlington Memorial

Bridge, wearing placards with the names of the dead, it was an attempt to restore each demolished man's individuality—to show that casualties were creatures, not mere numbers. There was almost an atmosphere of resurrection: an effort to revive particular persons. The names came with all the diversity of the continent: Glenn Nobuyki Nichizaura, Jimmy Lee Cook, Manuel G. Yberra, Arie Terry. Walking alone and far apart stressed the singleness of the dead, their isolation. Candles glimmered through cupped hands as in the seventeenth-century paintings of Georges de la Tour; shadowed faces were lit from below. Some looked rather haunted, as though briefly possessed by those whom they symbolized. Warren O. Kneppery. Balades David Zalada. Roy Smith. Perfecto M. Lorez. Albert Glanton. As Murray Kempton said, many of the Wasp names probably belonged to blacks: the descendents of slaves who were given their owners names. Mine was Ronald Powers. Wearing the name made one wonder what he was like, what he looked forward to. Passing the White House at night, power has never seemed so blinding: for "security," the lawn floodlights were reversed so that the building was almost unseeable—it was hard to imagine that it was actually there. Dropping the names into the coffins to the recurrent drumroll, watching the steady line of candles still approaching: that was as repetitive as death itself.

Of course, some of the young men marching were also making a plea for their own lives. Although many cheered up later—"See you at the big cock" (the new name for the Washington Monument)—some appeared as bleak as the candles which had been extinguished by the wind.

Trust is so lacerated and suspicion is so lavish that, if there had been rain throughout the Moratorium, it would have been tempting to deduce that Nixon had seeded the clouds. (During one downpour, a man in a drugstore said, "He's taking care of those dirty hippies out there." God or the President?) But, by asserting that violence would occur, the administration tried to frighten away some of the potential demonstrators, and also issued an invitation to possible psychotics.

During the Chicago convention, two sixteen-year-old waifs and I foolishly accepted a lift from a crew-cut stranger, a professional ballplayer from Florida. (There was a bus strike and a taxi shortage, hence many were offering rides.) Ignoring the boys' street directions, he drove us further and further into the deserted outskirts of the city, and then stopped speaking to us altogether. At that point, we noticed his stunning resemblance to Richard Speck, the mass murderer. We asked to get out, but he wouldn't stop or reply. Really alarmed by his silence, the boys asked him how long he'd been in the movement. "I'm not in any movement," he hissed, "I'm here for the action, for kicks, like anyone else." We spilled from the car at the next red light. "Man!" said one boy. "That was really feeling like croaksville."

At any rate, there could have been a few like him in the herd that played games around Dupont Circle and the South Vietnamese Embassy in Washington. Also, the crowd may have contained some provocateurs, fulfilling prophecies for Agnew. Many seemed propelled just by curiosity. Others kept losing their affinity groups. But it was the only truly provocative group I've ever seen. Just as those in the front ranks stood nose-to-nose with the police, a man offered some of us poppers from a paper bag: "You want some courage?" Afterward, some were brave enough to trash the windows of parked cars or small shops. Later, two cackling Weatherwomen described how the wicked pigs had been gassing innocents. They failed to arouse a resentful audience of over a thousand marchers. There was also a man who claimed to be a Panther from the New York chapter. I doubted it, because I knew that group fairly well at the time, and because he got a lot of the Panthers' ideology and slogans wrong. But he was urging his hearers to "bring it all down tomorrow."

Despite the debates about violence that are continuing among militants, many agree that November 15th was the wrong time for it. Then, the most pungent way to defy the administration was to be peaceful. But some Weathermen hadn't combed out the difference between thrills and results. The issues got lost. If you kick a cop and he kicks back, you're a hero and he's a villain. Many black people know it's not that simple. In October, Fred Hampton, the chairman of the Illinois Panther party (who was killed by police in December), called the Weathermen "anarchistic, adventuristic, chauvinistic, masochistic, and Custeristic," adding, "We don't dig confrontations that lead people into struggles they're not ready for."*

Obviously, no street event is worth an ounce of the persistent long-

---

* As Tom Hayden later wrote in *Trial,* "The Weathermen believed in 'war,' chose an arbitrary date, and then just began it. But most young people could not relate to scheduling a riot . . . mainly because it was not a spontaneous reaction to an immediate situation." (Holt, Rinehart and Winston, 1970.)

range organizing for change in specific areas, from the military to the ghetto, in schools or throughout the whole system. However, demonstrations do tend to commit those who have been present. Still, while swaying within the Moratorium mass to "Give Peace a Chance," sharing tangerines, cigarettes, Hershey bars, blankets, and gum, warmed by hugs and smiles, the whole experience made many of us feel more helpless than ever about Vietnam. Futility filtered through the sunlight: some later agreed that the sensation of being in that crowd was to be invisible—along with a multitude. Few could agree with Howard Samuels that the Moratorium was "more consistent with American tradition" than the war is. Meanwhile, trying to catch Nixon's attention or concern is like waving at a drunk across a canyon. What someone called "the flexibility gap" seems to yawn wider than ever: the grin of a dying dog.

Hindsight: On April 15, 1970, there was another modest Moratorium, which ended up behind the New York Public Library, where a couple of small groups seized the mike from one another. I saw only one person I knew, and we wandered about rather sadly, agreeing that if demos were held, we would always join them for the old reason of increasing the numbers. I felt that the attitude towards the war had subtly changed. Quite a few seemed able to live with it, even though it still gnawed at them—rather like a person who's learned that he has an incurable disease which isn't going to kill him . . .

So we all went on other marches, none of them very large, and they really did begin to seem like picnics. But fiercer occasions felt just as pointless. Dodging gritty snow and iceballs hurled at policemen's horses outside the New York Criminal Courts, or scrambling out of the path of yet another guerilla theater, growing more expert at running away from gas—it seemed that the numbness of re-run scenarios had weakened almost any crowd's effort.

□

One of the most radical events I've covered was the Gay Liberation march of June, 1970. Striding up Sixth Avenue: thousands of young people, many in plain jeans and work-shirts, flourishing their fists, marching with a determination that had been scarce in recent peace demonstrations. Spectators squinted for clues; another Panther rally?

A draft protest? Then they heard the rousing chants: "Gimme me a G! Gimme an A! Gimme a Y! . . . GAY POWER;" "Less pop-u-la-tion/More de-via-tion!," and "Ho-ho-ho-mosexual!" Agog and aghast, the faces on the sidewalk curdled as they saw placards reading "Sappho Was A Right-On Woman" and "Release Oscar Wilde." A boy on the pavement gasped, "There's my *mother! Marching!*" As they surged into Central Park for a vast Gay-In, many wished each other "Happy Birthday." Visiting heterosexuals worried that they might not be recognized as such; in much of that crowd, it was impossible to tell who was gay and who was straight. A news photographer murmured, "Everyone looks so . . . normal." In that long afternoon, lots of labels got lost, and it appeared that the gay community was over-riding a history of self-dislike and fear.

I was also impressed by the way that gay men sympathized with women: for the inadequacy that both have been made to feel. (At that particular period, the lesbian groups were wary of talking to a reporter—saying that they themselves must write up their own themes —but some of the men were very open.) One said, "While homosexual oppression is different for men and women—we can also oppress each other! Gay men have many of the habits of straight men: we talk abstractly, argue competitively." He described a meeting where a gay woman kept banging the floor with a baseball bat; he finally told her that the bat symbolized oppression to him—all the sports that had dogged his childhood. She replied that it meant liberation to her—since she'd never been allowed to be aggressive. But they combed it out.

The feminist march of August 1970 bestowed confidence to some who were fairly new to the women's movement. It also inspired the most hostile crowd reactions I've ever seen. Yelling and jeering from the sidelines—all the way from 59th Street to Bryant Park—were a mixture of hard hats and men in neckties who'd just emerged from their offices, plus many women, their faces knotted with contempt. "You should all have been aborted!" was a recurrent cry. The counter-demonstrators from MOM—"Men Our Masters"—absent-mindedly held a lot of their signs upside down, reading WOW. It also looked as though the 42nd Street skin-flicks had shooed their audiences out to watch us: there were some spastic faces among the spectators which appeared to be waiting for titillation, or tits.

Walking slowly down Fifth Avenue, I thought about my own lateness in realizing that I was part of the women's movement. I'd ignored it for several reasons. First, I felt that it distracted people from the facts of racism—which I'd been concentrating on almost exclusively for a number of years. I was also influenced by a few militant black women, who—in the late Sixties—still thought that sexual politics were apt to obscure most others. (And it still troubles me that some have used the women's movement as an escape from the issues of racism.) Second, I come from a liberated family; my great aunt, born in 1880, was one of the original Suffragists, all of the women in the last three generations had worked, I'd always had lots of encouragement about my future professional life—so I'd cheerfully assumed that women had won their rights long before I was born. The men in my family also took a very dim view of women who expected to be supported; I'd been raised knowing that I would have to earn as soon as I finished college. And Radcliffe in particular had nourished a tendency to be snotty about other women: to be impatient with housewives' complaints, or scornful of those without good educations or jobs. I'd failed to evaluate all the poor salaries I'd been offered, or the frowns and sighs and little headshakes that I got when I asked for a raise, or the depressions of job-hunting when—again and again —the interviewer praised my qualifications, adding, "But you'll understand what we mean when we say we want a man." However, as a freelance writer, I'd had more equal pay and treatment than most women do in offices. So I didn't fully catch on until a man—an old schoolmate—rebuked me for saying that women's issues were out of date. He added, "Just because you've had it good shouldn't let you forget that lots of other women *haven't.*"

The second stage in my education was talking to a number of women (and men) at *Newsweek* and *Time Inc.* for a piece on women's jobs in the media. From questioning amiable male editors at the news magazines, I finally learned why women can't write: it's because they get cramps. ("Oh, I'm sure *you* don't"—a freelancer is no threat—"But, *you* know, sometimes lots of them have it at once.'") So Mark Twain's old definition of women as "beautiful creatures with pains in their backs" helps to perpetuate the nurse-and-surgeon mentality of *Time* and others. The expectation of seething female distress recalled a nice slip I'd just heard on the radio: "The defendants filed emotion, uh, I mean, *a motion* . . .''

But by 1970, women were weary of hearing that they were irrational and unreliable—while being told that they were also more stable and less sensitive than men . . . Meanwhile, the wit of decades continued to decorate the magazine researchers' role: there was (and maybe still is) a senior editor at *Newsweek* who affectionately addressed the researchers as harlots, sluts, broads, and little bitches. He had a favorite joke about "greasing the researcher." First you strip the researcher, then you grease her (like a pig), run her down the hall, and whoever catches her can have her for the night. My father contributed a *Time Inc.* belly-breaker of the Forties: at *Life,* the researchers sleep with the writers; at *Fortune,* the researchers sleep with one another; at *Time,* no man would *ever* sleep with a researcher—because they're all so ugly and intense. As a *Newsweek* woman said bleakly, "The assumptions are rather hard to change." Still, the mossy gags have the aggression of desperation, since many large offices are so exhausting as to be de-sexing. But the tired verbal assaults can make the female staff feel like collective ass. A woman editor at *Esquire* quoted a male colleague's remark from an editorial meeting about women's liberation: "Give them some dildoes and they'll shut up."

Next I read some recent issues of the *Ladies' Home Journal,* having been rather surprised that Media Women had selected it as the magazine most degrading to women. But they were right. Many articles and ads evoked life as a perpetual apology: for being inefficient, helpless, thick-headed, or charmingly incompetent—for making a mess. In 1970, *The Journal's* typical protagonist was apt to burn the roast, dent the fenders while backing the car into the garage, fudge the income tax, blow the budget, or dye her hair the wrong color. You could easily imagine her losing her children in a tornado, setting the house on fire, or starting an avalanche. Hence "salvation through housework"—the only way to ask for your husband's forgiveness. You feed him Baked Alaska *because* you fused the new power lawnmower or scorched all his shirts. This relates to the psychiatric columns on "what to do with your husband's ego," how to build him up (after you've broken everything in sight?). And *The Journal's* "Newsletter of Involvement" was far from liberating: "Across the nation, women are rolling up their sleeves to get at society's laundry list of urgent problems."

So I got the message which so many women in the movement had been repeating: that their male colleagues expected them to limit their political commitments to mailing, filing, and stapling—plus some dusting and coupling. As one young woman said, "Licking stamps began to taste like licking boots." Away from the type-writer, a lot of women found themselves welcome only in the sack. Power to the People didn't quite include both sexes. Contradictions about the nature of Peoplehood impelled some women radicals to try to make radical changes for all kinds of women. Then, many sexual moderates and even some former reactionaries discovered the contagion of concern.

As of '72, we're getting used to living with the backlash: the enormous resistance to such old-fashioned subjects as equal pay, and the need which many insecure men have to keep putting women down, or to demand that women behave deferentially to them—even if the respect isn't there. It's now obvious that some men are even greater victims of machismo than many women, and I'm grateful to Hortense Calisher for her observation that "Penis envy is really *male*."* So I've reviewed some history because many men (and some women) are still asking what feminism is about.

□

From the women's movement, I came to understand my own personal loathing of violence—while continuing to agree that this country brings violence upon itself. As street fighting ebbed after the summer of 1970, so did most dissenting political actions of any sort; it also seemed that many had come to associate all politics with violence—especially since Weatherman and others had told people that they were useless *unless* they were violent.

But in the spring of '72, we all turned out to protest the war again and again; I especially remember one huge march down the West Side in a downpour—for rain-wear, many wore butterscotch-colored plastic garbage bags with holes cut for heads and legs and arms. In front of me, a young man shouted, "Nixon is a cunt!",

* ". . . it's you men who envy penises. The one you never can be sure of is there. Till it's there. Then of course you admire it . . . And pretend we do . . ." (*Queenie*, Arbor House, 1971.)

and several other men reproved him—"Hey, we shouldn't use it that way any more."

Recalling so many marches, I feel that the helplessness and the seriousness of many demonstrators was distilled by the quiet crowd of several hundred which gathered near the Manhattan Tombs after George Jackson was shot at San Quentin in August 1971. The marchers raised fluttering red silk banners stencilled with Jackson's portrait, while the press photographers talked about cameras and the cops beside me discussed fishing.

Unresolved.

CONVERSATIONS IN WATTS
January 1968

You CANNOT leave Watts regretting that there was a riot. The visiting radical or liberal departs with the donation that Watts forces on an outsider: a new moral teething ring, plus the sensation of swallowing your own blood while trying to learn how to use it. You are not allowed to regret that in August 1965, there was killing and burning and thirty-four people dead. And some nine hundred were reported injured. But it's ridiculous to claim that the holocaust "helped" in a tangible sense. As so many have noted, the "war on poverty" has hardly made a dent in the ghetto; Paul Jacobs wrote in *Prelude to a Riot* that "the amount of money spent thus far has been less than $100 per poor person in the country and a sizable percentage of that has gone to administrators." (This week, LBJ's State of the Union message contained exactly one sentence about civil rights, and it got no applause. But he was cheered for his "anticrime legislation," which is especially aimed at rioters.) Yet Watts gained by "the Revolt," as it's called there: there's a new energy and confidence, combined with self-determination and outrage, and the revelation that black Americans do, after all, have a weapon. Many don't want to use it: the older people, the educated, the employed. But they, of course, are a shred of a minority. And so many speak of the Revolt with pride; they ask, Where were you when it happened? Did you understand the news?

The young militants stress that patience, reason, and nonviolence did nothing whatsoever for blacks—and no one can disagree. There's no way to refute Ron Karenga's remark: "Only thing nonviolence proved was how savage whites were." Yet if you deplore killing in Vietnam, you can't sanction it in U.S. streets. However, future riots could have a purpose and a rationale that the Vietnam war does not. Having appreciated what the last rebellion did for Watts, you dread the next: which is very frankly expected. You can agonize over the shattered skulls or spines, each body on the pavement, the bullet in any inch of flesh, down to the pain of a broken leg. But you can't call black riots unreasonable: indeed, they've made more sense than much of our recent history. Meanwhile, no one—black or white—can pretend to discuss them unemotionally. So you end by supporting what the militants say, and fearing what they will do —while remembering that their own death will come sooner than yours. You don't want to share their fatalism—yet you can't unfurl resounding alternatives. So the teething ring grows bloodier as you chew, while you talk to yourself about programs . . . solutions . . . and all the words that failed to become facts.

Beginning with a guided tour of Watts, you visit job-training courses, where sewing is called Garment Technology and typing is Secretarial Science, some private and public agencies that appear to be well run, and an impressive new health center. A series of solid programs, administered by blacks who explain all of the possibilities —and then burst into cases about funds that haven't arrived, the snarl of conflicting outside interests, the paralysis of liberals' "research." People have learned new professional skills, but employment is brutally sparse. Typically, one program trained a hundred workers, but had only twenty-five jobs to fill. Many projects weren't refunded after ten or sixteen months of work, and many who'd been hired were back on welfare. One young politician said, "Why is that fellow back standing on the corner? He *had* a job, he learned how. But it's over. He's got nowhere to go. He can't even go home. Mom's watching *Peyton Place* on TV in the living room, where he sleeps. He doesn't have a room of his own. Doesn't want to see *Peyton Place or* Mom. Doesn't want to stand on the street corner. He's feeling very sore."

And the theme expands. The Office of Economic Opportunity—

"Hah!"—gives only year-to-year commitments. No housing has been built since '65, although there are plenty of plans on paper. Public transport hardly existed, now it's been slightly increased—"But have you ever *seen* the bus?" No. "See, we got an *imaginary* bus. Or maybe invisible." (The nearest hospital is twelve miles away. Anyone with a job outside Watts would have to walk to it—for several hours.) Even the new health center, with all its fine facilities, may not fully serve Watts in the long run, since in two years it will be administered by the University of Southern California, a private and conservative university outside the area. Some fear that it will then be used for research rather than for curing local patients. Currently, it's the main center in the U.S. where black physicians can get experience. But it will be very difficult to keep it that way.

Community involvement has been attempted on all of the programs. The participation of the poor is still the most important—and the most controversial—concept that arose from the poverty program. The Watts boards of citizens have been carefully chosen as cross sections from young and old, moderates and militants, men and women. One administrator said, "My board is pretty rough. All the emotions of the whole country bust out when these people sit down together. Sometimes I wonder if they were chosen *because* they could never agree." And certain boards have only notional power: for example, they may not be able to fire an outsider whom they find useless. And, as one young black official said, "Community action *must* be based on aggressive saneness. Yet how can you balance sanity and aggression over a *long* period of time?" He added that his board is so shot with internal combat that "some feel that community action is just a frustrating thing designed to wear you out." Then he magnified another point that echoes through Watts: that the battles of the sexes and the generations are also raging there—and that these are related to many aspects of the racial war.

A black man of about fifty said: "Two revolutions are needed: racial *and* sexual." He and other men spoke volubly and bitterly about matriarchy—referring to the days when female slaves worked in the house and slept with their white masters, while their husbands worked in the fields. "The black woman is killing the black man," a man repeated—looking straight at a black woman who neither flinched nor replied. He added that equal numbers of

GARDNER WEBB COLLEGE LIBRARY

men and women on one community board resulted in the women "shouting the men down and chasing them off the board—so you got a ladies' majority." While 63 percent of Watts's population is twenty-four and under, "Women over fifty have too much power here." He noted that the young Nationalists are "teaching their women to sit back." Ron Karenga, the local Nationalist leader of US—a separatist group that rewrites most of its maxims from Malcolm—instructs that the black woman should be "submissive." Karenga's followers are told that "Male Supremacy" is natural, and that "Equality is false; it's the devil's concept." Women have two rights: "consultation and separation." At Karenga's headquarters, you see quiet young wives in floor-length African print gowns; their appearance, at least, is meek. Meanwhile, most of the older blacks are still cautious and timid about challenging whites: "They want their social security and their retirement pay." But they are scorned by the young, who condemn their parents for "sandpapering their feet and scratching their heads."

After a general tour, it's possible to persuade your hosts to introduce you to the militants. Accents thicken ironically to inform you that Watts has been "*re*searched" and "*e*valuated" by thousands of sociologists, writers, planners, and meddlers. "We're still the basic test tube, the ghetto *laboratory*." "Yeah, we get a lot of visitors with plantations in their heads. You know, the Albert Schweitzer complex. They say, 'Let's all be brothers—and I'll be the oldest!' " The Sons of Watts and the Young Men for Total Democracy and SLANT (Self-Leadership for All Nationalities Today) are sick of talking to strangers, and a few of them sometimes charge a fee—usually about $100. (I'd certainly do the same if I lived there.) One group told me that they captured NBC's camera—until they were paid to return it. The idea of expenses diminishes later—eased by conversation itself. Of course you expect to feel hostility against whites directed personally at you. But I never did, although naturally I heard it—including the jokes about whites "who think they're doctors of niggerology." But everyone I saw was cordial, and very ready to answer questions.

The cordiality increased when I ran out of cash and had to borrow $15 from a white woman. A militant was appalled: *"What* kind of magazine do you write for, anyway?"* He urged that I apply for a job at *Time* or *Life:* "Now *there's* the bread." I explained my own notion of editorial freedom, which brought snorts of laughter and the indulgent pronouncement of "Crazy." Naturally, the choice of earning less than you *can* sounds mad to those who are hardly yet allowed to earn at all. But these particular young men didn't yet seem aware that the lettuce-lined middle-class life can be mortifying (meaning both deadening and humiliating), although so many black leaders have made the point with more precision than any author of a gray-flannel lament. James Baldwin wrote that "the American dream . . . has become something much more closely resembling a nightmare, on the private, domestic, and international levels." It doesn't seem as though that fact has yet reached Watts, where most assume that outsiders are richer and happier than they—which is certainly a sickening half-truth.

False promises made the poison. "After the Revolt, they came in and filled people with hope—hope up to here. Now that hope's run out." There will be another Revolt because "Hope's made things worse." As well as the discontinued programs, there are jobs that need to be done now: which are not filled. But the young men don't froth when they talk about killing. They are the same local leaders who meet to discuss highway and transit systems and urban renewal, who have run summer work programs for teen-age gangs (who cleaned lots and were not allowed to fight), who think that the Job Corps is a good idea but that it needs detailed revising—especially that it should include camp counselors from their own neighborhood. Veterans of many beatings by the police, and some jail terms, they still talk about "being involved in your community," and say that a new city could be built in seven or ten years. They've been using sensitivity sessions to heighten and test their blackness, and sometimes to confront whites. They have the certainty that their elders lack, plus guns.

When you think of the false promises, it's odd to see all the childrens' paintings of Jack Kennedy displayed in the health center, including many bitter pastels of the assassination: Kennedy as a felled tree or a lost sailor. Again and again, the Statue of Liberty crumbles or collapses in the background. Is Kennedy forgiven because he's dead?

The refrain is "Peace and equality by any means necessary."

Everyone knows that different groups are arming themselves, and that they keep meeting to discuss some kind of revolution. (Here, the nationalists, who study Swahili and shave their heads "in mourning for the black living dead," stress the need for an independent Afro-American culture, while the militants appear to want advancement as Americans—theirs seems to be a very Yankee determination.) But no one's shy of explaining that "the next Revolt will be organized, not spontaneous. *If* things don't change very soon." A fledgling riot was suppressed by some militants last summer: because they "still had hopes of the promises that had been made." Now they speak about choosing "the right time." "But we would stop any outburst if it happened at the *wrong* time." Laughing, one said, "The most beautiful thing the government did was to take our fellows to Vietnam and train them and bring them back. Now they're skilled at guerrilla warfare, and they know the area."

The concept of revolution is in a wingless, larval state; most of those who discuss it are talking well into the future. And you have to remember that overstatement is not only the language of the ghetto but of this whole country, from our ads to our politicians' speeches. Still, Ron Karenga has his lively moments: "When the word is given we'll see how tough you are. When it's 'burn,' let's see how much you can burn. When it's 'kill,' let's see how much you kill. . . . And when it's 'take that white girl's head too,' we'll really see how tough you are."

The militants say that some of the middle-class blacks—who came from outside Watts to run the stillborn programs—will be erased in the next Revolt. When they repeat that "our next one will be against the middle-class *Nee*-grow," you feel that black people are still the victims of divide and conquer. "It's the Toms who sold us out. They helped themselves: they took all the gravy off the top. They come back with meringue around their mouths, and we say, "Where's the pie?' And *they* say, 'It's *alllll* gone.' " These "house niggers," accused of "lipping the songs," are also called "hat-trick men" and "Whip-Me's." Contempt and fury erupt when they're mentioned. The '63 March on Washington is known as "The Sell-Out." Militants add that "slatting up against liberals" is worse than dealing with racists— "who don't feed you a lot of songs. At least they're straight." However, "We'll accept whites' support—*anyone's* support."

Wrath against the system coincides with a desire "to be part of the structure—while keeping your identity with blacks." Perhaps the moral—and the discussion does become very moral here—is that a black who makes personal progress in Watts should continue to keep battling on behalf of those who haven't yet made it, should "bring back what he acquired from the system." One man said, "I want what's mine here." The point is "here": in his own town, not in some "better" neighborhood. Escape: "That's not *my* bag"—a theme that rings through Watts.

One young activist, who guided me through Watts, scolded me like an indignant nursemaid when I wandered away from him to buy cigarettes. "You want smokes, you say so, we'll go get them. But if you're on your own, suppose some eleven-year-old kid throws a rock at you, and another does, and the cops come, they use gas. That's how shooting starts and our people get killed. So we're having no riots *today*." Because he didn't want to be seen too long in the company of a white woman, we sat talking for hours in a parked car in a burnt-out lot. I asked what he did during the Revolt, and he heaved a huge laugh out the window. "I made twenty-seven thousand dollars!" He picked up a lot of color TV sets—"and I know where to sell them quick, because I used to be a hustler. Any man who didn't take advantage of the Revolt I feel sorry for. You had Mom out there looting too—got herself half a cow from the supermarket. What's to be afraid? Everyone you know is on the street. Then a lot of us took trucks—we just blocked traffic and made the drivers get out. You had to have a truck to move all your stuff."

Fatalism about dying alternates with the talk about what *could* be done for Watts, with the angry amusement at "liberal" mediators, with the advantage of having your own car. Death seems to be accepted as a matter of timing: "No one's running from death. You say, Well, I guess this is my time." Those already killed "were there at the wrong time. That's the breaks, Jake." In a society of hoaxes, put-ons, lies, public relations, imagery, and political charades, you feel that the Watts militants mean what they say. These are private citizens—unlike the public revolutionaries who enjoy raising the rhubarb on TV. But these young men's feelings about death should be believed: it is the measure of their seriousness, the proof that life in Watts is as intolerable as ever.

After talking about violence for over an hour, my guide in the car sighed deeply and said, "Perhaps, perhaps the *threat* of violence is even more important than violence itself." He felt that the threat could be used as a substitute: "If only people could fear what we *might* do—enough to make things better for Watts—then we could really save some lives, instead of risking them." But Washington's reply is new police weapons and "riot control," fuelled by what Dr. Kenneth B. Clark has called "the democracy of American racism, which includes *all* Negroes." The level of national comprehension seems equal to that of a rich Californian woman, a diet specialist, who deduced that everyone in Watts eats "hostile foods." She offered to change their nutrition and their emotions through a program of "neutral foods."

Hindsight: By late 1970, the press reported that unemployment among blacks in Watts had increased by 61 percent between August 1965 and the end of 1969. Had there been any substantial improvements in the early Seventies, we would have heard a lot about them. Still, in April 1972, Watts got its first hospital, which the *New York Times* called "a most imposing response to the riots of 1965."

January 1968 was still pre-Panther time, even though the Panthers had been formed in Oakland in the fall of '66. But they were hardly mentioned in Watts, beyond a couple of admiring references to the occasion in May 1967 when twenty-five armed Panthers made a visit to the California State Legislature in Sacramento. But the themes of this ghetto show how many were going to listen to the Panthers.

In '68 and '69 one lived with an apprehension of summer—for those who might suffer in their own neighborhoods. But one administrator in the Watts health center very firmly predicted that the next confrontations would be on campuses, not in ghettos. By late '68, community control was more than ever a theme; Tommy Jacquette, the head of SLANT in Watts, said, "The brother is too busy getting his thing together to think about riots. But Whitey's funny; he worries like hell when we riot and he worries like hell when we don't."

Meanwhile, the press continued to focus on new "nonlethal weapons," including "instant banana peel," a substance to make streets slick. A Los Angeles police chief warned his staff: "Don't throw your guns away. Let us not be seduced by the naive philosophy that foam dispensers or slippery substances can summarily pacify rioters, looters, and arsonists." In '69 Julian Bond was still trying patiently to explain that "what you have now is a conflict between black people and white institutions." But by late 1970, my anthology of white supremacies was richer than ever; for example, this remark from Major General Walter Johnson, commander of the Mississippi National Guard, in his testimony before the White House State panel that investigated the two killings at Jackson State: "There is a difference between stealing watermelons and stealing color television sets."

What remains as the main lesson from my visit to Watts was the way that things had been structured to turn black people against one another: the economic classes and the age groups and the sexes. I heard far more anger of blacks against blacks than against whites. Our institutions, like OEO, have a talent for perpetuating systems which force people to deeply disagree and then to fight one another. (On a much lower level, just think of any office you've worked in lately.) And of course the spectacle of divided blacks satisfies the majority of whites—it's even better than when radicals or women battle among themselves.

Starting in '68, until about the midsummer of 1970, I heard so many (especially white activists) say that they were ready and willing to die. I didn't believe most of them for a moment. But in Watts, the discussions of death were undramatic, very quiet. Death as a fact of life.

BLACK PANTHERS AND WHITE RADICALS:
Oakland, California July 1969

DURING those July days of the Moon and the Pond, the lunar dust and the bubbles from Teddy Kennedy's car, "the astro-pigs and all that moonshit" and one politician's panic were ignored by some three thousand people, who were attending the Black Panthers' conference for "a United Front Against Fascism" in Oakland, California.

The conference was neither a failure nor a success, as varying voices pronounced it.

Contrary to the Panthers' intentions, those three days of forty-five speeches and panels didn't establish a new party of blacks, browns, Third World forces, and whites. But it tried to be "a preface," as Chairman Bobby Seale called it. He welcomed the audience to a "mass workshop," stressing that "You came here because of heads bleeding . . . you came because you related to the reality that people suffer." In a period when dissent is as diffuse as frog spawn, the need for unity is so acute that each attempt raises momentary hopes.

Clearly, the Panthers were determined to forestall the types of tumult which dismembered the SDS June convention in Chicago, when the Progressive Labor party was expelled and Weatherman was founded; in Oakland, you felt the influence of that frenzied prelude. Hence debate or even discussion of ideology were not allowed on the platform—which distressed a good deal of the audience. (Elsewhere, the Panthers have been clear in their conviction that capitalism and democracy cannot coexist, and that the poor are the victims of class as much as race. But many at this conference knew very little about the Panthers' ideas.) Seale made the mistake of equating rhetoric and ideology: "When you start a united front, you do not start with some jive ideological struggle." But he and others did unleash enough rhetoric to kindle a longing for more theory behind the action—as well as an ex-minister's remark that "We're all in the movement. But any movement without thinking and a program is a *bowel* movement!" After all the species of shit that had been mentioned, many gasped at this image, and a lot of shoulders heaved.

The emphasis was on practical action which people could take in their own neighborhoods, in labor unions, church groups, in dealing with the law and with hospitals. The aim was to provide the poor with information that could help them to help themselves. This plan reflected the Panthers' efforts to be "a service organization to the community"—which they would like to extend well beyond the ghetto to include Puerto Ricans, Indians, Mexicans, and poor whites, as well as working people throughout the U.S. (Although it's probably too late, some do wish to reach Wallace's audience.) It was repeated that so many people are treated as objects—that valid modern terror which strikes even the middle class—as well as those robbed of hope or dignity by racism and poverty, or the mere acknowledgement of their existence.

During one panel, Andy Chavez, of the Farm Workers' Union, condemned the Defense Department's doubled purchase of grapes for soldiers in Vietnam, and urged a boycott on Safeway Stores, which still market California grapes. He remained committed to "militant nonviolence," even though his co-workers have been beaten and sprayed with insecticides in the fields. Other speakers called for strikes in plants that contribute in any way to the Vietnam war. A white man from the Chicago branch of the United Auto Workers said that white workers in skilled jobs must realize that "sweetheart agreements" (which exclude blacks in unskilled work) with employers will only result in "being tied to *and* screwed *by* the union boss. . . . You're with the boss *or* with the black worker. There's no third path."

However, a good 80 percent of those present were white; there were many of the same faces that I've seen in Chicago, at the Pentagon, on peace marches: those who are already converted. Quite a few tend to spin fantasies around the Panthers, evoking them as pagan animal deities in male or female form—excitingly nonhuman. Jungle thrills tinged with mysticism allowed some to forget the issues. Others were huffy about having to listen to people less educated than themselves. And some are privileged, querulous innocents, who—as one observer grimly remarked—"wouldn't recognize a worker if it came and peed on their leg." Not that they should have stayed away. But their presence underscored the absence of working people and the poor, and—above all—the scarcity of blacks who weren't Panthers. It was odd to hear so many speeches about the community —when the community wasn't there.

Despite the Panthers' breakfasts for children, their programs to inform welfare clients of their rights, their advice on dealing with bad landlords—it looks as though they may have lost the neighborhood support which they had in Oakland until recently. Several rueful militants said that perhaps the Panthers are forfeiting the trust of impoverished blacks because of the collaboration with whites. This is of course Stokely Carmichael's charge. In his July letter of resignation from the party, Carmichael wrote, ". . . any premature alliance with white radicals has led to complete subversion of the blacks by the whites. . . ." Yet this hasn't happened to the Panthers. Since they reject black separatism along with "reverse racism," the Panthers may be the last black organization willing to work with whites. Bobby Seale said, "We're setting examples: that's why we're so hard on black groups that are racist." However, if the white backing that the Panthers have received is hurting them, if the best aid that radical whites can offer them is withdrawal, then many white conservatives will be delighted. Yet the white left may have to accept a period of black separatism—without wounded resentment.

While some of the recent altercations between the Panthers and the cultural nationalists have been magnified by the press, one clash did result in two murders. In January '69, two of Ron Karenga's US group shot and killed two Panthers at UCLA. (One of the dead was John Huggins, whose widow, Ericka, was later acquitted in the New Haven Panther trial. The two accused members of US gave themselves up to the police soon after the UCLA killings.) The January dispute hinged on whether the Panthers or Karenga's group would run the black studies department at UCLA. If Karenga had been in charge, only blacks would have been hired; the Panthers were expected to employ a range of colors. Karenga, like some other nationalists, has no tangible program beyond "self-determination, self-respect, and self-defense," and his particular expression of race pride swims close to racial hatred. The Panthers also accuse Karenga of being a capitalist and of "enslaving" the women of US.

Currently, few black militants are eager to discuss the pros and cons of nationalism; one quoted Malcolm X: "When you have problems in the family, solve them indoors." Cultural nationalism, which is still in a liquid state, is apolitical—nor is there any radical demand for a restructured society. So far, it plays nicely into the hands of white conservatism: by implying that dashikis, black theaters, Afro jewelry, and some tom-toms are all that's needed to satisfy black discontent. Sometimes, it looks as though black art is in danger of being used as a hush-puppy. Last spring, a young Atlanta activist told a reporter that he didn't wear Afro clothes—"the beads and bones"—because "it costs more to dress for the revolution than to run it." His crack sounds rather like a warning to some cultural nationalists: style's no substitute for liberation.

Culture was hardly mentioned at the Panther conference, where the liveliest session analyzed the abuses of medicine. A group of radical doctors assailed their own profession. They stressed that a lot of medical care is hardly intended as a cure, since mere symptoms are often treated without much probing for their cause—a practice which plumps up profit. One doctor said, "Illness is one of the most lucrative products of this country. . . . Every health professional can be paid by propagating your suffering. . . . We've been carefully groomed *not* to relate to people or to suffering, but to meat—to carnage." (He was talking about the tendency to experiment on the poor.) He added that "the health industry creates the *shame* of illness"—which so many do feel, due to the cost that sickness wrings from their families, as well as the sense of personal humiliation that some of our public hospitals administer along with the brutality of their treatment. This doctor and others urged a "demystification" of the industry, announcing that they want to teach the poor how to look after themselves, and about their own bodies. A very graphic pamphlet on diseases, injuries, and short-term remedies was given out. The pamphlet, which explained medical rights in hospital and in jail, treatment for bleeding and shock, lacerations and bruises, also contained a section on different tear gases, nausea and blister gases, and Mace. For nausea gas, "masks are dangerous . . . as the gas is absorbed in the skin . . . and you can choke in your own puke." Reading the pamphlet in a sunny Oakland park, surrounded by teenagers nibbling bright green sherbet, I was reminded that this was the neighborhood where such information had already been needed.

Deplorable health conditions for workers were also described; in addition to the contagious diseases that they take home to their families, black lung, cancer from fumes and radioactivity, joint and bone destruction, are all abundant. (Some tunnel workers were about to have a wildcat strike because the air they breathe will incapacitate them in about ten years.) A dilating health crisis was declared: "A death on the job, in a train, at the movies, in a doctor's office: what we're living with is daily death!" Above all, "Health is *essential* to revolution or social change. You've got to be well to fight, you can't if you're sick."

Finally, a psychiatrist gave his views on mental health and capitalism: "Depression and neurosis often occur because of the oppression that people are living under. This runs through our whole society, and includes the rich and even the oppressor—he gets ugly in the head. . . . Emotional illness can come from being fucked over by the system." He described his very poor patients, who have just lost their jobs or have been thrown off welfare. Naturally, they are depressed, and many assume that they're worthless—since that's what they've been told by the ethic that surrounds them. "The idea that some people are better than others" is quite literally sickening. He denounced much of the "mental health industry" as "a pacifying program—to get people to adjust" to abnormal conditions, and he cited the expanding desire to believe that social rebellion is caused by emotional illness.

A lawyer's panel explained some of the legal rights which many do not know they possess. William Kunstler also declared that bearing arms is the only way to keep the police from savaging the ghetto: that the fear of retaliation is the only protection. "If you have the power to defend yourselves by weapons that are legal, then you have the power to rid the ghettos of the paralyzing fear that invites repression." He said that he hoped that retaliation would not be needed. However, "if you [tell] the power structure that they need not fear you, [then you] open up the whole sad trail of misery and depredation that has characterized life on this continent for so many years."

Later, a band of rebel clergymen attacked the corruptions of the church, including its loss of moral and ethical values, and insisted that the public must help to reform it—"especially through your concern for others than yourself." There was lavish disgust at the churches' economic greed; one ex-minister cried, "I didn't leave the church, the fucking church left me!" Several expressed the dilemma which has racked many churchmen in the past year: the use of violence. Quite a few priests have found it impossible to instruct their congregations just to go home and be quiet. One said, "God gave us all life, and life exists primarily to be preserved. When you see a pig moving toward you, I can't tell you to get down on your knees and ask God what to do. . . . The best prayer I can suggest is: to defend yourself!" Throughout, the clergymen demanded that life on earth must be salvaged; none even mentioned the afterlife. For them, Christianity now means serving and protecting other people— immediately.

Indeed, despite the infinite confusions, fragmentations, vicious or silly feuds, and all the gargle within the movement, you feel that its members do have one thing in common: an awareness of suffering, in the ghetto, in Vietnam, next door or in Prague, in the subway or the laundry—a painful consciousness that simply won't relent.

Still, the Panthers' conference had its frustrations—which may have left some groups farther divided than ever. While almost everyone agrees on the goals—such as peace abroad and liberation at home—few can harmonize about tactics or priorities, and the alliances will keep dissolving. (Currently, you simply cannot summarize the convictions of SDS, since so many within it are denouncing each other's beliefs.) Since the movement is deeply anti-individualistic, many of its members do try to eschew ego trips, and attempt to submerge themselves in their groups. But groups can fight with the same gusto as individuals: the result is just like a collision between warring personalities. Perhaps the history (or the tragedy) of the left springs partly from honesty—the refusal to work with those whose methods you cannot accept—while many conservatives cherish party unity beyond mere questions of honor.

So I could see why the Panthers feared that ideological battles would dilute or destroy the drive for unity. However, many found them far too authoritarian. The Progressive Labor Party—which was barred from the conference due to their denunciation of the Panthers as "bourgeois nationalists"—tried to distribute leaflets, and were beaten up for it. PL members also slugged some of the SDS. And one random incident confused witnesses about the nature of brotherhood. Toward the end of one panel, a middle-aged man who seemed rather drunk kept asking in Spanish and English why there weren't more Mexican-Americans at the conference—as had been announced. Panther officials told him to stop interrupting, and advised him to go consult Bobby Seale. The man mumbled, "I've tried to—but I can't find the motherfucker." "WHO you calling motherfucker!": five Panthers hit him until he fell crashing among the folding chairs. The term, uttered every few minutes by many speakers, couldn't be used casually by an outsider. A friend of mine caught the man's watch as it sailed through the air, but when we gave it to him, he was still muttering, bloody and groggy, "I just want to talk to the motherffff—."

The conference yielded some other distressing lessons. After all, dodging ideology hurls you back to the stock responses to rhetoric and clichés—which aren't just aesthetically depressing. Deadened language is dangerous and corrupting because it makes perfectly good words and phrases meaningless—with the consequence that the *ideas* behind the words can seem to weaken. Now, when the word "revolution" is flying around like an old frisbee, when "fascism" twangs like a wornout rubber band, even "racism" may become too familiar—a word and a concept that may already have ceased to shock a numbed society. (Since both SDS and PL delegates shrieked "Racist!" at each other in Chicago, what new term can emerge?) This fascist tablecloth, that racist tree, those imperialist soap flakes—you start entreating others in the movement to preserve their ammunition, to allow language to keep its force. Even "violence" is a furry notion, befuzzed by more than leagues of eager cops. We're still far from a revolution—when so few have entangled the nursery tales about "good" and "bad" violence. For example, how provocative are you going to be in order to stimulate suppression—simply to prove that suppression exists? And how do you know how you will react when the moment comes? After the ferocious police siege at People's Park in Berkeley, a former civil rights worker told me that some of those who had been shouting "revolution" all winter were the first to run away, while he, who had always been devoutly nonviolent, found himself picking up a rock and belting someone.

Yet the Panthers seem to know the dangers of thoughtless action; as many Californians keep saying, Oakland itself was expected to explode long ago. The Panthers have worked to prevent this; they stress that the local police would welcome an excuse to move on them. On several occasions, Panther leaders have told black high school students to cool it, and many have mentioned how they warned the young against rioting after the murder of Martin Luther King. But some of their white fans are still very naive; the hairy notion that "the blueprint will grow out of the struggle" has kept some on what's called "the praxis axis." How often I've heard lines like: "The thing to do is to break down old forms and not worry about coming up with new ones." That kind of spontaneity has worked for some strikes and demos, but it fails completely as a recipe for changing society.

Another confusion that needs flushing is the association of life styles with revolution or even reform. Drugs and flowers and fun and beads and horoscopes have been grafted onto rebellion—mainly by overnight hippies. (They weren't at the conference, but they scramble into activism at Berkeley and elsewhere.) None of the charms of stylistic experiment has any kinship to politics. When protest means nudity, social criticism sags. (No one needs to write satire now. Especially in California, it writes itself. Parody made flesh means that urgent issues can be fudged or obscured by the merriment of fringe style.) A woman who had been one of the early Panthers told me that she thought the party was fading—not only because of the FBI's faithful harassment or because most of the leadership was in jail—but also because style had become too important: from the shiny black jackets to the slogans. She said that she and Huey Newton had originally agreed that style was useful in appealing to the young, "But now the Panthers are holding press conferences, getting into public relations—so much is getting lost in the image." Other concerned leaders groaned when black students at Merritt College used time and energy to win the right to black vanilla ice cream in the cafeteria—"all that jive *licorice*"—or when women's groups fought for two days about what to wear to the demonstrations at People's Park: overalls? red stockings? (Finally, it was decided that everyone could wear what she wished.) When I was at Berkeley, there was a "militant fly-in" to defy the banning of frisbees on campus: about a hundred protested what their leaflets called "another attempt to repress . . . our youth culture in general." Also, despite sympathy for those who were badly beaten by the police, the late May battle of People's Park was considered frivolous by some members of the movement.

Among all the muddles about relevancy, the Panthers' conference showed that women were hardly included in any revolution. On the first night, a women's panel was unexpectedly postponed by a long, old-fashioned speech by Herbert Aptheker (who probably had no idea of the evening's agenda.) During his talk, some women—who feared that their speeches would be eliminated altogether—stood up in protest; others clapped. Masai Hewitt, the Panthers' Minister of Education, warned the women: "You want to act bad, you get treated bad," and told them they were "pigs and provocateurs." Some walked out.

Later, some women Panthers were very frank about the sexual strife within their own party. In his lectures of '68, Eldridge Cleaver praised "pussy power," announcing that "political power grows out of the lips of the pussy. Ladies constitute a strategic reserve for the revolution." He urged women to "cut off the sugar" from reactionary or uncommitted men. "If you're part of the solution, how can you justify laying up with part of the problem? You're giving aid and comfort to the enemy when you lay up with one of those chumps." He added that, for women who did reject men with lame politics, "there are plenty of us who will come to aid you in your hour of need."

Cleaver's bawdy charm made both sexes laugh, and—since he was mainly talking about who *not* to ball—many of us missed the point that women would be pressured to hit the sheets with any man who called himself a brother. Soon, other Panthers' reiterations about pussy power made black women extremely angry, since the theme developed to that famous line, "The only position for a woman in a revolution is on her back." One young woman Panther said, "The brothers expect us to stick to typing and cleaning the office and all that shit. They forget that lots of the sisters can shoot as well as they can." Aside from more bitter discussions about who they were supposed to sleep with, both black and white feminists agreed that women must purge themselves of the old "ruling class" notion that "what we want most is houses, furniture, clothes, and all the commodities that we're supposed to love"—the possessions that have made women eager consumers "who please the capitalists."

On the last night of the conference, Bobby Seale and a white lawyer tried to outline a plan for community control of the police to a weary audience of a few hundred—the remains of the three thousand who had originally attended. Many white radicals associate police brutality with simply being hassled by narcs—just as some assume that freedom merely means legalizing drugs; and some don't yet seem to understand what cops do in ghettos. But Seale was a weak and rambling speaker, and he couldn't hold the tired listeners who kept straggling out. (It's said around Berkeley that he was always a good organizer, but was never meant to be a public figure—that was left to Newton and Cleaver.) When the evening ended, a few dozen Panthers—waving their red books and stamping their feet in rhythm, swaying and bobbing—chanted *"Pow*-er-to-the-*peo*-ple, *Pow*-er-to-the-*peo*-ple . . . *Pow*-er . . . *Pow*-er,"* and I chided myself for thinking that I'd rarely seen people look so powerless.

If the movement sometimes resembles an overturned basket of marbles that are rolling apart or away, the upheaval may partly result from the concept of polarization—a word that's already so mossy that it needs more than a good shave. Sometimes, both the left and the right seem to be trying to create one another—in order to sculpture their own identities. I've met a number of militants who said that they voted for Goldwater or Nixon; some have even said how splendid it would be if the U.S. made a disastrous invasion in Latin America. The theory is that if the forces of conservatism grow uglier, then the left will finally organize itself—that everyone will line up. (Few who think this way remember that the left could also be a pushover.) On the right, certain professors seemed truly disappointed that last spring's campus revolts were not bloodier: there was the desire to point at smoking ruins, to affirm that the moment for galloping suppression had arrived. On both sides, the occasional longing for a holocaust is also due to the tension of waiting; it's rather like the agonized impatience of a body that must vomit. And it's human enough to love being right: all factions agree that the country's in an appalling state, and that *something* is going to happen.

And maybe it isn't. Some of the most committed black and white radicals feel that this is a time for temporary withdrawal: to rethink, to regroup later—and certainly to stop fighting those who are supposed to work together. One said, *"If* there were a revolutionary party, I would join it. . . ."* Those in retreat concentrate on tangible actions: tutoring poor children, organizing tenants' groups, starting a cooperative store, helping with the Panthers' hot breakfasts, trying to reach those in their own block or neighborhood. They agree that it's not enough. But some still express a hope that there's a new awareness of need and "the meaning of pain" that has never quite existed before.

BLACK PANTHERS AND WHITE RADICALS:
Philadelphia, Pennsylvania September 1970

THE EXHAUST fumes from the Mister Softee truck mingled with the baby-powder smell of the creamy cones, while bongo drums thudded throughout the crowd of ten thousand waiting to hear Huey Newton speak at Philadelphia's Temple University—a crowd throbbing with suspense, elated by anticipating their own celebrity. Political proximity has a new tang now: sniffing Softee, I remembered inhaling the mixture of tear gas and maple syrup that suffused a Washington waffle shop near the Department of Justice in November '69, where some of us raced for shelter. But one of the points of the plenary session of the Revolutionary People's Constitutional Convention—which was sponsored by the Black Panthers and other black groups in September 1970—was the absence of CS gas or violence. And when an excited young group from North Philadelphia's ghetto started to march toward City Hall, the Panthers stopped them and made them go home. Just as they had been relentless peacekeepers on Yale's Mayday—when some fights began on the New Haven green, while the Yale radio station repeated "The Panthers ask you to go to your rooms"—so the Panthers used their authority in Philadelphia. When it came to the crunch, they saved skulls and probably lives: to the astonishment of some Philadelphians, who later said that they'd been "sure of" a riot. The Panthers' military discipline, which is very disturbing to their white supporters, is certainly respected by many of the ghettos' young, and even by the white revolutionary trippers who appear half-stoned at Panther conferences.

In the week before the Philadelphia convention, one policeman was killed and three were wounded. After five suspects from a group calld "The Revolutionaries" were arrested, they were shown to be unconnected with the Panthers. Still, these events inspired a raid on the Panther headquarters. (A former Philadelphia policeman told me, "The best publicity any police department can have is a dead cop.") After a shootout, the police made fourteen Panthers strip naked against a wall and spread the cheeks of their buttocks so that "body cavities" could be thoroughly searched for weapons and explosives. (Bail was set at $100,000 apiece, as "preventive medicine," but it was soon lowered to $2,500 and much less.) Police commissioner Frank Rizzo, who at first referred to the Panthers as "yellow dogs" (because they submitted to the search) later tried to retract this image. He did say, "Imagine the big Black Panthers with their pants down!"

However, the savagery of Rizzo's troops had already generated a lot of neighborhood support for the Philadelphia Panthers—which had been one of the Party's weakest chapters in the country. The dean of Temple's School of Social Administration said that the raids were in response to dissent, rather than a reaction to any activities of the Panthers. One U.S. district judge issued a very unusual temporary order restraining the police—announcing that "a madman out of control shooting policemen is not much more dangerous to the community than a policeman who loses control and goes shooting up people's houses and raiding them"—while a black judge, long known as a moderate, called the raids "outrageous," also "totally unnecessary, uncalled for and really improper." He added that white Philadelphians "were hopeful of violence [during the Convention, so] they could retaliate."

As a New Yorker, I found Philadelphia so jammed with hostilities and hatreds that Manhattan seems gentle and pastoral in comparison; although I'm perpetually exasperated by Mayor Lindsay's many bunglings, I felt a wave of appreciation for his efforts to curb cops— as opposed to the police-camp vibes which shiver through Philadelphia or Chicago. (Rizzo: "The only thing we can do now is buy tanks and start mounting machine guns.") During the convention, no white Philadelphian would give me street or bus directions to the ghetto; most just turned away, shrugging or scowling, though one cab driver said, "You want to see stabbings and killings?" In fact, the only violence I saw was in the dining room of the Benjamin Franklin Hotel, where one middle-aged man began to slug another in the belly and the throat, finally pounding his head against the table. As they pummeled each other toward the doorway, a waiter said, "They're only brothers," and the audience of diners seemed relieved.

During the unviolent convention, the Panther speeches—although

pruned of much of last year's rhetoric—weren't lamblike. Michael
Tabor (of the New York Panther 21, an ex-addict who is defending
himself at his trial)* and, later, Newton, sounded as disgusted as
William Lloyd Garrison must have been when he called the U.S.
Constitution "a covenant with death, and an agreement with hell"
which "should be immediately abolished"—because the document
which gave whites their human rights excluded blacks. Both Newton
and Tabor quoted the Declaration of Independence, including the ever
more popular passage about "the Right of the People to alter or abolish" a government which is destructive to their rights, "and to provide
new guards for their future security." Tabor, who spoke for over two
hours, views the Nixon Administration as part of the native tradition: "what they're doing is the natural outgrowth" of our history
and its Constitution. "The Founding Fathers started this show. . . .
[Genocide has continued] since 1607 when those racist bandits
landed on that rock." Moreover, "Nixon ain't in control of this
government . . . he's just a paranoid with a loser's complex." He piled
contempt on the Pentagon, corporations and their directors—
"They're the true dope fiends—hopelessly addicted to money"—white
and black capitalists, denounced all "murder on an international
level," and said of Vietnam: "That war is over. It's over. It's over.
The Vietnamese have won. So why is fighting still going on? Why?
Because here in America, we have not done our job. . . ."

He said that "a lot of people are confused about the whole issue
of self-defense." He cautioned that an unarmed man can't protect
himself against a cop who menaces him at noon. "But, come sundown, come sundown, when the streets are dark and deserted, and
you go up on the roof, and you take your action out, fix up your
sights, put your index finger on that trigger, and you pull that trigger
—that's self-defense, that's self-defense. Because if you don't get *him,*
he's gonna get *you* the next day." (Roars of delight from the crowd.)
He continued, "We have enemies who are dedicated to killing us, to
offing us. If you're a masochist, then you'll just allow your life to be
snuffed out. . . . History will look at you not as a martyr, but as a
goddam foooooll." He added that violence or nonviolence isn't the
issue: "The issue is whether we want to live or we want to die. We're
all here today because we want to *live.*"

* Tabor later jumped bail and joined Cleaver in Algeria.

"America today has one foot in the graveyard and the other foot on a banana peel, and they're slipping fast, fast. . . ." (Cheers.) "Lots of people think they're going to get through this by playing cool. . . . But the name of the game in America is tag. And specifically, black people is *It*. . . . But I also think Kent State was It. . . . They have turned on their own sons and daughters." He repeated the Panther commitment to a class struggle as an alternative to racial war, and the need for a socialist government. (Actually, the Panthers' brand of socialism sounds quite similar to that of Clement Attlee after World War II: the skeleton of a welfare state which has since been dismantled by British Socialists and Tories alike.) Tabor underlined the seriousness of writing a new constitution—and of preventing the U.S. from dispensing further death. "If we do not do our job effectively, mankind is through dancing . . . it'll be *all* over with."

Among the later responses to his speech, some thought that he referred to shooting *only* cops who had attacked you: others felt that the whole sundown passage was a fantasy. Personally, I was less concerned with his intentions than with the question of who was listening—especially the handful of spaced-out teen-agers who nodded through most of the program, but would jerk awake to cheer at the most dramatic moments.

After Tabor finished, two tear-gas canisters were found near the speakers' platform: which could have sent five thousand people stampeding up the wooden bleachers of Temple's gym—an ideal scenario for broken legs. Many had complained of the Panthers' stern security measures: all the frisking and "patting"—"You been patted yet?"—which was required before anyone entered the gym. Yet the canisters had slid through; later we were told that there had been two telephoned threats on Newton's life. Still, much of the crowd was unnerved by the searching; a jittering matron yelped at a boy behind her, "You blew on my neck!" When he apologized, she said indignantly, "I don't let even my *husband* do that." Otherwise the waiting crowd was cheerful and friendly, although there were little clusters of racial shyness. About half the mass was white. But the neighboring ghettos turned out more fully than for any Panther gathering I've seen: it was indeed a grass-roots audience.

The press was closed out of the hall for Newton's speech. Crammed up against a huge glass doorway, reporters rumbled with resentment, and one man began to mutter, "Press—op*press*ed, de*press*ed, sup-

*press*ed." In the past, all the Panthers I've seen have been helpful to reporters. But now, all journalists are associated with the oozing distortions of all the media. And I can't be totally indignant—since I've seen how often the Panthers (and most dissidents) have been wildly misrepresented. (WBAI titles some of its reports, "Forgive Us Our Press-Passes.") Hence, in Philadelphia, many of us wanted to disassociate ourselves from the rest of the press; not wanting to be lumped with oink pig media pollution, we sometimes behaved as though the others had contagious cancer or inflammable VD. (After two days of walking freely in and out of the Church of the Advocate, the convention's information center, I was banished simply for standing next to two black reporters from the *New York Times* and the *Washington Star.*) Later we were told that Newton was displeased at our exclusion from his speech, supposedly due to "a mix-up with security." We also heard rumors that CBS—and perhaps ABC—had had a rumpus with the convention's sponsors (which included the Muslims, African Unity, the Nationalist Separatist Front, the Black Vanguard, and others besides the Panthers) over the question of paying $25,000 for exclusive coverage. It was said that the sponsors had argued about the possible shakedown until Newton began his talk, and also that the networks had finally refused to deliver the sum.

For the next session, we were assured that we'd all get in; then, told that only one reporter would be allowed; then, that we ourselves must choose ten representatives—out of thirty. Soon, some of us loathed each other: it was a fine case of divide and conquer. Finally, everyone was admitted, after being made to march rapidly, two abreast, from one locked door to another, circling the building several times, yielding "anything sharp," such as a random nailfile. (One reporter asked forlornly, "Can I keep my ballpoint pen?") In some ways, the hassle was a healthy reproof to those who control the established press: to the arrogance which has betrayed facts for so long. ("My editor rewrote it" gets no forgiveness now. Reporters who can't be responsible for their published pieces will soon find all doors closed.) Still, as some of the Panthers became more dictatorial, a sentence from Daniel Berrigan kept swimming through my head: "A revolution is interesting insofar as it avoids like the plague the plague it promised to heal." And, if you consider yourself a reliable reporter—and yet refuse to be a flack for the movement—muck-ups of this kind will only become more frustrating. Who will be allowed

to speak? Who will be allowed to hear? Who's a pig in a poke? As
Eldridge Cleaver said in a speech in '68, "People are so confused
nowadays that they don't know who their enemies are and they don't
know who their friends are." Philadelphia reflected that confusion.
So we heard Newton on tapes and read his speech. His style was
far cooler than Tabor's, but the vast audience was ecstatic. He said
that "a nation conceived in liberty and dedicated to life, liberty, and
the pursuit of happiness has in its maturity become an imperialist
power dedicated to death, oppression, and pursuit of profits." (Cata-
racts of applause.) "... we will not be blinded by small changes in
form which lack any change in the substance of imperialist expansion.
Our suffering has been too long, our sacrifices have been too great,
and our human dignity is too strong for us to be prudent any longer."
("RIGHT ON!") He stressed that the Constitutional Convention
should produce "rational and positive alternatives." As for self-
defense: "People are never violent... until they are aggressed."

Afterward, the crowd surged to the streets around the Church of
the Advocate. In this ghetto, the gashed sidewalks sparkle with
broken glass—it's not yet paved with diamonds by OEO. Standing
on a ravaged curb, I learned from a former Urban Coalition staffer
that this was a Model Cities area, where $25 million had already
been spent—too much of it on office space and salaries. He described
job programs which allowed participants to earn less than welfare
recipients—"people working for their poverty"—and said that the
techniques of "trying to create a golden ghetto" only intensified segre-
gation; the housing plan ties residents to dwellings they can't afford to
leave, while the jobs which would pay them better are in the suburbs
—remote from local transit systems. Around us, the packed streets
seethed with the hope that Newton would appear; he didn't, and it
was then that the Panthers prevented a possible explosion.

Each of the next day's fifteen workshops produced a paper which
would serve as a recommendation for the final draft of the new
constitution.* The two sessions I attended—on "the Distribution of

---

* In November 1970 the Panthers tried to arrange the next convention that
would complete the constitution in Washington, but it ended in chaos because
they couldn't obtain a large meeting hall. Howard University turned them
down when they didn't pay expenses in advances, and Washington's blacks
didn't support the Panthers; many are middle class, and others were nationalists who can't stomach an alliance with whites.

Political Power" and "Control and Use of the Educational System"—kept breaking into smaller groups. Many delegates were haunted by the question of whether *any* eventual government could be trusted, and whether there's any alternative to voting: "Isn't it worse if we never vote at *all*?" Later, I heard that some other workshops came close to punch-ups. But the proposals were finally thrashed out, and were then read aloud to all the delegates.

The recurrent themes were decentralization and self-government for numerous groups. Self-determination for women and homosexuals was a very new position for the Panthers, who, until recently, had derided both. (Many of us who were moved by much of *Soul on Ice* had also been disgusted by the attack on James Baldwin.) But Newton wrote a supportive statement for both Women's and Gay Liberations, admitting that "sometimes our first instinct is to want to hit a homosexual in the mouth and [to] want a woman to be quiet. We want to hit the homosexual . . . because we're afraid we might be homosexual; and we want to hit the woman or shut her up because we're afraid she might castrate us, or take the nuts we might not have to start with." (He added, "Friends are allowed to make mistakes"—a notion that's scarce among revolutionaries.) From several workshops, there were repeated demands for community control of the police; others focused on the military ("No genocidal weapons shall be manufactured or used"), the legal system, environment, religion, drugs and health, and "internationalism—relations with liberation struggles around the world." An ovation burst for "a redistribution of America's wealth to the have-not nations of the world . . . and acceptance of a more modest standard of living that such a move would require." Many papers leaned on the phrase *"after* the revolution." The street people's paper stated that acid, mescaline, and grass "are instrumental in developing the revolutionary consciousness." The crowd whooped until the ceiling rang. However, *"after* revolutionary consciousness has been achieved, these drugs may become a burden." Small response.

The next morning, while crowds swirled around the Church of the Advocate, I listened to Charles X Kenyatta—who was once Malcolm X's bodyguard, and was very active in helping to calm Harlem streets after Martin Luther King was murdered, when he volunteered to man a sound truck—describing the international Congress of African

People in Atlanta, which had taken place on the same September weekend. The congress, which included such diverse speakers as Whitney Young, Imamu Baraka (Leroi Jones), and Roy Innis, largely favored black sepaiatism ("White cooperation is white co-optation"), the use of the existing political system (by running more black candidates), and nonviolence. Kenyatta said that the Atlanta audience was professional and middle class in contrast to the Philadelphia convention, which had drawn so many from the streets. He expressed his own doubts about black-white coalitions; he feels that the priorities are too far apart. "The black radical is fighting for his freedom, while the white radical is fighting for power. The white's free already. So they don't really need the same things."

At this point, a Philadelphia TV crew started to interview Kenyatta. He said that he didn't believe in the gun, although he would defend anyone's right to have it. He added that he was worried about "diffuse hatred"—and he should know, since he was gunned down and badly wounded by unidentified blacks a year before. Just as he began to say that the one thing he can't forgive whites is their ability to make blacks turn against each other, two teen-aged Panthers stopped the interview, by making it clear that they would hit him if he went on talking. They told the rest of us, "Don't listen to him, he's been purged from the party." Kenyatta told me later that he'd never been a member, that he'd always differed with the Panthers and had often told them so. He added that he expected the nationalist movement to develop, but admitted that it didn't yet have a political program.

On another street corner, a young white man dressed as an Arab, complete with flowing headdress, engaged in a testy rap with some young blacks. He said that he was an Arab "sometimes," which annoyed them immensely. As he gurgled about roots and origins, he mentioned the *Mayflower*. One replied, "Well, *we* came on slaveships. And anyway, the *Mayflower* was full of thieves and prostitutes—the un-de-*sir*-ables." The sometime-Arab insisted that he was helping black people against a common enemy, but they told him he was crazy; also, "Your enemy is *you*."

Next I talked with a Panther who said that the party was trying to establish some "unofficial alliances" with separatists and cultural nationalists, despite all the disagreements. Newton had told the Liberation News Service that "blacks have a moral right to separate," but that separatism is a poor "political strategy." Later, a young Panther said of Ron Karenga, "Every time he opens his mouth, he's sick." He began to expand—"We're just as alien to African culture as the Atlantic is to the Pacific"—but someone down the block shouted, "Pigs are beating the sisters!" Warning the crowd to stay put, he and other Panthers dashed to the corner, and learned that the police had merely answered a house call from the neighbors of a brawling couple. The Panthers quickly killed the rumors that were rippling through the neighborhood.

At the end of his Philadelphia speech, Huey Newton said, "It is a fact that we will change the society. . . . It will be up to the oppressors if this is going to be a peaceful change." The point has been repeated so often, but Washington still seems clueless. Last May, before the big peace demonstration, when Nixon "talked to" students at the Lincoln Memorial, they later told CBS: ". . . people were asking him questions, and it was like he didn't hear them at all. He ignored them. And finally, someone shouted out a question, I guess loud enough that it snapped him out of it, and he answered the question. But his answer made no sense. Someone asked him about the Black Panthers, and whether he thought Bobby Seale had gotten his constitutional rights in Chicago, and his answer was that when people stab each other with ice picks, they are still entitled to their constitutional rights, and we still have no idea what that meant."

Hindsight: As of '72, you can't yet tell where the Panthers' new programs will take them. Looking back on their earlier years, I still think that they were very useful in many ways—even though some of their local chapters were really destructive. But the main spokesmen did provide an amazing amount of public education: about racism, about unjust trials for black people, about the problems shared by the poor of any race. At a meeting of the poor during the 1969 Washington conference on Hunger, the blacks, whites, and Mexicans all withdrew and caucused. Finally, the blacks produced a list of demands, the whites had a list of goals, and the Mexicans presented grievances. The lists turned out to be very similar indeed. That was the kind of point the Panthers were trying to make.

The Panthers arrived after liberalism had lost its legs: because it had come to mean hypocrisy—the promises of "economic advance-ment" that weren't refunded, plus the notion that the Vietnam war was a moral exercise, and, above all, the habit of rationalizing: "seeing all sides of the question, and then walking away." (One Panther told me, "The liberal really is a threat—because he can rationalize *any*thing, like overkill.") It also appeared that the Panthers were one of the few groups in the country which reached both educated and uneducated people. In the midst of a fairly horrified reaction from the press, the *Wall Street Journal* ran a lengthy, carefully researched piece which described the respect which the Panthers drew from the ghettos—especially because of their efforts against hard drugs—and many white-collar blacks said that the Panthers were expressing things that they themselves had often wanted to say.

So . . . the language of violence. Throughout the late Sixties, I continued to think that threats were quite valuable as a substitute for violence itself. And, as the language grew fiercer, more and more black faces appeared on TV, in offices, in schools and universities, in ads—the hasty but much wider tokenism in hiring appeared to be a direct response to militancy. (Now I see that it benefited only the middle-class, professional, already well-educated blacks—but not the ghetto, where most of the threats were made.) And of course the threats soon became dangerous to those who made them, and hastened them to jail. James Baldwin offered a helpful reminder in one speech: "White people seem to think that when any black cat says woof, he hates you. But he wants a job, a roof, a raise, to breathe." Baldwin had also written, ". . . when white men rise up against oppression, they are heroes: when black men rise, they have reverted to their native savagery."

Yet it grew harder to know what was really meant by some state-ments. In '68 and '69, when I saw quite a bit of the New York Panthers, including some of the eventual 21, some of these particular individuals stressed that guns were merely for self defense. Numbers of black moderates said they agreed that the ghetto needed such protection against assaults by the police. And others talked about offing or icing the pig so casually that it sounded like a form of shuffleboard. Meanwhile, nonverbal actions accelerated. Pickets, marches, and seizing buildings had been symbolic speeches—which were noticed less and less as the press and the public became accustomed to them. By '68, some seemed to be regarding death itself as a form of speech, a way of asking to be listened to. In April '69, the eighty-year-old Arnold Toynbee said in an interview how much he deplored violence, and: "You have to shoot somebody, burn yourself alive, do something violent, in order to get any attention at all, however good your cause or causes, however patient you have been, however well you have put your case. There is an absolute stone wall of indifference. All over the world." About the same thing in '69, a black woman said to me, "Many of us die all the time. That's not new for us. But the *purpose* for it: that's what we have now. A new strength."

The theme was changing from defense to the possibilities of attack. But if you argued that the innocent would suffer, you were reminded that they were suffering already, from malnutrition to murder, from the diseases of poverty to the black babies who die at six times the rate of white ones, from lead poisoning in slum tenements to the throngs of blacks who die from the nature of ghetto life. Again, if you objected that devastating retaliations would overwhelm any shape of organized revolt, you were told that "more people will join in as blacks are killed off. They won't just stand back and watch it happen." (That wistful argument was very common.) Some accused the Panthers of romanticism, and others angrily charged that the Panthers' young white supporters were just being romantic about black people getting killed. At the same time, you heard middle-aged and even elderly white speakers telling students that they must be prepared to die, "ready to go to the wall," and that "you may ultimately be bathed in blood"—always "you"—an easy shove from those who'd already had some fifty years of life. Hence many were reasonably confused by the death talk—it was so difficult to untangle image from fact.

By 1970, Cleaver, in his Algerian sanctuary, was openly encouraging people to kill cops, and many who had respected him earlier had to write him off. (Most of his statements have sounded frantic ever since.) Long after their split with Cleaver, Newton and Seale were still denouncing him and repeating that they'd "rejected the rhetoric of the gun." But the battles within the Panther party later provoked James Forman to quote an African proverb: "When two elephants fight, only the grass gets hurt." The reputation of poor *or* militant black people was damaged when the Panthers fought each other—since much of the white world was only waiting to hear the worst about all of them.

The Panthers' macho, which suited the Sixties—when I heard a man chide his wife for being "a sissy about violence"—was unacceptable by the end of 1970. The irony was that the Panthers functioned very well as policemen—at the moments when certain communities needed cooling—and at other times, they maddened their supporters by policing *them.*

Also, when most of the Panthers I met talked exactly alike—in identical slogans—I wondered if that extreme effort to suppress all individuality wouldn't result in an almost inhuman experience—as it did for quite a few whites in the movement. (Hence, by '71, the acute introspection among many who were once so doctrinaire. It seemed an inevitable reaction for some who'd tried to have no personal character at all for a few years.)

During 1970, Tom Wolfe's famous Bernstein piece frightened away much of the support that had been building—even though most book reviewers subsequently knocked Wolfe sharply for obscuring the issues of racism and preventive detention. (Later, someone remarked that, since the Bernstein guests had been doing a worthy thing,—i.e., raising bail—that it was natural that sophisticates would be ridiculed for an activity that was so *un*chic.) When the remains of the New York 21 were acquitted after two years in jail, the case had become an embarrassment to many who'd seemed roused by their arrest, and Bobby Seale's release in New Haven was barely noticed. The murder of Alex Rackley, and later, of two Panthers caught between the Newton-Cleaver factions, seemed to echo Fanon's thesis that "oppressed people . . . kill each other all the time"—thus expressing what they'd like to do to their oppressors. But those who prefer to see blacks fighting were rather smug about the murders; some even talked as though they were social gaffes on the level of Leonard Bernstein's. And the Panther leaders' own discovery that some hoods and crazies had entered their ranks had come too late.

Throughout, some whites had expected the Panthers to be morally superior (also forgetting that most of the chapters were staffed with young kids). This tied into the old American notion that people are ennobled by being oppressed. Hence the shock and dismay when the Panthers made many mistakes—which made their documentation of racism easier to forget, or so it seems.

SHOOTING REVOLUTION
January 1970

LIKE SOME hapless Victorian waif, ripe for rape, the left has rarely been lucky in its allies. Besieged from right and center, punctually lacerated from within, the movement faces yet another problem: how are you going to make a revolution when your enemies keep joining it? Industry has long been into revolution, which has already lost some of its language to ads for lipsticks and vaginal sprays, while Bergdorf Goodman and Kenneth have announced "Right On" styles for next fall. And Hollywood—equally inspired and unnerved by the success of *Easy Rider*—is producing "Now-movies" by making films about "campus disorders." In *The Activist* (from the *Ride the Wild Surf* team, Art and Jo Napolean), student radicals have been smeared with sympathy, as they probably will be in most revolution pictures— since Now movies have to be aimed at a young audience. M-G-M has filmed James Kunen's *The Strawberry Statement* and has also bought Abbie Hoffman's *Revolution for the Hell of It.* Elliott Gould has just made *Getting Straight,* Stanley Kramer is producing and direct-ing *RPM**, footage has been shot for a movie on the Chicago Seven, and others are being packaged with a haste that's almost outpacing the politics of genuine protest. Richard Kleindienst has announced that "While Nixon is President, random civil disorders will not be seen in America." But it will be seen in many movies.

However, as an independent film maker admits, "The trouble with Now-movies is that they're often Then-movies." What may happen on the campus or in the streets before a picture's released may worry the publicists as much as it worries Martha Mitchell. How can your product maintain its appeal for those who provide the material? Only fest films, like *Woodstock,* seem safe in this sphere, since cul-ture isn't changing quite as rapidly as politics.

However, some of the current styles of movie making still seem influenced by the techniques of promotion. As many have noticed, parts of both *Easy Rider* and *The Activist* resembled TV commercials: filming attractive bodies within nature at its nicest suggests the hint of menthol, or seems to advertise the life style that's depicted. (And, although *Easy Rider* was the ultimate Now movie of '69, quite a few have remarked that it seems at least ten years old—a nostalgic belch from the Beats and *On the Road.*) But the moral stance for filming revolution will be slippery: are you trying to sell it outright, or must the conclusion be an awful warning? (Of course, good intentions can't validate any movie: as an English critic said of Antonioni's *Blow-Up,* that wopsided view of London, "He got it all so *sensitively* wrong.") Meanwhile, young film makers are being hired to help the industry to reach the audience which it's trying to portray. As Graham Greene wrote in 1935, "There's always money to be picked up in a revolution."

One movie that's braving these problems is Stanley Kramer's *RPM*,* starring Anthony Quinn and Ann-Margret. The confrontation scenes were filmed at the University of the Pacific in Stockton, California—it's one of the few universities which will permit the miming of revolution on campus.

Like a professional army, the crew and twelve hundred extras—including many real students from Stockton—stand about on location, where the bushes around the college buildings have been sprayed with yellow paint to make December look like fall. A chorus of responses punctuates the shooting. "Quinn's finished. They knocked him down and they've been kicking him in the head."

"Were there some nice kicks?"

"Yeah."

Policemen scrape dirt and leaves from their uniforms, rub their sore ribs and knees, compare shattered visors and broken clubs; students press icebags against bruised faces, share bloodied bits of Kleenex for cut lips. Some pat each others' backs or shoulders, others scowl. All wade in succulent mud, which clutches their boots and streaks their thighs. One says, "The vibes are getting ungood." Two crewmen recall the styles of riot control which they once saw in Italy: "We should have the kind of equipment they have. They squirt guns full of red stuff all over the leaders, the inciters—it dyes their skin. Then it's easy to arrest them later."

"That's good. Not messy, you know what I mean?"

The *RPM** script is by Erich Segal. Anthony Quinn plays the acting college president: one of the world's most distinguished sociologists, author of *Studies in Alienation*. A radical in his fifties, he has been chosen by the students to replace the president they've forced out. (The faculty agreed to his appointment, since the other choices were Che and Eldridge Cleaver. And at least some of them are flexible: one professor admits, "We've been absentee slumlords in the ghetto of the mind.") Stanley Kramer, who cheerfully refers to himself as "a discarded liberal," focuses the movie on the aging rebel who's racked by conflicts of responsibility when the younger militants outdistance him. At one point, the Quinn-president protests, "I marched for the Textile Workers' Union! I fought against Franco. . . . I spoke out *against* McCarthy. . . ." (Throughout, he gets limited comfort from Ann-Margret, cast as a student body, whom he urges to "Read Talcott Parsons . . . *and put on a bra!*") He does satisfy most of the radicals' demands, but balks when they insist on hiring and firing faculty and abolishing formal courses. So they threaten to wreck a two-million-dollar computer in the building they've occupied. Quinn accuses the white student leader of having "a pathological need to destroy." But the latter's unmoved by Quinn's earlier defense of private property; the student replies, "Private property is the jockstrap of the American conscience." The anguished president orders a friendly police chief to clear the building, stressing that there must be no violence. But, as the students are gassed out, a psychotic badmouth woman activist attacks a cop and inspires a bloodbath. After a giant bust, the president is hissed, booed, and pronounced Pig! by even the moderate students, who continue to jeer as he walks away. . . .

Filming is slow because the weather's unreliable. Someone says, "It's all in the lap of the gods."

"Yup. And sometimes the gods stand up."

□

Sweating beside a swimming pool before Christmas, drenched in steam and cooked by lights: they're shooting an earlier scene in which Quinn mingles with the students just after his appointment.

"You gotta look radical," a makeup man says, pasting sideburns and a moustache on a sulky extra. "Yeh, like one of those goddam hippies." The one-line actors explain that they were cast as left or right according to their looks.

"Oh, but I was left yesterday and right today."

"Well, I was left in my last picture." Then they talk about the word faggot, its multiple meanings, and what it stems from.

Blue lights are arranged to shine on Quinn's scene with the right; later, a red glow bathes his consultation with the left. The two groups assemble at opposite ends of the pool. The conservative students keep telling Quinn that they deplore the left's tactics, that the university should stay the way it is. One actor keeps fluffing "Maoist" for "Marxist"—a slip of the Sixties.

Just before I came to Stockton, a couple of young New York militants were disturbed to hear that such a movie was being made at all. One said, "That really hurts. What will they make of us? Brutes or clowns?"

Disgusted with the right, Quinn dives and swims down the pool to the left. They keep telling him, "You're beautiful." The president basks in their admiration.

Then they say, "No more classes!"

"Unstructured things, no tightness."

"No more goddam science requirement."

"Science is killing Vietnamese children."

Quinn says, "It also cured polio, guys."

They tell him, "Back to nature!"

"Let the flowers grow straight and tall!"

He mildly defends classes, but they explain, "The important thing is communication. . . . *We* are the only subject. We've got to relate to each other."

"No more classes."

"No more ghettos."

"No more wars."

Quinn surfaces from the pool between takes, shaking himself and scattering water like a formidable sea god, shedding the kind of charm that makes the soles of your feet sting. No wonder he has eight children. It's nice to hear him speak without an accent, after all those life-affirming Mediterranean roles.

As a tenth-grade dropout, he describes preparing for this film. "I really crammed—I've read forty books for this part. I even read Abbie Hoffman and those dirty newspapers at Berkeley." He and Stanley Kramer visited universities, questioned many students, attended classes. He says that the theme of *RPM** is "Where does permissiveness end and authority begin? There comes a point when you have to say, Here's the line. Right, dad, it stops here." (He doesn't think highly of Dr. Spock. "I think he was well-meaning, like Emily Post—but so many sins have been perpetrated in his name. I just bought his book in Italian and threw it down the toilet.") He praises students for their instincts and their ideals, but he considers the rebellion to be psychological rather than political. And yet he hopes that a third political party will come out of the student movement. "If the students could ever unite, they could put this country on its ass economically. . . . I don't think a lot of them are morally against the Vietnam war; instead, they know they're being exploited as slave labor. But nowadays you don't need kids to fight a war—you can have old men pushing buttons. If my generation wants this war, let *them* fight it. With their buttons."

He says that he refuses "to do anything outside the system." Still, he was recently touched when the Brown Berets asked him to be a spokesman for them (he's a Mexican Indian). He visited the Indians who were occupying Alcatraz, has given speeches on their behalf, and was chided by George Murphy for his efforts.

Quinn says that he and his family came to Stockton from Mexico when he was a boy, and that they were migrant fruit pickers, traveling in cattle cars with wooden slats. At first, they didn't know that the California workers were on strike, that they themselves were being used as scabs. Now, he says he's left of center, although "my son thinks I'm one step behind Nixon. . . . But don't make me sound like one of those far-out leftists." And yet: "The public doesn't do a shit. . . . If tomorrow a shooting war started, we'd all run and hide." Suddenly, he's furious: "We've reached the same point that Nazi Germany reached when they were killing the Jews!" He's fiercer than I've seen him on the screen. Then he shakes his big head; there's a pause; the outrage subsides. He talks quietly about the power of economic boycotts: "A twenty-five-million Negro boycott would really hurt. . . . But I still wonder how far the balloon can stretch

—like a balloon, you've got to say, This is all the air I can take. You've got to stay within the balloon, within the system."

He takes off his robe, stretches, swats his toes, prepares to dive for a retake. "Some people are buying good will from the students by saying Go! Go! Go! kids. I don't agree with that."

He swims off; soon, the radicals who will later defy him are repeating that he's beautiful.

□

Stanley Kramer, whose productions include *Home of the Brave, The Men, High Noon,* and *The Wild One,* and who has directed *Judgment at Nuremberg, It's a Mad, Mad, Mad, Mad World, Ship of Fools,* and *Guess Who's Coming to Dinner,* among others, says that he'd like to be "a leader of the counterrevolution"—which means "hope against frustration. Life against death. Many of the films of the moment have a death-in-life motif." He emphasized that *RPM**'s student revolutionaries "must appear pure and idealistic. I take very seriously the responsibility of having people understand them. I dig the activists. If I were black I'd be a militant now. And I also think that tyranny is worse than anarchy." However, he feels that some students have carried their tactics too far. He's already been attacked by some: "I told them, 'I've been fighting the establishment for thirty years, and I can't find out what it is.' And they said, 'Because you're it.' " To refute them, he cites some of his earlier films, which were considered radical. The Navy objected that *The Caine Mutiny* was anti-American; they protested that the character of Captain Queeg gave them a bad image, and that they'd never had a mutiny. The government refused to lend him a nuclear sub for *On the Beach,* and he had to defend himself before a congressional committee concerning "world guilt" about nuclear weapons.

Now, stressing that no single movie "can tell the whole truth," he underlines his identification with the college president played by Quinn. "Yet I'm part of the system that's financing me." He looks momentarily wistful. "Isn't it possible to be someone who has a little compassion and awareness—and work in your own area? Isn't it possible to wait a little while, until things become clear? Before you choose sides?"

☐

I'm up against the wall, standing with my back to a college building: the police are about to charge. That sickening suspense—of waiting to see if and how the cops will move—uncoils from the experience of Chicago, Paris, even Washington—from covering so many confrontations of the past two years. . . . Now, as the sun winks on visors and helmets and the revolving red lights of police cars, I shrink as the uniforms and boots hurtle toward me and past me. But it's only a rehearsal; those who practice tussling with each other have to be reminded not to laugh. *"Please! No* more laughing!" Smoke billows from the windows: it does look exactly like tear gas, and dispels a mildly unpleasant stink of inner tube. I remember how gas can make you hate your own lungs, detest your throat.

Two young cops twirl their rubber guns, fencing lightly with their plastic clubs. One, mishearing directions says, "Hey, the riot starts now!"

"No, we don't get to be violent until after Christmas."

Most of the cops are from UOP's student football team. The black football instructor and the president of the Black Students' Union tell me that UOP is very conservative, very expensive, and that many undergraduates are still apolitical. Atmospherically, the Stockton campus seems a solar distance from most impassioned universities—few of the student extras seem to have many feelings about the war or the draft. However, when the BSU demanded a number of scholarships for minority students, the administration granted more than they asked for. Still, verbal agreements have outstripped concrete action. . . . The football instructor talks about white activists; he says that "their main project is to get rid of football; they forget that it gives scholarships to blacks." He adds that whites at so many universities are especially isolated from politics due to their recent discovery of drugs, which absorb so much of their time. "Drugs have done a flip-flop. They were a black thing for years. Now they're white." He and I share a queasy sensation that this movie's being filmed far from the experiences on most campuses. Yet my own actuality bump is dissolving: at moments, the movie jolts into what one knows so well—at others, it jars because it's so remote. Sometimes the *RPM** company seems to distill most of the opinions and quandaries of the whole country, with all of the contradictions which are thickening up around us. Only one ingredient is missing: militants.

Now they're making some close shots of the left. I chat with an amiable old lady from Stockton who enjoys watching the shooting. She has a library face, haloed with the transparent Martian pleats of a rain hood. Apropos of nothing, she asks if I believe in giving eighteen-year-olds the vote. I say yes, and she says, "But look at the kind of people they turn into! *Look* what they did to Sharon Tate." She points at the college building, occupied by actors and some extras, who are leaning out of the windows for a close-up. "You never know," she says, "they might do anything."

Rap groups tend to form around Gary Lockwood, of *2001* and the TV series, *The Lieutenant;* he now plays *RPM**'s leading white revolutionary. Young actors and extras close around him, arguing, asking questions. He talks about redneck California, the world he grew up in, which is now hostile to the abundance of his (not very long) hair. (Thus, the problems of hitchhiking: "You can't get a ride with long hair. But you can't get a free bed on the other end with *short* hair." "So go buy a hair piece.") Shaggy Californians are used to being called dirty faggot hippies, but mere insults in the East can be threats fulfilled in the West. Although *Easy Rider* isn't Lockwood's favorite movie, he and others agree on the validity of the theme: you really can get killed for the way you look. He's regretfully giving up his place on the Colorado River "because of the polarization": those who yell at him when they drive past his house could one day start shooting. . . . Of course the police are equally suspicious at the sight of him; he describes being frisked at gunpoint by a cop who snatched a small brown box out of his pocket. "What's *this?*"

With his hands over his head, Lockwood meekly replied, "That's my electric garage opener."

"Your *what?*"

"You press that little button on and off and you can dig my garage door going up and down."

Still, he was held for several hours at the police station, where a boy who was descending from acid was weeping and rolling on the floor. Lockwood mimics the two cops who bent over the writhing boy: *"Seeing a lotta monsters,* huh? Having a *bad trip,* aren't you?" Yet he has a rueful sympathy for tough, rural whites—after all, he was one.

Two crewmen disagree about Vietnam; both fought heavily in World War II. One says we should withdraw. The other insists that we've got to stay. Someone asks him why. "Because of the minerals."

Meanwhile, the local police of Stockton, who patrol the location, are very friendly to the company; they admire the professionalism of Stanley Kramer's staff. They snort with disgust in referring to M-G-M's *The Strawberry Statement,* which was filmed very freely in Stockton a month ago—the police call it "Fruit's Delight." "Those hippies were so disorganized, and they used four-letter words that were eighteen inches high." The City Hall was used as an administration building, and the city manager was staggered to find his office being occupied by extras. He said that he had to get into his desk, but they said, "We're making a movie, daddy!" (The bona fide policeman loves imitating them; he switches his hips and snaps his fingers.) "And *he* said, 'Let me in or I'll call the *real* cops!' Ha!"

□

One theme that drifts around the lot is the plight of the huge Hollywood studios. Many have been bought up by business companies, attracted by the vaults of old movies which are rented to TV, and the profit from selling the valuable property which the studios own. Bob Yaeger, the unit publicist for *RPM** (which will be released through Columbia), remembers the lush years of Hollywood, "when the golden goose was erupting eggs from its backside." Of the takeovers, he says, "There are more laughs in a heart transplant." He describes Paramount trying to endure: "like a convict under water breathing through a reed while the dogs are after him." Others repeat that the businessmen who now dictate to film makers are crushing the chance for experiment or change. "All they want is to make money. They bring in their IBM machines and their MIT graduates in tight-ass dark suits. But they don't know anything about pictures." It's stressed that big business is strangling big business. But when the voices of seasoned Hollywood protest, they may not realize that they sound rather like student radicals deploring capitalism.

Anthony Quinn thinks that the movie business has been its own worst enemy: by pandering to popular taste. "They want fucking— so we'll give them fucking! There's this twelve-year-old girl, we'll have her fucked by a horse. . . . It's our own fault that people don't accept movies as an art form." Younger actors love listening to him —they nudge each other's ribs when he roars with disapproval. (He detested *Oh! Calcutta!*)

The extras even repented having to shove him off his feet. "He *is* beautiful. He's much too good for lots of his crappy parts."

Gary Lockwood is having another rap group. Someone's talking about survival. He says, "You dig plants?"

"Uh?"

"Man, plants are outtasight! Say you've got a sick plant—he's got so many ways of trying to tell you. He puts out tendrils all over the house, his leaves will change color or droop in a certain direction. If he can't make it—if you don't understand his signals—he just dies. But the plant that survives! He's stronger than any of the others. Sometimes you even have to starve them to make them strong."

Someone objects that starvation isn't equally good for humans.

Lockwood doesn't fight it. "Look, man, all I mean is that you've got a very complex society—it's like onions growing under roses. . . . You can't store apples and potatoes in the same cellar: they don't like each other. I do think there's a weird connection between people and plants. But I don't think people are really into people yet. . . ."

On the set of *RPM**, an echo steadily recurs: so many kinds of Americans can no longer stomach living with each other. Later, several crewmen reminisce about "how the boys who came home from the war cleaned out the zoot-suiters in two weeks—they strung them up and had them hanging from the lampposts in L.A."

"Oh, I don't think they actually *hung* them."

"Well, anyway, they got rid of them."

Bob Yaeger says, "Well, time's scythe has reaped another day."

□

Gentle and cordial, Ann-Margret is reflective when asked for her views on revolution. "I've never been in a riot," she says, "I'm not an intellectual." But she's sympathetic to student protest—"I think its very healthy." Still, "I find so many of the kids so mixed up, they don't know what, because the world is going so fast. I wish there were more leaders than followers. The leaders know exactly what they're doing, and sometimes they're doing wrong.

"You get a sixteen- or a seventeen-year-old kid, seeing their parents into the martinis and sleeping around, they tell them not to smoke pot, you know, blah, blah, blah, they're so confused, they'll grasp at anything. Some of them find it.

"Lord knows it's ten thousand times harder to go to college now than it was for me." (She went to Northwestern's School of Speech.) "I don't know how the kids remain sane. And some don't, and we know that some freak out, and some are insanitary. They've got to have something, or else they'll go completely out of your mind."

□

The film company grows restless during its week on location in Stockton. Someone says, "This is a one-horse town. And they castrated the horse."

Mounting toward the confrontation, a female militant, played by Linda Meiklejohn, yells at the police chief who has ordered the students to clear the building: "Thanks to you, and to our *noble* president, maybe our citizens who are so unmoved by our use of force overseas and in our own cities will wake up when they see hobnailed boots in the Garden of Eden . . ."

Between takes, Graham Jarvis, of Elaine May's *Adaptation* and her movie, *The New Leaf,* tells me that he initially hesitated about playing the police chief. He accepted the role when Stanley Kramer assured him that the students "would not appear in a bad light." Now, it does seem likely that the audience may leave the theater thinking that the rebels are sick adventurists. I know that Stanley Kramer doesn't intend this. But Jarvis and I talk about how easy it is to play into the hands of the right. After all, this subject is in the public domain—it merely belongs to everyone in the country.

ABC-TV is filming the filming; Gary Lockwood makes some shots with his hand-held camera; a still photographer snaps pictures of Lockwood and ABC filming the filming. Bob Yaeger says, "So this is not just for The B'nai B'rith Bugle."

☐

Teda Bracci is setting her hair for tomorrow's confrontation. She plays the ferocious activist who mauls a cop, shouting "Pig bastard!" and thereby touching off "the riot." She loves her part. Now, her eyes glow and her excitement kindles as she anticipates the shooting —she throbs like a Tolstoyan heroine looking forward to her first ball, or National Velvet before the great steeplechase. Her bony face ripples with a flurry of rapturous smiles; she has the kind of ripe, husky voice that can slide from a whoop to a croon. Meanwhile, Audrey Hepburn is having nun's trouble on TV. Teda says, "I mustn't have any breakfast, or there'll be something *else* all over the ground." Audrey Hepburn says, "How can I be a good nun if I cannot get the Congo out of my blood?"

☐

Agitation rustles through the location, despite the fiberglass vests and shin guards, and the plastic skullcaps which some stunt men wear beneath hairy wigs. Waiting for planned chaos pinches some nerves and mouths, tautens the skin stretched over cheeks and around nostrils.

Teda Bracci kicks her cop's feet out from under him, flinging him prone. She's a magnificent fighter; someone says, "She knows where a man's castanets are." Hundreds race and leap to beat each other's heads against the ground, to wrestle in a mud-rich fleshpack that grows angrier every hour. Arms, legs, fists, knees, clubs reassemble again and again to punish one another. When the action's cut off by the bark of a gun, they stand panting and gasping and glaring. After all the rehearsals, the preparation, the choreography with stunt men, much of the crowd starts punching from the heart. Later, it was discovered that some who swung hardest weren't even student extras, but were unpaid visitors simply fighting for free.

Many grudges build up through the reshooting: "*Next* time, I'll get *him*." A cop slams a student hard against a car; a student knees a cop repeatedly; many skulls are cracked together; one policeman socks a student six times after a take is finished. The casualty list swells. Blurts of blood glisten through the glycerine and the red paint, and lots complain of having been bitten.

Older professionals talk indulgently about "body contact": they think that's what makes the crowd grow wilder. But it's also the period: by December 1969, the real students who play students can't help reacting against the symbols embodied by their classmates who play police. And the latter do hate being called pigs. One says he'd *never* join the force: "like it changes you." Another adds, "I used to wonder why they called cops pigs, and now I know why." A shortish boy in uniform has been jumped five times by the same group. Another extra tells me that he overheard them saying, "Let's get him—he's in ROTC, and that's Communist, you know!" (Later, Gary Lockwood unpicks the initials: Russian . . . Oppressive . . . Terroristic . . . Communists.) Now, Lockwood's astonished by receiving his first mouse: he was doing elaborate fllips and rolls with a stunt man, when a student ran up and belted him in the eye. "Man, I've been in at least five hundred fights and never had a mouse!"

A black student playing a cop says happily, "Pig hit a pig" He explains that a few of the students are actually police trainees, and two have just accidentally clobbered one another. Later, two of the fledgling cops recall the flaming ping-pong balls which they encountered on a stretch of duty in Washington after Martin Luther King was murdered. "They're worse than Molotov cocktails. You take a hypodermic needle and inject the ball with fire-lighting fluid. After it's lit, you can bat it through a window with a tennis racket."

"It's not just an amateur thing."

Meanwhile, a cop and a student—who have been pounding each other into the mud—spring up beaming, and slap each other's palms. At least a few remember that this is a movie. But, as the days of shooting have accumulated, many have started weighing the issues that *RPM** has shoved at them. Some seem to have acquired more respect for student revolt: "They're trying to tell us something, but nobody listens, so the next time they try harder. What else can they do?"

Gary Lockwood says, "If enough people are okay financially, there won't be a revolution. And if enough *aren't,* there will be." He talks about ghettos: "Like I'm glad I'm not sort of black, man." Since he was poor for years, he's personally irritated by those who call him a copout because he now earns well: "They attack my eighty-dollar desk. But why shouldn't I groove on my own?" I press him again about student revolution. "Man, I *gotta* be for it! I just *have* to think it's good. But there's a lot of . . . elements I don't go along with. If you go ripping down the street with your bayonet, chanting from Mao, that's cool, but don't come yelling to me if you get shot. . . . But if this white conservative middle class doesn't come around, then it looks like we're moving toward civil war, man. Sometimes it seems inevitable. But I don't want all those people killed, or the rest of us. I like my old lady, I like my dog, I like me. And I'd like to be seventy, man."

Someone else says, "But what do we *do?*"

Small arguments continue about violence and repression, plus the likelihood that both will ripen soon. But there are others—including some high school students—who gleam with the sheer exhilaration of the fighting. "We're going to miss this when it's over."

"Man, we've never had such fun."

One murmurs, "Right on," as though he's never said it before.

Later, I learn that it cost over half a million to film the confrontation—including the price of keeping the company at a motel for twenty-six days. Abbie Hoffman wrote that the Yippies spent under $5,000 on the Chicago demonstrations, and that the Yip-in in Grand Central cost $15.

The flesh pile is heaving and hurting again. Paul Winfield—who plays the key black militant—and I compare our confrontations: he was in the antiwar crowd that was savaged by blue power at the Century Plaza Hotel when LBJ visited Los Angeles in 1967. While we agree that most of *RPM**'s combat scenes are painfully accurate, we're startled when so many students jump on cops' backs, and send them rolling over and over on the ground. We've never seen anyone attack the police so blithely, nor cops who are so easy to knock down. However, today's action is being shot in blur and slow motion, so perhaps the fuzz won't look like such a pushover.

Winfield, who grew up in Watts, describes being shot to death in his last picture, *The Lost Man*. Pellets of pseudo-blood and gunpowder were taped to his body beneath his clothes; when an electric switch was pressed, blood and smoke stains burst through his shirt. He says that it wasn't unpleasant, although the electrical aspect did make him uneasy beforehand.

The last gun is fired to end the shooting. Teda Bracci lies on the ground with a cop in her arms, patting the back of the man she's just been kicking.

The real Stockton police produce a huge cake with blue icing, inscribed To the *RPM** Crew/From the Boys in Blue.

Bob Yaeger gazes benignly around the location. "Well, as they say in the hardware business, God bless 'em and screw 'em."

Hindsight: For me, the filming of this movie characterized the end of the Sixties. A few young actors on the set had just been at the Rolling Stones' concert at Altamont, where the murder confirmed their impression that it was all coming down, that the ordinary life they knew might be over very soon. There was a sense of inevitability about violence—but none of them liked it. Some tried to ignore what was happening outside the movies, but they didn't succeed very well.

When the revolutionary movies were released, almost all of them had deservedly poor reviews. As was predictable, the film-makers had known far too little about their subject. *RPM**'s reviews were perhaps the worst, but *The Strawberry Statement*'s were dreadful, and many found *Getting Straight* the most offensive: revolution as a real gas—where all involved were stupid or crazy. *RPM** was much more respectful of students than those other pictures, and all of the silliest lines I quoted were cut from the final version, as was the swimming pool scene.

At any rate, Hollywood hastily abandoned revolutionary flicks and Now-pictures. Then we had *Love Story*—but few of the expected imitations followed. By early '72, *Variety* was predicting a wave of wholesome family movies. *The Last Picture Show*—which I thought was one of the most boring films in years—entranced the audience which had recoiled from "relevant" movies: good ones as well as bad.

At this writing, these conversations on the set of *RPM** seem fairly amazing in retrospect, muddled as many of them were. In '69, it seemed that few could escape the questions of the country, not even movie extras or movie stars.

VOICES FROM THE GI MOVEMENT
February 1971

HEAVY PEACE rings worn like brass knuckles; military bases where STOP signs have been repainted to read STOP WAR; young officers' cars bristling with antiwar stickers. "Dissent? It's more like contempt. Dig it: disgust." For many, loathing their personal experience within the military is the first step toward deploring what it represents; the next stage means rejecting U.S. foreign policy and its kinship with racism and poverty at home. Desertions and AWOLs are up as never before; reenlistment is at its lowest since 1955. Many refuse to carry out orders; a Vietnam returnee can't stop laughing as he describes how often his team neglected to set up ambushes in the jungle, and just blew grass for hours while they radioed back false information about their activities and their locations. You even hear about pilots who drop their ammunition in unpopulated areas, far from their targets. Members of the GI movement agree that they're still a minority—"But how we're growing! Just since early in '69." Until a couple of years ago, the civilian peace movement concentrated on draft resisters, and tended to ignore or scorn those who were already in the service. "People weren't upset back in '63— when only Green Berets were getting croaked. The hollering didn't start until lots of draftees were killed." Today, Vietnam vets and returnees are the marrow of the GI movement. Hence those about to leave Vietnam are kept apart from "the new meat," since their views are "bad for morale and discipline."

The antiwar GIs I met weren't drafted campus radicals. Most were from the working class, the sons of hardhats or blue collars or random hair-haters. Few had been to college. Among those who said that they'd grown up apolitical or reactionary were an ex-biker from the Boston Hell's Angels with an Elvis ducktail of the Fifties, who did five years in jail before his induction; a forlorn welder who reenlisted only because of the job shortage in his home town; a trainer of horses and grade-riders who went to a Seventh-Day Adventist school and was once the 4-H Canning Boy of the Year; a cross-country wheat harvester and street chemist; a deepfreeze salesman; the son of a policeman. Most remarked how the military had exposed them to their own racism, which had altered when they discovered that black and white GIs have the same problems: "only the black dudes get even more shit from the lifers than we do." Several stressed that the conservatism of working people was starting to change within their generation: "The army's beginning to turn out left-wing rednecks or greasers. Like me." Lately, the GI papers have carried detailed reporting on labor news, strikes, and unemployment—since so many of their readers come from or will return to the realm of unions. The papers also aim at educating GIs about their legal rights, and pool bad information about the military. "See, the army's the tie that binds—because it's so goddamn stupid."

□

What turned you against the war? Or changed your politics?

Bill (enlisted, reenlisted; 4 years): "You shoot a little gook kid and they give you a medal. I've got the Good Conduct Medal, the Bronze Star, two Purple Hearts, and some other shit too. I was very gung-ho in basic, fight for the flag and kill-kill-kill and all that."

Tom (enlisted, reenlisted; 4 years): "When I got back from Nam, I was a plans clerk for the Battalion, during August and September '69, and I worked at writing invasion plans for more than seventy countries—all for the **** Corps. We're ready to go to *any* country in Africa, every country in Central and South America, and part of Europe—like Germany and East Europe. And there's a plan for the Middle East crisis now: we're fully ready to support either side. . . . I was always antiwar, but that's what made me revolutionary. It's amazing what the army does to nonviolent people like me."

Buckwheate (drafted, reenlisted; 4 years): "The way guys collect souvenirs in Nam. Trophies like heads or breasts or ears. We had Head-Hunters painted on the nose of our chopper. And cutting off the penis and shoving it in the mouth. I saw that five times. The sixth time, I pulled a Thompson machine gun on a guy who said, 'I think I'll cut me some nuts.' I said, 'You start cuttin' and I start shootin'.' There weren't any more mutilations while I was around."

Paul (enlisted; 2 years): "At first I dug the excitement. I'd been in my unit fifteen minutes when we went into contact; since I was a cherry—after I'd made a kill—the guys stood around in a circle while I took the ear, and they said, 'That's the way we like to break them in.' That first time it made me feel queasy, but I didn't later, the army does wonders. We used to do it all the time and laugh about it. That was in the Boogaloo Renegade Rat Control—Second Platoon, E Troop, 17th Cav. I didn't get my head changed until it happened to one of my buddies—what we did to gooks all the time. They cut off his fingers and ears and wrote Ho-ho-ho across his chest with a knife. At first I wanted to go out and kill all the gooks I could find. Then I realized they're human, like I'm human. . . . How come? Well, when I was ghosting, I had a house in Ben Cao, I'd like to be there now, it was so nice. The Viet navy used to take me out in their PT boats, or I'd float around in the sampans; a kid would paddle me on the river. I used to leave my weapon behind, or give it to the mama-san; she looked after my billfold when I was all fucked up on dope. I knew I could trust her. When they started liking me, they just gave me my dope free—when they could have made money off me. So I started selling their dope at camp and bringing the money back to her. She had old Beatles records, and what I used to dig was doing dope during the monsoon and listening to the rain on the roof. I'd get stoned and swim and listen to music. It was so nice."

Jake (enlisted; 2 years): "Blood on my clothes, on the walls, on my hands. Not my blood. It was when I was flying Medevacs, picking up wounded guys. Their blood would be sloshing all over the chopper by the end of the day."

George (enlisted, reenlisted twice; 6 years): "All the lies on TV. They said there would be no troops in Laos, but—being in the military—we *knew* there were. Last June or July 1970, hearing some senator say the 82nd *wasn't* on alert for the Middle East—when we knew we were. Everybody's lying, the president's lying, it blows your mind, if you've still got one."

□

Again and again, you hear the rebellion against treating people as objects—GIs refer to this as often as feminists do. After all, it's how the army treats them—and how they're told to treat the Vietnamese. "You're always hearing: 'They're not people, they're just fucking gooks.' Your platoon leader will tell you that if you hit one with a truck or a jeep, you should back up and hit it again—to make sure it's dead. Otherwise, it'll sue the American government, and maybe sue you too."

A few said that their hatred of the war was fueled by the kinds of weapons we use; several had researched the weapons outlawed by the Geneva Convention of 1954—which the U.S. didn't sign. "In Nam, you see people literally nailed to trees by fleschettes—those are beehive artillery rounds. That's definitely against the Geneva Convention. So is Napalm B: that bursting white phosphorous which we use all the time. It sticks to the skin more than the old types of napalm. Oh man, they've got a lot of neat things. Let's see, other goodies: the army says a flamethrower is humane because you only die of suffocation, not burning. That's true if you're in a bunker. But if you're outside, the body fats burn, it cooks you alive. Nothing like being a torch."

"You know how they kept saying we found such big munitions caches? Well, in Cambodia the enemy had old rusty weapons—which the Vietnamese had already replaced. The only weapons I found were useless to the Cambodians."

"What gets me down: my parents treat me like a big shot because I've been in the war. But I know I'm just a big shit."

Another Vietnam returnee said that U.S. card companies send whole decks of the ace of spades to Vietnam. "Dudes tuck them in the camouflage bands of their steel pots. When they kill a VC, they nail the ace of spades to his forehead." Discussing the constant mutilation of the Vietnamese dead by American GIs, one returnee said, "We were fed a whole lot of propaganda about its having such a terrible psychological effect on Charlie. In their religion, if the body's mutilated, the soul can't get to heaven or something like that. But lots of guys do it just to do it."

"And revenge. Because you hear it's done a lot to Americans—although I personally never saw an American body that had been mutilated."

"I was there in '66, when helicopter crews were pushing Viets out of choppers. They took one prisoner and dangled him from a fifty-foot rope from a chopper and dragged him through the trees.

It was strictly Americans doing this: the 326 Engineers, attached to the A Company 327th Infantry. When I first got there, I thought that was how war had to be fought."

"I wonder what our psychiatric wards will be like a few years from now?"

□

In Haymarket Square, the movement coffeehouse near Fort Bragg, in North Carolina, table after table was awash with notes by GIs who were filling out their applications as conscientious objectors—some for the second time. Many were recently back from Vietnam. Some tablehopped to advise others about the procedures for CO. A white captain and a black first lieutenant—both members of the Concerned Officers' Movement—were also applying. A few weeks later, the lieutenant received an honorable discharge; he was the first West Point graduate to get CO. The captain, a dentist who wore a vast mushroom felt sombrero and loops of brown glass beads, had already been reprimanded for talking politics while his patients' mouths were jammed with metal—"I just lay some antiwar rap on them when they can't answer back." Among those rustling through their notes, there was some outraged talk about army chaplains, who are said to be most unhelpful to potential COs. "Those old rinkydink chaplains—they shock the shit out of you because they still think Christianity is the tool for fighting communism."

"Yes, and they tell you it's OK to burn babies with napalm because it keeps them from burning in hell later—because dying keeps them from sinning, and all Vietnamese are sinners anyway."

"Ahhhhh, Churchianity is just a capitalistic plot."

Some of those applying for CO said that they'd split if they were turned down. In California, a lawyer told me that some GIs who work in offices (especially in Germany) have become expert at writing discharges for one another: "And by the time the brass wakes up, all the files on those guys have disappeared!" One of the nimblest forgers was finally detected, so he wrote emergency leave orders for himself, boarded a military plane, and is still enjoying his freedom.

You hear about a galaxy of actions against the military, from numerous groups of GIs who file petitions to have their officers replaced, (an Article 138 gets an officer investigated), to some who try to have their officers court-martialed for charges like "communicating a threat," or assault and battery, plus all the fragging in Vietnam. Thus, from the flight line at Quan Loi in late '69, in the Bravo First Squadron 9th Cavalry, the First Air Cavalry Division: "Once we were pulling inspections at night and we all had our various means of relieving tension. A CID man saw us smoking; he whipped out his badge and said, 'You're all busted!' And those were the last words he *ever* spoke. Three guys fired on him at the same time."

"Fragging used to be mainly for racism, or too much harassment. But it's up a lot now—guys do it to almost anybody they don't like. After you've been in Nam a while, it's not too hard at *all*."

"I had a section sergeant in Camp Holloway, in Pleiku, who gave us twenty-hour workdays, seven days a week. He was found from the waist down."

There were also references to putting prices on officers' heads. Someone with a private income may offer $1,000, "plus legal fees if necessary," or a group will take up a collection. The Fort Bragg GIs told me about two officers who are now said to have expensive heads; one is a general in Vietnam who "initiated the policy that enlisted men who failed to salute officers were sent to the forward firebase"; another is a major at Bragg who's considered "big on racist repression." Someone added that the price on officer removal is rising due to inflation.

It was mentioned that some buildings at Fort Bragg were nearly burned in the summer of 1970: "It was close. Guys were coming back from Nam, realizing they were being used here just as they were used there, hating the war, hating the army." Last year, two messhalls in the Special Processing Detachment at Fort Ord, California, were burned down. (SPD is used for pretrial and posttrial confinement, and is usually crammed with AWOLs.) This account comes from a civilian who visited the SPD about an hour after the fire: "That night, an MP busted one guy for not wearing a hat, and another for keeping his hands in his pockets. So about twenty stoned the pig car and demanded that both men be released. Then about a hundred and fifty guys smashed up the cage—that's the only locked part of SPD, where the new arrivals are kept—and sprang them. After they burned the messhalls, they decided to burn the dayrooms, but they didn't want to burn up the pool table, and it was too big to carry through the door. . . . Well, the brass got wiggy after the torching, and some discharges were speeded up, especially for political types."

Mutiny?

"It's hard to have a mutiny in Nam. When guys are over there for only a year, they just cover their ass and wait for the time to be over. But you could have strikes in the form of massive sick calls. And you could organize sympathy strikes back here. The real test will come for a lot of bases when guys are ordered out for riot-control duty or told to break up a labor strike."

Some at Fort Bragg told me that they would refuse riot duty. They praised the forty-three black GIs at Fort Hood, Texas, who refused to be sent to the Chicago Democratic Convention of '68.

"I'd love to get orders to fight my brothers. It would be so easy to fuck up riot control!"

"If there's riot duty, there are some of us who'd like to keep some units here—if only because the brass is worried about what *might* happen. If we keep them here through rumors, that's cool too. Anything's possible, but it's up to the brass to find out the differences between plans and rumors."

From the alumni of any base, there are many accounts of low-level sabotage. Sugar or mothballs often appear in officers' gas tanks, with certain regional variations: maple syrup is popular with New Englanders, but Southerners favor molasses. I learned that "peanut butter saturated with gas explodes, although you need a cap to set it off." At Bragg, the technicians were very explicit. "Sabotage—oh wow! Every time my unit goes into the field, the machines are in perfect running order. In five miles, they break down. Turning the ignition on and off blows pistons out nicely. You can take the sparkplugs out and bang them with a hammer. There are other neat things, like not putting the lug nuts on tight, so that the wheels fall off, or loosening the bolt in the steering wheel. What else is cool: broken bottles beneath the back wheels of two-ton trucks."

"Take the air inlets in the cheeks of army gas masks—if they get wet, the mask is useless."

"I used to work at the airport, but now they've decided they can't have me around half-a-million dollar aircraft."

"In Nam, when you hear there's going to be a bad mission, you can say there's something wrong with the bird. Then you make it wrong. Put a scratch on a rotor blade, or scrape the insulation off the wiring, or loosen the fuel lines, or spray oil on the engine so it looks like it's leaking."

"See, we're just using intelligence that the army taught us."

A statue of a World War II paratrooper, known as Iron Mike, is rather wistfully mentioned as a symbolic target.

But there are many other GIs who think that further revolutionary actions within the military "would only result in sheer terrorism." One militant added, "You've got a lot of dudes who are into any kind of violence. Sure, that's how the army schooled them. But luckily, they haven't done much about it yet, because the targets they'd choose would be the wrong ones." A spokesman for the GI movement said, "Some of us find it difficult to decry sabotage, because we know that GIs have no political power. But we also tend to discourage it because it won't build a wider GI movement. . . . Still, the result of fragging in Vietnam is that guys aren't ordered into a combat situation. So maybe fragging's a form of pacifism?"

☐

"You know how the brass uses racism? It's a way of keeping people in line: by turning them against each other. Last Halloween, at Fort Ord, the army tried to provoke a race riot in SPD. The black GIs were told that if there was another riot, blacks would be thrown in the stockade, but not whites. There were rumors that whites would burn the place down, and rumors that blacks would beat on them if they did. But nothing happened." From those who've been in the stockade, there are recurrent reports that guards threaten blacks with punishment for what the whites might do—which increases the possibility that blacks may attack whites, and vice versa.

Although black GIs get most of the worst jobs and much of the fiercest combat duty overseas, you're told that "Black guys really have it together in Nam," where many officers look the other way when blacks "give dap" (the power shake); however, many have been hassled for flashing the fist on bases at home. A number have faced court martials rather than trim their Afros. In October 1970, a black GI at Fort Lewis was given three years' hard labor and forfeiture of all pay for refusing to part with his Afro and his beard. A few months earlier, some white Marine reservists who wouldn't cut their hair received fourteen days' hard labor. All in all, it's unstartling to hear that "Some black guys are joining the marines to get training for the war. Not the Vietnam war."

Racism in the military surfaced like a sperm whale at the Alameda Naval Air Station in California, where a white staff sergeant produced, dittoed, and distributed a drawing of a naked black man tied to a stake, his penis bound by a string attached to a pistol pointed at his head. A naked white woman crouches in front of him: when he has an erection, his brains will be blown out. The drawing is titled "HOW TO ELIMINATE THE NEGRO PROBLEM!" Several white NCOs helped to circulate the drawing in the fall of 1970. A black lance corporal took it to a lawyer, and they filed a writ of habeus corpus for the lance corporal's release from the marines—on the grounds of the racist nature of the military. More than two-thirds of the petitioner's detachment of some hundred and fifty men signed a solidarity statement concerning the case—and only seven of these were black. However, the judge dismissed the case.

□

During my first evening's conversation with GIs at Fort Bragg, I was staggered to hear four of them contemptuously referring to some others in their unit as sexist pigs. Almost all of the antiwar GIs I met were stronger supporters of the women's movement than many civilian radicals—perhaps because GIs are beginning to rebel against their own experience with machismo. One huge, crop-headed GI, just back from Vietnam, said, "Macho is still the army's biggest drawing card for enlistment—it's even more powerful than patriotism or opportunism. So many of us have been programmed to this compulsion: it's what sucked us into the military. There's got to be a way for young men to learn that they don't need the army to make them feel worthwhile—the army's still capitalizing on their insecurity. So I think civilians and women's liberation groups can help GIs a lot: by continuing to expose the absurdity of the male role."

"Right on!" came from the GIs in earshot—to my astonishment. (And I didn't bring the subject up; they did.) They went on to stress how badly the army treats WACs and army wives: "WACs are just supposed to be a handy lay." Distilling the army's attitude toward women, someone mentioned a friend who had refused to wring a chicken's neck during survival training in basic; his colonel had shouted, "If you can't strangle a chicken, how can you ever make love to a woman?"

Two WACs later told me that their daily assignments were pointless "jerk-off stuff that's too dumb for GIs to do." Their bubble gum popped softly as they angrily snapped and shuffled a deck of cards. "If they need us in the army, they better give us some goddam work. We're supposed to look busy in the office, but I don't even have a goddam desk—I'm supposed to look busy standing up?" Their descriptions of army life sounded like a caricature of a 19th-century girls' boarding school, stiff with humiliations and "piss-poor morale." They added that their major keeps a baseball bat by her desk, and their first sergeant has a billy club in her in-tray.

I also learned that homosexual GIs are discussing the possibilities of Gay Liberation groups on several bases. "At induction centers, you can tell them you're gay and you'll still be drafted. So if you're gay, you're going to Nam—and lifers'll tell you that you're going as a lay." Although homosexuality can mean a dishonorable discharge, some are convinced that coming out will be useful in further weakening the army's reliance on macho: "The last stereotype to fall could *really* fall!"

As for wives, the military sometimes tries to use them as a conservative force—in hopes that they'll pressure their husbands to stop their antiwar activities. The most political GIs are fined repeatedly for indirect reasons, such as untidy lockers or lateness for formations. (Fines are taken out of the paychecks, hence the married are particiularly vulnerable. And families are easily divided.) One black army wife of twenty-two years—"I am now violently against the war"—told me that she would like to organize GI wives around the issues of peace and pollution. "But they threaten you with your husband's rank. If you do anything they don't like, they *suggest* that he won't get promoted." Her own husband is now in Vietnam for the third time, he also spent eighteen months in Santo Domingo, and has been wounded on three different occasions. Half in tears but trying to stifle them: "God forbid that it should happen, but if my husband is killed—and I really mean this—I feel he will have died for nothing if he dies for this country. And if they give me that flag and those medals—they pin those medals on you and I'll rip them off my chest, and I'll tell them to send that stuff to Nixon and tell him to *shove* it . . ."

□

The notion of liberalization unleashes a series of hoots and snorts; *Time*'s December cover story, "The Military Goes Mod", brought some gut-spilling laughs from a number of GIs—especially because the "people programs" described have no relation to their hostility to war. Longer hair and rock and beer in the barracks hung with psychedelic posters don't make them more eager to fight: "Raising a 'fro is supposed to make me dig Waste-More-Land?" Many are very cynical about the Enlisted Men's Councils, which allow them to "voice grievances," but give them no authority. At Fort Carson, some GIs yelled "Safety-valve!" and "Pacifier!" at officers who were offering them culture in hopes of making them fonder of the army. At Fort Bragg, which is supposed to be a liberal base, GIs say that their NCOs often fail to carry out "all that public relations crap that the brass dishes up. So they've abolished reveille—and our field first sergeant keeps threatening us with a 5:30 A.M. *work assemblage.* Haw."

Quite a few said that they'd reenlisted just to get out of Bragg. "After a year or eighteen months in Nam, you can't stand the way you're hassled here." And the living conditions for GIs aren't as swinging as the media suggests: some showed me the broken windows—long unrepaired—which makes their temporary World War II troops barracks so cold that ice forms overnight in the water cans they use as ashtrays. Ravaged boilers and toilets often stay that way. Bragg is so blanketed with coal dust that many who blow their noses on awakening complain of having black snot.

"I lived so much better in Nam than I do here."

"Well, at least it's warm in Nam."

But both enlisted and drafted GIs said that they were appalled by the idea of an all-volunteer army: "It'll be all pigs—except for the kids in civil courts who are forced to enlist by judges who give them a choice of three years in the army or five in slam."

"A volunteer army is *really* frightening—when you think of all the wigged-out guys we've got now. The enemy will be anybody who doesn't wear a uniform."

□

Within the bleary glare of Fayetteville, N.C., a town with no character, which is merely a strip of rip-off stores and drive-ins to tempt GIs, plus eateries and topless Live Entertainment, signs winking "YALL COME HEAH," the Pop-a-Top Lounge and the Pink Pussycat, John Wayne or skin-flicks, bleak trailer camps filled with Mobile Unit Homes, lunch counters, where, "If you're a black dude, they fix you food to go," and the juicer-joints disdained by the grass generation, a GI called the antiwar coffeehouse "an oasis of enforced peace." At Haymarket, posters announce "GULF KILLS" and "This vacation visit beautiful VIETNAM," bulletin boards report the latest in lettuce boycotts and officers who demand war crimes inquiries; sweatshirts are stenciled with the Statue of Liberty looking rather like Che and giving the fist, and buttons support Nat Turner or Tom Paine. While the Nitty Gritty Dirt Band or the Youngbloods or Led Zepplin get some assistance from twanging Jews' harps, and "The Sounds of Silence" begins to sound like the national anthem, GIs can buy or browse through I. F. Stone, Fanon, Leroi Jones, Mao, and Juan Bosch, or "Cuba for Beginners" or "The Myth of the Vaginal Orgasm," or chalk up more graffiti on the black walls: "I am a captain in the U.S. army and I think it sucks;" "They put in my mind the ways of truth—in my hands the weapons of war!! Then they take my sanity!!"; "My country right or wrong, but right the wrong in my country." And everywhere there are signs forbidding the use, possession, or dealing of dope.

□

"Listen, that whole war's being fought on dope!"
"To stop dope, you'd have to jail the whole army."
"For a while, I thought I'd stay in Nam—just sitting back and getting stoned. I could dig being over there now for a lot of that cheeeeap grass, and those sweet little vials of liquid dex."
"On patrols, we used to carry speed right in the kit."

"The day I reenlisted, I was skagging so much I was nodding, but they managed not to notice."

"In Nam, our CO told us, 'I don't care what you use as long as you get the job done.' "

"I wasn't doping much in Nam—it's mainly since I came back here."

"I was. That's the main reason I went to Nam."

Despite billows of puffery—about burning occasional fields of marijuana in Vietnam, or opening drug centers on bases—it's obvious that the military has indeed been permissive about drugs, as the Defense Department has openly admitted. But GIs say that their COs have been reluctant to confront the subject, since the evidence of drugs will blacken their own records. "But the brass is getting scared now. They're striking out sporadically, here and there, which makes people schizzy. But they'd rather have guys around on dope than going AWOL to look for it—they'd rather have them stoned than screaming. In Nam—where so many start doing smack in the combat zone—there's very little real effort to unhook them. The army knows that smack-heads can function on heavy drugs for a year—which is all that's needed."

"I worked in a clinic in Nam, and I saw the same thing happen over and over: when guys came in and smack was proven—unless they were withdrawing and *had* to go to the hospital—they were sent right back to their units, where they got more smack and went right on."

"Sure, the army lets H happen—to keep people quiet. If they *really* wanted to bust the dealers, then they would."

It's steadily repeated that many become addicted to hard (or robust) drugs in Vietnam. Black-market speed comes from Vietnamese pharmacies; one favorite is known as "mop juice," since "mop" is the Vietnamese name for fat, and the product (Obisotol) is used for dieting. "Number tens" or "BTs" (binactols) are also popular: "They're superdowners, it's just like being drunk. They appeal to juice-freaks who want to get into the dope scene. BTs make you very hostile: they get you into the guerrilla bag."

It's said that quite a bit of heroin comes from the Thai troops. Also: "We wonder how much money the Saigon government is making on dope. Air America, that thing the CIA uses, flies opium—

from the Meo tribes' crops. The U.S. Air Force supplies planes to fly it when Air America can't. We have armed guards protecting opium fields in Laos and Cambodia during the harvest—especially Laos. We heard this a lot from our friends in the Special Forces; they said the guards were sometimes discharged Special Forces guys."

"And I've heard that our planes have even destroyed a competitor's aircraft—like Air Vietnam or the Cambodian Air Force—so the product can't get to market."

References of this sort have been trickling into the press for a couple of years. In a speech by Representative (now Senator) John Tunney of California on March 24, 1970, there were charges that "We are . . . engaged in a secret war in Laos, a tribal war in which the CIA has committed the United States to support a faction of Meo tribesmen led by General Vang Pao whose sole function is to dominate other factions of this opium-producing Meo tribe through northern Laos. . . . The Administration has deliberately veiled in secrecy our deepening involvement in an opium tribal war . . . clandestine yet official operations of the United States Government could be aiding and abetting heroin traffic here at home." Of course there are many who want a thorough investigation of these matters.

At Fort Bragg, heroin usage increased so much in 1970—mainly due to Vietnam returnees—that Bragg is now called the second largest heroin market in America—after New York City. Quite a few GIs told me that they often see others shooting up in their barracks. But Bragg's much-publicized drug-treatment center, Operation Awareness, was derided as "a farce." "Officially, no one's a doper if he's been in there. But they're just barely rehabilitating guys so that they don't have to be immediately discharged from the army."

One ex-addict—who said that he'd finally gone cold turkey in a friend's apartment while on leave—gave this account of Operation Awareness: "First you rap to a bunch of shrinks. Then you start earning points, like a little kid at camp. More points get you out sooner, and patients even get points for telling other people on post that the program is good. That's lying, man. Then you go to the shoot-up room" (where emetics are injected) "and puke your guts out. And you get some Methadone: I was really stoned on that. But some guys are bigger junkies when they leave than when they go in —smack's so easy to get from the corpsmen. One dude I knew came in with a twenty-dollar-a-day habit, and he left with a forty-dollar-a-day habit. So you just puke and earn points and don't get cured. I think the whole setup is only political propaganda. They just want the public to think they're trying."

The most political GIs stress that they're "very down on dope," and some said that they themselves had given up hallucinogens "for political reasons." They said that they try to tell others, "Skag wastes you worse than it wastes the army," and they continually warned them to keep any kind of dope away from Haymarket. But several admitted that it's tricky to put down psychedelics without turning off their audience. "Yes, grass and acid can be radicalizing—to start with. But how can we tell people to stop after a little?"

"The biggest problem I have rapping to the guys is that they're too stoned to hear me."

□

Naturally, political dissent within the military means lots of assignments for agents—either federal or military, as well as the GIs who are busted for pot and told, "Be nice, inform a little, and we'll take the heat off you." Traditionally, drugs, or planted drugs, or those where "the flakes were lost in analysis," yield the most convenient charges against an individual or an organization. However, "outside agents used to be the easiest to spot, because they offer you some grass right away and offer to blow up a building for you at once."

During the week when I visited Haymarket, the civilian staff was acutely worried that the coffeehouse might be closed. They expelled all known dealers, held an antidope panel, and distributed warning leaflets. Someone wistfully suggested building stocks and a pillory. But, since the Fayetteville police had shut off the local park a few months before, contacts and dealing had accelerated in bars and coffee joints all over town. High school students especially liked to go to Haymarket. Therefore, new dealers (who aren't old friends of FDR) kept wandering in. Most were strung-out teen-agers in velvet jeans or fringes or capes; some twirled their rolled-up umbrellas far too casually on their way to and from the bathrooms—while the staff grimly wondered what kinds of agents might be watching.

So it was helpful when a federal narcotics agent introduced himself to me. On learning that I was a reporter, he asked to see my credentials and then unbosomed himself. I think his motive was simple megalomania: he kept saying how professionally expert he was, what a lot he earned, how much he knew—the power glands were buzzing. He was almost romantic about the perils of his job, and told me that "There's nothing like the touch of cold steel." Throughout our talk, he constantly pointed at himself: he kept tapping his chest, where his notebook of dealers was, tapping his leg to indicate one gun, jabbing at his jacket for the other. (He was indignant because I initially thought he was an army narc: "No, no, the *Federal Bureau*.") He had fake army ID, and looked like a basic trainee: his reddish hair was strikingly short, his moustache very small, and his fatigue jacket was well pressed. So his appearance would have jarred within any Aquarian landscape; however, he had the virtue of being inconspicuous, except for flyaway ears. He repeated that he was a good actor, which I doubted. Nor was he likely to blow dope with his suspects, as many agents do; he said he'd had one joint in his life—by accident, when he was drunk.

Wagging his head, he promised that Haymarket would soon be closed and the staff busted: "It'll just be a matter of time." He insisted that two members of the staff were dealers who were making a lush profit on the coffeehouse. He then named two Fayetteville natives who I knew weren't on the staff, but he wouldn't believe me. While he explained the ultraviolet test for the strength of acid, and documented the range of drugs which he said dealers had offered him on the premises, I realized that his was a rum blend of efficiency and sloppiness. He didn't know any of the staff members' names, or that they lived in a collective, or even that they had a policy against dope. And it wasn't very bright to talk to a reporter.

He was very vindictive about all drug users, and spoke scornfully of the organizations that work with heroin addicts—"They only try to *help* them, I'd jail them for ninety-nine years"—but occasionally he tried to sound like the movement: "See, I just don't want my brothers and sisters out there to get hooked." He added that his stint at agenting was a substitute for military service, and that he'd done "big jobs" in New York and Oregon. He mentioned a vast supply of heroin he expected to arrive in Fayetteville in three days. Although he had recently fingered one civilian for an acid bust, he said it was worth waiting for more detailed information on dealers and suppliers, hence he was ready to let the heroin reach its source— the microboppers or GIs who would be easy to arrest later. All in all, he couldn't separate the politics of the GI movement from the presence of teen-age dopers.

When I told the staff about him, they were distressed but took it calmly. Some considered asking him if he was an agent—if he denied it, he could still arrange arrests, but wouldn't be able to give evidence in court. (I was touched when he was referred to as "Nora's pig," and found myself talking possessively: "Please don't blow my pig until I've milked him.") But they finally agreed that "It's better to deal with a narc you know" than with a stranger, and that it would be useful to note whom he talked to, since they would then know who to toss out. Since some of the dealers thought the staff were informers, they were amused to hear that the agent thought they were dealers.

On the next night, the agent left the coffeehouse after a brief visit, and a member of the staff followed him. The agent went to a phone booth and made a call. He didn't return, but soon three policemen strode through Haymarket, and then frisked three civilians who had just gone to a car outside. They were clean, and had to be released.

A few weeks later, the staff reported that the agent had widely admitted his identity, that he'd told them that he liked Haymarket, but was still repeating, "Just a matter of time." Not long after, he suddenly claimed that "his head had changed and that he didn't want to be a pig anymore"—and pointed out four others who he said were agents. The staff, which couldn't believe that he'd flip-flopped, thought that he was probably trying to ingratiate himself and to learn more about them—since he'd already blown his own cover.

There are plenty of other places in Fayetteville where dealing and contacting are the norm. But military and federal authorities are naturally eager to eliminate the actual locations where GIs can talk freely about the war and the government. There have been (unsuccessful) efforts to close the Oleo Strut, at Fort Hood, and the Shelter Half, at Fort Lewis; the UFO, in Columbia, South Carolina, has been shut down. Yet antiwar groups like GIs United and MDM

(Movement for a Democratic Military) continue to expand. The civilian tax-exempt United States Servicemen's Fund and similar nontax-exempt organizations, such as Support Our Soldiers, help to support some twenty projects by providing money for educational materials, lawyers, and speakers, and also finance the largest of the seventy-five GI newspapers.

At Haymarket, I was told that pro-war GIs also make visits: "They fall by to argue. It's the usual stuff—either, 'You fight a war to win,' or 'If you don't stop communism in Asia, we'll have it in Brooklyn!' So we try to make them aware of facts, to give a direction —rather than impose an opinion."

Early in '71, quite a few at Bragg were wondering if they were going to be sent to Jordan on an alert. "They're building up troops to full strength now—why? And we're being trained in desert-type tanks. Jordan's been mentioned quite a bit, and they keep pounding it into us that it's not just Nam anymore."

"If we ever get out of Nam and Laos, I wonder what'll be next? Bolivia?"

"Chile?"

"Peru?"

Hindsight: Since Vietnam was bombed more heavily in 1971 than during any previous year of the war, and since more GIs in Vietnam freely expressed their astonishment to the press when they heard that they were no longer in combat but merely in a " 'defensive' position," Washington's insistence that the war was winding down meant little to those in the military.

In May 1971, a psychiatrist from the Bronx who worked in a drug rehabilitation center in Long Binh, told the *New York Times* that "the men were reacting to Vietnam much like the deprived in the ghetto.

"Vietnam in many ways is a ghetto for the enlisted man," he said. "The soldiers don't want to be here, their living conditions are bad, they are surrounded by privileged classes, namely officers; there is an accepted use of violence, and there is promiscuous sex. They react the way they do in the ghetto. They take drugs and try to forget. . . ."

It was also discovered that, while the heroin in America is of about

5 percent purity, the heroin available in Vietnam is of about 95 percent strength.

In early '72, some of the "liberalization" programs in basic training were discontinued, the beer machines were removed from the barracks, private cubicles were abolished, and the new recruits received a 30 to 40 percent increase in physical training. On some bases, the "people programs" persisted, while others pushed for a tougher army.

Within the year following my visit to Fort Bragg, the Haymarket staff shut down their own coffeehouse because the drug problem was inescapable throughout Fayetteville. Instead, they opened a bookstore, which served as a meeting place for GIs and offered counseling and legal services. The location chosen was outside the town but still near the base. Other coffeehouses have gone through a similar transformation, and legal counseling has accelerated. Certain projects, like the one near Fort Hood, at Killeen, Texas, are working on the life problems of GIs and their dependents, especially bad housing. There have also been boycotts and pickets on stores in army towns which pressure GIs to buy expensive products which they can't afford. Thus, the focus on the military has expanded beyond the antiwar movement.

In '72 activities increased in the navy and part of the air force. There have been Stop Our Ship campaigns. In April '72, seven crew members of the U.S.S. *Nitro* jumped overboard when the munitions ship pulled out of New Jersey; they were cheered by forty-five demonstrators who were paddling canoes and lifeboats near the ship. Those concerned said they wanted to prevent the ship from delivering ammunition to aircraft carriers in Vietnam. (Some of the sailors had already sent a telegram to the Navy Department, stating that the ship was unsafe—mainly because equipment was out of repair and there were some fire hazards. Sailors on other ships have made similar complaints.) In October '71, eight sailors from the U.S.S. *Constellation* refused to sail to Vietnam with their ship; they took sanctuary at Christ the King Catholic Church in San Diego, California. (They later received "general discharges under honorable conditions" from the navy.) Some on the U.S.S. *Rush*—which left Newport, R.I., for "a friendly tour" of Angola and Mozambique—sent petitions to Congress protesting these trips to colonies of the Portuguese regime. And there have been vigils at air force bases in Idaho and Texas.

Amid all the stories of defiance and the tough talk I heard at Bragg, one of the sturdiest GIs I met left me with an image that won't retreat. When he was in Sydney, Australia, on leave after combat duty in Vietnam, he decided to treat himself to a fine dinner to celebrate his first night away from the war. Perusing the menu in a posh restaurant, he ordered Steak Diane, not knowing what it was. The waiter brought a dish to the table, poured on some fluid, and the thing went up in flames. "I jumped back and crashed into the wall. It looked just like napalm. I couldn't stop shaking—and I don't usually shake." He paused. "You know what the steak reminded me of."

FRANK RIZZO AND PHILADELPHIA
June 1971

BABIES FOR Rizzo: blond and bald and rosy brunette, dribbling or chuckling, babies studded with Rizzo buttons, which click and clank whenever they move, even when a deep breath's drawn. The babies cry when the pins prick them. All the mothers and daughters and fathers wear so many buttons that three or four buttonless visitors are stared at with suspicion; those who don't accept buttons must be creeps. Chesty teen-aged boys and youngish jocks strut about in lemony, grape, or lime pastel T-shirts stenciled with RIZZO RIGHT NOW—surely a mating of Right On and Peace Now—at this backyard rally in Richmond, where some hundred and fifty people sip soda and munch a frank for Frank, while the crewcut guitarist gives them "Jailhouse Rock" and "All I Have To Offer You Is Me." Rizzo's own small band sinks the singer's voice with "O Dem Golden Slippers," and a few older women in smocks and spoolies twirl each other around in the sunlight, laughing a little when their buttons clack. Rizzo, like most behemoths, looks ready to burst his suit, but he signs autographs and then nods quite amiably when a small, neat, middle-aged housewife calls out that she has a question for him. Suddenly, two Right Now sweatshirts grab her and haul her away, she shouts *"Helllpp"* while the drums crash louder and Rizzo begins a speech about creeps who don't get up until three in the afternoon, bums who don't work like the rest of us, and the woman gets the bums' rush because this is private property.

Trembling on the sidewalk, she explains that she wants to ask Rizzo what he will do about drugs when he is mayor—what methods will he use which weren't employed when he was police commissioner? She says that, as the mother of a fourteen-year-old son, she's terribly worried about drugs in schools. Two weeks ago, she waited outside Sears Roebuck to ask Rizzo the same question. But his staff wouldn't let her near him, and one man put on a gefilte-fish accent and said, "Vot are you doing here, Mrs. *Cohen?* Vy don't you go away?" She objected to his inflection, but he said that his name was Weinberg, so how could he be anti-Semitic? (Rizzo's assistant campaign manager was Martin Weinberg.) Then a young Rizzo staffer asked her, "Do you want the Zulus to take over the city?" and his female colleague added some remarks about niggers, and the woman was ordered to leave.

On her second appearance, Rizzo's campaign workers recognize her and make certain that she won't be able to speak to him. Still on the pavement, she repeats, "Why can't I ask a candidate a question? What's happening in this city? If you can't ask a question?" Several young boys look disturbed and say she's right, it's true, there's a lot more drugs at school this year. She rubs her cheek with a hand that still shakes: "So why can't I just ask a question?" To avert this danger, Rizzo is filtered out through another entrance, while a few goons chortle at her and say, "Have some nickel-bags"—"Yeah, have some"—and they tell her to beat it, don't make trouble, stay away.

□

In Philadelphia these days, much can depend on who looks guilty. Last winter, near Society Hill, the neighborhood was intrigued by seeing a couple on a rooftop in the early morning: the woman wore a nightgown, and the man was naked. Police cars hurtled to the spot, and Rizzo himself rushed inside the house. The couple had actually been threatened by a man with a gun—before they'd dressed for the day—and had rushed to their own roof in fright. The assailant was still walking around in the streets, openly carrying his weapon, but the police didn't notice him or nab him. A neighbor said that—in Philadelphia's current mood—a gunman wouldn't attract attention: the guilty person must be the naked one.

□

Philadelphia: a town of harmless drunks and mean little old ladies in information booths who give you the wrong information; the lacy, flowing script of compulsive young black graffiti artists— Cornbread, Chewy, Kool Kev, Tity, and Kleptokid, who proclaim themselves King of the Walls or paint crowns over their names (the fiercest graffiti I saw were WATCH MY SMOKE, and, in the ghetto, Irish Power Is Boss, chalked in letters that grew smaller and smaller); soft pretzels—"there's a lot of crooked dough in this town"—and wistful jokes, and news features on Princess Grace's "Fifteen Years of Serenity." A city where the words "gorilla" and "guerrilla" fly around so fast that it's hard to distinguish them (even though gorilla means right and guerrilla means left), of shining shelves and floors and banisters and glistening oilcloths on tables in ultraclean Italian homes; sequestered nuns in shocking-pink floor-length habits roller-skating behind their convent; where a man in drag won the "best life-style expression prize" in 1971's Easter Parade, and mud-brown skirts droop over the shins in Bonwit's windows, while a Presbyterian church announced its Sunday sermon: "The Importance of Being Properly Dressed."

A very puzzling town for a New Yorker. The city's brave enough to number the thirteenth floors in many buildings, but—against a new guest's pillow—hotels prop cards reading CAUTION (Please Turn Thumb Bolt, Also Attach Chain . . .). Poe drafted *The Raven* in Philadelphia, Zelda Fitzgerald took dancing lessons there, Pound went to Penn and later wrote the alumnae secretary, "All the U. of P. . . . does . . . for a man of letters is to ask him to go away without breaking the silence"; Eddie Fisher and Mario Lanza and Frankie Avalon and Fabian all came singing out of South Philadelphia. They have one of the world's best zoos, plus something called a Sinatra-rama.

Many old houses have slanted, reflecting mirrors on upper floors, which enable house owners to see who's at the front door. These are called *busybodies,* which seems appropriate for a town of intense gossip: everyone tells everybody everything, and most of it is at least two-thirds true. Not lies, not malice; what you hear may be merely incomplete. And you're sure to get the story again soon: the source may be next door or across the room. (You also hear correct accounts of what appeared in the press—where the facts were fudged.) So you learn who had shad for lunch yesterday at which Bookbinder's, who was (or wasn't) a bagman for the Mafia in Seattle, who had just switched laundries (and why), and that Cornbread is dead (he isn't). There are various versions of who punched who among those who are working for the same political party, and lots of recycled yuks about piles, since both Rizzo and retiring Mayor James H. J. Tate had operations described as "their lobotomies. We call this our hemorrhoid administration." (Mayor Tate, said to have "delusions of mediocrity," was mainly reelected because of Rizzo, who ran his department as "a private army" and was answerable to no one.) And there are endless discussions about Rizzo's youthful case of diabetes, which got him an honorable discharge from the navy in 1939. He explodes when questioned about his war service, and has asked the Navy Department that no information be given about his record—which is now in the Pentagon's file of "prominent persons." Eager newsmen keep trying to trace down the crew who served as Rizzo's shipmates on the U.S.S. *Houston*—in hopes that a few of them can clarify whatever he seeks to hide. But his supporters say that his hysteria about the discharge is merely due to the shame of not having fought "a man's war." The gossiping Philadelphians also tell you where sheets and towels are on sale.

In the Philadelphia evenings, I go back to my hotel, where Dutch Schultz is dying on TV and a cop fires shots into a muffler, hyping Lead-Free Amoco, and read *Kitty Foyle:* "Philly doesn't want to feel things unless they've had a careful okay from yesterday." William Holden and Clifton Webb appear in dog collars, coping with the Chinese; one of them says, "Now they're spreading disease along with their propaganda." Kitty Foyle says, "I suppose Philly is the last place in America where it still matters to be a gentleman." The Warwick Hotel recoils from my Master Charge card, calls my editors, then says accusingly, "They say you're not there." "No, I'm here."

Then they call my New York answering service: "They say you're here." "Yes, I know I am." But they insist that the N.Y. phone company has never heard of me: "You have no number." "But you just talked to it." After yards of Pinterish dialogue, they announce that I'm here, but that, since they don't know me, they might have had to lock me out of my room. It makes me happy to say that I would have called the police if they had, and I switch to the Bellevue-Stratford, where the toilet flushes by itself so often—and especially when I'm phoning—that someone kindly suggests that the room is bugged. I shout *What?* above the roaring waters. "Maybe it flushes when the tape is changed." But the Bellevue-Stratford, unlike much of Philadelphia, doesn't seem suspicious of strangers, and is willing to let them pay to stay there.

By this time, I'm ready to let Philadelphians tell me that they're masochists: some really boast about it. A native dwells delightedly on the subway system: "We're packed into cattle cars by conductors trained in Auschwitz—if we get home alive, we're pleased. A city that can elect Tate twice has to be willing to tolerate *any*thing." (Rizzo disclaimed responsibility for safety on the subway; he said that was up to the transit authorities.) Another added, "Philadelphians love to wear the hairshirt and beat themselves," love hearing bad stories about the city, constantly cite the paint-spray amendments to the Schuylkill Expressway billboard—"Philadelphia Isn't as Bad as Philadelphians Say It is/NO, IT'S WORSE"—and seem proud that Lincoln Steffens' phrase, "corrupt and contented," was invented about their town. (In 1903, Steffens discovered that Philadelphia's votes were padded with the names of dead dogs, as well as those of small children and imaginary persons. A native told him, "At least you must admit that our machine is the best you have ever seen.") Today, you hear lots of bleak bragging about graft and payoffs and deals: "Suppose you wanted to support motherhood or to give City Hall $50,000—they'd still say, 'Now wait, we have to make a deal.'" Some stress that docility, torpor, and indifference are intensely Philadelphian traits, which serve as fertilizer for many seething local problems.

After all the triumphant put-downs, you rather desperately ask what natives like about the city. They talk about intimacy, easy mobility, also a security in the notion that nothing will change—unlike the headlong New York temperament that clamors for changes (and helps to keep New York exhilarating and destructive). But Philadelphians cherish their own territory—and you can quickly appreciate the charm of small, leafy side streets and envy the modest rates for renting or buying homes. In fact, the possibility of liking where you live and being able to afford it is astounding to a New Yorker. (How many New Yorkers apologize before letting you into their apartments for the first time, explaining, "My place isn't me.") Since Philadelphia's property taxes are still low, and it's cheaper to buy than to rent, natives can even afford to embellish their dwellings, paint their front doors, buy trestle tables and embroidered donkey bell covers and wrought iron twisted to their taste, and can actually expect their surroundings to reflect them. (In Manhattan, more and more grow wary of possessions: you rather assume that what you own will get trashed or ripped off or somehow mangled.) But when Philadelphians want to offer you something very nice, they take you home; it's also their way of showing why they do like Philadelphia.

So the city is run by neighborhoods; natives really have the decentralization which some other cities (think they) want. And it all comes down to possessing your own turf: the discreet liberal watering his own lawn in Society Hill or planting his tulips seems to have much the same feelings as the teen-aged gangs do about their own blocks of the ghetto, where young boys have been killing each other at the rate of 158 in the last four years. (There, some graffiti read DTK, meaning Down To Kill, if you set foot in our nabe. Others elaborate: DTKLMF . . . like a mother-fucker.) The old liberals buy guns and Mace and pens with tear gas, and the kids croak one another, especially because the presence of a stranger seems so threatening. (Even the most impeccable outsiders are unwelcome; Richardson Dilworth told me that he was called a carpetbagger when he first ran for mayor in 1947—because he came from Pittsburgh.) Meanwhile, unwanted change accelerates: no city I've seen changes so rapidly from block to block, from white prosperity to black poverty to the modest, gleaming lower-middle-income areas, where residents hose their pavements daily, polish their brass, and go up the wall when newcomers don't do the same. The traditions of solidity and serenity continue to amaze a visitor: our battered national landscape reveals few pockets that appear so comfortable or so confident.

And Philadelphia is also the most frightened city I've ever seen. Fear in the air: trickling and leaking across sidewalks, under doorsills, between the buttons of so many suits, crawling up sleeves. Reasonable persons tell you that they've given up the movies or the ballet—that they mustn't leave home at night. At midday, walking for several blocks behind a severely limping black man, who was shabby but not ragged, I noticed the twitches of fright in most of the white faces coming toward him—their eyes flew to the fact that one hand was in his pocket; they clearly imagined a gun. (Since his limp was so bad, I wondered if he was holding onto his wallet.) Sometimes you feel that you're wading in Philadelphian fear: knee-high, waist-deep, finally eye-level fear. Although—as in most cities —a majority of the most serious crimes occur in the ghetto, inflicted by blacks on blacks, many white Philadelphians seem convinced that the youthful gangs are going to carve their giblets out in center city. At moments, there seems to be a whiff of voluptuousness in some Philadelphians' dread—perhaps it's more of the local masochism.

The task is to comb out the difference between rational and irrational fear. Just before leaving New York, I was prepared for Philadelphia by being held up on my doorstep by a small addict with a chisel. Our conversation—"You're gonna give me all your money!" *"Damn"*—cost me six dollars, but I've had worse for free. All my neighbors said that it was my fault for walking home after midnight—hence none were alarmed. During my first three days in Philadelphia, a nine-year-old was shot dead while playing in the street, and a man—whose sixteen-year-old son was killed by a policeman who now faces manslaughter charges—lost an eye defending his own windshield; both were victims of rival gangs. Both were neighborhood crimes, in North Philadelphia, where many citizens are very bitter about the lack of protection. (As one said, "Law and order *only* means keeping black crime from spilling into white neighborhoods.") Although most of the gang killings have been solved, Rizzo and his troops haven't reduced the murders. For him, punishment takes a huge priority over prevention. In 1970, he and Mayor Tate rechanneled $400,000 which the City Council had marked for gang control into police overtime and armored police buses. (The city has 93 gangs and about 40 men in the gang-control unit.) A popular technique for dealing with gangs occurs when the cops catch a boy outside his turf; they deposit him in a rival gang's area, and suggest that he won't get home alive.

□

So you can slice Philadelphia like a four-layer cake: it's a ter-rified city, but is supposed to have the lowest crime rate among the ten largest cities in the United States; while some calm citizens repeat that much of the city is quite safe, many have lately ques-tioned the official crime statistics—on the suspicion that adequate figures aren't given. Other studies announce that Philadelphia's crime rate rose by 23.4 percent between 1970 and '71, which equals four times the national average for cities of more than 250,000 people. According to the FBI, Philadelphia rose from 126th to 58th place among all U.S. cities in the realm of major crimes —during Rizzo's years as commissioner (1967–1970). Hence con-cerned Philadelphians emphasize that, despite the folklore, Rizzo has not been effective when it comes to reducing crime. Spencer Coxe, the executive director of the ACLU, who feels that the causes and amounts of crime have little to do with police work, added, "If Rizzo wants to take credit for an allegedly low crime rate, then he has to accept the blame for a great crime rise too." Yet you also hear: "Frank's kept the lid on and kept *them* in their place." Some Philadelphians, including many cops, refer to the ghetto as "the jungle," and insist that "they" drum on cars and garbage cans whenever a stranger comes near: a percussion that no one I met had ever heard. Those who know North Philadelphia well stress the general passivity—even the conservatism—of its ma-jority. There are no strong black militant movements at present; the Panther convention of 1970 drew most of its leadership from other parts of the country.

With all these contradictions afoot, Rizzo and Mayor Tate have been deft at manipulating the fears of all kinds of Philadelphians. This city is the place to study the political use of fear, the value of scare tactics. In '69, Rizzo said, "Look at the city after dark.

Grown men walking down the middle of the street. Women afraid to venture out of their homes. You leave your children out at night, you're frightened to death until they come home." In 1970, he evoked Philadelphia as a vast combat zone: "It's exactly what it is . . . a war. Almost as severe as the war that's going on in Vietnam. We've run a comparison a couple of weekends in our city against the casualties in Vietnam. And, surprisingly, we had more homicides and deaths and casualties than they did in Vietnam."

Aside from those who live in rugged neighborhoods, it's Rizzo's liberal supporters who are the most intriguing. Many consider him a practical (not an admirable) choice: "Frank's the man for the times. Normally I wouldn't vote for him, but kids are breaking windshields." These can be the same people who want an end to the war, support equal opportunities, study ecology. One said pensively, "Philadelphia used to have good race relations: due to the Quaker tradition of tolerance. The whites were content to be on the top, and the blacks were content to be on the bottom." He referred to the "hopelessness" of trying to educate some black children: "Maybe we should do what they do in Spain: let kids drop out at eight or nine, since they're uneducable." Actually, Philadelphia has an estimated twenty to thirty thousand students who just don't go to school; no one quite knows who or where they are.

Suddenly you realize that visiting Philadelphia means time-traveling: you're back in the Fifties, even racially and socially, when upper-middle-class whites talk about self-improvement for black or poor people, and shy, formal, middle-aged men peer bleakly down women's dresses while making awkward cocktail conversation. Few in Philadelphia seem to have discovered that the word liberal isn't lovely anymore, or that it's come to mean hypocrite—when it doesn't mean Commie. Those who want to stop gang wars or expand education are still talking about charter reform. Alvin Echols, director of the North City Congress, a community action group, observed that most liberals are still hung up on the notion of a fair chance, assuming that if people work hard and save and hustle, they'll earn well—whereas, "You're always going to have poor people; you mustn't tell them that they'll never be poor again." As one who believes in supplementary payments to those who work but can't ever earn enough, as well as direct incomes for those who can't get jobs, he agrees that this defies the whole American ethic: that effort's certain to put you ahead. Hence "giving direct dollars will upset the liberal bag." Meanwhile, "Liberals think, 'Well, a *little* repression right now wouldn't be too bad,' since Rizzo is focusing on the white fear of black militancy and the black hatred of white recalcitrance." There are also your burned or ex-liberals, some of whom are Jewish; they vibrate easily to the anti-Semitic statements of young blacks. You also feel that some in Philadelphia are withholding their full opinions. Perhaps ladies with glass finger-nails and Pucci dresses, wearing peace buttons and crying "Right on!" for Rizzo's opponents, may finally be willing to sacrifice civil liberties in order to think that they can walk down the street.

□

Outgoing Mayor Tate, who naturally backed Rizzo, may be one of the most unpopular mayors in the U.S.; "incompetent old-time party hack" is one of the kindest terms you hear applied to him. Elected in 1962, Tate is said to have been "sucked to the top by the vacuum"—a seasoned Philadelphia joke. However, from 1951 to 1962, Philadelphia had a reform government, under Democratic Mayors Joseph Clark and Richardson Dilworth. Many Philadel-phians explain Tate's election as part of the inevitable political cycle; they feel that the reform movement had run its course, and that the reformers lacked professional political staying power. Meanwhile, as the likeliest supporters for liberal government moved in greater numbers to Philadelphia's suburbs, the city became more and more the province of conservative working people who would auto-matically vote for a Tate or a Rizzo. (Rizzo's Republican opponent, Thacher Longstreth, a city councilman, was regarded as a well-intentioned liberal who would continue to serve the moneyed inter-ests of the city. Therefore, many of his supporters lived on the Main Line and were unable to vote for him.)

In 1971, most were sure of Rizzo's election; some wondered if "tough cops" in municipal saddles might emerge as a national pat-tern. (Mayor Charles Stenvig of Minneapolis was previously a police lieutenant.) While kids turned the *z's* in Rizzo's name into swastikas, and revived old Goldwater rhymes—"In your guts you know he's nuts"—some of his most dedicated opponents stressed that his personality was less important than the likelihood that he would perpetuate the Tate machine. Also, many mused on the fact that a man from the extreme right of the Republican party would represent the Democrats.*

□

Although black people will suffer most from Rizzo's election, many who detest him agree that he's not anti-black—despite his often overheard remarks about niggers, and his famous cry of "Get their black asses!" to his men when black high school students demonstrated outside the Board of Education on November 17, 1967. (Heard on TV and by many individuals, the blackness of the asses has often been denied, and it's said that the TV prints were destroyed.) Witnesses stressed that the demo was disorderly but under control and that the cops themselves were restrained until Rizzo appeared—and whipped up the police. Richardson Dilworth charged that the police "provoked" the holocaust that followed—which scattered students all over the city, where they did beat up some whites. A few weeks later, a group of white South Philadelphian housewives demonstrated in the same place, to protest busing; they pushed and tore the clothes of some school board aides, while the cops stood by and did nothing.

Despite Rizzo's '67 statement on black power—"The only thing they understand is force, and they have to be crushed before they destroy the community"—one black writer said, "No, Rizzo's not a racist—he's a sadist." Although the cops are at their fiercest in the ghetto, and are said to be more trigger-happy of late, many repeat that Rizzo has been just as ready to savage whites as blacks. In 1957, when he was still a captain, he blinded a white Italian in one eye and fractured his jaw with a nightstick—for not moving his car at Rizzo's request. (That'll teach him to park illegally.) The case is often mentioned as proof that Rizzo treats all races equally.

* In 1972, he supported Nixon.

☐

Creeps, kooks, liberals, phonies, fags, ultraliberals, lefties, hoodlums, and bums—Rizzo's morality dictates that he must save his city from the shaggy perverts whose politics or culture spread like dandruff. In 1959, when he was captain, his raids on some six new coffeehouses inspired cops to rip Vivaldi off the hi-fis, drag away bearded chess players and espresso-heads, and book them at the police station. Although Rizzo insisted that drugs and homosexual solicitation were flourishing in these dens of poetry reading, not a single conviction resulted. Still, it was Rizzo's obsession that the coffeehouses thrived on immoral profits, since they made so little money. (He is always frantic on the subject of homosexuals; almost anyone he dislikes gets called a fag.) Richardson Dilworth, who was then mayor, says in retrospect that those who lived nearby were indeed alarmed by the coffeehouses—since Philadelphia had never had an equivalent to Greenwich Village—and that many were outraged by the intrusion into their own neighborhoods. In '69, Rizzo told the owner of the Electric Factory, Philadelphia's first rock club, "You brought these people to Philadelphia and you're going to pay for it. I'm gonna make a parking lot out of this place." Precisely one patron in over 100,000 was convicted on a narcotics charge. After terrorizing visitors with onslaughts of cops, Rizzo had the Factory closed because of "the rise and fall of sounds." He hasn't yet come down on the Academy of Music for playing Stravinsky.

Known as a puritan—"I never saw my mother or father without their clothes on. My children never saw me without mine on. What are these kooks trying to do?"—Rizzo still felt free to call his primary opponent Bill Green "a fucking bum" in front of reporters, and to joke winsomely about the photographs which show his nightstick rising out of (or "protruding from" or "jammed into") his cummerbund. Many Philadelphians call it the phantom phallus. But his morality demanded that the Playboy Club mustn't open in Philadelphia—although many observed that the bar investments of Rizzo's friend Frank Palumbo would have suffered from the Playboy Club's competition, as well as some of the profits to Palumbo's associates. For years, Palumbo supplied enormous organizational help to the Democrats in South Philadelphia, hence most politicians have been cautious with him.

Meanwhile, the clip joints along Locust Street, which Rizzo raided enthusiastically when he was a captain, have been thriving since he was appointed commissioner. Philadelphians believe that most of these bars are owned by the local Cosa Nostra, which Rizzo appears to tolerate. Since the bars are distinguished for prostitution, watered drinks, serving minors, and other violations of the liquor code, many natives suspect payoffs at the lower levels plus accommodation at the top. Some forty to fifty policemen are quietly fired each year for graft, but it's assumed that many cops earn well on the side. (It's also said that prostitution doesn't perturb Rizzo, although he thinks that most women should stay home and bake.) Yet his morality can sometimes peak to a passion that starts him talking in the third person, rather like Henry Adams: "Ask Frank Rizzo if he's ever hit anyone with a pipe to take his money. Never did that. Ask Frank Rizzo if he ever took a gun and shot someone else . . . to rob him. Never did that. Ask Frank Rizzo if he ever burglarized someone else's home . . . or took someone else's belongings, that didn't belong to him. Never did that. So if this is the standard that we're going to measure any individual by, I say that's the proper standard."

The moralist has files on some eighteen hundred persons he disapproves of; reporters have heard him repeat, "Get me their weakness" to detectives, who then research a man's tendency toward booze, women, drugs, fags, peace demos, or past charges. (A few young men were arrested for "conspiring to commit litter"—putting up posters which criticized the police.) After the '67 school board explosion, he told the Board of Education, "I have a file on every one of you," and also boasted to the press that he had "something on" all the other candidates running against him in the 1971 primaries.

Rizzo's campaign manager, Albert Gaudiosi, who has defined Rizzo as "a big cuddly bear," wrote a series of pieces with Bayard Brunt called "The New Revolutionaries" while Gaudiosi was still at the *Evening Bulletin*. Despite the searing implications that "fragmented" Marxist groups were preparing to bring the country to its knees, the revelations were on the level of: "Membership in these revolutionary organizations, notably Weatherman, is highly secretive"; that one *Philadelphia Free Press* staffer "is very domineering . . . and her 'bag' is opposing male chauvinism"—also, her three-year-old son "has been known to shout obscenities and epithets at the police." In the "Pepperpot" section of *Philadelphia* magazine, an editor questioned whether Brunt and Gaudiosi had ever interviewed a single "revolutionary," adding, "the core of the information obviously came from the files of the Philadelphia Police Department and the FBI." Rizzo has denied this. However, as a result of the series, the *Free Press* was closed, and its Canadian editor is being deported. All in all, there's an extra tang of fear in Philadelphia, even among very moderate dissenters: fear of the police. Some of Rizzo's power rests on "the *uncertainty* of what he'll do": no one knows when or if he might be followed, suddenly arrested for an unpaid parking ticket, beaten, charged with resisting an officer, or whether drugs might be "found on his premises." As many remark, people are simply afraid to tangle with him.

□

As the ACLU has noted, Rizzo "has a long history of publicly accusing organizations of criminal activities, but failing to produce evidence that results in convictions." Some dud stories received huge initial coverage, although charges later had to be abandoned, and sometimes no one was even brought to trial. The ACLU's report added, "The media bear a heavy brunt of the blame for playing the police game." But the newspapers are understandably reluctant to expose these fluff-outs, since such an admission would reveal their own distortions.

In 1966, in "the SNCC dynamite plot," Rizzo had nine people arrested, and gave the impression that they were preparing to blow up the city. "Acting on a tip received three days ago that the SNCC quarters were filled with 'hoards' of dynamite, guns, and ammunition, four 20-man squads wearing bullet-proof vests and armed with machine guns and other weapons struck the four buildings shortly after midnight" (*Inquirer,* August 12). On August 13, Rizzo told the *Daily News,* "Five sticks of dynamite could reduce Independence Hall to rubble." On the same day, from the *Bulletin:* " 'I know they have more arms,' Rizzo said." On the 16th, the *News* reported: "Both Rizzo and Tate said they believe a major incident had been averted by the raid."

In fact, only two and a half sticks of dynamite were found—which a man (who was soon placed under psychiatric treatment) admitted that he had stolen from a construction site. A few of the defendants had worked for SNCC, but they weren't "members," nor were their apartments "headquarters." There was no plot, and charges were quietly dropped.

In '69, Rizzo said that "people . . . have had too much of crime and disorder and the SDS. As far as I'm concerned, the SDS can drop dead. . . ." In March of that year, he reproduced and circulated to all the major media a publication called *Your Manual,* which contained recipes for homemade explosives, and was published by the "3-R News Service" of San Francisco. Rizzo told the press that SDS "is the moving force behind the circulation of this booklet in Philadelphia." However, when challenged that it was circulated by anyone but him, he fell silent. Philadelphia's district attorney concluded that the circulation of the leaflet—by Rizzo or anyone else—didn't "constitute a crime."

On November 30, 1970, Philadelphians read about a plot to kidnap Rizzo and hold him as a hostage for Angela Davis—with the alternate possibility of using him for "target practice" by black militants. Bombings of two police buildings were supposed to bracket these events. A "People's Liberation Army" was held responsible, and the press coverage was meaty.

In April 1971, a very different kind of story was released. An Alaskan-born Oriental called Sulieman, who said he was an agent sent by Mao and claimed that he had fought with Che and with the NLF in Vietnam, had conned a group of young blacks into believing that the U.S. government had a plan to provoke ghetto riots and to put black people into concentration camps and to exterminate them. (Most of the revolutionary warriors of November were characterized by the *Inquirer* in April as "not militant . . . ordinary wage-earners . . . middle class types.") Sulieman persuaded his young listeners that they must prepare to defend "the helpless people of the ghettos" against "the King Alfred Plan," which he said that Chinese Communists had stolen from Washington. Arms were collected, and suddenly two members of the group were shot dead because Sulieman decided that they'd betrayed him. Over a month later, another member discovered that the King Alfred Plan was lifted from page 306 of the novel *The Man Who Cried I Am* by John A. Williams (published by

Little, Brown and Co.), and he told the FBI about Sulieman, who had already disappeared. In the long run, the Angela Davis kidnap plot was discounted as "wild talk" of Sulieman's—even by the police who investigated the case. But again, the public mainly remembers the alleged threats to Rizzo. The national atmosphere, which suggests to impoverished blacks that whites may suddenly overwhelm them, and which made Sulieman's manipulations possible, wasn't really acknowledged. One of Sulieman's eighteen-year-old followers later said that Sulieman's style was hypnotic, and added, "He played on all our fears." In Philadelphia today, you feel that dangerous fantasies or accusations can be accepted with more ease than in some other towns —whether they come from gifted con artists or from the police.

□

The Philadelphia Police Department is acknowledged as one of the most efficient in the country. Their communications, mobility, and command systems enable them to respond to emergencies far more quickly than the police in most other cities. Although Rizzo absorbs the credit, many Philadelphians say that it should go to his predecessor, Howard Leary, who initiated the rapid communications. (Leary headed New York's Police Department from 1966 to 1970.) Rizzo despised Leary's restrained methods, and often called him "a weakling." Newsmen reminisce about the time when Rizzo was chasing a boy and Leary intervened—and got socked by Rizzo. Rizzo told the press it was an accident.

However, even Rizzo's critics agree that he is a quick learner. For example, he has not allowed his men to freely maul demonstrators since the '67 outbreak at the Board of Education. However, some Philadelphians are increasingly worried about police actions against individuals—especially against any black persons found walking after sundown in prosperous white neighborhoods. The phrase "unnecessary shooting" recurs. Rizzo's own favorite unit is the highway patrol, known as "The Boots"; clad in shiny black leather jackets and crushed hats, they're assigned to holdups and shootings. They're also the shock troops who ignite much community outrage. "Even the other police hate them," said an expert.

But Rizzo always supports his own men lavishly in "the line of duty." In South Philadelphia, in November 1970, where a policeman had wounded a boy whom he said had pointed a shotgun at him, three reporters heard Rizzo questioning a cop: "Are you the officer who just shot that kid?" "Yes." "Good work. What happened?"

Rizzo loves arriving at the scene of action—the press constantly repeats "Rizzo was there"—and has been photographed dismantling a bomb with his bare hands.

In 1969, Mayor Tate abolished Philadelphia's police review board as a Christmas present to Rizzo. On learning that the Legal Aid Society was referring citizens with complaints against the police to various neighborhood organizations, and that Legal Aid was supported by the United Fund, Rizzo announced that policemen would no longer contribute to it. Legal Aid finally issued a memo instructing its employees to refer complaints about the police to: the police themselves. Complainants had to take lie-detector tests administered by the police. But Rizzo is confident of public support: "The only people, black or white, who hate us are the criminals. Sure, if you ask them they'll tell you about police brutality. But when you want to find out about police, you don't ask Al Capone."

Rizzo skirts the issue of organized crime in Philadelphia, and has said that Angelo Bruno, who is considered to be the head of the local Cosa Nostra, has been properly questioned and has denied ever bribing a cop. One student of Philadelphia rackets mused, "We have a very peculiar Mafia here—like the rest of Philly, it's dull." Bruno doesn't believe in violence, and there hasn't been a gang killing in Philadelphia for years; he prefers legitimate business. Bruno's interests include John's Vending Machine Co., and his wife owns the Miami Pest Control Co., plus a couple of other outfits in Florida. Rumors concerning Bruno's other holdings could make a book the length of *The Sot-Weed Factor,* but the complexities of nailing him down are distilled by this excerpt from the Philadelphia Police Department's interrogation of Bruno in 1957:

> Q.: Tell us how much money you made last year from the ironing board cover business?
>
> A.: What?
>
> Q.: Ironing board covers.
>
> A.: I don't even know what you're talking about, chief.
>
> Q.: You know what we're talking about.

A.: Ironing boards?

Q.: The cover a woman uses to cover an ironing board when she irons.

A.: I don't know what you're talking about, chief. Are you serious?

Q.: Yes, we are serious.

A.: Do you mean something else or do you really mean ironing board covers?

Q.: Ironing board covers.

A.: That's a new one. Am I supposed to be in that business?

Q.: You tell us.

Q.: I told you we are not particularly interested in . . . gambling and any income tax . . .

A.: I know that.

Q.: We are interested in major crime. We are interested in homicide.

A.: That's out of my line.

□

Some years later, it appears that heavy investigations of the Mafia are out of the police department's line; what the *New York Times* calls "reputed rackets chiefs" have gone generally unmolested.

While Philadelphia's heroin scene isn't as ferocious as New York's —"But just give us another six months"—many natives have been staggered by Rizzo's observation that drug traffic isn't connected with organized crime, and that drugs haven't really increased in Philadelphia. Bill Green's researchers retorted that Philadelphian drug deaths have increased thirty-seven times in the last five years; in 1966, there were five drug deaths—in 1970, there were a hundred and eighty-seven. Mayor Tate didn't apply for the federal funds which the government makes available for drug-abuse programs.

Although policemen pursue grass users and small-time peddlers, and are said to hassle addicts outside clinics, there are few arrests of professional suppliers or dealers. At 17th Street and Norris, quite close to the local police station—in an area saturated with police cars—pushers operated freely until the *Bulletin* published pictures of their transactions; only then did the police make arrests. As many say, the police reflect Rizzo's indifference toward the problem: "*Either* he doesn't give a damn, *or* the cops are paid off and he doesn't want to upset them. But you have to hold him responsible: because the cops take their coloration from the top, as they do in any city." (Rizzo complains that "soft" judges should be blamed for the narcotics trade, and he has threatened to campaign against certain judges before elections.) Witnesses say some Philadelphia bars are supported by drugs—that you can sip a beer and buy stuff under the counter—and that much of the numbers profit now goes into drugs. Yet some shapes of public tolerance persist; one moderate Rizzo supporter said, "Maybe heroin isn't that bad: it might keep them quiet. In a permissive society, you give everyone what they want, and perhaps it'll keep them off each other's throats."

Rizzo is praised because Philadelphia had no racial riots while he was commissioner, although some black citizens tartly remark that their neighborhoods should receive the credit. In 1967, Mayor Tate banned all public gatherings of more than twelve people; Rizzo signed this proclamation, which later became an ordinance—under which peaceful demonstrators have been arrested. In '68 and '70, a "state of emergency" was declared. While civil libertarians feel that the ordinance could be reasonably used in troubled areas at certain times, they're appalled that it now applies to the whole city. Anyone "disobeying" the ordinance can receive up to two years in prison. Even the Young Americans for Freedom were against it.

□

Famous for fresh shirts and for redying his hair once a year, Rizzo usually sits with his back to the wall, like someone expecting to be shot. His hands often open and close while he talks. Ham and beef are mentioned when his fists, face, or torso have to be described. During the Democratic primaries, which he won with a 40 percent plurality, he was about as available for interviews as Huey P. Newton has been since his release from jail. As a primary candidate, Rizzo made few statements beyond observing that lots of air pollution comes from the suburbs, not just from cities. But he used to shower editors and reporters with wallets and police lieutenants' badges, and take his favorites, like Walter Annenberg, for rides. (Since most fledgling reporters in Philadelphia begin by covering the police, favors win over many at the beginning of their careers.) He made it easy for his friends in the press to get gun permits quickly—"You have a problem? Just come in"—although he fought hard for gun control a few years ago, with the implication that students would arm themselves.

Rizzo has a habit of ringing reporters and asking, "Is it going to be a good story or a bad story?" At times, he practically assaulted those who were questioning him—springing up behind his desk and jabbing his finger at their chests, turning maroon while yelling about his own integrity. He responds to tape recorders the way Dracula responds to the cross, and often tries to retract some of his hairiest statements or actions. In 1970, after the celebrated stripping of the Panthers, the assistant DA told the press that the Panthers had stripped themselves—"to have a case against the police."

When Rizzo learned that a *Daily News* reporter was consulting some of his critics, as well as his admirers, for a series of articles, Rizzo demanded to know why he was talking to "those creeps." The reporter replied that he wished to be fair to all sides. Rizzo said, "Fuck this fair bullshit. If you were to find yourself in jail, I'd be more than fair. I'd violate my oath and let you out." The management at the *Bulletin* has always been tender of Rizzo; as long as Annenberg owned the *News* and the *Inquirer,* there were few anti-Rizzo stories. Now, although all three papers have run unflattering pieces and editorials about him, their coverage is still amazingly mild. Some reporters complain that references to Rizzo have been constantly cut from their columns, and that they've been taken off assignments that would concern him, or transferred to harmless topics. Even so, some of his fans were indignant when a couple of papers ran photos which rather resembled Mussolini. (Old joke: "I hear you've been in Philly. Is he still making the trains run on time?") Again, the intimacy of Philadelphia seems to feed inertia: some reporters don't want to raise dust, let alone rake muck, or to ask questions that would disturb him. Others are just intimidated. However, he has been very pleased with a few articles which actually put him down—which he failed to realize, since he was proud that they made him sound tough.

Since he revels in the range of his powers, he should have been delighted with Joe McGinniss's column in the *Inquirer* in August 1967, which described Rizzo "gleefully" telling "a small audience of reporters" about beating a man up. Rizzo "told how he chased the man, caught him, and finally threw him to the ground. 'Then I come down with the old Number 12,' Rizzo said, stamping his foot on the floor, 'and that guy ain't walking right today.' Then Rizzo did an imitation of a man who cannot walk right."

Hindsight: There are those who think that Mayor Rizzo of Phila-delphia might some day be as important as Mayor Daley of Chicago, even though Rizzo has done nothing very conspicuous since his election; he has just been quietly gathering support. But there are also rumors that he may fancy himself as an eventual successor to George Wallace.

THE JOHN BIRCH SOCIETY
The 9th New England Rally for God,
Family and Country July 1971

BLUE FLAMES bursting through the darkness, jouncing to the beat of "Hey, Look Me Over": held high over waiters' heads, fifty bombs of baked Alaska speed to our tables, while everybody cheers. When the lights go on, the snowy crewcut on my right says, "Pass the Rockefeller cream." He explains that the food business is part of the Conspiracy: the communists are weakening and starving our bodies so that we'll knuckle under more easily. That filthy socialist Rocke-feller controls the milk industry, and he uses that foundation of his to research formulas for polluting dairy products. "Not *poison*," he grunts, holding up the cream, "*Just weak*." We compare our tastes in salads. It's very easy to talk with Birchers and their friends: you befoul Nelson Rockefeller, praise watercress and radishes, agree that Washington's gone bananas, and curse inflation. The doctor across the table repeats, "Nixon should be tried for treason." Fine. Here, in the Boston Statler-Hilton's ballroom, when the swing band plays each state's song. Ohioans or Rhode Islanders or Virginians whip to their feet and whirl their yellow napkins in wide circles at the ceiling (as usual, most New Yorkers fudge that line about "Me and Mamie O'Rourke" from "East Side, West Side.") After "Dixie," the rebel yell sounds very much like the cry of the Algerian women or the Yip whoop—perhaps because most larynxes are withered or worn.

For five days, I've been clutching my collarbone to pledge allegiance, and jumping up to sing the national anthem again and again, or bowing my head for benedictions. (The only way to report on the

John Birch Society is to be invisible and follow the crowd.) Hence it's soothing to sit still and hear Art Smith sing "The Hawk and the Dove" —"They're two different birds,/They'll never make love"—and the evening's most popular song, "Accentuate the Positive," which makes me hope for "Celery Stalks at Midnight" or "Fry Me Cookie with a Can of Lard." But we never get beyond "Don't mess with Mister in-between." At Smith's request, we all hold hands around the table while he sings "A Closer Walk with Thee." There are some little yuks about sensitivity training, which the Birchers deplore, and a murmur of distress when he says that a song was inspired by Plato ("That homo, Socrates"), but Smith is far better received than Rudy Vallee, who doesn't seem to understand his audience. He carries a plumber's friend—"Is he going to clean up the cesspool?"—tells dozens of shattering drunk-jokes, ("After the Taj Mahal cocktail, ya won't know what got India"), shocks his listeners by saying that he campaigned for Nixon, and confuses them with "The Whiffenpoof Song" and "Winchester Cathedral."

Therefore, my table is grateful when (some) conversation can be resumed. Still, the man on my left—who looks very much as Lee Harvey Oswald might have if he'd passed forty-five—maintains a nervy silence, aside from saying that he's heard there are a lot of patriots in Florida. (Some Birchers immediately tell you that they're members, while others never do—they just talk about patriots.) The rather charming elderly Bostonian describes how she tried to prevent a college scholarship from being given to the son of an Italian work-man in her family's granite business. "His father has $187 take-home pay a week. For only five people! Scholarship indeed." So she gave the boy a bad reference. The old man beside me asserts that some public figure will be assassinated this year: the communists—in league with part of the establishment—will kill someone *in order* to make the public clamor for gun control. Then everyone will have to register their guns, and "they'll know who and where we are." The sole point of the assassination will be the identification of the Birchers, since they're such a threat to the Conspiracy. Hawaii may be used as a refuge for "some of the big boys—to sit it out until the shooting war is over."

The Conspiracy may sound like a boutique to you, but it's plasma to the Birchers. Basically, much of the U.S. federal government and the rich are plotting to bring about world government, which will eventually mean communism—which has *always* been financed by "the international bankers." In a wonderful lecture by G. Edward Griffin—whom some expect to be Robert Welch's successor—slides and diagrams of triangles and arrows and circles show how the Conspiracy learned its techniques from the 18th-century Freemasons of Europe. Those at the center control the dupes or lackeys in the outer rings. After references to the Warburgs and the Rothschilds, accompanied by drawings of dusky, shifty-eyed men whispering behind their hands, I thought that the Anti-Defamation League would have some fresh ammunition. However, "*not* all international bankers are Jewish." (Even the Panthers have never been so unkind to the Rockefellers, who may be the wickedest tycoons of all.) Our politicians have had a secret agreement with the "private banking dynasties," hence "the total control of the nation's money fell into private hands." Suddenly, the name of RUSKIN! flashed across the screen. Ruskin's "ruling class ideas" influenced Cecil Rhodes, whose secret society was inherited by Lord Alfred Milner. . . . In the U.S., this pattern is imitated by the Council on Foreign Relations, which is a front for J. P. Morgan and Co. While the council isn't the absolute center of the Conspiracy, it "governs the country" through its control of education and the media. However, some of the council's own members don't realize that it's a front.

Those who plan a "world superstate" pay and incite left-wing groups to start confrontations—so that the terrified public will accept a police state, martial rule, and a larger government. In fact, world government will be offered as the only alternative to violence. The Birchers don't seem much alarmed by the movement, since it's just a tool of the establishment—which "needs chaos and crime in the streets and the threat of nuclear war."

The Strawberry Statement was cited as an example of "an intelligent programmed mind thinking it's acting against the establishment." Stokely Carmichael was respectfully quoted as saying that the Morgan Guaranty Trust and the Chase Bank "own most of the mortgages in Harlem," and Griffin suggested that Carmichael was expelled from SNCC and the Panthers because he knew "the truth." (The Birchers would loathe all those rumors about Carmichael being a CIA agent.) So "the establishment publicly condemns but privately supports the revolution." And the communists are secretly encouraged because the Conspiracy "needs a huge foe." (Here, my neighbor crooned the Birch bumper slogan: "Get the U.S. out of the UN and the UN out of the U.S.") Griffin urged his audience to "challenge the establishment's candidates," and "to return government to the hands of the people." He added, "Is it possible that the communist and capitalist conspiracies have one more inner circle? We don't know, but it seems likely." My neighbor sighed, "One ball of wax." Griffin concluded by quoting Looney Tunes, "That's all, folks!"

Since the long arms of the Conspiracy reach out to clasp so many institutions, there has been some confusion about tentacles and testicles. The testicles of the Supreme Court? Anyway, "the greatest threat to constitutional government is not communism from without, but the Supreme Court from within," according to Congressman John Rarick of Louisiana, who kept calling Chief Justice Burger "Booger"—nearly "bugger"—throughout his speech on "We Live and Serve for Those We Love," which was mainly a disgruntled listing of federal expenditures.

During long days of staring at liver spots on the backs of bald heads, and wondering where the men found those old seersucker jackets of the Fifties, I unwound by chatting with a very pleasant judo instructor in the hotel's basement, where he taught self-defense to children and adults throughout the rally. Small Birchers tumbled in cartwheels around his knees, while he explained to me that it takes only three pounds of pressure to break someone's finger. Few at the rally looked younger than fifty; a trickle of teen-agers had clearly been brought by their parents. They had discussions about "whether rock music is part of the Conspiracy," and practiced singing "Gobless America" for the final dinner.

Quite a few Birchers dozed or took little naps as soon as the speeches began; others applauded at the wrong moments and were gently reproached by the speakers. With nine hours of lectures a day, many seemed quite exhausted, and they wandered off to the exhibition halls, where booths were staffed by sympathetic organizations. (The rally is said to be sponsored by "a coalition" of conservative groups, but the Boston press sets it firmly in Birchdom.) The bazaar of Birch-related products ranged from alfalfa sprouts and little dishes of seeds, which you should grow and can to become SHELF-SUFFI-CIENT—as riots, pollution, and strikes increase, you won't be able to leave your house, and the supermarkets will be empty—to rhinestone flag pins, or an LP on "The Child Seducers" narrated by John Carradine, pamphlets on "Freedom's Judas-Goat" (Fulbright, sometimes called Fooldull), bumper stickers—MY GOD IS ALIVE, SORRY ABOUT YOURS; SHOOT LOOTERS; SEE AMERICA FIRST, IT'S A RIOT! —or Orwell's *Animal Farm,* a great favorite of the Birchers.

Spooning up wet cold beans and apple mush, dispensed by the Hippocrates Health Society, you could watch Devin-Adair Garrity presiding benignly over Devin-Adair books, while Taylor Caldwell autographed her latest, or read the riveting hand-outs on devil worship in America or how to massage your feet to regenerate other parts of the body: pressing your big toe to relieve the back of your neck, or squeezing your heel for the sake of your hips. ("Two persons can accomplish wonders by working at each other's feet at the same time.") At the Birch Society's own tables, *Teddy Bare,* a rightwing analysis of Chappaquiddick, was this year's best seller. The usual Birch front groups offered their regular literature: TACT (Truth About Civil Turmoil), which connects black groups with the communists; TRAIN (To Restore American Independence Now), which belts the UN and the peacemongers; SYLP (Support Your Local Police); and MOTOREDE (The Movement to Restore Decency), which fights sex education, birth control, and abortion. These organizations recruit citizens who may not realize that they're halfway into the Birch Society. There wasn't much evidence of SHAME (Stop Helping America's Marxist Enemies). They recommend boycotting stores which sell Polish hams, Czech toys, also Camel, Winston, and Salem cigarettes—which are supposed to be made with Yugoslavian tobacco. In the past, SHAME has intimidated even Sears Roebuck, Woolworth, and Kresge out of selling products from East Europe.

You can easily predict what Birchers hate: disarmament, socialized medicine, busing, programs to aid Appalachia, the *New York Times,* taxes, John Dewey (who is still being "exposed"), and of course any Kennedy. Throughout, we were swimming in Chappaquiddick jokes: "Teddyboy laid down his friends for his life"; the races run by the Kennedys include "the race to get out of a submerged automobile"; the Democrats, who will definitely nominate him, "can swallow a bridge or two"; "Some condemned Teddy for wearing his neck brace to the Kopechne funeral. But he needed it: to hold his head up." (These are in keeping with the Birchers' old gags about JFK's funeral: "Jackie got a Jack-in-the-box.") Only Pat Nixon escaped: "Isn't it nice to have a *lady* in the White House again." (Timid applause.) Certain names are magic: Bernadette Devlin, "who won't know the *color* of her child—black, white, or Red," Jane Fonda, Walter Lippmann. But only Sammy Davis, Jr., got hissed.

At other moments, when the Birchers repeat: the government's lying to us! the media distorts! public schools are disintegrating, the establishment is exploiting us all ... you wonder if you ever left home. The Birchers are fascinating because they're half right on some points, also because they're fueled by a period in which it's often hard to know what's true or crazy. They also dislike the CIA, the AMA, the National Council of Churches, and "capitalists"—meaning "rich socialists" who don't practice free enterprise. They're not a bit fond of John Mitchell, and even Agnew (who was hardly mentioned) is understood to be a "phony conservative"—a front for the left-wing government we actually have. As for the Silent Majority, it "never saved any nation," and it stood back while Jesus was crucified: "the Silent Majority is yellow and always has been."

It's beguiling to hear the Birchers use certain phrases when they're obviously innocent of the source: the AMA and other medical organizations which deny individuals their rights are "*not* part of the *solution,* but part of the *problem*"; what the U.S. needs is "people power"; those who are ruining America should be lined "*up against the wall*" (before a firing squad.) At times, I felt as though I was again covering the Panther conventions of the last two years. Still, nobody said Right On.

The Birchers naturally uphold the Vietnam war—but they don't love it. Robert Scott, the retired brigadier general, author of *God Is My Co-Pilot* and its recent sequel, *God Is Still My Co-Pilot,* survivor of 388 combat missions in World War II, mentioned that Douglas MacArthur and others advised against a land war in Vietnam, and added, "then we sent our sons away to do the dirtiest job in the world." Lecturing on "The Poison of 'Peace,'" he said that "our carefully planned failures" were conceived by "very intelligent men"; again, they're part of the Conspiracy "to unite with Soviet Russia." (Birchers refer to Russia much oftener than to China.) God willed us to have the atomic bomb—not only to win World War II, but for peacekeeping. However, we've been sold out by the Conspiracy. Scott blames the military's drug problem—"if there is one"—on letting the war "get boring." Also, "the uniform has lost its glamour." (He and others were very reluctant to believe that the army's stoned; narcotics programs can be just an excuse for raising taxes.) Proudly, he said, "I was as much a murderer as ten Calleys." But his home town gave him a hero's parade, and even rented a water buffalo—"at great expense"—for him to ride on.

The Birchers cherish their weapons for self-defense: "Take up a relevant sport—target practice." Although the speakers weren't inciteful, a couple of men in the audience chuckled over the possibility that Mike Mansfield might get shot during the next hunting season in Montana: "He better stay out of the woods." Patriotism may indeed mean risking life. But of course the U.S. itself is "underarmed." William McBirnie, the executive director of "the Voice of Americanism," urged his audience to press their congressmen for the rapid development of "exotic weapons," such as more bacteriological warfare and the "neutron bomb," which is "destructive to human tissue," but leaves most buildings standing. It removes people, not cities, and "doesn't make rubble out of the land."

Nixon? Some were hopeful at his election, but he's now despised as "the liberal he always was." And "trading LBJ for Nixon is sort of like getting custody of your ex-wife's parents." Nixon was used by the Conspiracy during the Hiss case, when "only *one* communist was exposed, and the public was placated." After many sneers at Keynes' homosexuality, plus references to Keynes' "*dear* friend, FDR," it was stressed that "Franklin Delano Nixon" has finally "confessed that he's a Keynesian—though that doesn't mean he's a homosexual." (For some reason, the Conspiracy didn't want Humphrey for president, and they elected Nixon by saying that a vote for Wallace was a vote for Humphrey.) Hence Nixon, like the CIA—and its employee Daniel Ellsberg—feeds the Conspiracy. "Let's fly above those silly Pentagon Papers"—which were leaked by the government to make the public demand peace, which means defeat.

Old Birch buffs say that many who embraced the Conspiracy theory used to be openly anti-Semitic—despite Robert Welch's efforts to keep racism at bay. (Welch has written that anti-Semitism is a weapon of the communists. Others have claimed that the Birch Society has been plagued by "anti-Semitic infiltrators.") So most Birchers are extremely cautious now. They even produced a couple of black speakers. One, named Charles E. Smith, who edits and publishes the *Voice of Watts,* said that he first picketed Robert Welch—before joining the Society. Smith explained that employers who wouldn't hire blacks were "sitting on the boards of the NAACP and the Urban League"; the same people "were making the problem and financing the protest." Later, I questioned him during a whispery rap session in the hall, while square dancers in mammoth crinolines thundered by. He confirmed that "colored people" and whites can get along—it's only "planned class warfare that makes them fight." He referred to "those Hollywood movies that make colored people look dumb—and on the boards of those movie companies, you'll find the NAACP and the Urban League." In fact, "civil rights leaders" really deprive other blacks of their rights.

The square dance caller shouted "Do-si-do!" The black Bircher began to weave a wild parallel between the United States and medieval Europe: "See, the squires finked on their own families, to get themselves up the ladder—"

"Allemande left!"

"And the fiefs—"

"Swing your partner!"

"What's Queen Elizabeth ever done against the communists? Nothing. They help to keep her in power."

"Do-si-do!"

"Shoot a leader—like Joe Columbo or Martin Luther King—and you solidify the people. They think there's a plot against them—so they're ready to fight other races."

"Now I want to see a graaaaannnd chaaaaaaiinn."

At a reception for some hoop-skirted women, who'd dressed themselves and a collection of dolls in the style of Godey's Ladies, an excercise which was somehow plugged into "the priceless heritage of being an American woman," it was repeated that the Alabama Negroes love Governor Wallace. The Birchers paid tribute to "predominantly Negro" colleges; Daniel Payne College is one of the few in America "that's never had any violence on campus." Moreover, the aim of integrated schools is "*not* to educate Negroes but to keep whites ignorant." (The "purpose of keeping people ignorant is to make them more malleable, easier to lead.") Prior to integration, the all-black public schools were very good—and so were the white schools. Now, most public schools are bad, while the "private" black schools in the South are doing fine. Still, it's "not a racial question."

Beneath the emblem of a broken hammer and sickle, superimposed by a sword-tipped cross and flag, speech after speech confirmed the Birchers' beliefs. "The poor of America own more cars than *all* the people in Russia." Hence, "Mostly, poverty is a state of mind. . . . Money and education cannot end poverty." Higher education is "the most overrated thing since Jackie Kennedy." (Cheers.) There *is* no population explosion, so there's no excuse for birth control; also, "Have you noticed that those who support abortion are against capital punishment?" Sex education is designed simply to distract children from learning anything else. Students take drugs "because someone wanted it that way, and industriously promoted it." However, all drug users should be jailed. This may be the age of Aquarius, but the water in that sign "isn't being used for purification, but for *brainwashing* our youth." Modern women are "immodest and unclean." The churches could have prevented the communist take-over; instead, they promoted it. And the "pagan" peace symbol is an inverted crucifix, designed by Nero, and was originally used for crucifying St. Peter and others upside-down. (It has also been identified as "the witches foot" of the Middle Ages and "a symbol of the anti-Christ" used by Satanists.) Throughout, "You can't play down the possibility that the same group may be running the capital-ists and the communists."

Although "We depend on the press for information as a child depends on its mother's breast for milk," all publications which aren't produced by the Birch Society are toxic. One white reporter was forced to leave the rally when he tried to cover it for the *Boston Herald Traveler,* and was threatened with "personal assault" if he returned. A Black cameraman who had the Society's permission to film the rally for a Boston TV station, was kicked, kneed, and carried out by a group of men who didn't want their pictures taken. He reported that one of his thirty or forty attackers said that he hit him "because I am a patriot."

The Birchers are anarchists—if only they knew it. They detest most professional politicians, except for Wallace, and they don't seem to like any form of government. "Our authority is *not* the President, but the Constitution . . . anyone who sabotages the Constitution should be resisted"—like Richard Nixon. The audience loved a story from ancient Greece: "When a senator made a proposal, he stood on a box with a rope around his neck. If the people liked the proposal, they took away the rope. If they didn't, they kicked away the box." Huge applause.

Any kind of liberal should be flattered to learn that the Conspiracy is brilliantly organized, and that its members have been very well *"trained."* The world is laced with corridors and wings: FDR was "waiting in the corridor"; communists "always have a student waiting in the wings." But the Birchers' strength springs from their knowledge: again and again, speakers told them: You *know* so much, you're the only ones who know what's going on in this country. Hence their sense of superiority. Certain as any astrologer that he knows what lies ahead, the Bircher feels a titanic responsibility: to tell others about the Conspiracy. "It's *our duty* to inform them, and to *name* the culprits."

There's great emphasis on organizing in your own community to fight the local Job Corps or the school board or the library or fluoridation, or to harry the sponsors of TV and radio stations who finance unpatriotic programs. Speakers stress that "We have *only fourteen months* in which to do something for America" (convince students to vote against Teddy Kennedy); "we have *only thirty-six months*" before the Russians "force a confrontation in the Middle East." Yet they know that many Americans will ignore or try to suppress them. "If there's a murderer *crawling* into your bedroom at night, and your dog barks in the yard, you have two problems: discomfort at being awakened"—and the suspicion that "something's wrong with the dog." But if you shoot the dog, you've lost your protection from the murderer. And that's how the spiritual watchdogs of the Birch Society feel that they're treated today.

Aside from the ego biscuits, part of the Society's spell may be cast by the vagueness and the rambling contradictions of the speakers.

The polite audience sighs or gasps in response to passwords like
Conspiracy or fluoridation, but few can explain the concepts to you.
(Does the Conspiracy direct the communists, or vice versa? You hear
it both ways.) Most of the Birchers I met were doctors and teachers
and small businessmen; all were from the professional classes, and
there was no mention of Middle America. Yet, unlike the yelling
uglies I've seen at Wallace rallies, or the smug "realists" who turn
out for Ayn Rand, many Birchers seemed quite forlorn or wornout
people. The hatred and rage which they were known for in the past
may have ebbed, although many are very bitter indeed, and their
jokes have a queasy malice. But they didn't gleam with the confidence which you see at most rallies—that exhilaration which often
peaks when any kind of faithful get together.

So you feel that the Birchers are losing the momentum which they
had in '66 or '67. Last year, even the Young Americans for Freedom
broke with them, and denounced Lester Maddox, their prime speaker,
for his racism. Empty of all political sophistication, the Birchers seem
unable to capitalize on most conservative sentiments in the country
now. Yet, although they seem rather powerless en masse, I'm sure
that they can still exert furious pressure in their own small towns or
neighborhoods. It was said that some three thousand registered for
the rally, and officials claimed that it was the largest they'd ever had.
After all those long and boring speeches, many kept saying what fun
the rally had been, how lovely it was to see each other again, and how
much they looked forward to meeting next year—if only the Conspiracy doesn't kill a lot of us off, if only we can work fast enough
to prevent it.

STRIKES AND LULLS: HARVARD
July 1972

"Si, si, Sihanouk!
Rotcee's building's gonna cook.
Workers, yes! Harvard, no!
Racist Rotcee's got to go."
                    —April 1970

I COVERED the Harvard strike in '69 and the Yale strike in '70, and wrote rather hopeful pieces about both. At each university, the issues seemed very clear—although so many commentators insisted that the upheaval was psychological, not political or social. (There was a lot of stuff about sons battling fathers, and one Harvard dean even had a biological interpretation: he declared that student protest was engineered by "the sons of communists.") At both universities, I was also heartened by the fact that those who disagreed were still talking with one another, still arguing and listening. By early '69, that had almost ceased in New York; a tired satirist said, "If we don't confront our polarizations, we'll have to polarize our confrontations—*then* maybe we can have a dialogue."

Despite the nationwide lull that followed the university strikes— from about October 1970 through March of '72—it was plain that many students' convictions hadn't changed, even though the campuses were comparatively hushed. (Also, as one of my friends said, "Whoever expected a revolution from the children of the ruling class?") But in '71, I even heard old-style liberal professors—who had hated the strikes—contemptuously putting down their own students for being "docile."

In May and June of '72, I returned to Cambridge and New Haven, simply to ask a lot of people what they thought about their strikes in retrospect. The seniors of '72 were the freshmen of '69: the last Harvard class to have lived through the strike. What direct or indirect results did they see? Or side effects?

Near Harvard Square, where many used to try to sell you dope, people were pushing kittens—little, mewing bundles were thrust at me while I read the sign on the Unitarian church: "It Is as Much a Sin to Take Offense as to Give it." *(What?)* And the voices of Harvard rose to battle with each other:

"The strike changed everything!"

"*Nothing's* changed."

"So you give the ruling class a heart attack. Then it recovers."

"Dig it, the war's not over. But people grew a lot in awareness."

"Five or six years ago, radicals were a fringe group. Now they're the mainstream."

"There's a new course in revolution, which is terrible."

"I have a really rough time thinking about bombing. I don't want anyone hurt. But I was glad to see the bomb in the Pentagon. But I do know that bombing's a male chauvinist pig fantasy."

"So what's new? Harvard still houses Handlin, Skinner, Bell, and all those end-of-ideology creeps from the Fifties."

"I think—at its best—our generation is the conscience of the country. And we'll *never* be the same as we were before the strike."

"People offed LBJ. Then they found you could change the person, but not the system. From Pusey to Bok: the only change is style."

"The peace movement picked up again, then it died, then it picked up, then it died."

"There are some people it's still hard to speak to—it's been like the aftermath of a civil war."

So, as a Radcliffe graduate from the Fifties, I did a bit of time-tripping: in '69, when one of my favorite professors asked me what kind of piece I was writing about the strike, I said that it was a term paper which would please no one: neither students nor faculty, not moderates or militants. I added, "Pleasing no one was exactly what you taught us to do up here." He snorted and agreed. I also remembered the experience of majoring in English: they told us that generalizations were evil—sloppy and perilous—and then they asked us to make them, demanded the very thing which we'd been warned against. So I'm always uneasy around Harvard: what's required is also what's despised. Uneasy and also scornful: an institution which teaches you to be so critical can't ask for respect in return. (There used to be a dredging firm near Harvard called the Veritas Sludge Company, which pleased a lot of students.) And yet I've a reluctant soft spot for the old dinosaur: I liked what they gave me to read, liked so many people who are still my friends, am (unwillingly?) grateful for the skepticism it bred. I also think that part of the Harvard-Radcliffe education means deeply disliking the university itself. That was true for many I knew in the apolitical Fifties—even though we didn't know the facts which students do today.

In '72, almost all the undergraduates I met said that the strike had been a major part of their education—execpt for a few, who sounded rather as though they'd once performed in a school play. (One of these said, "It made everybody try out radical politics to see if they liked them. Lots *didn't* like them.") But those who still felt that the strike had been valuable spoke of the lessons about power and how it operates: "having the university exposed as the monster it is." Another said, "When I came here, I had no use for the government, for Washington. But I did think the one thing you could trust was the university. Now I know you can't." And another: "When Mother Nature turns out to be an old bitch—that really hurts. But it's useful to know it."

Throughout, the discoveries about Harvard were mentioned in a positive way: as a preparation for a society which can't be trusted and should be changed. A close observer remarked, "Like other school strikes, it showed a lot of people the political limitations of struggling with academic institutions. So they've left—to start struggling with the problems of the country." An alumnae of the graduate school said, "The strike changed the administration's behavior. Now, all their stalling mechanisms are so finely honed. They know it can happen again, and I think it will, since they've resorted to so many Nixonish techniques, like the stalling, or saying they'll do things which they don't. It's like saying you'll end the war —and you don't. They say, 'Sure, We'll hire more blacks'—and they don't. Yet I still feel I have to try to change things, even though—as a *non*politico—I feel it's all rather hopeless. But I can't be passive any more. The strike did that for a lot of us: and that's a *huge difference.*"

The same person reflected on Harvard's resistance to reforms: "When you take these things on, you feel angry all the time . . . Harvard's so cynical. For example, the Design School has listed one black Mexican woman three times—as though she fulfilled three different categories! She's listed in the percentages of women, blacks, and 'other minorities' enrolled in the school. So many of us feel we're insulted *all the time* with these tactics. Do they think we're so stupid that we don't *know* what's happening?"

Indeed, trust has disintegrated like an old shower curtain—the one you bought at Korvette's seven years ago. Almost none of the professors I saw really trusts the administration; some said they didn't trust students either. The three words I heard oftenest in Cambridge were "impotent," "nefarious," and "manipulative." ("Impotent" came up, or maybe down, in nearly every conversation; it was always used socially, not sexually, and was uttered by as many women as men, equally among faculty and students. I wondered why they didn't say helpless or powerless. Perhaps a number have been reading Wilhelm Reich.) One professor believes that the strike has meant long-range disappointment for everyone: "For the administration, because they couldn't control the students. For the students, because they didn't change the administration. For the faculty, because they felt they couldn't affect either the administration *or* the students." He and other professors (including some who aren't political) agreed that one prime result of the strike was that the administration swiftly became more conservative than ever, also even more bureaucratic. One added, "My students don't yet know that counter-revolutions happen oftener than revolutions. Life is so *much* messier than they realize."

President Derek Bok has hired four new vice-presidents, whose experience is considered to have more to do with management than education. One came from the ITT Sheraton Corporation. Known to some as "Bok's goon squad," their sense of priorities has displeased certain teachers. At a time when every university is panicky about money, some of their suggestions for economizing are considered alarming: proposed cutbacks in tutorials, also for new appointments, or charging rent to faculty who now live free at Radcliffe. "Sure, Harvard has to save. But there are other ways of doing it. They say to us: 'There are items which we must prioritize' and then they try to economize on meals for tutors. Now, money's the easiest way of saying no to *every*thing: to every new idea *or* innovation." Quite a few also feel that the conservative elements in the faculty have taken over. (Lunching in the Faculty Club, I felt that the chilly smugness was unchanged—although it's even more conspicuous now, since much of the social atmosphere has relaxed.)

Meanwhile, the graduate students formed a union in March of '72 —in response to announcements that there would be big cutbacks for them. One said, "There are situations where a third-year graduate student can earn approximately $3,000 a year and then pay Harvard $3,000 a year. . . . We feel that if *we* strike, the university could fold, because we do so much of the teaching." In reply to Harvard's claims that money is minimal, they charged that far too much is being spent on new buildings and on athletics, and that many millions were earned on the university endowment last year, which some think has been unwisely reinvested. (They feel that the investment portfolio could earn a good deal more, but that antiquated methods are being used.) Also, it's believed that the four vice-presidents earn $45,000 a year. Some think there may eventually be a faculty union, but that it will take many years. Throughout, several (not very radical) professors at both Harvard and Yale told me that they hoped student protest would revive: as fuel for future change. Some of the younger faculty, who had worked hard for curriculum reform—which hasn't moved far—felt that students had retreated from the issues. "Of course, the university relies on the fact that students are transients—it can shrug off a year or two of their anger."

From the faculty to the graduating seniors, many suspect that the admissions department has been screening students for potential radicals—although this will always be denied. But many have remarked on the degree of squareness in the recent freshman and sophomore classes ('74 and '75). Bridge is back and so is booze; jocks are conspicuous, you hear the word "dating"; there was even a formal last year, also a panty-raid. One instructor referred to the freshman class she was teaching in the fall of '70: "The culture shock of who I was talking to! They weren't with me at all when I mentioned Cambodia. They came from very unaware families—I think some were admitted for their backgrounds."

Although it can never be proved, some students believe that there's a profile of "the radical troublemaker": an Easterner who's often from New York, probably Jewish, apt to major in Social Studies or History and Lit., a likely candidate for a magna. In January '71, Chase Peterson (then the dean of admissions) met with a group of Jewish faculty who felt that Harvard was taking fewer Jews. (It didn't appear that they were inquiring about radicals.) Peterson said it was his "impression" that Harvard was simply admitting fewer applicants from "the doughnuts around the big cities"—meaning the suburbs. He referred to students with good grades from local high schools. One professor retorted, "Dr. Peterson, those aren't doughnuts, they're bagels." The doughnuts-and-bagels are constantly mentioned when Harvard indicates that it has an obligation to educate the elite. "Look, Harvard could go into the subway and choose twelve hundred people and they'd *become* the elite."

Radcliffe students—who are grimly observing Harvard's resistance to admitting equal numbers of women and men—also think their admissions department has grown much more cautious. One said, "No one *ever* got in here without good marks." I objected: I did. "Oh, then *you* were on the freak list." (Indeed, I have some evidence that I was admitted as one of those known as "interesting risks.") There were lots of those—I mean, us—in the Fifties and early Sixties. But the Radcliffe students I met feel that diversity's decreasing.

□

These were the themes which swirled forward when I asked about the aftermath of the strike. Quite often, I had to keep pulling the conversation back to politics, or to some of the main demands of '69. ROTC has been abolished; its former building is now a day-care center. But there's no applause, since some think it may return—as is being considered at Dartmouth and Brown. Army ROTC has been reinstated at Princeton (without the naval and air force programs). Many are convinced that intelligence-related research still continues, along with investments in "pig products." As for the university's expansion into the poorer communities, no one seems really sure of what Harvard has or hasn't done. (Harvard did donate a small lot —for ninety-nine years—on which some housing for the elderly was built with federal money. Some feel that this would not have happened before the strike. It's also been announced that Harvard will build housing for residents as well as for the Medical School in Roxbury, although some don't believe it.)

Expansion was an impassioned issue in '69, but few seem interested now. Yet I also found many individuals—at both Yale and Harvard—who'd gone off to work in neighboring community projects such as women's health collectives, tenants' organizing groups, or welfare rights. One instructor added, "But you can have people in tenants' groups who aren't interested in welfare; too many are isolated with their own issues, and don't realize that it's all related." Another added, "You can be *into* day care or *into* food co-ops, to the exclusion of other things: including human pain."

Which brings us to the loss of momentum—not merely on campuses, but in the movement throughout the country. (Enquiring after one radical of '69: "Jack? Oh, he's into primal scream now.") A librarian said, "Kids are aware of their limitations now—as they weren't before. Some students feel very threatened by the possibility of big political reinvolvement. So they try to develop healthy interests —like suburban husbands doing woodwork—such as working for McGovern." One senior said, "Now that Nixon's changed the draft laws, men are dropping out like flies again. For some, the war is really over." He and others spoke rather sternly about "instant gratification": wanting immediate results from any protest. Another senior said, "This place is screamingly apolitical. It's a point of honor that *one* does not get involved in political issues. After the Cambodia actions, it was a disaster here. When the government didn't crumble to its knees in ten days, lots of people threw up their hands and said: 'I can do nothing.' Cambodia helped students to construct a very sophisticated defense against *any more* antiwar activity."

In '69, I wrote: "Anyone who has seen (or shared in) some fighting and bleeding and weeping cannot escape the issues that began it. Romanticism ebbs; sore heads and soreheads have to consider what has hurt them." I now see that I was wrong; many want to forget the varieties of hurt, and some issues were partially obscured by pain.

A Radcliffe junior, who had taken one year out, was eloquent about dwelling amid the conflicts: "When I came back last fall, I was grateful for the apathy because it allowed me to immerse myself in work. And people are much more into personal relationships." (Others said that they'd had no personal life at all when they were spending ten hours a day in meetings. Also, Harvard's health and psychiatric services reported that fewer students sought aid throughout the strike.) "Because of '69 and Cambodia in '70, people have come to feel that they can't change all the shit around them, so they might as well have full private lives. They won't listen to the news or read the papers—they know it's all there, it won't go away. But the feeling is *impotence.*

"After '69 and '70, I felt all that euphoria was a dirty trick, somebody's dirty trick. After Cambodia, when we felt *some* feedback— some reaction from Washington—it was so brief. *So* temporary.

"The atmosphere for head-changing isn't what it was two years ago. Then you had to talk about the issues."

Not now?

"You don't *have* to talk politics now. But the trouble with that is— when Nixon decides to bomb Vietnam again, people say: Oh hell, it's one more thing.

"Cynicism really runs counter to the undergraduate experience. If you're cynical—as many were after 1970—you can't relate to Plato or Ibsen. You can't study if you're cynical." (She referred to the numbers who she felt had dropped out for that reason.) "A lot of people feel they can have some power over their lives—in terms of this place—I think that's an illusion.

"Listen, the strike made Harvard a better place *and* a deader place. It opened things up, academically and between people. It was even a stab at community democracy. And it was ultimately deadening *and* liberating."

All the students to whom I later quoted her views agreed. One said, "No wonder I've been feeling funny."

□

And a few are still nostalgic about the strike.

At the height of the '69 bust in University Hall, one student saw a friend of his being badly beaten in the Yard. "That set something off inside me, so I jumped the cop. He beat me on my back. Then I broke away. Every moment of fury and rage I've ever felt in my whole life was concentrated in my body at that moment. I felt completely impotent, I didn't know what to do, I threw rocks: from a pile of dirt from some construction work. Then the cops bore down, and I ran, I tripped over that same pile of dirt—which may say something psychological about me. They ripped my jacket and I slipped out of it. . . . Afterward, I was in a state of shock, I just walked around, glaring at the deans and wishing them all good morning. For an hour after the bust, *no* one was in charge of Harvard —not SDS, not the administration. *Anything* could have happened, but no one had prepared for that moment.

"For seven days, anyone could walk into the Yard and communicate intensely with anyone—on politics *or* personal things. That never happened again.

"But I think it was the taste of what a revolution could mean. 'The transformation of everyday life.' "

□

Behind Widener Library, I heard two middle-aged white men— neatly buttoned into their jackets—chatting about "the brothers."
"How are the brothers doing?"

"Oh, the brothers are doing fine." Somewhat startled by their apparent concern for black militants, I eavesdropped until I discovered that they were talking about Brooks Brothers. One was worried that the firm might be bruised by recession.

Among the white undergraduates and teachers I saw, almost none knew any black students. They referred to the strong black separatist movement which is current at Harvard: "Blacks make you feel that you mustn't intrude on them." Some sounded rather forlorn about having no black friends—especially those who'd had a number in high school. Some said that individual blacks might mix with whites when they were on their own, but would not do so in front of other blacks. One instructor described a paper written by one of her black freshmen: about continuing to mingle with whites while experiencing the scorn and anger of his black classmates. Certainly not all black students are separatists, but it appears as though they have to make a choice when they arrive at Harvard. A black man with a white woman will probably be ostracized.

White students spoke respectfully of the separatism; they said that it was clearly a source of strength and reinforcement. A black faculty member who is especially close to black students explained: "If a white wants to be liberal, he has to accept black separatism. Sure, it makes whites uptight—but they've got to realize that it's not animosity toward them: it's solidarity for us. But we can't have our causes co-opted by theirs, we can't have our minds infiltrated by their issues; we've got to work full-time for ourselves. And we've learned that it's possible to survive without sharing white values. . . . You learn you don't need white people! . . . Because of their mutual support, I think the black students' morale is better than the whites'. Also, because the Afro Department was established in '69: black students got more out of the strike.

"I feel that most of the faculty don't know anything about black people—and they don't bother to learn. Many black students feel that they're here for the *benefit* of white students—to broaden their horizons."

There are some four hundred black students at Harvard now. The few I did meet were enthusiastic about being there. One said, "It's easy to become a black activist here—this place does heighten *all* the contradictions." But he and others kept stressing that they enjoyed the university's variety: "Where else would I find so many kinds of cats? Even the ones who are into the conservative bag—I won't come down on them. That's what's solid about Harvard: you can have both radicals and conservatives here." (*"Solid"* seems to be replacing "Right on," at least around Boston.)

In April, President Bok announced that Harvard wasn't going to sell its 683,000 shares of Gulf Oil stock—as had been demanded by the Pan African Liberation Committee (PALC) and the Harvard-Radcliffe Association of African and Afro-American Students (Afro): in their protest against Gulf's involvement with the brutal Portuguese colonial regime in Angola. The future president of Afro told me that black students had been working on the issue since September 1971, that they had steadily sent petitions to Bok, but were unable to see much of him. They'd asked for a decision on Gulf, and when they got it, about thirty-five occupied Massachusetts Hall where Bok and his administration have their offices. The blacks held Mass Hall for six days. Bok did not call the cops. Instead, he obtained a court injunction which meant that if the occupiers did not leave, they could have been sentenced to six months in jail for contempt of court. During the occupation, there was a supportive picket line outside the building—at times, it reached a thousand.

The PALC and Afro tactics, which impressed many white students, were carefully considered. There were different roles for different temperaments. Some of the most militant blacks occupied the building; others helped to organize the pickets, delivered food, or gave information to the press. "It would be ridiculous to force someone to occupy the building if he didn't want to. But he can do other things. . . . We do encourage white support—we couldn't have succeeded without it. But when SDS wanted to take over another building, we asked them not to. We didn't want occuping buildings to be the issue—*Gulf* was the issue." There was a five-day strike by some of the white students—against the renewed bombing in Vietnam, as well as in support of the Gulf action. However, this strike wasn't directed against Harvard itself. On quite a few campuses, the university is less of a target than it was three years ago.

The corporation announced that Harvard would ask Gulf "to set forth its plans for further improving" the employment and treatment of black Angolans, and the corporation would send a representative to Angola to gather information on Gulf's performance, "thereby to help us determine our future actions as a responsible Gulf share-holder." Meanwhile, black students were researching the amount of Gulf stock owned by other universities; they hoped to make it a nationwide issue and to organize a boycott on Gulf. "Gulf should be a continuous process—*not* a mass event where people discharge all their emotions. *Not* like Mayday at Yale."

In '69, the issue of black studies was initially separate from the general strike. But, when black students learned that the proposed program might be merely a "Committee on Degrees," which would offer only tutorials, and would have given degrees only to students who had fulfilled the requirements of one of the other departments, they joined the strike and won their demand for a full academic department. Three years later, professors in Afro-American Studies say that there have been growing pains—in part, because the program was assembled so hastily; also, because Harvard has been careless in its requirements; for example, African languages aren't required to teach African history—"But would Harvard hire someone to teach German or Asian history if he didn't know the language?" And some feel that outsiders, including one black professor, have sought to damage the department. Also: "Afro Studies are a threat to profes-sors in established fields, like history and economics. They should have done their homework, but they say, 'We haven't had the facilities.' So it makes them uneasy that the department even exists." Obviously, no outsider can really judge the department. But the black students I saw were very keen on their Afro courses, especially literature and languages.

□

When you pursue the current weaknesses of SDS—which, at Harvard, is dominated by the Progressive Labor Party—you hear a lot of grunts and sighs from former members, as well as from inde-pendent radicals or moderates. Of course the '69 split in SDS—when Weatherman was formed, and others were left to fight one another—was very crippling. Now, some feel that PL was never serious about the war: "Sure, they surface at antiwar demonstrations. But people who care about the war just can't make it with PL." Also, many repeat that SDS and the movement in general sagged due to the lack of long-range plans or a blueprint. "If you think the world is ending in three weeks, you can't plan a movement. But many *wanted* to think there was a very short deadline—because that was the only way to keep up the pressure."

Some think that SDS developed a talent for picking the wrong issues. Garrett Epps, president of the *Crimson* from '71 to '72, wrote in '71, ". . . as the bombs dropped on North Vietnam, SDS held a demonstration against Harvard's system of parking fees for workers; as crowds marched to Boston Common to protest the invasion of Laos, SDS demonstrated at Holyoke Center against Harvard's apprenticeship program. . . ." SDS still attracts a small new membership; one activist explained, "If there's no doctor, you take the guy who has a Band-Aid."

But manipulation is the theme that recurs again and again: from those who feel that SDS and PL were able to tyrannize others by denouncing them as ideological scum or political pukes—including many in the movement, who were working on the same issues. The rigidity of PL—with its assumption of moral superiority—drove away some with deep political convictions; the style was far too authoritarian to build a "mass base." One veteran of '69 said, "There was the pressure to have a total analysis of *everything*. Your intuitions weren't trusted or valid, unless they related to politics. You were being *judged* all the time. You'd say something, anything, and then the counterattack would begin: they'd say *'That's not clear,'* and then they'd rip you apart. A lot of people couldn't deal with that. . . . Once I was taking half an hour off, listening to The Band, and loving it, and I was told that it was capitalistic, rock revisionist music. I was *really* shamefaced. I got so I didn't want others to hear me hearing it."

Did the standards seem inhuman?

"Yes. People are reading a lot of Orwell now. He said that zealots or purists are always in danger of changing into their opposites—because they've let go of human values.

"Weatherman was the logical extension. Because you've been raised in a sick society, blah, blah, blah, you have to smash yourself. Weatherman said: Okay, we're going to be *perfect*. We're going to smash bourgeois experience. But most people can't keep that up. And they can't be perfect."

I've always felt that Harvard teaches self-doubt. Along with recurrent dissent—the carping and the sneering and the most valuable dogfights, searing self-criticism makes many far too skillful at putting themselves down. Truly scorning the self can follow easily. (Again, I can vouch for the Fifties.) And I've felt that many alumnae were hampered by this; quite a few I know have large egos but very little confidence indeed. It's the mark of our common schooling, and I can often recognize it in strangers. So I can well understand those who were vulnerable—in '69 or '70—when told that they were lousy. One student who said that the movement had made him feel that he ought to "negate or dissolve" himself—that he should "abdicate" his judgment to his superiors, "destroy your own identity to serve others" —gave me this description of street fighting in the Square in April 1970: "I loved it, I thought it was great, that kind of chaos. I ran back and forth, though I didn't throw rocks. It was danger and chaos and everything being transformed—like the streets you know. It was a form of self-obliteration. No thought. I wasn't frightened at all. Maybe because I placed a low value upon myself."

What else did you like about it?

"The feeling that you are out of yourself, your revolting, imperfect . . . corrupt . . . self—and you're into something that requires no decision. You're part of the flow. A feeling of transcendence—transcending yourself, transcending reality. I think I was basically out of my head—on adrenalin. . . . Placing no value on yourself—the way Harvard makes you feel."

We chewed over that, and he went on: "The distrust of yourself that is taught here—I bought the whole thing. My freshman year, I'd start reading—it didn't matter what it was—and I'd feel too ignorant to understand it. To read a piece of literature, I'd feel I needed to understand economics, linguistics. Before I read Chaucer, I'd have to know Latin and Greek. I felt like an idiot, more and more."

Another student said, "Yes, that's where Harvard still destroys people. Meanwhile, everybody here is used to being told they're Number One—but they know that's phony! Although they may look good in the eyes of other people—outside Harvard—they know that's just bullshit."

However, some in the movement who were reviled by their own classmates have rebelled against that abasement. A radical senior's summation: "People here never learned from SDS, and SDS never learned from the people here, so everyone stayed stupid."

☐

This is a period of rethinking and regrouping. There's some interest in the New American Movement (NAM), which one student called "a healthy version of SDS for the Seventies. NAM is clear about alternatives, and they understand the need for leadership." NAM has attracted some of the old New Left, such as Staughton Lynd. (While PL and Weatherman were hefty on campuses, some of the older movement people grew very quiet.) NAM is still fluid, and there's said to be a commitment to democratic socialism. "People know that what should be done will take a long time—whereas PL sounds as though it will be ruling the country tomorrow. But it's important to avoid the mistakes of the last few years. For example, the foreign-vanguard-peasant type revolution didn't relate enough to the *American* experience."

☐

"Hey, I'll tell you one result of the strike. You haven't heard anyone mention a 'generation gap' up here. Right?" (Right. Not a word.) "Because the Sixties are over! We all passed through them together—parents and children. Now, due to the sad facts of the economy, kids are understanding what their parents went through—how they compromised." An alumna said, "The strike blotted out a lot of generational differences. Because people divided politically. And that was the only thing that mattered." In '69, I heard about a student who accused his parents of "knuckling under to the Depression." But in '72, I heard no one knocked for being a parent—or for being any age.

☐

One senior looked back to '69: "Everyone was talking solidarity. That was a party line that no one could live up to. So it just produced more loneliness. People tried *so* hard to merge with the group, then they felt *more* isolated than ever."

There has certainly been a recoil from mass participation—even if it's only temporary. (At the end of 1970, at a Yippie workshop which was expected to be totally political, I was astounded when the theme became "cultivating personal relationships"—though none I questioned had heard of Bloomsbury.) In universities, many have withdrawn to lead acutely private, often introspective, lives. It's the revival of individualism that you see everywhere, and I'm sure that it's a reaction against the conviction of late Sixties that ego is ugly: from SDS to Timothy Leary, you heard that the sense of self must be dumped. In the name of politics *or* acid, many Aquarians tried so hard to suppress their selfhood. Now, it seems as though many egos have sprung up like toast from a toaster.

Meanwhile, some of the more political students in Cambridge are impatient with others who have been lulled with life styles. "You know the old one: that society can be changed with life styles. But the relation between smoking a joint and stopping the war is just too tenuous!" Another said, "There's lots of consumerism. Buying expensive hiking boots. Fancy dope—being a connoisseur: like winesmanship. Waterbeds . . . The basic thing that Harvard runs on is that people here deserve to earn a lot of money. And so a lot of my classmates will go on to perpetuate the system; they'll be doctors and lawyers, and they'll say: I'm going to do a lot of good things for other people, radical things, but I must be well paid for it. Lots of people live with accepted schizophrenia: they know the system is shit, but the sugar at the end of the trail is just too sweet: the promises of jobs and money."

The puritanism of some of the left has abated. "I expect to be a radical all my life—but not to give up going to the movies." These days, although the general morale at Harvard seems very low, you also hear quite a lot about "the quality of life" from political animals. "I began to realize that radical politics wasn't just SDS screaming about imperialism, but that politics related to personal experience and daily living." And I met quite a few who certainly aim to stay outside the system. Planning to live cheaply—while running small summer camps or play groups, being a carpenter or driving a taxi—but hoping to earn just enough to travel, to explore. Of course the groundnote is freedom—especially from a brutalizing high-powered job which gives no nourishment to the self. My Fifties concept of freedom was quite similar, except that it hung on a compulsion *to be grown up:* to be treated as an equal by adults, to pass as one of them—which sounds hilarious to students now.

"People are willing not to have much security. Desire for success? No, not much, we know that what the employer wants is bullshit. But there's a desire for a *niche.* To be in your own place, to be with friends. Who wants to go up some ladder? *Less* desire for fame—not wanting to go out and beat T. S. Eliot or Albert Einstein." (That was a Fifties hangup at Harvard: some fledgling writers would measure themselves against Proust or Dostoevsky or Melville—and then despair.) "Trying not to be part of the economy, still living the student life style: in small towns, communes, not big cities. I'll get a room in someone's house for ten dollars a week, spend ten dollars for food. We'll live on the underbelly of society."

A Radcliffe senior said, "I look around me and I don't see anybody doing anything I want to do. So I'm going to spend a few years being a bum." She and her friends kept razzing each other about not being "directed." One punctuated the conversation with "That's *irrelevant*" while she doodled on a paper napkin.

A young man said, "I thought of teaching in public high school. But I hear the kids just sit there and stare at the teachers. They know they won't learn anything. They know what the school system is doing to them."

"I'm going to work with a group that's organizing sharecroppers in Louisiana. But I think doing one thing for a whole lifetime is ridiculous."

"I had a summer job in Washington with Nader. I'm not sure muckraking is useful, but I enjoyed it."

"You're not directed!"

"Who is?"

"That's *irrelevant.*"

"You see, Harvard's standards have lost their legitimacy: in terms of what they expect of graduates. Or Harvard's idea of success."

"That's irrelevant too."

Another disagreed. "Harvard just wants you to be good at what you do—whatever it is."

"Like being a good Panther?"

Many expressed disgust because they feel that Harvard trains students only for academic work—"And many think that's not worthwhile. So what you've been trained for you don't believe in."

"I've talked to professors who say their profession is bankrupt."

"We're trained for nothing. We have twenty-thousand-dollar BAs, and magnas, and no skills, just a lot of nothing."

□

Ex-President Nathan Pusey, who had outraged so many when he called the police to clear University Hall in '69, got a standing ovation when he received an honorary degree at commencement in June of '72.

STRIKES AND LULLS: YALE
May 1970

"Fuck Dick, *fuck Spiro!*
Bobby Seale's *the people's hero!"*

THE BUS driver spat out the window as we approached the New Haven Green, where crowds were massing for the Mayday rally in support of the nine Panthers going on trial for the murder of Panther Alex Rackley. The driver said, "At least they're mostly white. But it's gonna be disgusting." The bus rumbled with agreement. The fourteen passengers were so nervous that they kept talking compulsively to one another: as though words could ward off the menace of the next few hours. An old woman jabbered: "I wish I had a penny for every mile I've walked my dog. She's six years old." Someone said, "I wish I had my dog with me right now." "Oh, dogs are the best protection." The old woman hardly heard them: "These days, dogs don't have a chance. The way people want them policed—tied up." The driver growled like a mastiff—"Look at that crowd"—while her voice spun faster: "You must always talk to your dog. That's how you educate them. They like to be treated human."

I went to New Haven a week before Mayday: just after some undergraduates began carting their stereos out of their rooms and leaving town. Local shops had boarded up their windows; all over the plywood, students had stenciled WHY BE AFRAID? (On one, someone had written, "But what about Alex Rackley?") A truck carrying 280 weapons—including riot guns with fixed bayonets—was stolen in New Haven and found empty in New York; a fire in the Law School Library burned $2,500 worth of books; fires in abandoned buildings in the ghetto have caused the police and the Panthers to accuse one another, while some of the neighborhood suspected right-wing arsonists. A lot of liquid mercury—which can be used in making bombs—had been swiped from the chemistry lab; it was found in the apartment of a revolutionary dropout. There were rumors that the Gutenberg Bible would be stolen, replaced by a fake, and that the original would be sold and the money given to the poor. There were even more rumors about white vigilantes and Weatherpersons and Hell's Angels and out-of-town adventurists arriving. It was said that certain outsiders—who later preached non-violence in New Haven—had invited large audiences in Boston to come and help trash Yale. Some felt that others had decided that the Revolution would start on May 1st in New Haven, Conn.

Medical centers were ready to go on full-time alert: they especially prepared for head injuries. Volunteers were organized to drive ambulances or station wagons to collect the wounded. Some prepared water bombs to be dropped from roofs to extinguish Molotov cocktails. There was also talk of "comfort stations," where medical students would soothe those who had witnessed bloodshed but had not been badly hurt. The police and the National Guard would be backed up by some four thousand army paratroopers and marines, which Connecticut's Governor John Dempsey had requested from John Mitchell as "a precautionary measure." Many felt that their presence would be highly provocative.

In late April, walking through New Haven, I looked at all that brick and stone and glass and saw how perishable that stern New England permanence might be. (A new sensation for an American; one that older Europeans would understand.) I also saw some haughty faces that looked as though they'd been dropped from a great height, and privately, I was glad; those faces appeared as though they'd been certain of their superiority—until about five minutes ago. And yet the town's terrors seemed irrational; it was easy for a visitor to think that many middle-class natives were over-reacting. (Regrettably, I now know that the dangers were greater than they seemed at the time: in terms of what a few hoped they could make happen.) Still, Harvard Square had been severely trashed the week before.

Meanwhile, Yale's neighboring black communities had a reasonable dread that if there was a holocaust, their own teen-agers might get excited and involved, the police would chase them back to their own turf, and a real battle might begin. There, police violence was greatly feared. A middle-class black, who was far from radical, told a friend of mine: "If there's a white riot—if *they* start it, *we're* going to finish it. If it means going to the barricades, then we're going for the last time." Meaning that he and others would fight to defend their children if they were incited by revolutionary gamesters, and then shot at by the cops.

There was the sense of being on a conveyor belt; as the whole town was tugged toward a date which threatened to extinguish the issues, some worked hard to keep the priorities clear. Yale was less on strike than in the midst of a vast moratorium. (One activist told me, "Basic-ally, most of us like Yale. We're not interested in hustling deans out of their offices or destroying files.") The black faculty had asked for "the suspension of normal academic functions" as an acknowldeg-ment of the oppression of the Panthers and of all black Americans. President Kingman Brewster helped to reword the proposal to "normal academic expectations" being "modified." "FUCK NORMAL EXPECTATIONS" became a slogan.

Many (but not all) classes were suspended in support of a fair trial for the Panthers, with particular concern for Bobby Seale, who had been charged with ordering the execution of Rackley. (To me, it seemed more than forlorn that the dead, illiterate young man in his early twenties, whose torture-scarred corpse had led to the shutdown of Yale, was rarely mentioned.) But there was solid alarm because George Sams, one of the chief witnesses for the prosecu-tion, was "an alleged dangerous mental defective" who had spent four years in institutions. Sams alone had accused Seale of ordering the murder. Out of twenty grand jurors, twelve were friends of the county sheriff's, who had chosen them, along with his barber and the barber's landlord. By early 1970, many middle-class Americans were aware that the trials of dissidents or black militants should be viewed with the famous "skepticism" which President Brewster voiced. Some students were cynical about the sincerity of his "appalled and ashamed" statement; they called him a shrewd hypocrite. But even the cynics seemed glad of his support.

Most of the Yale students I met were moderates who were worried about civil liberties; only a few radicals demanded that the Panthers be freed. Throughout, the long-term abuse of black defendants by American courts was analyzed. Novelist John Hersey (then the master of Pierson College) and some distinguished New Haven attorneys set up a trust fund to defray the costs of the trial, including witness and subpoena fees, special investigators, transcripts, research, and attorneys' fees.

Meanwhile, many white students were perplexed by the Panthers' rhetoric, and assumed that the Panthers' language was responsible for their being jailed. Some black professors and students replied that the Panthers were repressed for being black and for challenging the system. One thesis, restated from Eldridge Cleaver, emerged in many discussions: if whites didn't commit themselves to working for change, then black people would be left on their own, and then the country could have a racial war. It was repeated that the choice was up to whites.

But it wasn't clear what the Panthers specifically wanted of Yale students in the spring of 1970. (To me, the campus seemed like 1966; despite the strike, many undergraduates somehow seemed to have missed the late Sixties.) David Hilliard, the Panthers' national chief of staff, had turned off an audience of some forty-five hundred when he told them ". . . there ain't nothing wrong with taking the life of a mother-fucking pig." Some booed him; he said, "I knew you mother-fuckers were racist," and the boos grew louder as he denounced them. Then he added, ". . . although you don't agree with what I have to say, you should be intelligent enough to tolerate that rather than boo me." Eventually: "Now you got me talking like a crazy nigger. . . . And I want to compound my sin by calling you long-haired hippie Yale mother-fuckers. Fuck you." Hilliard then said he would "take it all back . . . On the grounds that you all repudiate your boos." People sprang to their feet and applauded, holding their fists high. At an earlier meeting, students cheered non-violent speeches, cheered those who attacked nonviolence, then booed *and* cheered some speeches favoring violence. Sometimes, mass emotions seemed to be whirling in a giant centrifuge.

The theme at Yale was Either/Or: as many buttons announced. It was understood as a statement from black people: either you're with us or against us—for or against equality. (It obviously came from Cleaver's motto of '68: "Either you're part of the solution or part of the problem.") No one was supposed to be able to escape taking sides. (Later, Tom Hayden envisioned a day when Nixon and Agnew would move heavily on Brewster: "He and other people like him-self are caught in the middle when the middle is disappearing." But Yale without a middle is impossible to imagine.) Some also wondered if Either/Or meant: either you pick up the gun or you get shot down. So the Panthers had the (reluctant) support of many—who wanted a fair trial but couldn't swallow the notion of guns.

There was (or seemed to be) an equal focus on Yale's relationship with New Haven's black community: the land-grabbing which oc-curred as the university enlarged, and the false hopes which had been raised among black citizens. In May '68, Yale did give an $111,000 grant to the Black Coalition, which represents over thirty groups in New Haven. But Brewster had given the impression that he would help raise $1 million a year for ten years for the coalition, and that money had not materialized. (Later, it was known as "the $10 million misunderstanding.") Also, a health center which the university had initiated was desperately low in funds, since the federal money which began it had dried up, and Yale had not assumed the responsibility for continuing it. Yale's administrators argued that, for legal reasons, they could not give university money which is tax deductible for education—although they repeated that they were ready to help black groups gather money through grants. But many felt that Yale had planted seeds which it refused to water. "The community is tired of having programs come and go at the whim of Yale." Some felt that there was no way for Yale to be neutral: "Just being here is a promise."

The other demands of 1970 were that the proposed Social Sciences Center should not be built (since the money could be spent in better ways), that day-care centers should be set up for the community, that Yale provide unemployment compensation for its own employees, and that low- and moderate-income housing should be subsidized by Yale. Many felt that the ghetto had too long been used as a laboratory for Yale's "research." As someone said, "Privacy is the only luxury of the poor."

Kenneth Mills, the black Assistant Professor of Philosophy, born in Trinidad and educated at Oxford, who was one of the main forces behind the strike, said in a speech at the Yale Medical School: "Yale symbolizes—and is—the contradiction that plagues our society today: the elite and the oppressed." He developed the theme of "people living in an enclave of privilege, surrounded by those who are suffering." Later, in another speech, he called Yale "a jewel in a swamp." Like so many others, he stressed that the black community would suffer most if Mayday was violent, and that New Haven should be a better—not a worse—place for them to live after May 1st. (On Mayday itself, he said, "The determination to be nonviolent is the determination to be militant." Many also realized that a savage Mayday would be damaging for the Panther defendants.) In conversations and teach-ins, the question expanded to what the rich should do for those who have nothing—or what comfortable whites owe to beseiged black people. Momentarily, Yale seemed like a giant membrane through which a lot of social change might be passing. Meanwhile, it was said that the black faculty wanted "to defend Yale by reforming it."

As the university prepared to open its colleges to house and feed the arriving crowds, solidarity sweatshirts—stenciled with a bulldog and a Panther—appeared, along with signs like THE BLACK PANTHERS' RIGHTS ARE YOUR RIGHTS TOO. While fear kept quivering through the spring daylight, I heard many amplifiers playing "Here Comes the Sun" again and again: like an incantation or a spell cast against destruction, almost a prayer: "It's alllll right . . . *it's* all right."

Meanwhile, the black students I talked to were very dubious about Yale's concern for the community or for the Panthers. They thought their white classmates were very naive, and they were certain that any commitment to the black or the poor would vanish rapidly. "It's just self-interest, they don't want their dorms blown up. The weekend *ought* to be a small bead on a very long chain. But it'll be like a big stone dropped in a pond: it'll sink out of sight." And: "Sure, Yale realizes its debt to the community. But Yale will try to fulfill it as little as possible. . . . People *are* wide awake—and looking in the wrong direction. They know what the facts are, but they don't want to see them." A group of black students stressed that so much of their experience is inaccessible to whites. One senior described being jumped by two cops when he was unlocking his parked car in order to remove his camera—which he thought might be stolen if he left it there. It took a long time to convince the police that it was his car and his camera. "We're all supposed to be Yalies. But a black person here has no immunity. Two feet off campus, we're treated like criminals."

Yale opened its colleges not only in self-defense, but also because some were determined to build a base of protection for the Panthers, so that the police wouldn't feel as free to raid their headquarters as they had in cities across the country, as well as in Chicago, where Fred Hampton and Mark Clark were shot and killed. "The People's Yale," as some renamed it, echoed with rock bands in the college yards, and oozed with Familia. (After tasting the stuff, one New York Panther remarked that it could be used to provoke a riot, since it was "subpoverty level.") The fact that the weekend itself was quiet was a poke in the snoot for Agnew, who had called for Brewster's resignation. After that statement, Yale students collected fifteen hundred signatures in an hour in support of Brewster. (When these were presented to him, outside the administration building, applause rose even from passers-by in the street. Brewster was slumped with fatigue and hardly seemed able to respond.) After the big rallies, the crowds drifted calmly away, some picking up papers and a few playing leap-frog. It was apparent that black families had kept their teen-agers at home; there were very few kids of that age in sight.

Cambodia had just been invaded. But there wasn't a great deal of reaction—perhaps because the weekend had absorbed so many energies.

On the morning of Mayday, Jerry Rubin told an audience in Woolsey Hall that the most oppressed people in America were the white middle-class young—more so than blacks in the ghetto. He said that schools and colleges were simply ". . . an advanced form of toilet training. . . . Number One on the Yippie Program is kill your parents . . . they're dictators, teaching you to be a capitalist, a consumer—school is a concentration camp! . . . Parents eat their children—it's a children-for-breakfast program." He shouted that the only reason that "fancy liberals" are against the war "is because we're losing. If we were winning, they'd be standing right behind the flag." And: "Everything comes out of the university—Che was killed by university research." He referred to the case where a vice-president of the *Reader's Digest*—who had been lecturing around the country about the necessity of taking the young in hand—was stabbed severely by his teen-age son, who punctured his lung but did not kill him. "Our parents kill *us* at birth—we've got death-before-life, we've got to be reborn again." The crowd whooped and roared. Later: "It's the fucking alcoholics who are putting the pot smokers in jail! Alcohol is a part of capitalism—it makes you aggressive, makes you beat your wife. . . . Arresting us for smoking dope is like arresting Jews for eating Matzohs." He told an old Ted Kennedy joke (about crossing that bridge when we come to it), adding: "If Bobby Seale had been in that car with Mary Jo, he'd be hanging from a tree, he'd be lynched!" His hearers began to bang the wooden armrests of their chairs and stamp their feet until there was an ovation.

That night I listened to Tom Hayden in a Yale courtyard. He asked for a show of hands among the group of several hundred to determine where they came from: there were many from New York and Boston, but fairly few from Yale. He told them: "It's possible for us to go beyond spontaneous action: we had a peaceful rally that was not a copout." However: "If Yale shelters those who want to do something about Bobby, the government will move on Yale the way it moved on Cambodia." He stressed that May 1st was "the beginning of a struggle, so I'm not disappointed that more didn't happen here today." Some of his listeners shouted "Co-optation!" and tried to goad him into telling them to bring it all down—which he refused to do. Adding that sporadic busts and gassings make it difficult to sustain radical programs, he emphasized the value of teach-ins—because so many are still politically confused—and expressed the hope that a new strategy for change was developing at Yale.

Hayden said that New Haven could become a sanctuary for the movement, that students should remain in the summer and that outsiders must return, and urged that Bobby Seale Brigades should be formed throughout New England, in order to mass at the trial. "There's no contradiction between trying to organize people and —or—getting into heavy shit." He recommended the formation of an underground railway. Moreover: "We're divided unnecessarily about tactical issues." He said that there was a valid reason for staying in school, stemming from Castro's idea of organizing cultural guerrillas. "Consciousness is to us what hunger is to the Third World—momentum." (A friend stirred uneasily beside me at that last point: "*That* sounds pampered.") Hayden said that "It's the fault of the left—not society—that the left hasn't worked yet." Stressing the need for discipline, he went through a self-criticism passage about male chauvinism, individualism, and public figures: "No movement should be organized around media freaks like ourselves."

Later, a sham Panther borrowed Jerry Rubin's microphone while Rubin was speaking at Branford College, and (untruthfully) announced that Panthers were being arrested on the Green. Rubin cautioned people against going. But some of the hot white blood on hand strode off for some senseless (but not drastic) scuffles with the National Guard. An outsider explained, "I'm here to *free* this place, man." The Panthers—who didn't know the provocateur—were so helpful in crowd-cooling that Brewster praised them afterward. They shouted through bullhorns and loudspeakers and worked to head the mainly white crowd away from the Green. Later that night, three bombs went off in Ingalls Rink, but there were no serious casualties. The police later indicated that a right-wing group was responsible.

The next day, on the Green, Hayden blew many minds, including mine, when he announced that "Facts are . . . irrelevant in this case." All my reporter's cells protested, aided by my recurrent anger at those chunks of the press which betray facts in a way which helps the public to believe lies. But I also remember an elderly woman from Boston mentioning the fights she'd had with her older relatives about Sacco and Vanzetti. She'd told them that it didn't matter whether the two were guilty or not (she was sure that they weren't, but was even more concerned with the larger questions of justice). So I could see what Hayden was probably trying to express: that the overwhelming existence of racism was far more important than the question of who killed Alex Rackley. But I thought that he'd unintentionally confused a lot of people more than ever; others had so firmly insisted on the Panthers' total innocence that few could deal with the notion that Rackley had died at their hands—not those of the police.

Returning from New York to New Haven, I was writing a respectful piece about Yale when the news of Kent State came through. That and Cambodia made the New Haven weekend seem like a charade. Only three weeks before, some NYU students—who were supporting a cafeteria workers' wildcat strike—had liberated some frozen steaks from the faculty club kitchen, and had gleefully given them away in the streets. Now, games with steaks seemed as remote as the swallowed goldfish of the Thirties; bombings, which had been deplored as "the politics of despair," began to seem almost inevitable to some who still disliked them deeply. The anguish of that spring of 1970, after two more were shot dead and twelve were wounded at Jackson State, and the killings abroad accelerated, and more bombs flared across this country, made many feel that there was very little time to turn around in.

June 1972

When I revisited Yale in November 1970, it seemed as though there had never been a strike; one day-care center had resulted from that tumultuous spring. When a *New York Times* reporter, who had been covering Panther Lonnie McLucas's trial, came to talk to students about the case, not many showed up, and they had few questions. Those I met recoiled mildly from the subject.

□

Whenever I'm around Yale, I begin with the illusion that I'm in a familiar place; since I know Harvard so well, it always takes me a few hours to discover that the references don't apply, that the territory is very foreign. (Lifting a glass in a master's lodge, I read Lux et Varitas, and am startled that Veritas has been improved on. And somehow, light does sound more like luxury in New Haven.) But what amazes me most is the real affection that so many express for Yale—as they did even during the strike. I've rarely heard such sentiments in Cambridge. I'm accustomed to Harvard's sour energy, the perpetual bad-tempered Yankee griping, the capacity for indignation that was taught us—until we learned to level it against Harvard itself. This education for malcontents has produced constructive rebels, snarling conservatives, reformers, and bad losers. (Dissent at Harvard dates from 1776, over the issue of rancid butter: "Behold our butter stinketh!") Students and teachers, stamping across the buckling brick sidewalks of Cambridge, have been denouncing the university, its practices, and each other for decades. That's my idea of normal college life. So I'm astounded by all the good manners I encounter at Yale, and the apparent self-confidence of the students, and the scarcity of much strong criticism. I find it all very pleasant indeed, and at times, I wonder: what are they taking up here? There must be lullabies in the water supply.

Since being deeply fond of your university is incomprehensible to me, I'm further amazed that everyone seems to agree about the reasons: they mention the intimacy of the college system, which means that students live much more closely with their teachers than they do elsewhere, and that their faculty are also their administrators— there's no loathed impenetrable bureaucracy, as there is at Harvard. Yale also has fewer deans; the administration has been kept small and supple: "When the kids want walls to break down, they find we have no walls!" I found no shortage of trust in New Haven, and no one seemed to think that applicants were screened for their politics.

In June of '72, the signs on the churches near the Green were hearty: the United Church asked, "Is Your Religion A Spectator Sport?" and the Methodist Church was almost hysterically jolly:

YES TO STRIVING
YES TO HOPING
YES TO LIFE!

The latter reminded me that Yale students may have the illusion of having more power than they actually do.

Many seemed glad to talk about the strike, and a few students said that it was still very important to them—especially because it had influenced their choice of work for the future. Some black students felt that the strike had succeeded in its purpose of drawing attention to the trials of black militants: "Without all that exposure and pressure, Bobby Seale and Ericka Huggins and the Soledad Brothers and Angela might not have had the just trials that freed them."

But the word I heard oftenest from white undergraduates was "embarrassed." One said, "*Somebody* killed Alex Rackley. We thought the Panthers were framed—we didn't look any further than that." But there was no evidence to convict Seale. Didn't it help that he and Huggins were released, that the others—most of whom were very young—were judged to have been terrorized into the murder by George Sams, and that their sentences were comparatively light? "Not really. I still feel embarrassed." And the concern for the black community? "Next to nothing. The impact was zero." However, Yale did receive an anonymous gift of $1 million to be used for economic development programs in the community.

A faculty member said, "You don't hear boo from the black community now." He added, "Many students truly feared that Yale would be damaged. The more upset they got, the more they wanted Yale to be an agency of social reform—they wanted it to be an instrument of change *in order* to save it. . . . Protecting the university was protecting themselves. The colleges are their homes, we're like their family, and who wants his own home trashed? Holding certain social opinions—for three or four weeks—was in many cases sincere. Their concern was honest, but it had no staying power. As the black students were right to perceive."

A black administrator described the meetings held by the black community about a possible explosion on Mayday. "*They* drew the line, and they told white kids and Black Panthers not to step over it. They said: Hey, you cats are having a circus. But you better keep that crap downtown and not bring it into our neighborhood." He and many others spoke of how sternly the black population had warned outsiders against disrupting their lives.

One master rather ruefully called the strike "a catharsis that didn't work." Afterward: "Many felt that a breach had been made in the stone wall, but that the wall was rebuilt brick by brick." He compared the Harvard students' occupation of University Hall in '69 to the general use of Yale's buildings in '70: "There, they claimed a piece of territory. Here, they were *given* it—and discovered that they weren't well organized. There's no reason why students shouldn't take over everything. But they find they can't sustain it. They learned a lesson in their own incompetence. Which is sad."

A dean said, "In 1970, there was the notion that the nation would listen to Yale. That the country would follow the elite. The touching naiveté of the students: they despised elitism and yet partook of it."

A woman graduate, now a teacher who plans to become a therapist, and who was deeply affected by the strike, recalled: "A lot of very repressed students had a chance to throw shit at society. You don't get into Yale without having worked hard, or having been quite intense. *Then* you become disenchanted with American politics, with the university—you feel you're being lead by the nose, as tenderly as any ass. . . . For many of us—for people who were stifled and resentful against society—it was a *huge* release. Yet I'm embarrassed, by some things I rejected at the time."

How so?

"I thought it was a confrontation between good and evil. We wouldn't listen to anyone. We were dangerous in our idealism, I think. Now it's hard to tell who was good or bad. We thought one significant encounter between right and wrong was going to change society. . . . Yet I might do it all again."

She and others spoke of Kent State murders, which followed the Mayday weekend by half a day. (A dean said, "Yes, that was very instructive to students.") A black male student remembered: "In 1970, people didn't know they were going to get croaked. After Kent State, they said: God*dam!* I could get killed doing this! . . . Maybe it was the first time an American government has taken a part of its population and said: We gonna bust their ass." The same woman described the signs that read Four of Us Died Today. The number was crossed out to read "Six" after Jackson State. "Everything we thought and feared had come true. It felt like us against them—a personal attack on students and nonconformists. It showed that they were going to shoot us down if we got in the way."

She mused on the outcome of the strike: "Then, realizing that the world won't change, you ask: how am I going to dig my feet in and keep struggling? I still believe you must be on the right side. Even though I don't believe in progress. I think there's just an exchange of problems. Some people said fuck it altogether. Others flooded the Med School and the Law School:

"The strike gave some of us the feeling that no work or job could be good or untainted. Teachers still oppress children, most industries make products that oppress people. There was *nothing* that *wasn't* part of the problem. So some went to Vermont and baked bread—because that was untainted.

"Perhaps there's no way? To be part of the system and maintain yourself."

Then you and your friends are extraordinarily different from Yale graduates of the past.

"Listen: this is very important: we thought we bore more guilt than others for being the leaders of a society that's morally bankrupt."

How do you feel now about politics?

"My radical sense says that it doesn't matter who's president. Maybe it's better to have Nixon, because he makes the static. But—even though I can't believe it will work—I think McGovern would make people's lives better. Then people tell me I'm a liberal, not a radical. The strike gave me a terror of being called a liberal."

She spoke of "looking for a middle way that's all right." (This theme recurred with almost everyone I saw.) "Two years ago, they said: You'll change your mind. We said: *Never*. But we've changed a little and it's not so bad.

"Someone made a good movie, which juxtaposed scenes of the strike with the reunions. I thought it was a stunning put-down of reunions: grown-ups acting like children—their funny handshakes.

"Later I saw the movie again. It seemed different. The students looked as ridiculous as the alumnae. I was suddenly frightened by it—had there been wool over my eyes?

"The strike seemed simpler than it does now. . . . I was willing to let blacks get away with a lot more shit then." (She referred to some rough experiences working in a community project in the summer.) "They're *not* morally superior, they don't need a revolution *more* than anyone else. They should be able to see that women and homosexuals are oppressed too. . . . We're all capable of these big guilt-trips about blacks: like the strike. But I have no truck with blacks who just want a middle-class life."

□

I have to keep remembering that there was no bust during the Yale strike. Listening to a live recording made in Harvard's University Hall, at the peak of police violence—the cries, the crash of battering rams, the scared narrator's cracking voice—a cheerful child asked me, "How many people were killed in this?" I said none. "Oh. Then what was it for?"

□

A black Yale graduate, a former radical who was particularly active in 1970, said, "The thing was storybook for so many people to begin with. A play thing. With white students, it was a freedom-justice-and-*equal*ity thing. You had kids running around like they were ten years old. For the blacks: we were here with the Panthers. Some of them tried to push us around. But we refused. We watched those cats every day. I knew who the jive Panthers were and who the righteous ones were."

Yale and the community?

"I'll be cautious, but I think some good and quiet things are going to be done. Not flamboyant. Maybe we *need* more flamboyance. I don't know if Yale will ever give night courses for the people of this town." (Some feel that Yale could best serve the community by establishing more educational programs.) "But Yale won't face the question of open admissions. This is Ivy League, man." He and other black students agreed that there wasn't much separatism, although there are black entryways and floors for those who want them. "Some don't talk to whites, but most do." There are about three hundred black students: "The morale goes up and down. Some play supernigger, and others bite on the Protestant ethic. A lot find the experience of Yale was hip *after* they've finished. But we're the first generation of blacks here—we're told we're the cream, and that's a burden!"

He doubted that black Yale students would care much about Yale owning Gulf stocks: "Everybody here makes their money off somebody's back. People say: let's take care of ourselves for a while before we go out to change the world."

He said of the strike: "I believed in it then, and I believe in it now. But . . ." But? "I'm a cynicist. But I *was* a politico. I nearly went nuts. Finally, one day I stopped. Went back to my music, tried to get my head together for a while." Why nuts? "You carry the weight of the world on your shoulders, you gotta go nuts. That's true for whites, but even more so for blacks. . . ."

Are drugs decreasing, as some think?

"Here, we've got *quiet* junkies—they're studying. Not flashy junkies, like Harvard. . . . There are going to be a lot more crazy white boys. Blacks who strive hard to come here don't want to blow it. Yale is lots of striving young intellectuals who don't know why the hell they're striving. Now striving is cool—if you have a goal. Striving just to be striving is madness.

"Yes, I'm fond of Yale, I call it the nipple factor. Mother Yale . . . People say we were co-opted. So I was co-opted—so what? We got a black study program—before Harvard's—without any hassle. . . .

"Brewster—he's something else! The problem at Yale is that we have a good president. That's the problem! He does have a great sense of how to defuse things. . . ."

Indeed, not many students seem to know what they feel about Brewster now. A senior said, "In 1970, the university sanctioned civil disobedience. Brewster made it look as though he was *leading* the strike." Some still think Brewster very courageous. Others speak of him as "a slick operator," who is basically conservative, and they expect him to make Yale more so in the future. "But it's all so damn subtle! The trouble is, nobody knows what's true around here. For example, they don't know what admissions are really based on. . . . There's no real *center* to the administration: you try to find it and you can't." "At Yale, 'the enemy' is such an elusive thing." At this point, one familiar paradox reels out of my mossiest cupboard: that Harvard, with its hard-line administration, still seems a far more liberated zone than Yale. In Cambridge, people can unite their feelings against a bureaucracy. In New Haven, where many enjoy their apparent freedoms, "We have a progressive administration that's really conservative! And that's bewildering." (Another senior said, "You get some real screwball professors at Harvard. They just wouldn't be tolerated here.") But it's a lesson in the old uses of liberalism, and quite a lot of people seem happier at Yale than at Harvard.

And Brewster still keeps them guessing. Some who graduated in '71 were infuriated by the speech he made at their graduation—"I have not quite reached the great glad state of Hubert Humphrey's 'politics of joy,' but I do think things are looking up. There is a lot which is right about America and it is time for us to 'accentuate the positive' as the old song said." One graduate of 1971 said, "He was kowtowing to Nixon and alumni and parents, and I was just burning." In '72, I was told that Brewster's baccalaureate address "really slapped Nixon and Agnew around."

I also heard some haughty and derisive remarks about blacks and blackness from some of the liberal faculty, and some lofty comments on students in general, some of which were couched as compliments: "People like undergraduates because they're pure potentiality —which is over the day they graduate. They're pinned down immediately afterward, and they're less appealing after one year out." I heard about "molding" at Yale, which isn't a word I'm used to.

It was repeated that there had never been many radicals at Yale, that SDS was always minimal, and that undergraduates mix very little with graduate students—as opposed to Harvard, where that contact is thought to enlarge political involvement. At Yale, business and finance have been waning for years, but now they're reviving, and many are far more concerned with good grades than they were in the Sixties. "Yes, they're being more commonsensical now."

□

A woman explained that the strike had made some more determined than ever not to be like their parents, and to resist traditional jobs and marriages: "To avoid the tremendous pull of our backgrounds, and the need for security. Fearing to wake up at thirty-five and to find that we were doing what they said we'd do. It *was* Either/Or: to avoid being *sucked* into your past. It's still difficult. . . . For example, I like flowers, and my mother likes flowers, and all the flower-arranging she does is part of the ritualistic life style that she's in. It terrorizes me that I like flowers too, it feels like Either/Or again: oh my God, I like flowers, I'll have a life just like hers. Even though I just pick wild ones."

□

In a sharp contrast to Harvard, I found that when I asked Yale students about the strike, some soon began to talk about their parents or their sex lives. Sometimes it was very free association: "I don't oppress women in my fantasies. Or do I? Once I dreamed about tying my girl friend up. But we'd been out looking for *string* that afternoon, for our kite, and we couldn't find any, it was Sunday, and string got to be an obsession, so I dreamed about *rope*. You see, I met her during the strike, and what I was going to tell you . . ." But, since women are so very new at Yale (the first ones arrived in the fall of '69), the relations between men and women overlapped and mingled with questions raised by the strike, especially since some men kept saying that women's issues "weren't political." After feeling that they were unwelcome, or being sexually stampeded, or treated like Martians, many moved rapidly into the women's movement—perhaps even more swiftly than they might have done elsewhere.

One woman student, who had transferred to Yale from a coed university, said, "Here, lots of seniors were scared of us. And there's a sophomore male myth: that if you find a girl, all your problems will be solved, your grades will improve, and so on. So freshmen women get a big rush at first—then it all stops. And due to the shortage of women, men who are just your friends make you feel guilty —because they're *not* your boy friends, and they may feel they're not masculine if they don't sleep with you. But I think having more women here will help."

Another said, "I used to think that women were catty and boring.

Then I discovered women were unhappy here, and I shared some of that unhappiness. . . . The men were schizzy about us. At first, it was hard for women to get dates, yet the men were all horny as hell, and so were we. Dressed-up girls from other colleges were coming on weekends, wearing makeup. Should we dress up too—even if we weren't going out? I found a boy friend quickly, as an anchor, to give me friends and an identity. He was a male chauvinist pig and I broke up with him. . . . After the strike, I went through a phase of not being able to deal with single men—I dated married men, and blacks, and got interested in women. Because I just don't want a marriage like my mother's."

At Yale, as on other campuses, I heard much intelligent doubt about one-to-one relationships. But since sex is as available as Mars Bars, quite a few young men and women have started to mention love again—mainly wondering if it's possible, or possible to sustain, which many feel is unlikely. I met few who thought it realistic or desirable to spend a lifetime with one person. "But that doesn't mean that some of us aren't going to try. What's torturing is not believing that it's possible."

A third woman said, "The first year at Yale was just insane: all those guys who thought you'd been shipped in for their express pleasure. I even had a heavy pass from my favorite English teacher. I had several boy friends who were a pain in the ass. I thought all men were fucked up, and that all couples were fucked up. Some women turned lesbian, though I wasn't ready to. Though I did have a lesbian relationship during the strike. But I prefer heterosexuality.

"The whole gynecological scene at Yale is a drag. There's a Yale doctor who's all for the pill: like he thinks it's his job to see that Yale men have all the *intercourse* they want. Yale has a little sex book. They think it's so hip to give advice.

"When I went to Yale, I stopped feeling I could do *any*thing. I had this feeling: oh, men are good at things, and I'm not. So I stopped doing things like writing."

One Yale student said that she thought Yale might be simpler for women to contend with than Radcliffe, "where you're *supposed* to be equal. Here, at least we don't have a college with a different name—which can be a pathway to discrimination." It's true that the sham equality of Radcliffe was perplexing for many in the past. An old schoolmate of mine remarked that, in the Fifties, Radcliffe never really acknowledged that its graduates might have careers. Then why did they want to educate us? "Oh, they thought it was a nice idea for the mothers of intelligent children to have good educations —not just be hausfraus." We talked about the bind that many women are in, especially those who went to New England schools: from childhood to college graduation, discipline meant studying hard, putting work first. Then, after an early marriage and an immediate baby, the discipline was *not* to work—or to put work last. At least fifteen years' training had to be promptly reversed.

□

After some three weeks' saturation in Harvard and Yale, I spent my last night in a commune of some ten Yale dropouts, in the country well outside New Haven. It was a miniature farm, lavish with lettuce. There were chickens and a pig named Sabrina and goats (for "g-milk"), and stuffed zucchini for supper, before which almost everyone gave thanks: for a truck which had worked that day, for a small raise on a job, for the weather, for a newborn kid, for Sabrina. Later, they played the *Missa Luba* during a sudden thunderstorm. I went to bed in an attic insulated with silvery paper which fell in great folds, like a deflating circus tent, with light from a glowing red lampshade flung against the silver. It was a fine place to comb over all that I'd seen and heard.

This commune is about two years old; a few of the founders have remained, and quite a number have passed through it. (One of the virtues of certain communes is that they suit transitional periods in people's lives; no one has to promise to have and to hold, or to stay forever.) Some may buy land together later on. For others, "This is a good halfway house. And a way to get out of Yale and into other things." Some potential members stay for a trial period, and then the group decides if they live flexibly with the others. "That's a problem. We don't want it to be like a fraternity, to make people feel that they're being discussed. But it has to work. . . . We had a difficult guy staying here last year, rather crazy, though every time he got mad, he'd take his temper out on fixing an engine or digging or putting up an electric fence! Which was helpful, but it was a relief when he split."

I've seen some distressed communes, but this one really seemed to be beating the economy. The house cost $250 a month, which was divided between about ten; they produced much of their own food, and also traded their vegetables for oil and grains; most managed to earn approximately $35 a week: working in day care or a record store, a small offset press, a lumber mill, or a health food store. One had made money by folk-singing, and several men and women had been paid to do nude modeling for New Haven art classes. (Since I spent three years scratching the soil at an expensive progressive school, I have to remind myself that some people really *like* farming. But they seemed to.) And they clearly enjoyed living together; their festive supper, around a vast gleaming wooden table, had a relaxed gaiety many families might envy.

One woman, who had been on the Strike Steering Committee, had set up the first mass meeting, coordinated the marshals for Mayday, and had made many speeches, pensively made buttonholes while we mulled over 1970. "We all believed every word we said—and I still do. (I just don't believe it can all be changed as quickly.) I still go to demonstrations, keep in with the movement. I went to Washington this spring—but it just felt useless. How silly we felt and how useless. . . .

"When I was first at Yale, I tried to be what I thought was a really good Yale student. Trying to conform. It's not that easy to be an ideal student. . . . Then I read a lot of political stuff. Everything seemed hopeless. . . . Some of the political dudes were doing smack—that was the *heavy* thing to do. Because that was what the lumpen proletariat was taking." She chuckled. "Acid was bourgeois. I did smack too, for about a week. It was despair. Oh, I enjoyed it. Though it made everything seem worse when I was off it. I didn't think I'd get addicted. I liked jazz—which I usually hated—when I was on it."

At this point, it should be mentioned that this person of twenty appears to be pushing sixteen. Her experiences, as she cheerfully—and often ironically—unwound them, seemed deeply felt but well in the past, and no stranger could have guessed what she had passed through.

"I used to be a heavy smoker too." She described joining a revolutionary group which was off campus in New Haven. "They were supposed to be lower-middle-class whites, so they didn't like intellectuals, so it was shut up. Take the word from your leader. There were a lot of fifteen-year-old girls, treated as subhumans, made to clean house, expected to sleep with any of the men, or with the New Haven Panthers. (The Panther women weren't taking *that* anymore, so the Panthers moved in on these girls.) This group was big on discipline, they called it 'mudholing,' which meant getting the shit beaten out of you by the others. Punishment for your own good. . . . When I joined, the leader pinched my ass and gave me a long lecture, mainly from Stalin. We were told to go out and panhandle. We weren't allowed to return until we had fifteen dollars. . . . No, they weren't very political: it was more of a glory trip. The leader told one guy to go steal him a green velvet shirt with ruffles from a boutique: and be sure to get the right size. Then they mudholed a guy who left the door open—that was against security. Then I split."

She rethreaded a needle, and peered at a finished buttonhole. "I'd wanted alternatives. But that alternative was intolerable, unacceptable. So I worked a lot more on the strike, and with women's groups. Some women told me I shouldn't be working with men. Other people called me a fucking pig because I was a marshal. Some others were on huge power trips: they just couldn't resist having authority. And Yale's always looking for superstars: later, people began to treat me like that, and I began not to want to go out on the street.

"I was very tired and confused and I thought the revolution was right around the corner. . . . Each term, I let my parents talk me into coming back. Yale was very nice about giving extensions. . . . Before the strike, I was having hallucinations—which demonstrated to me how alien society was. I was sitting in an anthropology class: I felt my whole seat rising up, until I was about twenty feet above the floor, holding onto the arms of the chair, I was scared. I willed myself down again, left the class, and left Yale. I thought it meant I was alienated."

More thread for the needle. "Right after the strike, I didn't know where my head was at. Then I saw the revolution wasn't coming. That's what happened to a friend of mine—she saw it wasn't coming, and she couldn't handle that, she had a breakdown.

"I was away for the summer, but I went back to New Haven, I still hoped and thought the revolution might be there. . . . I lived in a collective in town, and a guy with a knife came through the window at five-thirty A.M. when I was asleep, and I got raped. Yale did nothing for me, and the cops said I invited it—when I was asleep?

My mother was so anxious to know if I was a virgin when I was raped. But *that* should have made it worse! For a virgin to be raped. The cops took my nice new bedsheet for 'evidence' and never returned it.

"All during the strike, I was so into being a free, independent woman, feeling physically free. So the rape—being physically overpowered, he was a big man, and I woke up with him on top of me, and he started strangling me—it was a shock.

"I dropped out. Oh yeah, the other thing that happened was I got pregnant. I don't know if it was from the rape or not. Maybe it was.

"At the Yale health department, they'd been giving me the morning-after pill. Then when I was pregnant, they told me that it gives you a 90 percent chance of having a deformed baby. Now, I wonder if that's true? But I believed it at the time. Maybe I could hack having an illegitimate baby. But not a deformed illegitimate baby. . . . I had a good abortion in New York."

She smoothed out her long skirt. "Well, that's where I was with the strike. . . . I still think the Panthers did a lot of good things, like their health clinic. It's very good, I've used it. And we did learn a lot from them, fast. But yes, this local chapter *was* fucked up. And we were naive: insisting that the others besides Bobby and Ericka had been framed."

Downstairs, someone was playing tunes that sounded Irish on a fife, and we listened for a moment.

"I don't know what you do. Group living—being responsible for your own food supply, living in a way that doesn't rape the planet, or other people—maybe these are steps in the right direction. It's such fun to live here. I'm working in day care now. But it's a partial answer—and not for everyone. Rural communes are lovely, but there's not enough land for everybody. . . ."

The sewing was finished, she stretched. "I love music, and I've worked as an electrician in a theater, lighting shows, but I don't want to get into that. Theater's hectic and stupid, licking asses and kicking asses. Too frenetic. . . . I still enjoy archeology, maybe I'll get into that some day. Now, I'm into mechanics and pigs." (She was in charge of Sabrina.) "Maybe I'll go back to Yale sometime: to become a veterinary."

☐

What do you remember about Mayday now?

"I made tons of Familia. I had a lot left over afterward."

"I was a medic. I squirted water in people's eyes—even if they hadn't been gassed."

"People disappear. One politico I knew is keeping bees in Israel now."

"I was radical then."

Despite all the reasons for the lull in the movement—the sense of helplessness, the occasions where some radicals tyrannized others, fears of federal reprisal, fears of increased violence, cynicism, the draft lottery, and, as one black student said, "confronting the situation in America is hard to do *all* the time"—it's still not easy to determine why the commitment on some campuses has been muted. You wonder if there's such a thing as a temporary learning process: if some views, quite deeply held, can just evaporate.

One Yale dean said, "Maybe the changing views just have to do with being very young: students don't like being confined by time and space—they want to be in several places simultaneously." (As a reporter, I sympathize. I like a gypsy life myself. But one's beliefs don't alter with personal mobility.) A master said, "Some were permanently changed. For others, being nineteen means shifting your commitments. And then feeling guilty." A radical Harvard instructor said, "You have to remember that most people just aren't political!" He added, "The real failure of the left was not having a program. But kids can't provide that, they've no experience. Maybe it has to be an adult movement in the future."

Throughout the late Sixties, I think that many of us expected too much of poor people and very young people, of blacks and students. Because there were so many of them, we hoped that they might have power as a pressure group, as smaller generations—such as those born in the Thirties—did not. But they were overloaded with the expectations of those who were better off or more experienced than they. I also recall that many older people—including certain professors—asked students to make sacrifices which they weren't prepared to make themselves. These ranged from "being ready to put your life on the line" to demanding that students remain in their university towns all year round, to work on radical projects—as their seasoned mentors did not.

As for Either/Or: if I were black, I would want to pose that alternative to any white—in terms of their commitment to equality, to fighting racism. However, Either/Or was also interpreted too loosely: in a way that made some feel that they must abandon whatever they enjoyed or found worthwhile—music or raising vegetables or reading fiction. But these can coexist with political convictions: neither need be a substitute for the other. And although culture sometimes seems like a middle-class luxury, I never met a revolutionary who hadn't listened to a song or two. Perhaps that was another error of the Sixties: the idea that politics must drive out every other experience. But of course none of these considerations would be valid in the ghetto, in Vietnam.

PART II:
UTOPIA AND
INFERNO

HERE ARE two pieces of personal experience which continue to haunt me. One school and one job, each deeply rooted in the realm of privilege: I'm still celebrating my escape from both. The claustrophobia that each instilled was oddly similar.

Since I wrote an anti-utopian blast concerning my progressive school, I've visited some communes and collectives which I liked very much. (Well, they weren't utopian.) But I'm respectful of many communal efforts, and also of experiments in education. What intrigues me here is liberal hypocrisy—or how a reactionary and intensely conventional society pretends to be liberal. The unacknowledged squareness and stuffiness of my school demanded a degree of conformity which I've never witnessed anywhere else. So I think it's useful to understand how whole communities can fool themselves.

As for life on a womens' magazine: the subject makes waves which have been unsettling for the womens' movement. For feminists, the question of how women treat women should be as important as how women are treated by men or by society. Of course, many women have been trained to be hostile towards other women, and the notion that women are natural enemies satisfies many men. (Certainly, women who put down their own sex are thought more loyal to men.) But when I wrote up my experiences in a womens' office, I wanted to shame the employers who positively encourage woman to behave badly towards one another. Also, plenty of men will recognize the habits of large corporations, which approve of games and in-fighting within the staff; what passes for healthy competition merely wastes time and ruins stomachs. The staff of the particular magazine that I've described did change enormously in mid-'71, and the fiercest I've known have retired. So I hope that the new regime has behaved more humanely towards its employees; they have already begun to change the product.

BOARDING IN HEAVEN
April 1968

I'd rather keep bachelor's hall in hell than go to board
in heaven if that place is heaven.
                              —Thoreau on Brook Farm

As PALESTRINA'S *Hosanna* poured through open windows, I reverently raised my rack of test tubes gleaming with the urine of diabetic rats, and carried it between lilac bushes that were rocking in the sun. The experiment had been successful, in that the urinalysis differed from that of normal rats, and predictably contained sugar. My latest sonnet had been completed the night before; a new calf had been named for me; my little production of *Sweeney Agonistes* had been applauded, and a teacher had told me that I was "incorruptible" (because I didn't play bridge). Sliding my test tubes into a giant kitchen freezer, I joined a Bach chorus rehearsal for Cantata 150: we sang "And so my soul shall rest content." Perfection seeped from the walls, and from the blossoming trees outside; there was health and happiness and praise; above all, there was the promise of one's own superiority. Costumed for life by accomplishments, lavished with credentials like "creative," "individual," "fulfilled," we would soon be bestowed on the fortunate world: by graduating from school in two weeks. I liked urinalysis and I loved Bach. It should have been flattering to master art and science in a single day: in a setting that merely asked one to unfold. Hence one felt a seedy ingratitude for failing to believe in this Utopia, a viperish guilt for longing to escape Elysium.

Perhaps the utopian temptation is particularly native. After all, this country was at first supposed to be a Utopia in iself, and disappointment drove various ciitzens to form their own Utopias as early as the 1690s—although the nineteenth century was of course the uniquely utopian era. As everyone's noticed, Americans were rapidly repelled by what their own society produced or became. Our Utopias, whether religious or atheistic, utilitarian or aesthetic, austere or epicurean, socialist or anarchist, primed by yarn pickers or rhyme strokers, whether based on the grittiest economics or the wildest worship of Beauty, reconfirm Thomas Moore's pun: Utopia can mean "no place" as well as the "good place." Their failures were usually tinged with irony: as if high purpose was fated to parody itself, to bite off its own tail.

At Robert Owen's New Harmony, the principle of equal sharing dissolved after the communal cashbox was quickly emptied by greedy colonists—despite the anticapitalistic doctrines which initially drew them together. The unit also collapsed, as one member said, from "too much democracy—the community was talked to death," especially because votes were taken on every pinching detail. The transcendentalists' Brook Farm, which Hawthorne hated, and even Emerson and Thoreau refused to join—Emerson decided that it wasn't necessary that "the writer should dig"—and also Bronson Alcott's Fruitlands, where "spade culture" exhausted those who meant to "make a new heaven and a new earth" after only seven months, both sound like succulent excuses for writers' blocks, although they were intended as shrines to the intellect.

The Oneida Colony, founded to nurture communism and polygamy, became thoroughly capitalistic, property-loving to the extent that it became "difficult to borrow a hammer"; soon, it dominated the steel trap market throughout America. Meanwhile, from an Eden where "amative intercourse" could become "a fine art," it lapsed into (jealous) monogamy. From Edward Bellamy to Upton Sinclair or Ayn Rand and B. F. Skinner, fictional Utopias show a ticklish similarity: in the assumption that everyone's needs and desires will be the same, and that, as Robert Owen wrote, "man's character is not of his own formation." The last point may be mockable when applied to adults, but it can be queasily true for many adolescents. My coeducational boarding school appears as one of the few American Utopias that has survived. It hasn't changed much since the 1950s, according to all I hear from recent graduates.

The school was founded in New England in the Thirties. It was designed to offer freedom, art, nature, equality, and ideals to students who would receive a sublime education while learning to be peerless citizens. Actually, it's a very old-fashioned place, engineered to grapple with the ogres of Victorian restraint. However, it appeals to parents whose own education was repressive or frustrating. And the school is violently fashionable, especially because so many famous people have sent their children there. Teachers, parents, and students, all vibrate to resonant names.

The institution has had a colossal effect on other schools, and it mirrors much that is occurring in our styles of education. But it can't be criticized. Those who love it and believe in it are more easily outraged by dissent than the devout of any faith—they're more dogmatic than Jesuits or the radical right. Perhaps Utopias must preclude criticism, or humor, or rage, or any jagged emotion, since the notion of perfection must be unyielding, and cannot allow defiance or burlesque. Laughter or doubt sap the certitude that's essential to fuel an impossibility, to make a mirage concrete. The school is an impossibility, and yet it's resplendently successful. Only a few traitors feel that it fails—and that the treadmarks left on its nostalgic graduates are symptoms of weaknesses which dilute much of our education, our upbringing, and help to congeal some national neuroses.

Perhaps the most enfeebling doctrine ballooned out of the hallucination that everyone's an artist. The refrain was, "If it's in you, it's bound to come out." Although the intestinal imagery suggests elimination rather than production, almost any adolescent would thrill to the theme. Many of the convinced poets, painters, playwrights, and composers fell apart at college, where the fragility of their talents was revealed. Some wasted many adult years in trying (and failing) to flourish in the arts. Practicing an art was supposed to impart a condition of being—which was superior to any other

state. During one commencement speech, the principal said that the
school had produced many artists, scientists, and teachers, "and
(distressful pause) . . . and lawyers . . . and (painful hesitation)
. . . well, *bankers*." We all knew that bankers, also most professional persons, were despicable creatures, wheezing away in the
offices that made them miserable, clutching at filthy cash—they were
quite justly gutted by the system that they helped to perpetuate.
Still, since we were meant to believe in equality, all of our own
schoolmates had to be thought superior.

There was also the conviction that everyone can be good at
everything, from calving to writing verse, the French horn or weld-
ing. I once took sculpture because I needed to fill an evening class.
Being bootless with my hands, I wasn't surprised when my kneeling
clay statue (called "The Outcast," subtitled "Cast Out") often
caved in at the chest and constantly lost its enormous head, which
rolled wetly across the floor after five minutes of wobbling on the
thin neck of that doleful figure. I thought it was hilarious, and felt
that it looked best holding the head on its depressed lap. But the
teacher was demoralized. She kept insisting that I could "truly be"
a sculptor. (I gleefully wrote this down at the time, along with the
other quotes that appear here.) "You are tactile," she said. "Just
as there is music in you, there is art." I disagreed eagerly, but tried
to cheer her by carving a hideous wooden fish. She cried when my
wild chisel shattered the tail into splinters. As a senior, fleeing from
what was called "your literary bent," I resolved to be a biochemist
—I'd been allowed to think that I was very good at it. (It would
have been a disastrous attempt at college, where I certainly would
have failed. I was lucky that false encouragement didn't propel me
as far into science as it shoved others in the arts. Also, I was three
years behind in preparation—in all subjects.) Ironically, the tyranny
of thinking that everyone has talent perverted the possibility of
developing happy amateurs: those who may sing or sketch for
pleasure, without trying to be professional geniuses.

However, artists couldn't be oddities. The school's most triumphant paradox was its extreme conservatism. (Due to peripatetic
parents, I went to fifteen schools, and none was so oppressively
conventional as this one.) There was infinite rhubarb about "individuality": the teachers twinkled, beamed, and breathed on us,

and urged originality. But students of that age are unnerved by hymns to freedom. Also, many teachers were so naive that the students recoiled from them, and rebelled by constructing the most rigid social system I've ever seen. In fact, the teachers' attempts at "permissiveness" resulted in conformity in the students.

Hence few had the courage of their eccentricities, since it was fatal to seem peculiar or even slightly inconsistent. Even absent-mindedness was an ominous trait. In a midwinter fog, I used to stand patiently knocking at the door of my own room: waiting for myself to let me in. This gave other students the horrors, despite my nice cousin's efforts to reassure them of my sanity. Loners were also disapproved. My faculty adviser told me to stop taking solitary walks and listening to music by myself, because it was upsetting for others—that they concluded that I didn't like them. Since we had no privacy, I said that I *did* often want to be alone, but would that prevent my making friends? She replied that it probably would; also, "Man is a societal being." Implying that solitude was unnatural, she stressed the charms of "compromise": to ask one person to share the walk or the music, then ask two, then three, and soon a group would feel more natural than any other context. Indeed, the alumni are very dependent on various forms of group reinforcement in their later lives: more so than many adults.

Psychology was an earnest hobby for most teachers: they did adore problem children, and sometimes sought symptoms where none existed. When I entered the school at fifteen, I had never made a bed, and didn't plan to start. So I kept the window shade permanently lowered in my room—to hide the snarl of sheets and blankets. Years later, I learned that several faculty conferences were held about my terrible emotional state. They thought I was curled in the dark in a foetal position—when I was really out riding my horse over the hills. No one looked in the room for months; they consulted texts. Finally, the unmade bed was discovered, and a teacher admitted that the truth was disappointing. However, a couple of students with severe emotional troubles went unnoticed, and nothing was remarked until their parents carted them away for medical treatment.

From Plato to H. G. Wells, many theoretical Utopias have been guided by an elite, where power belonged to the most intelligent members. Some Utopias have even admitted to the presence of "the base and the dull"—which our school could not dare to do. The teachers wanted us to like them, and, as a graduate remembers, "They were in real trouble when we didn't." Their lack of influence clenched that reactionary social structure which resulted from student power. (We had the sovereignty then that so many students demanded later.) While the faculty beseeched us to be unconventional, they didn't notice that a caricature of the public high school dating system was pleating our lives. It was crucial to be a couple: socially rather than romantically. There was a biannual dance for which we all submitted lists of preferred partners: it was an official popularity contest which meant far more agony for those rejected than it yielded pleasure for others. Girls cried and boys swore with disgust at the names they'd received: so many felt ashamed of one another. Couples were drearily faithful, although the one who severed the tandem was considered socially the more desirable. (Although the school's principal was a devoted feminist, most girls muffled their minds in class, convinced that they would be more attractive if they made the boys feel brighter.) While these patterns are inherent to middle-class America, it's startling that they should reach their zenith in a Utopia which kept gargling about its freedom from the orthodox.

Certainly, being violently in love at sixteen, amid baroque trumpets and in a beautifully tangled landscape, was an exhilaration that I'll never deny. The high pounce of those trumpets, as one raced down a hill, or embraced between the roots of a rustling elm, made daily life a pagan privilege—until one was interrupted. True, the sight of a flashlight still generates an adult phobia: the teachers were always hunting and finding couples under bushes, in haylofts, rolling about in fields and ditches, or clasped on the roof of the vegetable root cellar. Virginity was (sometimes barely) maintained, really because we had too little time to lose it—a bell rang, horses had to be groomed, or a meeting on World Federalism began, an arts conference opened, there was a rehearsal of Auden or Pirandello. Reeling and gasping out of one another's arms, we were kept exhaustingly busy. . . . Most graduates, including myself, were very grateful for coeducation. However, a couple of male alumni recently said that they consider fourteen too young for such proximity. The girls of their own age were often physically larger, and some even started shaving before the boys did. But I doubt that this would worry those who'd gone to co-ed schools from the first grade.

One's role in the community was meant to be equally strengthening to the self and the school. It was supposed to be rewarding to make a contribution. This charming concept often collapses because so few have multiple capacities. By my senior year, my deficiencies in leadership were noted. Hence I was made the head of a farm crew: to stimulate my executive talents. Mine was a dangerous little band, which achieved some expensive damage. We planted a whole field of gladioli instead of the beans which were meant to feed the school, demolished some stone walls which should have been repaired, and pulled apart some electric fences which released cows into realms of disaster. Some of this pandemonium occurred because I misunderstood the toothless directions spat through a pungent Vermont accent. But the kind farmer and I despaired together about my being a leader. My crew grew flaccid through a communal sense of failure. To preserve the farm from further destruction, we were assigned weeks of cleaning the chicken house. Choking on ammonia and chicken turds, dodging cross hens, scraping the dripping roosts and breaking eggs, I recalled my family's observation that this school cost more than any university, and that they hoped I was damn well getting a lot out of it. A final spurt of leadership resulted in feeding the pigs something that made them amazingly sick—since pigs are supposed to have such good digestions. Still, I never quite shared Hawthorne's feelings (after he'd milked the "transcendental heifer") on Brook Farm's barn: "Of all the hateful places that is the worst. . . . It is my opinion that a man's soul may be buried and perish under a dungheap or in a furrow of the field, just as well as under a pile of money." Later, he wrote, "Is it a praiseworthy thing that I have spent five golden months in providing food for cows and horses? It is not so."

Naturally, farm work was preferable to the tyrannical athletic programs that traditional schools insist on. And it was splendid for city children to be unleashed in the countryside. There was a voluptuous mud season, preceding spring, when the ground cracked and shone, liquid earth ran down hills, and the melting snow made small temporary streams full of mysterious shrimp. Still, "embracing nature" was a piebald principle: we were supposed to respond sensuously to soil and clouds and leaves, but not to one another. Hugging a tree "didn't even satisfy my *spirit,*" a classmate sadly said. Meanwhile, the idea that physical work and merging with nature are sanctifying was belted about with a lack of sophistication that would have sickened Rousseau or Thoreau. (The Brook Farmers believed that educated people should do some manual labor in order to free the working class for some hours of cultural pursuit. But we had no such excuse.) Again, our sensations were meant to make us superior: plunge your wrists into the potato field, and it will magnify your soul. Far more credit was given for hard physical work than for any mental effort. We heard a lot about "honest sweat," which made me wonder what dishonest sweat might be— sexual or cerebral?

In recent years, one graduate has personified the dilemmas of this heritage. An intensely urban man, he has occasional fits of feeling that he must move himself and his whole family to the country—as though a rural setting would make him a good person. Yet on mere suburban weekends, he often finds the sun too hot, the water too wet, the breeze too breezey; pine needles prick his feet and sand infuriates him. When he finally said that the ocean was too salty, I cautiously suggested that he didn't really like nature. He laughed and momentarily agreed. But for those of our education, a distaste for mud or wheat or birds can mean a sordid character defect. It's the knapsack mentality which haunts this kind of community: everyone simply has to revere the same things.

A maddened parent lately said, "They study only the snow up there." Many alumni agree that the teaching and the curriculum were phlegmatic—especially because each teacher was allowed to invent his own course. We were totally dependent on the personal skills or ineptitudes of each random instructor. In some courses, teachers deferred to the students, and asked them what they wanted to study. Thus, the already creaky tradition of making pupils responsible for what they learn: "sharing" in the educational process. So we played records of Edith Piaf and Charles Trenet in French class, learned a lot about using the metro, and were not pestered with grammar. There was some Maupassant and some Anouilh, the only apparent giants of French literature. Few teachers had much confidence in their subjects: they were afraid that we wouldn't like "old" things, and feared to impose the past upon us. (Contempt for the past meant that some subjects were superior to others—for example, Russian or Spanish was "better" than Latin.) Historical sequence was usually disdained. We paddled along on the comparative approach, which is still nurtured in many colleges which bend the knee to general education. In a sphere of "creative thinking," as they called it, anything may be explained in terms of anything else: King Lear is like Christ who is like Socrates.

The most deplorable exercise was the teaching of English, where the students' choice of matter was the freest of all. In three years, I was assigned exactly two Shakespeare plays (*Richard I* and *II,* for a paper on "subjectivity and objectivity"), yards of Katherine Mansfield and Archibald MacLeish, Upton Sinclair, *Patterns of Culture, John Brown's Body,* plus *A Passage to India* and *Darkness at Noon* (to learn how to hunt for symbols), and very little else—since no one wanted to rush us. There was one class where *Paradise Lost* was dismissed by giving each student a chapter to summarize; the teacher then said with relief, "There—that's over," and returned to the works of Edith Sitwell. I once asked why we weren't allowed more of the classics. I was told that we would have been bored by them, since the vocabulary was difficult and out of date. We were never supposed to be bored: another winsome preparation for adult life.

The English teachers were mainly capsized writers or would-be semanticists. They seemed so pleased with anything we wrote that there was no need to wrestle with the language. Stupendously bored in my first year, I ceased to work and failed three courses. My father said grimly that he could *see* how Latin and Algebra had gone awry, "But how in the name of Jesus could you fail English?" There was no honorable defense. We were supposed to work from inspiration, and I just hadn't felt inspired. For the last two years, I did work quite hard, and learned nothing outside of polyphony and photosynthesis. The music and biology courses were excellent, due to the luck of having gifted teachers.

The superb music department was almost another irony, since the brilliant man who ran it was a scholar sure of his subject, and unusually demanding: he gave difficult assignments and we loved them. His were almost the only courses which followed historical sequence. He also infused the whole school with a devotion to music —and to his shouting, irascible self. In his orchestra, chamber, and choral groups, students would strive for the precision that wasn't required elsewhere. The other teachers could have learned a lot from his example. But most of the academic experience was meant to be effortless: you lay back and allowed the text to stroke you. Acute mental exertion was considered a symptom of coldness or emotional limitation, despite all the benign nods to "the life of the mind."

However, John Dewey needn't be blamed for the school's character. Although he emphasized learning by doing, he often stressed that "the sort of material that instructs children or adults outside of school is fundamentally the same sort that has power to instruct within the school. . . ." He would probably have been appalled by the mental isolation that permitted us to float free from history, politics, and even daily events. One outraged visiting lecturer found the students innocent of the pope's death and the opening of the World Series, as well as the mere outlines of the international affairs he'd planned to discuss with them.

Competition and aggression ranked as vile qualities, and the school's ethic breathed contempt on hustling. Hence we had no marking system—which was also a wistful attempt to eliminate anxiety. Those who came to the school with headlong ambitions were whittled down. We rarely had to make decisions, or to find our own directions. Thus many became rather passive, and subsequent years at college were miserable for them. It's always been noted that the school had a far more lasting influence on boys than on girls. Many of the young men were especially vulnerable in later life: wavering, hurt, and bewildered. Those at Harvard used to revisit the school for constant weekends, telling us how dreadful it was outside. None I knew became cynics; some even wept as they talked, and it was the first time I'd ever seen male tears. Later, when I was at Radcliffe, most of the boys simply disappeared. Some left college quickly, others never found their feet in Cambridge— even though it was lavish with opportunities in the arts. Someone said that this school invented the dropout, long before the gesture became fashionable. In fact, many of our teachers had been dropouts from city life, or other jobs.

Perhaps an additional wound was gashed in the male side because students were deified for qualities which weren't much appreciated elsewhere: "ideals" (never quite defined), skill at chopping down trees, being able to do a sliver of everything, or gaining a cordial response from farm animals. But being successful in that community often meant being unfit for any other. Confidence in what one learned there rapidly collapsed because the world had such different standards. Bronson Alcott had wanted to restore innocence: our school synthesized it as an artificial product.

Throughout, there was the delusion that all problems have solutions. "Adjustment" was perhaps all the harder because of the hypocrisies that nestled in this Utopia. We were all supposed to be so free: but it was a conformist society. Competition didn't exist: but, socially, it was frantically competitive. The "community of equals" betrayed a fierce pecking order. All students were artists: but they weren't. Since capitalism was repulsive, the school was called "nonprofit," and no doubt it was; however, it was and is one of the most expensive schools in the country. (Lately, I suspect that it must rely on admitting many of the children of the rich.) "Helping others" was often a disguise for helping yourself—for example, improving your French by being a counselor in a French camp, which was merely being polite in admitting Americans. (There was jubilant scorn for tourism; rather, you went abroad to help the poor, shiftless Europeans upgrade their farms. There were many shocks when the French or the English showed that they were being patronized— or that we were simply a nuisance.) Also, the school was said to be a democracy. It was really run as a benevolent dictatorship, in a fashion that enraged many teachers. As at Brook Farm, there was meant to be "no strife." In fact, contentions crackled through the air, and we even had a turbulent teachers' strike: a pre-Sixties school revolution. The faculty's own ideals perpetually came undone before us; they were embarrassed, as though their flies were open. Hence the rifts between fact and illusion grinned at us daily.

A minor delusion even hung on our wardrobes. Most Utopias censure clothing—as though style or trappings were polluting. My school was antifashion, and dirndls were encouraged. We all wore slacks to classes, jeans and boots for farm work; and the girls' dresses for dinner were meant to be plain. Despite policy, most of us dressed as gaily as we could. But it was yet another hypocrisy: our denims and flannel shirts were conscious costumes—just as self-expressive as any cape or feather boa. While the teachers hoped that we would ignore our appearance, we grew defiantly proud of it, and were delighted when our Levis disturbed outsiders or older people.

In any history of Utopias, you see an (often elaborate) conception of virtue, while many deny the existence of vice. For us, both were divinely simple: it was virtuous to be an artist and a "well-rounded," useful citizen. Vices were smoking, drinking, making money, or any sexual diversion beyond holding hands. However, few agreed with these definitions of evil. Still, punishment bred severe quandaries. They couldn't punish anyone by assigning hours of shoveling coal or snow, since we already did both of these things, and were supposed to love them. Thus, a boy caught smoking or drinking or staying out late was sent to live for a few days in an empty chicken house, where of course he smoked and drank all night.

The faculty should have told us that things were uniquely styled within the school, that it was a garden of exceptions. Instead, we were meant to carry its traditions into later life—which many did, to their own loss. We didn't know that "educating society" might actually result in abdicating from it. Lewis Mumford, defining the differences between the Utopias of "escape" and "reconstruction," wrote: "The first leaves the external world the way it is; the second seeks to change it." Our school was designed to be the second, and we were shaped like little vehicles for its beliefs. Meanwhile the adults forgot that everyone arrived at the school with the luggage of his or her own background, the character laminations of fourteen or fifteen years. Perhaps this myopia about past or future experience is intrinsic to most Utopias.

There are naturally a few alumni who have done very well indeed. But the school's bulletin makes sad and fascinating reading. Many who graduated in the Fifties are selling insurance or trudging in their family's business; the names of Shell and IBM recur. Compared to the reports from my other schools, there's a stunning number of dull jobs, plus safe living in the suburbs, while desperate little notes assure others that "my interest in the arts" has been maintained. There's also a tugging, continuous appetite for news and visits from other alumni. Many disillusionments are described, as well as eternal Ph.D.'s or secretarial work, begun very late, after trying so many alternate careers. There seem to have been years of "research" before compromise occurred. Those who seemed so conventional when very young sound rather infantile in maturity, especially those who were afraid to grow up for fear of losing their vision. Maybe this particular neurosis should be embroidered on a special American flag.

The early-Sixties' graduates had the Peace Corps and other varieties of official social service: the Kennedy years did provide a role for them. (The school's very fuzzy idealism probably blinded them to the arrogant and colonial nature of the Peace Corps, which was so well described by Paul Cowan in *The Making of an Unamerican.*) A number teach at other progressive schools, and some returned to work at the school itself. A few have started similar schools. It's carefully noted that siblings or children of alumni compose the enlarging torso of the student body. (Also, some students married one another; many others found husbands or wives who function like honorary graduates.) Perhaps a whole race is being bred, by a school which may primarily equip its students for coming back to teach there. There's one rondo theme throughout the alumni notes: that the years at the school were indeed the best in very many lives. Few American schools manufacture such recognizable products: asteroids without an orbit.

Surely, the prescription of happiness in very early life is toxic, for two reasons. First, when nothing ever equals the bliss of someone's sixteenth year, it becomes the reference point for all that's later denied him. Second, the few who weren't contented felt mediocre and craven. It was rather like the spleen that erupts in Paris, or committing suicide in San Francisco in the spring. The miscreant realizes a disgusting dearth within himself—for not living up to his surroundings. Ever since William Dean Howells said that "the smiling aspects of life are the more American," many have felt themselves in disgrace—in a form that can paralyze them. However, not liking that school was also a salvation. For a few of us, college and the afterlife were infinitely preferable—and we didn't have to be grateful all the time. And I no longer regret my schooling: it was an education in contradictions which was oddly useful in living through the late Sixties.

The school was festooned with pleasures: from music to informal living. But the raveled ethos mainly created escape artists. It is all so native: the belief that happiness is the test of a character or a life —that good people are happy people, and that everyone deserves his slice of delight. The Declaration of Independence might have read "life, liberty, and the pursuit of property," if Jefferson hadn't corrected John Locke's phrase. The moral confusion can't quite yet be flushed as a cliché. Happiness as a standard still befuddles some of my old schoolmates, because—as a black militant said to me in Watts—"False promises make things worse." And it's ,merely a problem of honesty: being told how splendid you are, how happy you should be, or how inferior the world is, hardly prepares you for living in any kind of America—repressive or unbuttoned. Such an education produces the species of weak (as well as reactionary) liberals who help to strengthen the right. Often the school's theories remind me of Bronson Alcott's policies on manure—which he refused to use because nature mustn't be forced.

WAGES OF WRATH
May 1970

THERE WAS often someone crying in the ladies' room. Sobs or gasps (and sometimes retches) came jerking out of those grim cabinets, while others swiftly swallowed pills, choked, sighed, and recombed their hair—to prolong that moment known as "away from your desk." Due to some spasm of corporate economy, there were no towels of any kind, so we had to dry our hands on thin, dissolving toilet paper. My sense-memory of working at one of New York's choicest women's magazines has always been peeling those wet wisps of paper from my palms and fingers, as the notes of weeping receded down the hallway, while I reluctantly walked back to my office, bracing myself for a fresh burst of violence—plus collective confusion, paranoia, and fatigue. Recently, I admitted to a former colleague that the experience was the only one in my life which seems just as bad in retrospect as it did at the time. "'Even worse," she said, in accents of awe.

My job was a good one. (Veterans had warned me not to take
it, but I'd shrugged off their sordid accounts as exaggerations.) Being
in the features department meant seeing plays and movies, reading
some of the season's best books, interviewing luminaries, investigating the development of a new museum or Italian architecture or
Scandinavian design, and . . . writing. But each day's ferocity was
distilled from working for the kind of person who mistakes sadism
for authority, or hysteria for energy. Male or female, these quite
classical bone crunchers differ only in their compulsion to disembowel
their own—or the opposite—sex. The identifying trait is to swell like
a frog with rage; veins in the throat and forehead often stand out
thickly. The nose looks as though it may burst. (As in some other
firms, the company-founder believed that employees work best when
they are extremely nervous. Hence there should be one ogre in every
department. But the hours and days lost in illness might have implied the waste in productivity. Quite a few on the staff automatically
spent their weekends in bed.) At any rate, our employer zapped our
vitals by being (quite triumphantly) unable to give directions: to
merely convey what she wanted done. Unfortunately, some women
still lack this ability: it's a deficiency of upbringing and education,
which determine that women shouldn't be executives. But anger
accelerates from not being understood: the flush of frenzy reveals
the frustration of making almost no sense at all.

An average morning could begin with the furious question: *"What
are you doing here?"*

"Why . . . I just came to work."

"You're not supposed to *be* here! You know perfectly well that you
should be down . . . down . . . *down* there . . . Down there! Now!"

"Down?"

"Yes, you're interviewing what's his name, what's-his-name . . .
What's his *name?"*

"I don't know." (Evidently, an appointment has been made without one's knowledge. This happens constantly. Explanations are useless.) "Nobody told me."

"They *did*. I *did*. Why are you standing there? You think you're
a *guest* in this department?"

"Where am I supposed to be?" (Patience and cunning.)

"You know! You know! You know *perfectly* well! Get on *down* there. . . . How can you??? And Danes are always so punctual. And Oliver's on the roof."

Oliver is an eminent photographer, but who's the Dane on the roof? Ten more minutes of ardent detective work extract a reference to the Congo. So if Danish means Swedish—sometimes it means German around here—then the victim may be Dag Hammarskjöld, since the UN is downtown from this office. A photographic session on the roof? A heart-bursting race to the UN and into the building and up in the elevator reveals what tourists often learn: the guards don't want you to go on the roof. No trace of Oliver. Next, a conference with the dignitary's secretary, who gently explains that no such appointment was ever made, "And besides, he's in Geneva at a conference/dead/retired a year ago." A call to Oliver confirms some of these regrettable facts, but it's crucial to check the first assumption carefully.

"You mean you never heard a word about this?"

"No."

"You're sure?"

"Very sure. And I'm actually on vacation—as they *ought to know*. I only came in town to look for a tie."

Back to the office, armored for the abuse which no rational defense can forestall. It will be one's own fault that the great man was croaked or absent, or that no one ever called him. Still, there's a hideous suspicion: should it have been the Stock Exchange? Maybe the Aquarium. One clings to a few securities in life: it can't be the Guggenheim, that's uptown.

□

Some experts believe that a spell in a woman's office is an inevitable chapter in most young women's lives: a bath of fire that many professionals must pass through. Of course there are more writing or editing jobs open to women in this area than in the news or feature magazines which still imply that women can't write because their biological clocks are full of fudge, or because "they can't think conceptually." But almost every young woman I've met who's served on an all-female staff has found it just as mangling as I did. From the initial astonishment of the application form, which inquired, "Have you ever tried to overthrow the American government?" (no, but I'd love to), to the first day's intimate physical ("Have you ever had a miscarriage?"), to being savagely called *"Darling"* and *"Sweetie"* (and Pam and Jane and Doris) because one's name was punctually forgotten, dignity dissolved and the intestines howled.

There was no protection in refusing to play fishwife. Once, as I waited silently for a bottomless tantrum to subside, my editor flung herself hard against her desk—not quite cracking a rib, as I'd hoped —and yelled, "Don't-just-stand-there-being-*polite!*" Colleagues wove a landing net of sympathy; when office morale is in rags, there are gusts of desperate jokes and nervous laughter as partners in suffering try to cheer each other. Since then, I've always measured the health of a department or an organization by the character of its humor: compulsive clowning or rapid, forlorn gags mean that the staff is reduced to childishness in secret defiance of a loathed parent figure. Usually, in the offices where demoralization thrives, the employee is treated as a (good or bad) child.

Quite a few of my nicest colleagues had grim reasons for needing the money which shackled them to the magazine: expensive divorces, hospital bills, sick parents or children, drunk or unemployable husbands. So some felt trapped. (And it's still not acknowledged that most women don't work for fun, any more than men do.) As in the worst offices, many revealed too much about their personal problems, which made it awkward to deal with them professionally later: How can you ask me to check those proofs when you know I've just had an abortion/lost my lover/been kicked out by my shrink? Some have since remarked that the office was destructive to their private lives: shredded nerves and humiliations made them testy and dyspeptic with their men or their families; the stark self-control used on the job meant overreaction to small irritations at home.

Meanwhile, we all paid for the days when those above us were ripping one another apart. As they reveled in the mutual humbling process, we were lacerated by their brawls about the approach to Degas, vermeil, Sophia Loren, or Robbe-Grillet. (We'd keep rewriting our captions while each editor gleefully condemned the adjectives which had been requested by the others. Among enemies, the loser could become a stretcher-case: "Read this for me, uh, sweetie, my mind's all gone today"—which was true.) Reshaping senior colleagues' work was sometimes part of the freshman hazing system: during my first week, I wrestled with an older editor's account of her trip to Moscow. My favorite sentence was: "If you care about thickness, take Nescafé and towels."

Reeling out of the office, detailing my horrendous days to friends, I was rewarded by cascades of laughter—especially from men. "Oh, do go on being funny. Be funny some more about that." While I protested that it wasn't just a barrel of yuks—that in fact, my office mirrored many of the degrading experiences that we'd heard from men in advertising and news magazines or from those who worked for LBJ—some of my male schoolmates startled me by repeating how much they approved of my job: more so than of the straight reporting and reviewing I'd previously done. They thought my position was glamorous, even though I told them it was tacky and brutalizing. A few men seemed rather relieved that I was now out of their own field: of valid writing. Most asked eagerly if there were lots of lesbians on the staff. I said I didn't know, and anyway, the dump was desexing for everyone. They seemed disappointed about the lesbians, but urged me to stick with the job: "It must be good discipline—mustn't it?"

□

Over the decades, the magazine has published many fine articles and stories, as anthologies can prove. However, the staff-written text is adored by satirists, and pieces by the unfamous were often grotesquely restyled for "reader appeal." (I once spent an hilarious two hours helping a writer—whose essay I'd commissioned—insert lots of clichés and repetitions, so that the dizzy editors would cut them without mutilating the rest of the piece. It worked beautifully.) As with many other publications, the stylistic level had to sink when fashion magazines ceased to be aimed at the consumers, and were directed at the manufacturers—actually, written to attract and satisfy the advertisers.

The attitude toward the readers mingled flattery with contempt. The technique was to tickle their vanity by suggesting that they were bright—through spurts of culture—plus the assumption that they were actually interested in Cocteau, Zen, the paintings of Emil

Nolde, Milan's Piccolo Teatro, or the works of Marguerite Duras. However, they were expected to be stupid. Every reference had to be explained: Nixon or Wilde could not be mentioned without a first name and an identification slip. Each idea had to be pitched down to basement level, even though the language was contorted. "Ideas" indeed were frantically sought: the editors kept lists of titles in hopes that someone would invent a fitting topic. One author, offered the title "What to Use Instead of Money," finally wrote an essay on the joys of the five senses.

Throughout, a brief snort of great works of art was sufficient for the beef-witted army of subscribers, who were usually addressed as "You" ("You and the Atom," "You and Picasso"), in order to plug them into a subject which was presumably baffling for them. Meanwhile, art was mainly advertised through personalities—by portraits and paragraphs that skimpily summarized the work and underlined the life style of the practitioner. "Find a phrase for it!": the habit of reductio ad absurdum meant trying to tease language into little headlines—the slogan mentality which has curled so many minds. Here, I should hastily add that I like fashion magazines; looking at pictures of clothes is good for the soul, and a wild text bestows a pleasurable jolt. But having to package poetry and sculpture and snips of history as though they were blouses or scarves or shoes felt like a binge of perversion—especially if the readers were such idiots as we were told. Moreover, they had to be protected: I was once ordered to describe a movie about a black man and a white woman as "a sensitive account of an unhappy love affair."

But the clanking irony was that our fat and fatuous paragraphs were seriously regarded as *good writing*. At first, I'd (wrongly) imagined that parodying the magazine's style would produce what was required. But we were made to rewrite until the final word salad would have shamed an autistic child. The demand for "passionate" copy meant that we had to use words like "ebullient," "irrepressible," and "kicky" as often as possible. "Swerve," "veer," "sinewy," and "slithery" kept our pages effervescent—another favorite. "Implacable" also gained points, but I never knew why. Ideally, personalities were "amusing," or, failing that, "amusable"—which was even applied to Queen Sirikit of Thailand. Wit and wisdom often went together. Three adjectives were the norm for characterization:

thus, "bubbling, valiant, enduring" (an octogenarian actress), "tiny, mercurial, young" (Elizabeth Ashley), "austere, important, young" (Jasper Johns), "witty, beautiful, stubborn" (Mrs. Patrick Campbell). Marianne Moore was "gentle but not sloppy," Cornelius Ryan was "a gentle, bursting man," in contrast to "a bouncy, friendly, internationally famous astronomer." Only David Merrick won the space race: "a soft-spoken, good-looking, stage-struck, enterprising, single-minded, aggressive, rattrap-minded lawyer."

Novels were harder to nail neatly: "revolting, horrifying, funny" (*Naked Lunch*), or "a big, laughing, hoaxy book" (*Catch-22*), unless you could rise to the inspiration of describing Sybille Bedford's *A Favorite of the Gods* as "crisp and unsatisfying, like eating Cracker Jacks in bed." Once, praising an exceptional first novel, I found that none of my tributes were acceptable to my editor until I despairingly invented the phrase, "the cool bloom of his style." It took hours to recompose a finally approved passage like this one: "A loving grandmother with ash-blond-grayish hair and eyes the color of hazelnuts, she is right now finishing some works in mechanics and probability theory. . . . As a scientist and a woman, she has had a life rich in great experiences and full of rewards." And it's not easy to arrive at: "His intellect is all in his cuticle where it hurts."

Today, sifting through old issues, I savor passages like this description of the first Mrs. Nelson Rockefeller: "a brisk, lapis-eyed woman of polite but unwavering decision, has a refreshing approach to public life that seems rooted in playing herself absolutely straight. . . . Like almost all near-sighted women, she lives in a slight, steady wind of curiosity that leads her into turning interviews inside out with such questions as 'What kind of camera is that?' or 'Have *you* been to the Museum of Primitive Art?' . . . When all this begins to seem too guileless, a small crash of asperity makes it ring true. . . . When she was asked what she thought of a statement in the William Manchester book, *A Rockefeller Family Portrait,* that 'Rockefeller women are bred to be wives,' she said instantly, 'Now will you tell me what that means?' "

I also enjoy reading more recent issues of the magazine, still feverishly grateful that I didn't have to write about "the feeling of relief at storing away the 'sixties and jouncing into the 'seventies," or refer to "the clangour of the Vietnam war," or describe a TV series as "marvelous, chatty, a window opened by a man whose mind is an orchard of plums."

Naturally, the solution to a maiming job is to leave it, as many of us did. (It took less than a month to realize that a good salary makes no amends for deploring your work.) But several ugly questions lunge out of the closet of past experience. First: what (the devil) were we giving women to read? The magazine showed them marvelous clothes and some magnificient photographs. But our features department betrayed a bale of potentially good material. The well-educated can ignore the kiss-off approach to culture, but it's repulsive to think of its effect on those who backgrounds are meager —the many starvelings whom this country schools so poorly. Quite simply, the magazine insulted the readers' intelligence. Second: why are some women so horrible to women? In my office, the old easy answers of envy and competition didn't apply: the (already successful) tyrants weren't imperiled by those whom they reduced to hamburger. Perhaps the mere guilt of being female—fighting the instincts of inferiority—makes certain women despise others and want to punish them, resulting in what Evelyn Waugh called "the ruthless, cut-throat, rough-and-tumble of the . . . Woman's Page." Perhaps the yelling and threatening was merely a tradition of behavior —the way certain women think they should treat one another. Finally, one has to rehash the familiar fact that so much of our whole office system functions abominably. Granted that many departments are structured to make people dislike each other and to prevent work from being done, all that uproar seems like part of our rotting national heritage: toiling without questioning, accepting the product as the same old sausage comes grinding out of the exhaust.

PART III:
NEW YORK
FOR NATIVES

Thrice happy and ever to be envied little Burgh! existing in all the security of harmless insignificance—unnoticed and unenvied by the world, without ambition, without vainglory, without riches, without learning, and all their train of carking cares. . . .
> —*Washington Irving, evoking 17th-century New York in 1809*

MY TWO longest New York pieces were written in mid-flood, in 1969, when we knew that the town was in bad shape—but it wasn't as ravaged as it is now. Only in the Seventies did I realize that I might be seeing the end of something: New York as I've known it all my life. I used to defend the city fiercely against all critics; now I have to agree with all of them. Yet for some of us—for me, at least—the rewards are still as great as ever.

If you don't like New York, you never will. But one of its aspects which sustains some natives is the surprise—short of a dead body

—around any corner. Here's what Rupert Brooke found on Broadway in 1913: "A little crowd, expressionless, intent, and volatile, before a small shop, drew me. In the shop-window was a young man, pleasant-faced, a little conscious, and a little bored, dressed very lightly in what might have been called a runner's costume. He was bowing, twisting, and posturing in slow rhythm. From time to time he would put a large card on a little stand in the corner. The cards bore various legends. He would display a card that said THIS UNDERWEAR DOES NOT IMPEDE THE MOVEMENT OF THE BODY IN ANY DIRECTION. Then he moved his body in every direction, from position to position, probable or improbable, and was not impeded. With a terrible dumb patience he turned the next card: IT GIVES WITH THE BODY IN VIOLENT EXERCISING. The young man leapt suddenly, lunged, smote imaginary balls, belaboured invisible opponents, ran with immense speed but no progress, was thrown to the earth by the Prince of the Air, kicked, struggled, then bounded to his feet again. But all this without a word."

Between '65 and '69, when I reported on John Lindsay quite often, I was steadily rebuked for being hard on him. Now, many agree with what they reproached me for writing. I'd like to take a little credit for having described his weaknesses earlier than some.

1965 seems a very long time ago: a year that's sometimes remembered with nostalgia, as a time of hope, of possibilities. Quite a few New Yorkers were kindled by Lindsay's first campaign. Remember "He Is Fresh And Everyone Else Is Tired"? And he was constantly compared to the Kennedys.

There wasn't much serious criticism of Lindsay then. William Buckley accused him of "unsexing the Republican Party by flitting off with the Democratic majority," and of being "dangerously ignorant of the Communist problem." There were a few others who felt that Lindsay was a pseudo-liberal, who flew to generalities while trying to gratify all parties. Mrs. Eleanor Clark French—then the New York City Commissioner to the UN, and also Lindsay's congressional opponent in '64—said that Lindsay opposed busing when they debated it in a conservative district, but that he switched to her pro-busing position when speaking in a liberal synagogue. Lindsay's critics also noted that his congressional voting record showed that he sometimes voted for crippling amendments on liberal bills (to please Republicans), but when the amendments were defeated, he then voted for the original bills (to please Democrats).

Dancing the Watusi and the Donkey, inspecting six rats freshly killed by headquarters volunteers in Harlem, playing the drums in the Sanitation Department Band, singing "I'll Take Manhattan" in a Catskill nightclub, focusing intently on each pair of eyes that belonged to the clasped hand, Lindsay seemed to suggest that his success brought other people pleasure. As I followed his campaign through Staten Island, Harlem, and Spanish Harlem, while tomatoes and oranges hit the pavement as shopping women jostled for his hand, I found him rather like an old-fashioned debutante, radiant in public, but sulky in private—especially in interview. He had little to say, and was irritated by questions that had anything to do with black New Yorkers. I'd been impressed by a number of his aides, and they were troubled by the way he dodged questions—a couple of them urged me to talk to him again on the same topics—"He ought to say more on that." So I did, but he didn't. However, I liked his reply as to why he was a Republican: "My early admiration of LaGuardia, coupled with the historical appeal of Lincoln. And 99 percent of my Yale Law School class was Democrat—so my natural instincts as a rebel made me join the minority group."

Still, we were very patient with Lindsay then, realizing that a lack of practice made him slow on verbal uptake. In '64, a constituent who accepted his hand on the street said, "Remember the liberalization of copyright laws for American authors." *"What?"* The sentence was repeated, with a reminder that Lindsay himself had favored the idea, and had said so in a speech.

"Ah," Lindsay cried, "writer!"

"Yes, I'm a writer. Now, about copyrights—"

"Writer: that's a tough row to hoe."

"Yes. Now—"

Lindsay recoiled, shouting, "Tough row. Hoe! Row!" leaving a puzzled novelist on the pavement.

So enough of us voted for him. . . .

THE STATES OF MY CITY
January 1969

*The fury of sound took the form of derision . . . and
thus it might . . . have struck you as brazen that the
horrible place should, in such confessed collapse, still be
swaggering and shouting.*
　　　　　　　　—Henry James on New York in 1904

COMPOUNDING POVERTY and privilege, horror and delight, from the
ghetto to the penthouse, it has always been New York's nature to
seem on the shore of collapse. The city's only enduring trait is perpetual change. Long before 1842, when Dickens was appalled by
the wild pigs which roamed Manhattan's streets, and the black slums
—"where dogs would howl to lie, women and men, and boys, slink
off to sleep, forcing the dislodged rats to move away in quest of
better lodgings"—all but the richest natives have often declared the
town impossible. Mugging, which is sometimes now discussed as
though it were a new invention, was probably even more lavish in the
1850s, when politically powerful gangs like the Bowery Boys, the
Dead Rabbits, the Shirt Tails, the True Blue Americans, and the
Plug Uglies (who wore stuffed plug hats to protect their skulls in
battle) fought with guns, knives, axes, clubs, and spiked shoes in
the streets. In the Draft Riots of 1863, the city was nearly conquered by the mobs, which burned and looted slabs of midtown New
York; about twelve hundred were killed, and many blacks were
tortured, mutilated, and hanged.

Soon after the Civil War, residents deplored the city's "pace."
When Henry James visited it in 1904, he was agonized by "im-
permanence," the "sense of dispossession," and the "alienism"—
which showed most brutally in the treatment of immigrants. He feared
that they would inherit only "the freedom to grow up to be blighted
[which] . . . may be the only freedom in store for the smaller fry of
future generations." He was shocked by "the perpetual passionate
pecuniary purpose which plays with all forms, which derides and de-

vours them. . . ." The voice of New York seemed to say: "I build you up but to tear you down," and James saw citizens reduced to human rubble as swiftly as the *new* buildings that were demolished.

Last fall, Eldridge Cleaver told a friend that he wanted to leave New York even a few hours earlier than he'd planned; the city horrified and fatigued him more than any other he'd known.

Those of us who love New York cannot disagree with anything that visitors say about it. We simply want to live here—perhaps because this city rings a range of fascinations that seems unique. But many agree that daily life has become even fiercer than it was a few years ago—granted that it's never been celestial. It's a local joke that when there are certain strikes, it takes some neighborhoods a week to notice them, since the level of city services (like garbage and parcel delivery) is so low.

Morale sinks into the sidewalk, because our press and our politicians emphasize that New York may be "ungovernable." Natives feel an accelerating helplessness about this city, any city—especially since the "urbanists" are breathing doom. This coincides with the old Yankee notion that town is evil and that virtue resides in the country. Thus, we had an early hopelessness about cities; they weren't expected to be attractive or even decent. Living in the country was supposed to make you a good person, while cities were certain to be corrupting. Updated to the Sixties, this passive pessimism is truly dangerous for New York now.

In a period when politicians stress their own powerlessness, it's tricky to determine their responsibility. Certainly, Mayor Lindsay inherited a chaotic situation, one of the country's most crushing jobs, plus a Democratic city council which is grooved to oppose him, and an unsympathetic state legislature. But it's become apparent that New York has sagged under Lindsay and his staff, and that their incompetence has enfeebled this ailing city.

It's true that the mayor has style and that he is handsome. These two facts are all that some of his admirers know about him—and there's something wrong when facts are as elusive as they are at City Hall, where the big snow of public relations tumbles an avalanche of charm over the heads of reporters; they receive few solid answers about strikes or housing or welfare. Different officials dispense conflicting statements, enriching the confusion. And Lindsay once told reporters that he needn't answer questions *because* he was mayor.

Meanwhile, he and his aides have spent far too much time on personal publicity, on TV, and away from their desks; his first stack of commissioners was told to do this. The press has been amazingly cooperative, even to the extent of repeating the "ungovernability" theme—with the implication that if Lindsay can't run New York, no one else can. "That was a premeditated PR stunt," said a former official. "I was there when it was premeditated." (Since those in office must still function as charisma-cookers, many of my sources were ex-officials, who spoke freely when promised anonymity. They wished to be nameless partly because some will still campaign for Lindsay—on the gloomy but rational belief that a better candidate won't be offered.) A former supporter said, "Lindsay says what sounds socially correct. But he doesn't do what's socially necessary. He just uses his power to make people like him." An ex-commissioner said forlornly, "We really began to believe all the crap we were putting out." But—after the age of LBJ—political smog is harder than ever to live with.*

It's crucial to rack up the mayor's credits, because they are sparse. He established the long-needed New York City income tax, which also applies to commuters; it's considered superior to Mayor Wagner's habit of floating long-term loans. On the upper and middle levels, the tax is fairly graded to income—although it also descends to poverty level, and taxes too many of the poor. (Also, I suspect that it wasn't Lindsay's own idea, but that of his advisers. When I interviewed him in '65, he stated wildly that there must never be such a tax, that it would "ruin the small businessman." He was annoyed when I said that a lot of us favored it.) Everyone agrees that poverty is a national—not a local—responsibility, and that massive funds must come from Washington. Lindsay has been rightly impassioned on this theme.

With his energy and his actor's talents, he is also adept at performing the ceremonial functions of being mayor. And few doubt

---

* Woody Klein, an ex-press secretary, wrote in *Lindsay's Promise*: "The technique of leaking stories and then vehemently denying them was a sophisticated, often effective, method of leaking news." In 1971, we learned from the *Times* that Lindsay's public relations cost trebled since he took office in '66. As of '71, the cost was $3.6 million a year.

Lindsay's desire for decency. Even his sternest critics agree that his instincts are nearly always good—although he rarely knows how to translate them into practical actions. Despite the evanescence of his performance, liberals feel a particular urge to support him: because the right loathes him. In announcing all that he was going to do for the ghettos, he has enraged much of the white middle class, as well as many working people. Considering that very little has been done for blacks, it's unfair that the mayor should be called a nigger lover —a recurrent shriek of taxi drivers, which makes many of us want to defend him.

But it's difficult. Again and again, we learn of bootless "projects." As one expert said, "The *last* thing this city needs is another 'study' of *anything*." Lindsay paid the Rand Corporation $607,000 "to familiarize themselves with the problems of New York"—which almost any native could have told him. (Throughout the country, "studies" have become a substitute for action. Many suspect that social science isn't even a science—especially the ghetto dwellers I've met, who call it a hoax.) The city has been awash with "plans" and "programs," which are "hailed" by City Hall on announcement, and later go unmentioned—because so many failed to even get off the ground. (There were even promises to reform our public hospitals— which are as savage as ever.) Much time has been lost in "reorganization." The clumsy efforts to unzip bureaucracy have merely succeeded in adding extra layers to a fudged machine. Lindsay was warned against the irrationalities of the reorganization plan by the influential City Club of New York (since 1892, a nonpartisan civic organization devoted to "the advancement of good government" in New York, to which the mayor himself belongs), which stated that he was "in the hands of people who know all about management— or its vocabulary—except how to get a job done." He has reduced the power of commissioners, which hasn't increased his own authority, but lessened it. (Some feel that we'd have fewer strikes if commissioners were party to negotiations—which they rarely are.) Meanwhile, "the chain of command" is vaguer than ever. At the same time, Lindsay's incorrect when he complains about lacking power: changes written into the city charter seven years ago have enlarged the power of the mayor.

Many of Lindsay's supporters glumly agree that he's a weak administrator and a poor judge of character when it comes to hiring. At first, he attracted some excellent aides, most of whom have now resigned or been fired. It's said that he doesn't like "internal criticism," and that the favorites are those who constantly agree with him—"the back-scratchers." Much of his present staff is considered fearfully inexperienced: by those whose intimate knowledge of city government causes them to shudder. One specialist said, "These are kids with no background, no practice. Some are bright. But my God, it's frightening to think of John and those kids sitting down to try to figure things out." Another (particularly loyal) ex-aide admitted, "He has a lot of fools and yes-men, and a few who aren't, uh, honest." One of the mayor's most dazzling slips was the appointment of Water Commissioner James Marcus as Environmental Commissioner over Sanitation Commissioner Samuel Kearing in November '67. Many colleagues were appalled at the time, since they thought Marcus was a bungler, and Kearing was known as one of New York's ablest officials. In December '67 it was discovered that Marcus had accepted about $10,000 in bribes; he pleaded guilty, and is now in jail. (The FBI had known of his activities in the summer of '67.) But the scandal merely dramatized an inept appointment.

Recently, Lindsay said that his relations with labor "have never been better." Still, strike-stricken New Yorkers can choose among their favorite *Times* headlines or editorials for the tone of turmoil, from CITY ENDS STATE OF IMMINENT PERIL (when the fuel oil strike coincided with the Hong Kong flu epidemic, and deaths rose) to "The paramount—and immediate—problem is to get rid of the garbage before the rats take over the city" (during the nine-day sanitation strike, when millions of tons of garbage made towers on the sidewalks). For a week there was a slowdown on police and firemen's services in "minor" areas, such as illegal parking and fire-hazard inspection. The list winds back to our stunning transit strike on the mayor's inauguration day, January 1, 1966. Members of each department say that many of these strikes could have been prevented by sturdy negotiation. While many unions are full of grime, Lindsay has often been openly contemptuous of them, and it's constantly noted that he has no labor policy. It was naive to run for office by decrying "the power brokers" in one of the most potently unionized cities in the world. Commissioners often make plans without consulting the unions—which enrages them. Lindsay's attempts to limit the unions' power have made New Yorkers feel their power all the more.

Naturally, the most destructive strike was last fall's series of teachers' walkouts, when more than a million children were kept out of public schools. The union was supporting nineteen teachers who had been scheduled for transfer from Brooklyn's Ocean Hill-Browns-ville schools, where an experimental decentralization project (re-luctantly allowed by the central school board) had developed into an issue of community control. (Even neutral sources have remarked that these particular teachers were "provocative"—in harassing the local governing board.) The community is mainly black; the majority of New York's teachers are Jewish. While the mayor had initially backed decentralization, he dithered as the issues congealed; severe anti-Lindsay sentiments ripened among many Jewish groups, which also accused the blacks of anti-Semitism. The press intensified this theme, and concentrated on confrontations. What was lost in the uproar was the prime issue: the low reading level of the pupils them-selves—in fact, the failure of public education. The concerned black parents were impressed by the Board of Education's inability to expand their children's learning. They felt that through community control they could hire better teachers than the ones they already had. Incidentally, teachers are often transferred in New York public schools. But Albert Shanker, the union's president, apparently relied on the general ignorance of this fact when he reviled the Ocean Hill governing board for "arbitrary firings."

There's evidence that Ocean Hill has run its schools well, and that union provocation, especially through charges of "black racism," was responsible for the pandemonium—which has simply increased whites' fears of blacks, and has also highlighted the subject of black anti-Semitism. It's impossible to measure the latter's proportions, since the media has certainly inflated it. The mayor has panicked. Having given so much verbal (though not practical) support to blacks, he is now desperately trying to recoup the Jewish vote. He has assailed two black teachers from Junior High School 271, one for reading a poem by a fifteen-year-old student on the radio, and the other for criticizing the mayor's investigation of the poetry incident —adding that Lindsay was "in [a] hurry to appease the powerful

Jewish financiers of the city." Lindsay said that neither man had "any place teaching" in New York. The poem, now "under study" by the Superintendent of Schools, was dedicated to Albert Shanker. The first lines are:

> Hey, Jew boy, with that yarmulka on your head
> You pale-faced Jew boy—I wish you were dead.

Later, it continues:

> When the UN made Israel a free independent state
> Little four- and five-year-old boys threw hand grenades;
> They hated the black Arabs with all their might
> And you, Jew boy, said it was all right.
> Then you came to America, land of the free,
> And took over the school system to perpetuate white supremacy.

It's true that passionate anti-Semitism (at all levels) has flourished in New York for years—as few can bear to admit. But that a teenager's verse should result in the probable dismissal of two teachers shows what a frenzy City Hall is in: about its own image. And no one should be surprised to hear blacks make antiwhite statements—about any race of whites. Meanwhile, the mayor has been rebuked by various voices for fueling the tensions between blacks and Jews —through the mistake of seeming to hurl his total support back and forth between the two. Naturally, he has denounced racism of every stripe. But his awkward and hasty pledges have made both mistrust him—and each other. As Roy Innis recently wrote, "Black demands activate white racism [which] activates black reaction [which] activates racial confrontation."

Exaggerated promises to the poor and the blacks have of course been a national game. Lindsay said that 1966 "had to be the year of the poor" in New York—which it wasn't. He does deliver sympathy and concern, but little else. His famous shirtsleeve walking tours in slums—to show that he "cared"—were another brand of public relations. As an ex-commissioner said, "When the Mayor walks through the ghetto, there's an implicit promise. But three years later, the streets are still dirty." The local job program has been a farce. But the poverty program was a tragic jumble well before Lindsay's election. Under Mayor Wagner, Paul Screvane had the prime responsibility. When Screvane lost the Democratic primary to Abraham

Beame, Beame's staff ran the program. When Lindsay became mayor, New York was already seven months behind most U.S. cities. "Reorganization" took nearly two years, during which $10 million went up the spout because it wasn't spent by June 30, 1966. By late '67, the federal funds had dwindled: due to Vietnam. Soon, different communities like Harlem and Bedford-Stuyvesant were competing for cash: the money was then so inadequate that it became like bribes to keep a few people quiet. Hence much of the initial trouble was not Lindsay's fault.

But his agency has been particularly vulnerable to "poverty hustlers." On December 27, 1968, he said that the program had been purged of violations. On January 12, 1969, a colossal scandal erupted in the *Times:* MILLIONS IN CITY POVERTY AGENCY LOST BY FRAUD AND INEFFICIENCY. "The Durham Mob," from North Carolina, evidently rigged computers to write checks to imaginary persons for nonexistent jobs. Other stolen checks have appeared in Zurich—though, fortunately, these weren't cashed. Secretary of Labor Willard Wirtz said that New York "had the worst administrative problems of any antipoverty program in any city" in the United States (*New York Times.*) The Washington auditors who investigated the case said that New York's Human Resources Administration "is not fiscally responsible and should not be the custodian of Federal funds." Washington at first threatened to cut off funds on January 31, but later extended the deadline to June 30. On January 17, Lindsay defended the agency as "pretty good." On January 21, a former director of fiscal affairs was indicted on charges of stealing $48,340 in city poverty funds. An assistant district attorney said, "It's so bad that it will take ten years to find out what's been going on." Of course, the cruelest consequences are that the poor didn't get the money that was meant for them—and that the whole poverty program is now regarded with hairy suspicion by conservatives *and* liberals.

"In New York, *everybody* cheats. You *know* that," a former official told me. Indeed, the references to graft which came from every department I visited were a bit startling—since we're often told that "things have been cleaned up." But one fact is certain; few of eight million New Yorkers can afford this city. In the fall of '66, the Bureau of Labor Statistics announced that a New York family of four (i.e., two children) needs $9,075 a year "to maintain a moderate level" of living. The budget provides for one egg every two days, six cans of beer every two weeks, and $73 a year for "reading"—moderate indeed. But over 70 percent of New Yorkers earn even less than $7,000 a year. So it's time that the myth of our affluence was exploded. According to the City Club of New York, New York was the highest wage center in manufacturing among the twenty largest cities in the U.S. in 1947; in 1960, it became the lowest.

One of our foulest blights is the housing situation; rents of manic proportion ignore the facts of income. The poor, of course, live in realms of misery which are very similar to what Dickens described. The need for more public housing is supreme. Here, the Lindsay Administration has been incredibly slow. When he became mayor, New York had the money to build 28,800 units of public housing— but only 6,414 were begun by September 30, 1968. As for the middle class: within the last three years, rents on some uncontrolled apartments have risen 100 percent; many have risen 50 percent. For the same period, salaries are up 3 to 4 percent; the cost of living has risen almost 10 percent; all other rents are up by 20 percent. Hence most middle-income earners are rent-poor, paying far more than a quarter of all income to their landlords.* Billows of puffery continue to float out of the housing department, but most natives can't find dwellings which they can afford—especially since the vacancy rate is down to 1.5 percent.

Crime, housing, and education were the three major mayoral campaign issues of '65, and the only one that's progressed is crime —our burglars are doing splendidly. Meanwhile, the police are thoroughly confused about their role. Lindsay—despite good intentions —has multiplied their confusions. He campaigned on the issue of the Civilian Review Board—a good idea which was sure to lose, mainly because it was hustled through too quickly. ("He got credit for losing valiantly when he knew he was going to. Another PR gimmick," an ex-official said.)

So far, some New York cops have been more restrained than most—with some raging exceptions: they are always worst in ghettos; last summer, a batch of off-duty cops beat up fifteen Panthers in the Brooklyn Courthouse in '68; many were atrocious at Columbia

---

* In 1972, a *New York Times* survey stated that "the great majority of New Yorkers, perhaps more than 70 percent, can no longer afford unsubsidized housing."

last spring. Lately, there's fresh evidence of bribery in the force—
and a bulging cynicism. But it's apparent that the New York police
feel the need for more direction. With a very pleasant officer who
caught a burglar in my apartment last August, I spent many hours
in the Night and Criminal Courts. He was worried that the date of
the trial might postpone his yearly vacation. "It's not that I'm soft,
it's my nerves! my nerves! The strain of my job. Can you *imagine*
what it's like? You should see my stomach. The *strain* . . ." He
described all the rapid decisions which any day requires, plus the
fact that some laws don't make sense, and that few respect them
—and how it feels to be universally disliked. Clearly, many cops
might function better if they had more detailed guidance—as opposed to the right-wing howl for "Lawnorder." Meanwhile, the
mayor's latest project is "a big advertising campaign to educate
the public" about crime: how to use keys, lights, and so forth, for
self-protection. It sounds rather as though he's turning the problem
over to us.

Lindsay's newest announcement is that New York *is* "govern-
able"—and we're all delighted to hear it. Despite much of his
record, he did perform one particular service: that of making the
office of mayor important in the national consciousness—as it
hadn't been for years. Now, some of us wish that he might have
some special urban chair in Washington, where he could talk about
the problems of cities—which truly do seem to concern him—without actually having to run one.

LINDSAY'S REELECTION
November 1969

The Waldorf is going to pieces. The traffic towers have
been dug up by the roots from Fifth Ave. The green
line in the subway has been replaced by lights. The
hippopotamus in the Bronx Zoo is dead. . . . Life is
slipping away, crumbling all around us. Still, nothing
seems to make a dent in the town.
    —New Yorker, *Notes and Comment, May 18, 1929*

BY THE summer of '69, the mildest of New Yorkers were in the worst of tempers: as the fares rose, the subways grew more exasperating; as the sanitation trucks got bigger, the streets were even dirtier. Some looked wistfully back to Robert Wagner's twelve years as mayor, rather the way others reminisced about the Eisenhower era: "It was quieter then." (It was quieter because so many issues went unacknowledged, such as poverty and racism.) Later, as Mario Procaccino seemed to be crowding the other candidates with his one-note campaign of "a safe city"—urging that policemen should carry Mace ("It is better to spray than to slay"), that the "felonious length" of a knife blade should be shortened from five to three inches, and that thirteen-year-olds should qualify for adult jail sentences—black New Yorkers were growing more indignant at Lindsay; Roy Innis of CORE remarked that Lindsay was "a great guy to have over on a Sunday afternoon for cocktails," but stressed that he had little to offer the black community.

However, CORE invited the candidates to debate in Harlem in October, even though, as a spokesman said, "We're convinced that all three are bankrupt—in terms of programs for us." Henceforth, "We don't want any more politicians walking the streets and patting little kids' heads. Instead, we will bring these cats to us, and ask them, 'Why are you running?' We learn what kind of wares they are peddling. Then we decide what to do." Procaccino said that he would come, to show that "he had guts," but didn't appear. Lindsay refused, and spent the evening speaking at a showcase East Side public school. The waiting audience was deeply angry, especially at such a snub from a mayor who kept saying how much he cared for them. Marchi, who did show up, was tremendously booed. But many said how glad they were to have heard him; when he called one heckler "Buster," his reflexes became very clear to the crowd. So Lindsay did receive a much larger black vote than he had in '65, since black people knew exactly how Procaccino and Marchi would deal with them.

An extremely clever decision was made when Lindsay's mentors advised him to campaign on his mistakes: to say again and again that he had been wrong. (Arrogance pretending to humility has become a new national style.) Except for admitting that he mishandled the teachers' strike—which was excused because "information was so hard to get at the time"—the Mayor's taped confessional chant referred mainly to his smaller disasters, such as "unpreparedness" for the amount of snow that fell on Queens. However, honesty wasn't yet abundant in city government. Soon after the election Lindsay issued a statement that he had built a lot of middle-income housing—a fact which was easily disproved by simply checking the number of building permits. When the candidates debated each other on TV, Lindsay said that air pollution had been reduced (which it hadn't), and Procaccino denied several of his own recorded statements about the punishment of criminals. Marchi wisely kept appealing to the natives' daily experience. On radio, some of Lindsay's ads stressed that he's a Sagittarian.

But New Yorkers' moods and emotions can alter as swiftly as our landmarks: just as a parking lot can replace a skyscraper, so an overnight cordiality can overlay disgust. The native volatility keeps politicians frantic. Lindsay was finally aided by Golda Meir's New York visit, the Mets' victory in the World Series, and his own good handling of the October 15 Moratorium. (Even his harshest critics agreed that he was brave to make Vietnam the core of his final campaign.) Still, none of these had any connection with his ability to head a city.

Most experts thought that Lindsay owed his reelection to the character of his opponents; as a waitress said, "People don't like all three of them." Aside from many "negative votes," many in Manhattan apparently pulled the levers for him because "He has class"—a phrase which became a gleeful refrain in the last weeks before the election. Shortly beforehand, when Lindsay's next term seemed fairly certain, there was a new style of sneering in the air —not only at Procaccino's own clumsiness, but at his followers. More and more, one heard them called "greasy little people," mocked for their clothes and their accents.

Still, Lindsay's huge jolt of June '69—when he lost the Republican primary to Marchi—drove his staff to make more contact with bitter neighborhoods than they ever had before. They very suddenly discovered Queens (where he won by a slender margin), the Bronx, and Brooklyn (where he still lost). As the press repeated, Lindsay was reelected by the poor and the rich. One of his arguments against banning cars in New York was that chauffeur-driven businessmen would suffer—a constituency which he did partly understand.

Hindsight: Now it's slightly chilling to recall that one of the fantasies of '65 was that Lindsay and Robert Kennedy would be the two Presidential candidates for '72.

After Lindsay's disastrous 100-day Presidential primary race—his advisors truly missed the mood of '72 when they assumed that voters were hungering for a "media candidate," and Lindsay himself was innocent enough to tell Mary McGrory that he would regret drawing many of the young away from McGovern—the Mayor began to court the regular Democratic leaders. Hence, on his first anniversary as a Democrat, he was antagonizing many of the reform Democrats who had worked hard to re-elect him in '69. As he strove to please the "political bosses" whom he had so often denounced in the past, he even voted for the seating of Mayor Richard Daley's delegation at the Miami Beach convention. (At that point, some on the floor mentioned his seconding of Agnew's Vice Presidential nomination.) No one is ever sure of Lindsay's motives, since he has an aversion to answering straight questions. But it appeared that his chief mentor, former Deputy Mayor Richard Aurelio, expected a defeat for McGovern, followed by the disintegration of the reform movement, and a consequent renaissance for the party regulars. So Lindsay started to woo them for the future, while some of his friends told the press that he might want to leave politics for a while.

Since Lindsay's political career declined so rapidly, some New Yorkers became rather more tolerant of him. No one with his brains intact would hold Lindsay fully responsible for the condition of New York, though few could forget that the disintegration had speeded up under his mismanagement. (The *Times,* which had been soft on Lindsay for years, became tougher as the Seventies got underway.) Perhaps what had most troubled some of us was City Hall's pretense of achievements: programs which had barely begun were advertised as though they'd already been completed. But the tendency to blame each heatwave and mugging and cab-driver's insult on the Mayor was almost parodied when the *Times* reported that, before the Florida primary, when Lindsay had a "mixed" reception from a small group at a shopping center in Miami, "he was heckled by vacationing former New Yorkers."

NEW YORK FOR NATIVES
August 1969

My first day in New York has never quite ended. And eighty cents still seems too much to pay for orange juice.

—*Sinclair Lewis, writing in 1937 about New York in 1903*

ONCE I thought that I might hardly ever see New York again. Risking my plane at Kennedy Airport, I caught a cab, hurtled to the bottom of East 86th Street, and raced across the headlong pavement below the East River, up the crescent stone stairs of the Carl Schurz Park, to memorize the river in five minutes. The October currents blazed, the bridges swung, and I learned what most travelers regret: no landscape is portable. Meanwhile, scolding relatives pursued me, waving baggage checks and little canvas satchels. Eluding them, I wandered back into the street, swerving close to a bus, whose driver yelled "Wake up! Get off the needle!" Leaving New York, losing the river, I looked for substitutes, and found none.

The John Finley Walk—built in 1941 and named for a dead editor of the *New York Times,* who often walked around the entire rim of Manhattan—can still characterize much that (addicted) natives love about New York. Downriver was my daily walk to school, staggering with sleep, banging my stumpy shoes against the concrete—and hurling my unfavorite textbooks into the water at the end of term. Even then, I thought how lucky one was to be here, how dull life must be for those marooned in Hollywood, Hyannis, Mexico City, Philadelphia, Palm Beach—towns I already knew to be inferior to New York. The Finley Walk runs for half a mile from East 90th to 81st Street. Entering the park, you pass huge glacial rocks where climbing is forbidden. Other signs warn, "No dogs, skates, bicycles." The rocks are thick with children, who also surge along the river on skates and bicycles, dragging their dogs. At eleven, I used to haul a lumpy spaniel to the park, in order to tangle his leash with that of ex-Mayor LaGuardia's small white bulldog. LaGuardia was old and unwell; he looked cross. Each day, he shouted "Don't!" as I launched the spaniel at him. It was an honor to annoy the former mayor, who died soon after this abuse. A pleasing anarchy has always prevailed in Schurz Park, which is crammed with rhododendrons, laurels, firs, forsythia, swings, playgrounds, and sandpits, even a hockey rink. Winter milks the river to so soft a gray that the falling snow seems white.

The park spreads over two small hills and mounts to a wide esplanade, which is the roof of the East River Drive. Cars pound beneath your feet as the river opens out before you. Several ventilators from the tunnel are hidden among the bushes; sometimes the shrubbery honks at rush hour, and once I heard the oaths of taxi drivers coming up through a bed of daffodils. "Bastard," said one flower. "I'll get yours," said the other. Exhilaration springs from elevation: the river churns at about fifty feet below, while the tide runs in two directions. It feels like the top of the world. Here the river (really an estuary) is about eight-five feet deep—it seems little for so much life. Tugs, yachts, steamers, cargo ships, aircraft carriers, small oil tankers, and garbage scows slide past the boat-shape of Welfare Island, where hospitals are isolated in the middle of the river. Much of the river traffic is freight: wool, tin, bulldozers and lipsticks, coffee, wheat and TV sets, cement and bananas, railroad cars, are sailing past you. Ships from Israel, Iceland, Sweden, anywhere, decked with brilliant flags, must use this river. Slow barges are weighted with gravel, and jeered at by a speedboat. On certain days, clouds rest on columns of smoke from factories across the river. Mist makes the boats seem closer. On your right is the Queensboro Bridge; to the left, the looped arches of the Triborough and Hellgate Bridges, where cars glint jerkily in the sun. Standing there, you dissolve into the background of one of the most breath-stopping views of Manhattan. *The Great Gatsby*'s narrator felt that "The city seen from the Queensboro Bridge is always the city seen for the first time, in its first wild promise. . . . 'Anything can happen now that we've slid over this bridge,' I thought, 'anything at all.' "

On the Walk, black ribs of an iron railing curve inward at elbow height: people lean against them, while gulls flap before their faces. John Finley's small black silhouette is etched against the riverscape. No one is odd: on a bench at the brim of the river, two actors rehearse their lines—"You're sitting there knowing for certain that I'm going to give in—aren't you?—aren't you?" "Yes."—but get no attention. I once released twenty-five monarch butterflies—who must, in the fall, go south—standing on one of those benches. They made a quivering orange phalanx, beating out over the water toward Brooklyn. An Andover friend of mine, sixteen and drunk, raced a midnight tug from 90th to 81st Street, jumping over the benches. On top of the race and the champagne, he wrote a long, tightly metered poem in triolets, which he recited to the cops who finally led him from the park.

The river's brink attracts solitaries and couples; the friends and families stroll slowly past. At night, there is quite a bit of kissing. A huge sign across the river—PEARLWICK HAMPERS—reminds me of teen-age necking. This is also a reflective spot for partings: there may be a couple hanging over the railing in some dialogue of distress, filling the river with cigarette butts, staring out over the water. . . . At your back is all of Manhattan: towers and turrets that gleam pink and green at dusk. On some nights, the buildings seem to jump at your feet like giant typewriter keys. This is a good point to examine many architects' perplexities in finishing off skyscrapers; the tops are often absurd: domes, spiky minarets, and a few vast 1920-ish zippers, with the suggestion of sequins. Light lavishes along the river, strangely warm and gray in winter, cold with a shocking blue in the heat. The Walk's height feeds both fact and illusion, elaborates distance, until the sweep of clouds and bridges seems like one of New York's best designs. A range of motion, light, and water; car horns, boat cries, airplanes, shouts, barks, whistles, singing transistors, even the crack of hockey sticks. A pastoral prospect where the river is so urgent, intent on business. It is peaceful and tumultuous, the impossible mood of New York.

As any transient idiot knows, peace is scarce in what Henry James called the "vast hot pot." Since our calamities are notorious, since the daily awareness of so much suffering is now part of the pith of our lives, since decay is an accepted fact, many outsiders wonder why some of us still want to live here—or how we can so desperately miss it: even when we're in San Francisco or Rome, or being pampered on a country weekend. Clinging to the grit, the ugliness, the shrieking expense, dwelling among many who simply hate their lives, spitting on the sidewalk when lungs heave against the filthy air, the native sanity is questioned by disgusted visitors, who often exit a day or a week early, pawing their adjectives and their luggage, afraid that either may be wrenched away from them. (Dickens wrote, "Debauchery has made the very houses prematurely old"; James, horrified by the snarl of traffic and the trolley tracks, felt that "the New York predicament leaves far behind the anguish represented by the Laocoön.") "Sorry about that" is an old New York phrase, as is the sarcastic "Thanks a *lot*." All of the bad news is true. Hence those who are unhappy here should depart, if they can, leaving the town to those of us who think we own it, or feel that it owns us, that it's responsible for our characters. Relationships with certain cities can be as intense as those in private life. For some, New York is so emotionally demanding and rewarding that all of the struggles seem worthwhile. At least, for a while.

For over a century, New York's one unbroken tradition has been unceasing change—what William James called the "permanent earthquake conditions." But at least some of the mutations have been healthy.

As many have noted this is where the agony is—where almost everything happens first—where the issues surge and shout and glare until they can't be fled. At times you might almost think that New Yorkers are defiantly proud that their city seems to have the worst afflictions in the U.S. And it's typical of the past and present that few remedies are sought until a crisis bursts: in 1832, when the streets were deep in garbage, the city fathers finally had them cleaned when a plague of cholera struck. Among all the contradictions, our city belts us with its extremes. One resident, who settled here ten years ago, found his image of New York on his first night: during a fierce blizzard, he met a street shoveler on 42nd Street, wretchedly dressed in thin rags, pausing in his work to inhale voluptuously on a fine Havana cigar.

Naturally, change can be demoralizing. On a weekly level, you can't be sure of your own neighborhood. After a short absence, you may find that the delicatessen has been replaced by a discothèque, blunder into the new hairdresser's for a beer, go to the drugstore for your laundry, to the laundry for contraceptives. But change also means that the potentialities are staggering. Again, *Gatsby*'s narrator felt it ticking over: ". . . the satisfaction that the constant flicker of men and women and machines gives to the restless eye. I liked to walk up Fifth Avenue and pick out romantic women from the crowd and imagine that in a few minutes I was going to enter their lives, and no one would ever know or disapprove." Most of the glamor that Fitzgerald loved is long gone; "the iridescence," as his contemporaries called it, has drained away even more switfly in the last ten years. But New York is still romantic—even in his terms; it ignites the imagination more than any city I know.

Many find themselves adventure-prone. Here, you are perpetually exposed to the inventions and the fantasies of others—which can penetrate and shape and fill your own life. (Of course, there's the risk that they may damage it as well. Nonmasochists learn a lively kind of self-protection in this town.) And you can lead so many lives—among different people who will never meet each other. The same person, in his varying roles, can be a mentor for some, a clown for others; a grave, responsible employer may also be a maverick away from his desk. This personal variety is crucial for many of us, since the world of jobs and offices is horribly bracketing. Professionally, we're unfree. For example, few editors are writers, or vice versa; the two capacities are not expected to overlap.

Due to the range of its privacies, New York bestows the privilege of a mild schizophrenia: of having several characters at once. Paradoxically, the luxury of self-escape is enchanting for egotists—and here, a ripe ego is essential for survival. (In 1867, Mark Twain wrote, "Some day . . . may be, I shall acquire a New York fortitude, and be as shameless as any.") The egoless are soon lost: the city swallows them without leaving a foot or a handprint. Many who now flourish in New York have had a spell of this; few of them ever forget it. Hence it's easier here than in most cities to identify with those who are wasted or ground into the pavement. Almost all but the rich know what it is to be fired, to dread the doctor's bill, to find no work when cash is needed for tomorrow, or to lose a home.

In 1941 Sartre wrote of New York: "Nowhere more than here can you feel the simultaneity of human lives." And, as many say, it's a city where suffering is contagious—where intense poverty means the kind of misery which means heroin, which involves us all. As long as we allow so many to be so poor, we're going to pay for what hard drugs do to them, and they to us. In 1970, I. D. Robbins, the former president of the City Club of New York, said flatly, "New York is doomed unless we can raise the incomes of the poor." (He added that 51 percent of all New Yorkers earn less than $125 a week.) Cyril Connolly's New York notes from 1947 have a fresh irony now: "It is all part of the American tragedy—that, in the one remaining country where necessities are cheap, where a room and food and wine and clothes and cigarettes and travel are within everyone's reach, to be poor is still disgraceful." But even the richest can't escape the city's punishments: they breathe the same bad air, slide —almost skate—in the same dogshit, hear the phone squeal and die in mid-sentence; penthouses and limos can't shelter them from the traffic jams and holdups that entrap all of us. In Philadelphia, for example, the rich can still live in isolated neighborhoods, like Chestnut Hill. But there's no such sanctuary in New York—no defense against the entangling lives of strangers: you may sometimes get a bunch of flowers or a bullet that was meant for someone else.

New York has been called a devil's paradise: the great bazaar where everything is available. This is no longer true because of cost. My father, a long-term New Yorker, said, "You feel that a demon-core of public accountants has taken over. They pick up some twenty-five-cent corn plasters and say, 'Let's charge ten dollars for these!'" Many can't afford much of the cultural abundance; also, the expense of operation has killed some artistic outlets: much of the theater, quite a few magazines, and new experimental art galleries; orchestras and chamber groups are hurting. In the last two years, producers in various fields have made desperate statements about the swelling financial crisis in the arts. Therefore, many New Yorkers do feel a cultural starvation. While no other form of nourishment can satisfy that hunger, some can draw sustenance from experiencing the city itself as a limitless dramatic stage.

No one is daft enough to claim that New York is a work of art. But it's a series of theaters which can reward a participating audience. The (often compulsive) involvement with neighborhood is probably increasing—along with the themes of decentralization and community control. When physical realms outside your own can seem inhuman, the emotional dependence on a few blocks answers an almost animal need. (And certain New Yorkers seem almost helplessly committed to the crises on their own turf; a friend of mine, who moved to New Haven, felt lost in exile—and added, "I can't identify with the problems." *My* addicts, *my* muggers, *my* transit strike: these involve some of us more deeply than any national statistics.)

So whether you live in Yorkville, amid the German goosegrease and beer halls, or among the Czechs, Hungarians, and Irish of the East Seventies, among the Jewish colonies of the Lower East Side, where Puerto Ricans, microboppers, and a few lingering street people can still meet the price of kosher food, in Chelsea, where vine-laced elegance collides with ethnic outrage, or in the spacious, fortress-mute apartments of the Upper West Side (so rich in resident psychiatrists that one stretch is called Spook's Row)—your gut-attachment is apt to be intense. Some I know are urban gypsies, who can't pay for what's called a home; instead, they find pads or ledges in the neighborhoods that mean the most to them.

The New Yorker's irrational affection for his slice of the city spills through Claude Brown's delighted return to Harlem, after a childhood visit to the rural South: "This was a real Sunday morning —a lot of blood and vomit everywhere and people all dressed up and going to church. . . . I was so happy to . . . see it all. [Our] hallway looked . . . the way it was supposed to be looking on Sunday morning. Somebody had gotten cut the night before, and blood was still in the hall. And somebody had pissed on the stairs, and it was still there, just like it should have been." Certainly, some residents of the Silk Stocking District can greet their own streets with the same elation.

We live with lore: including small grim stories that appall outsiders but which rapidly become part of the folk-myth or the comedy here. New Yorkers still laugh at tales which simply sound like their own town. One man, whose ceiling—flooded by a neighbor's bathroom overhead—was close to collapse, desperately rang the Housing Authority for aid. An inspector actually arrived; gravely regarding the sheets of falling water, he said, "This isn't an emergency yet," and left. He did return after the ceiling was on the floor, but was unimpressed. Instead, he fined the tenant ten dollars for the (adjustable) bars on a window by a fire escape—which had been installed only after four robberies. . . . A tall black writer, leaving the subway on Lexington and 86th Street, saw that the middle-aged white couple walking in front of him nervously speeded up as he strolled behind them toward Park Ave. Flinging frantic glances over their shoulders, they broke into a trot. They tore into an apartment house, and when he came in behind them, the woman shrieked in terror. The writer told her to be cool, and that he was just having dinner there himself; he added later, "That's black power now!" . . . When I was twelve, my school advised those of us walking through empty side streets to carry a rolled-up copy of *Vogue* or *Harper's Bazaar* or *Fortune,* dangling casually at our sides. If assaulted, we were to heave it up beneath the villain's chin, coincident with swift action of the knee. (Some parents thought this excessive; mine asked me to be certain that the menace was not a family friend.) Like most New Yorkers, I've had a couple of unpleasantries—once I was trapped in a vestibule by two quite nutty young men; I escaped by pretending to have cancer, which caused a wonderfully quick recoil. But thoughtlessness is the mark of many victims. Three years ago, a boy who looked about eleven lurked at my side at midnight, murmuring, "Please, miss, give me your purse. Miss? Your purse?" Since he was small, and definitely an amateur—I suspected that his older brothers might have said "Tonight you go get your first purse"—he wasn't alarming. But finally, he began to tug at my satchel, so I let loose an operatic scream which I didn't know I possessed. He gasped and ran; immediately, four slightly larger black kids raced up from around a corner. "Man! What *happened?*" I explained, and one said, "We thought you were getting killed. Please don't make that kind of noise—just for a purse." They walked me home, clucking at the carelessness of being out alone. . . . Of course survival stories are less funny of late, yet we share them and expand our local mythology—which may be destructive too.

Perhaps you have to be rather eccentric to like New York, or to bear it. Professionally, there's so much sludge; it's no longer distinctly a town of winners and losers—that old seductive challenge for fledglings and new arrivals. Instead, you meet a lot of well-paid compromisers, who keep explaining, "My job isn't me." Some of those who seem to fare the best are adept at dodging the system, living in the present, spending amazingly little; their work can eventually thrive if they are stubborn about refusing to dilute it. But few can enjoy New York who try to plan for the future. The sanest New Yorkers may be those who cherish incongruities, or ludicrous degrees of contrast.

Things loved (and shared by some): the stomach of Grand Central Station, with the zodiac on its blue ceiling, and the mad visual spaghetti of winking ads; the impatient, greedy New York temperament, unable to wait for a green light, a bus, or a sandwich, which highlights the native conviction that life must be used—at once; dawn from any skyscraper; punctual derision of space programs in a local pizza shop; immense loyalty among friends, perhaps due to the fact that daily life in this city is so difficult that many offer mutual support; the New York logic, revealed when a taxi driver shouts, "If we can get rid of Lindsay, we can get rid of the traffic!", or when a member of the Sanitation Department—asked why so many public trash baskets were removed from Lexington Ave.—replied, "Because people were putting too much trash in them!"; eating artichokes on a roof on a summer night, hearing the Afro drums of the district throb from other roofs and fire escapes; infectious energy, which seems to leap from the pavements; a drugstore which serves as a communication center for its neighborhood: you can lean on the counter and learn *any*thing, from politics to love and real estate; infinite leafy side streets; the drastic, provocative New York sense of comedy—overstated in tone but not in fact—as from a beseiged friend who said, "If I weren't such a snob, I'd have a nervous breakdown"; the seals in Central Park, the arch-sensualists and exhibitionists of the whole city; a certain Italian butcher; the Unicorn tapestries at the Cloisters; the freedom to be furious: New York offers many valid reasons for anger, which is easy to express here; New York legends: for example, the Public Library lions roar whenever a virgin passes between them; concert rehearsals in nearby buildings: an open window means free Mozart; the statue of "Civic Virtue" in Queens, wherein a giant male nude strides over a prostrate woman, which was called degrading by early feminist groups and also defended as depicting the triumph of man "over graft and corruption"; the Olivetti typewriter (now gone) which was mounted on Fifth Avenue, where pedestrians typed poems, insults, and invitations; one or two good plays of the season; the Municipal Asphalt Plant; sun rippling down the avenues while one's pace springs faster and faster within a loose, swift crowd; slow walks where random lighting resculpts the city at night; the occasional sense that the whole town is an illusion, invented by some cosmic nut case, which allowed one to witness a myth—or maybe a movie.

BLACKOUT
November 1965

VICTIMS OF time and geography, who were not in Columbus, Ohio, on the Day the Dam Broke, hoped that James Thurber's ghost was in Manhattan for the blackout of November 9th. (It's a nearly perceptible spirit, since he was recently identified by an earnest graduate student taking an exam as "a muckraker in the age of Emily Dickinson"; also, most ouija board messages seem to be sent by him.) Lacking Thurber, it was pleasing to know that Federico Fellini was visiting New York—it seemed like an ideal sequence for him. Since capes are now fashionable, it was stirring to see mantled figures carrying silver candlesticks flickering through the East Seventies under a full moon. Discreet invitations to join a gangbang circulated through P. J. Clarke's when the darkness was only half an hour old, while candles sold for a dollar apiece from sidewalk entrepreneurs on Third Avenue. In subways and elevators, heart attacks were promised, threatened, and maybe a few were had. Citizens draped in white sheets, directing traffic with rolled-up newspapers, made it look as though the Ku Klux Klan had captured the city. The Statue of Liberty's torch remained lit by a New Jersey plant, but shocked airplane passengers arriving from Washington heard the pilot say, "And now you will see the fabled lights of Manhattan—*Oh*."

While national figures ponderously assured the public that it wasn't necessarily sabotage, numerous New Yorkers indulged their megalomania by claiming that they had personally caused the blackout. Police switchboards were clogged with calls (particularly from women) bewailing the electric egg beater, the hair dryer, or the waffle iron which must have fused the entire coast. The *Daily News* had the best headline—"NOBODY DIGS POWER FLOP"—but some residents still triumphantly insisted on their own responsibility. At my office, maintenance men apologized bitterly for the blackness until someone had the wit to look out the window. At home, I sang loudly in the dark until matches were found, while the telephone rang with rumors that Governor Rockefeller was "satisfied" (presumably by the mobilization of the National Guard and Civil Defense). It was comforting to imagine the not-very-popular governor —perhaps surrounded with heirloom hurricane lamps and vats of whale oil—in his state of satisfaction. His later observation: "This may be a blessing in disguise" (since "steps will be taken") evokes the Riverside Drive statue of Samuel J. Tilden, the New York governor defeated for the presidency in 1876, inscribed with his most famous remark: "I trust the people." One doubts the columnist who claimed that the eyes of polio victims in iron lungs dilated "in fear and wonder" as the machines ceased breathing, but the image serves nicely for the city fathers. Despite the next day's maudlin praise from sociologists, theologians, and politicians, New Yorkers were less noble than intoxicated.

The most unlikely people got drunk with determined speed, some on the 32nd and 50th floors of Wall Street offices. (Several men explained to their wives that walking downstairs is much more dangerous for the heart than ascending.) Five colleagues—one male editor and four secretaries—were approached by a courtly stranger wearing a private detective's badge, who asked if he could share the women. Leading them to a reserved table with six bottles of superb champagne, he alleged that he owned a fourth of Paramount, had married at seventeen but divorced his wife after she murdered their baby, but that he had managed to kill her lover first. Crawling up twelve flights of stairs on hands and knees at four A.M., the eldest and drunkest of the women realized that she couldn't locate her own apartment, and slept slumped across the stairs. She later described her host as a nondescript liar, but she loved her evening.

Despite stimulating transistor reports of "pillage and rapine" in Rochester, Manhattan's crime rate remained minimal, although fires increased by 300 percent. While Massachusetts convicts rioted mildly, New York zoo keepers succeeded in keeping even the cobras warm. Vladimir Horowitz, in mid-concert, did not miss one note of Chopin, and finished his complete program. Many heated their hands on the vigil candles at St. Patrick's, while others slept in the Lady Chapel; many complained because the cathedral has no toilets. While thousands were entombed in tunnels beneath the Hudson River, or walking across the Brooklyn Bridge, or having car accidents, women were still required to use the ladies' lobby at the Yale Club—although five women slept at the Harvard Club.

The city is said to have lost a hundred million dollars. Clay, New York ("a muddy hamlet," according to the *New York Times*), denied the guilt of its electrical substation, as announced by the Texas White House. The ultimate anticlimax came when the U.S. Department of Agriculture issued instructions for removing wax drippings. On November 10th, many employees returned to their offices already nostalgic, looking hopeful whenever a small bulb dimmed. Aside from those who suffered physically, plus insomniacs whose candles burnt too swiftly, many who love New York had enjoyed themselves thoroughly. Those who dislike the city were exultant in their outrage. The native temperament is often charmed by violent surprises, such as meeting their own neighbors, rumors of imaginary meteors, or poets who actually read well. Perhaps the only creatures unaffected by the blackout were the legendary alligators (flushed away as childhood pets) who matured to inhabit the sewers; their eyes are said to shine red in the dark.

Hindsight: A rise in the New York birth rate was noted nine months after the blackout. Sociologists were quick to go on record with two explanations: some people couldn't find their contraceptives in the dark; others, because they were deprived of their usual TV programs, "interacted with each other" more than usual.

Years later, I met an ex-biker from the Boston Hell's Angels who had been in a Massachusetts jail on that great night. He told me that the cells there had electronic locks; when the power failed, he and other prisoners were charmed to see their cell doors swing silently open. He and several cronies fought their way through a few guards and went over the wall, enjoying several months of freedom before they were arrested again.

UNDERGROUND MOVIES
November 1965

UNDERGROUND CINEMA ("a term invented from within") has had a flattering month in Manhattan: one festival at the Museum of Modern Art, another at the Film-makers' Cinemathèque, grants dropping like old apples from the Ford Foundation. Experimental movie makers receive the proceeds from the Cinemathèque and the Film-Makers' Cooperative, while the inmates bicker to define their themes. According to Robert Breer, who made *Eyewash,* the aim is "subversion—a revolutionary attitude toward society." For Stan Vanderbeek (*See, Saw, Seems; Feedback; Breathdeath*), "emotion pictures" will become a medium "in which we can talk to ourselves." Willard Van Dyke, the Modern Museum's film curator, praises "a personal cinema," stressing that most of the movies are made entirely by one person, "acting . . . under compulsion." Meanwhile, it's cheering to remember that the word *shambles* derives from the Latin *scamnum,* meaning the left-overs around a butcher's bench.

In fact, most of the movies carefully chosen for recent exhibition are "purely visual" (a screenful of boiling golfballs, or hogs wallowing in their own blood), or wistfully pornographic (men filling someone's navel with mustard, a couple slashing each other's underwear). Among the "retinal experiments"—which have included lights shining directly into the spectators' eyes, and lantern slides flickering over their laps—some images are ponderously repeated by certain film makers, proving Vanderbeek's point about internal dialogue. There are repeated shots of Jack Kennedy interwoven with bullfights (sometimes he seems to be the matador, and sometimes the bull), electric lightbulbs alternated with the dropping of the bomb, skulls for any occasion, bones and crosses, Christ and Beats. Often, the camera trembles as though some tic doleureux had slipped from the director's face to his hands. Audiences laugh hardest at brand names and protractedly blank screens. Extended humor: people dropping or breaking things, making faces at one another, moving large objects (like a chest of drawers), or rolling about in sacks.

Armpits are filmed as though they had just been invented. Vander-beek himself provides some pleasing sight-gags among his collages, such as a close-up still of Nixon, with a baby's foot slowly emerging from his mouth, like a helpless tongue. But few of the other meta-phors were as good as Vanderbeek's. After seeing thirty of these movies, you find that many have a communal quality: childishness. A man picks his nose and blows soap bubbles: this image from Ron Rice's *Senseless* characterizes much of the whole earnest movement.

Jonas Mekas is the resident archangel, and his work is far more in-teresting than many of the others'. Probably, the two most prominent *putti* are Kenneth Anger and Andy Warhol. Anger's *Scorpio Rising* was called "a masterpiece" within the cathedral hush of the Modern Museum, and it won the Golden Cup at Rapallo this year. The movie yields thirty-three minutes of homosexual iconography: boots, chains, deaths'-head rings, penises plunged through cardboard skeletons, while voluptuous motorcyclists assemble their machines. The motor-cycle is "a tribal token from toy to terror," so shots of Hitler (as well as Jesus) are heavily larded in to post the message. There are amusing moments: a black leather head and back are photographed slowly rising to look like a phallus, and the rock soundtrack is cleverly selected: "Wind Me Up" and "Sheeee Wore Bleeew Vel-vet" pound away while a vast blond slides into his midnight-blue costume. But it's all so dated and derivative. Blue shots of Marlon Brando in *The Wild Ones,* plus pinups of James Dean, slot it back into the early Fifties; the point has time-traveled very slowly and naively up to the filming of *Scorpio* in 1963.

In addition to his six-hour film of a man asleep, and eight hours of the Empire State Building, Andy Warhol is making "Reel-Reals" these days—meaning seventy minutes of his friends trying to be spon-taneous. For the Cinemathèque festival, Warhol offered *Camp,* which he advertised as a bad movie: "the camera work is so bad, the lighting is awful, the technical work is terrible, but the people are FANTASTIC!" Each one improvised his conception of Camp. A flabby man in Roman dress spun in a sad parody of ballet, "God Bless America" was played slowly on a sweet potato, there were feeble imitations of William Buckley and Yma Sumac, a Yo-Yo demonstration, and a poet reading: "Someone did me in the men's room at one of the posh discothèques. How can I face Flash Gordon and my father's friends?" Finally someone played with an electric train. Although the little skits were meant to be bad, the cast was trying so hard. Warhol's collaborators have been talking about "the space-time continuum and the need for communication before the bomb drops." He is now making a film of the audience.

At an embarrassing symposium at the Modern Museum, entitled "Whither Underground?," Susan Sontag tossed her leathery black hair and defended the "banality" of the movies. She announced that "works of art don't need to say anything." Applause. She later drawled that these particular films are helpful in destroying the connection between movies and literature, since they eliminate plot and character. (She came close to the statement which made her famous on British TV: ". . . there is a good taste of bad taste. I mean there is some bad taste that is good, and some—I don't know what the good taste of bad taste is exactly.") Robert Breer mumbled, "I find *motion* in films very troubling," and added, "My choice of images is random. Whatever I pick up is valid. What I don't pick up isn't valid." Sontag said that these particular movies shouldn't be criticized, but later added that she didn't like them. Van Dyke emphasized "the sincerity and honesty" of the film makers—and he was probably right.

The recent audiences were markedly middle-aged and sober; it wasn't what *Vogue* calls "a Youthquake." In the Cinemathèque's lobby, three irridescent pinwheels flashing *Now-Ow-No* were solemnly studied by a very mature couple. Woman: "Now see if it does something crazy to you. I don't mean ordinary crazy, but if it does something to your conscious." Man (ashamed): "No—not quite. Yet." One elderly man muttered "Early Man Ray" and walked out. And indeed some of these movie makers and their public don't seem to know that Dada and Surrealism have occurred, or that obscurity isn't very daring. The bored, the rich, and the innocent have a new toy; it can occupy the refugees from Pop and Op. While it's splendid that experiments can prosper, and that more movie makers can be subsidized, this batch of home movies has little originality or imagination. You can't blame the pretensions, since they spring from ignorance. But the Modern Museum's curators should examine the storage in their warehouse bins.

Hindsight: Back in '65, the general New York public hadn't yet seen mixed media or psychedelics. But some of the underground movies which were being shown then seem like the forerunners; the style wasn't yet born, but the embryo was stirring. Most of these films were very boring. But I now think that they were part of an important transition: toward the excitement of the best media mix which was to come.

THE CULT OF AYN RAND
January 1966

AYN RAND, the sixty-one-year-old abbess of the acute right, who sometimes wears a gold dollar sign on her lapel, leaves "any room" entered by William Buckley; the *New York Times* notes that he "presided over [her] excommunication." But he wasn't entirely successful. Her last two novels each sell between 100,000 to 200,000 copies a year; $70 courses in her "philosophy," Objectivism, draw some five thousand students; her tape-recorded lectures are given in fifty-four cities, and have been requested by American soldiers in Vietnam; Ayn Rand Clubs are formed at universities. Yet Miss Rand, a former Hollywood screenwriter, born in St. Petersburg, an Aristotelian whose favorite modern novelist is Mickey Spillane, says that the world isn't yet ready for an Objectivist political party.

Objectivism—as evoked in her last two books, *For the New Intellectual* and *The Virtue of Selfishness*—grafts old-fashioned laissez-faire capitalism onto a fresh branch of paranoia: Miss Rand's conviction that America is being destroyed by altruism and mysticism. Zen Buddhism is also part of the peril: the government is threatened by "doctrines created by and for barefoot savages who lived in mudholes." Plato and Saint Augustine are denounced as though they were modern liberals; "Plato was the transmission belt by which Oriental mysticism infiltrated into Western culture." Objectivism—the sole source of freedom and individuality—precludes "life as exaltation." (Miss Rand finds men superior to beasts.) "Reality" is easily understood, mainly because "facts are facts." Miss Rand has written that *"the achievement of his own happiness is man's highest moral purpose,"* also that "the words 'to make money' hold the essence of human morality." Intellectuals ("frightened zombies") have failed the businessman, who "looks at the universe with the fearless eagerness of a child, knowing it to be intelligible." Objectivists "will fight for Capitalism . . . as a *moral* issue." The choice between "Blood, whips, and guns—or dollars" is urgent now that the prevailing altruism is hastening "slavery, brute force, stagnant terror, and sacrificial furnaces." In fact, "the world is perishing from an orgy of self-sacrificing." Altruism includes any form of nonvoluntary taxation, relinquishing a career to support a crippled parent, or allowing your wife to die of a curable illness by spending the money which could save her on preserving the lives of ten other women. (Saving a drowning stranger is perfectly moral if the rescue includes no risk, but it's immoral if it's dangerous, and the would-be rescuer is accused of lacking "self-esteem.") Socialism is defined as "the grinning skull under bloody rags." America, a savagely liberal country, has enabled its throngs of mystics to weaken the citizens' self-confidence, which should inform them that they are heroic. (Moreover, humor is sometimes used as a weapon of destruction: collectivists may "kill by laughter.") Europe is full of bad examples: due to England's welfare state, that country has become "a mawkish poorhouse," where people sell "their rights in exchange for free dentures." However, rational egotism may yet defeat the contemporary lunge to sacrifice oneself.

Miss Rand isn't shy of self-quotation, and the patience of a prawn peeler is necessary to read *The Fountainhead* (1943; 754 pages) and *Atlas Shrugged* (1957; 1,168 pages), the novels which attempt to bring her notions alive. Yet they are chronic best-sellers. Sales may also spring from the rumored sex scenes. These have the tang of severe sadomasochism, but the most graphic word is "blending." Still, there are occasionally daring sentences: "I want you like an animal, or a cat on a fence, or a whore." Nathaniel Branden, Miss Rand's spokesman, calls her "a Romantic Realist," since she writes about "what *ought* to happen." Her happy endings eschew the "man-degrading nature" of modern literature.

The Fountainhead details the lumbering progress of an architectural genius. Mystics and liberals conspire to ruin him, but he eventually succeeds in rebuilding slabs of New York in his image. *Atlas Shrugged* is a fantasy of "the mind on strike." Because America is ruled by demented force, a brilliant inventor "stops the motor of the world," by persuading his fellow geniuses to disappear into a valley, where they continue to compose concertos, mine copper, sculpt, and build railroads; they use only gold coins. Without them, the world literally disintegrates—into starvation, bloodshed, and a total electrical blackout. Civilization must simply await their construction of a rational society. (Frustrated New Yorkers might enjoy imagining that one of Miss Rand's geniuses arranged the current Manhattan water shortage, the transit crisis, and other kindred problems—with the appropriate irony of a threatened welfare strike.) *Atlas Shrugged* ends with the hero tracing a dollar sign in space.

Both the vast fictional samplers are embroidered in women's magazine style of the late 1940s: "Nothing but your body, that mouth of yours, and the way your eyes would look at me if . . ." While Miss Rand insists that everyone can master reason and that success is accessible to all, her own gigantic heroes are biologically superior. You can recognize her good or bad characters by their physical traits: her two heroes have "trembling copper" and "ripe orange rind" hair—elsewhere, it's "liquid gold." One heroine, who runs a railroad, has "a sensual mouth held closed with inflexible precision." Both heroines embody intense fragility and discipline; one is so self-controlled as to marry two men she doesn't love, although her lover is an available bachelor. (Three men for each exceptional woman is the Realist's ratio.) Evil always has a lamentable physique: "Her skin was . . . dry, with enlarged pores showing on her nostrils"; "His posture had a limp, decentralized sloppiness"; "Her hips began at her ankles, bulging over the tight straps of her shoes." Clothes also reveal bad character: "She wore a filthy cotton dress and a crushed hat." Even names predestine moral quality: the heroes are Howard Roark and John Galt, while the villains or inferiors are Ellsworth Toohey, Wesley Mouch, Balph Eubank, and Lancelot Clokey.

Only those who have read and agreed with *Atlas Shrugged* are eligible for the Objectivist lectures. If a student attends only two lectures, he must explain why he has dropped the course. Nathaniel Branden recites the sermon, and Miss Rand answers questions afterward. It seems churlish to complain, but her accent really is a bit difficult: "Mahn muzbe guided eggs*gloo*sively by re-zhon." The audience is youthful, very well dressed, polite, and thrillingly quiet—when Branden asked if everyone could hear him, no one answered. The devout include some Young Americans for Freedom, many Goldwater fans—and a few I've met own a bit of not very valuable land, which the wicked government presumes to tax. A few black listeners appear; Miss Rand rebukes racists, but she says that the current black leaders have gone too far; "Instead of fighting for equal rights, they are demanding special race privileges."

The speakers' technique is making certain words interchangeable: communism, mysticism, Platonism, liberalism. The audience is clearly flattered by the repetition of "philosophy" and "reason," and the reassurance that everyone present must be intelligent. (Also, understanding Objectivism guarantees happiness. And some seem comforted because the enemy is so easy to identify, so swiftly labeled.) The questions I heard were rather timid: "As the author of the world's greatest books, please define the difference between an author and a writer." "As an atheist, do you deny the existence of God?" "How far will Objectivism go in one's lifetime?" "Will there be a movie of *Atlas Shrugged?*" Later, an MIT student told me that he used to flummox Objectivists by insisting that it was his inalienable right to uphold the freedom to relinquish his freedom.

Miss Rand scolded some of her questioners for sounding "subjectivist." She emphasized that "In philosophy, one does not fail to reach an answer if one works hard enough," and repeated that everyone has the intelligence "to guide their actions rationally." Asked why disbelievers and non-Objectivists are unwelcome, Branden rasped, "I won't have a mystic or a communist in my living room, and I won't have one in my lecture hall." Miss Rand explained that anyone who disagrees with Objectivism is despicable and self-destructive: she then shouted, "Let him go to hell his own way!," and stressed the application of reason to particular contexts. Afterward, a pleasant young man murmured to his companion in the elevator, "You do have to respect Hitler for his initial success in perceiving the reality around him. Of course he did wrong things. But he did comprehend his context."

SEDUCTIVE BANKS
February 1966

AN OCELOT, a giant, a Santa Claus who seemed on the edge of upchuck, Salvador Dali embracing Huntington Hartford, silver space helmets, kilts, and a mystifying number of air hostesses filled the Trade Bank and Trust Co. on Fifth Avenue. A woman guest in slashed gold lamé did deep knee-bends on a table, to the laughter of bodyguards, while the musicians revived tunes from *My Fair Lady*. Another woman, in a coronet, said, "I can't leave until I insult Hartford," and her escort answered, "Go ahead. He won't notice." Admittedly, it was midnight: a publication party given by Bobbs-Merrill for Nicolas Darvas' *The Anatomy of Success*. Editors, dwarfs, and ghosts, seemed the only absentees among the crowd which pressed past the Pinkerton detectives.

While it wasn't quite the atmosphere in which you open a savings account, it seemed only an elaboration of what may be found on a lunch-hour visit to a bank: a pianist playing cocktail music, surrounded by bright rubber daffodils, or two ice-skaters on a small rink, an art exhibit, orange trees on piles of pebbles, a red and white sailboat tipped sickeningly on its side. (Muzak is traditional, but it's unnerving to write a $20 check to the tune of "Big Spender," which is playing in many banks these days.) Spanning all styles from schlock to a deluge of dignity, New York banks have followed the advice of J. Walter Thompson Co. to the American Bankers Association, on how to make the public feel exhilarated, flattered, reverent, or flush.

Yet bankers must beware of a literal response to their invitations. One novelist, elated by receiving a sumptuous Ford grant, wandered into a branch of the Chase Manhattan and asked to exchange a Canadian quarter. Consternation and obstruction ensued. An official sternly inquired if he had an account there. No, he said, but he'd thought he had a friend. Indeed, Chase's altruistic advertising is desperately imitated by the decor of many New York banks. A psychiatrist recently remarked on the fortress style of post-Depression banks, which stressed the security and safety of your savings. But the focus is now on friendship, availability, and the impression that there's nothing between you and the money.

The exposure theme—typified by the suburban drive-in banks—is best expressed at the small, transparent Manufacturer's Trust Co. at 43rd Street and Fifth Avenue. It's one of Manhattan's handsomest buildings, topped by trees. The circular vault is in a ground-level window—the management boasts that a thief would need 380 years to find the combination—and the whole glass building remains alight until one A.M. Despite a menacing wire mobile resembling a huge handful of snarled hair, the aerial interior suggests a fantasy of enlightened finance.

Other banks have eliminated the tellers' cages and the brass rails which once surrounded officials, and another conspicuous motif is the (interfaith) cathedral. Some tellers stand behind marble altars which taper toward the floor, soaring lines proliferate, and the Personal Loan room sometimes appears as a small, discreet chapel. While it's almost impossible to deposit money without riding an escalator, the descent to basement level feels like a fall from grace.

Colonial banks are common; they evoke a reliable country bank in the city. The tone is gracious reserve rather than boisterous hospitality. A new branch of the Franklin National Bank calls itself "La Banque Continentale"; there are carriage lamps and urns at the entrance, and a mural of Benjamin Franklin at Versailles. Amid the facsimile petit-point and the new Louis Seize paneling, thigh-slapping cash display would be embarrassing. Actually, despite the gilt pineapples which are the symbol of hospitality, this bank seems fairly hostile to the public: a few of us who came in to inspect the decor were treated like small-time thugs.

The Chase's head office, near Wall Street, exhibits the dueling pistols of Aaron Burr and Alexander Hamilton. (In fact, the same pair of pistols killed both Hamilton and his son.) The murder weapons are startling since the welcome is like a blast of ether, and exposure amounts to exhibitionism. Tours—prefaced by a movie about how Chase makes "American dollars available to friends abroad"— commence every half hour, to reveal Noguchi's beautiful Japanese water garden, around which the tellers' desks are wrapped in a vast circle; the atomic clock which announces the building's age in years, days, hours, and minutes; and an art collection including Larry

Rivers' portrait of himself at the age of three and a West African water trough. There's also a fine Leonard Baskin owl, some 19th-century New England weathervanes, a Marin figure, and a Remington statue of "Rattlesnake on the Trail." As you plough across the caramel plush carpets, or hurtle thirty floors in an elevator at sixteen hundred feet per minute to the world's largest vault (behind bullet-proof glass), awe wrestles with revulsion. The 60th-floor view is worth remembering forever—"The irony," said Henry Hope Reed, the architectural historian, "is that it shows all the great towers of the 1920s, to this building's detriment." The vast clattering temple does indeed feel like the center and circumference of the financial universe. It also feels like the iceberg that sank the Titanic. The chill of the long, low, lit ceilings is paralyzing, and you appreciate the title of one of Albers' many "Homages to the Square." Humanity seems a shoddy standard here. Because, after all, the visitor is made to feel rich. What other interior bestows the sensation of seething personal wealth? In Manhattan, where a modest earner may feel mentally mediocre because his abilities seem to be notched by payment, it's hard for some to reject such an ego massage.

Again in the elevator, while two young financiers discussed the jeweled cuff links and stereos they'd been given for Christmas, I read Chase's own absorbing handout: "JUST FOR FUN. People are spending more for entertainment and amusement these days. . . . While some critics claim that our society has become too material-istic . . ." There followed some blurbs for power lawn mowers, bonded whiskeys, yachts, and pet foods, plus something about the "bottomless appetite for the good life." One of the young men said, "So I sold the cuff links, but the tie clip was just shit."

Meanwhile, throughout the friendliness competition, banks con-tinue to force gifts (such as bathroom scales) on those who open savings accounts early in January, or aim caressing ads at "the Maturing Man of Means," or "the New York Woman"—including "the heroic coed holding her own in the halls of learning." It all intensifies the notion that good people must have good money (earned or owned), plus the impression that banks give it away just to be charming.

PUBLISHERS' FOLLIES
Prize Novel Contests March 1966

LITERARY CONTESTS—theoretically conceived "to encourage new fiction"—often serve merely to discourage publishers. G. P. Putnam's Sons, which announced $210,000 for a novel which would be serialized in *McCall's,* reprinted by Fawcett, and filmed by Embassy pictures has just abandoned this particular philanthropy, after considering 3,262 manuscripts since May 1964. Meanwhile, other houses with less commercial ambitions are finding few candidates for the average $10,000 award.

Publishers haven't quite yet enlisted in the death-of-fiction academy, but some wonder why it's so difficult to bestow a prize. Naturally, most entries are first novels, since no contestant can be contracted to another house. Therefore, limited periods, such as a year (Harper and Row) or six months (Delacorte), curtail the lottery of applications. (Houghton Mifflin's undated $5,000 "literary fellowship" is much more practical.) But most gifted writers have agents, and agents dislike contests, since they can often sell a strong book for more than the prize sum.

Meanwhile, contests prove that those who will never be published do work painfully hard. I once read for a novel contest, and am in touch with others who are doing so now; we share a sad fascination concerning the subject matter and the styles of the thousands of hopeless novels which are diligently resubmitted—such as one leaf-brown manuscript denouncing Roosevelt's earliest proposals for Social Security, which hasn't been retyped since the Thirties. Amid the battered boxes full of fiction, there are certain recurrent themes, which show what's on the public's mind. Above all, there's the boredom of the peacetime army (post-Korea, pre-Vietnam—these are often set in Germany, where the always odious frauleins behave like World War II children, eager to yield themselves for a chocolate bar), and the sexually desperate housewife, who stares sleepless at the dim white square of the ceiling, lying beside a snoring husband. (A few country wives get comforted by farmhands.) Contest readers agree that most of the better efforts concern madness (especially in New York); sometimes, a mental crackup sounds like a form of social criticism. Of course there's lots of alienation and many identity crises; one submission began: "Permanence and stability are the two things I'd give my left nut to find in my own screwed-up life." Novels whose protagonists are recent BAs stress that a truckdriver or a milkman is far more intelligent than any professor, and that education clogs the mental pores.

The vast majority are quite illiterate; clearly, the models are pulp magazines or Westerns. Otherwise, you might expect such influences as Heller or Salinger or William Burroughs. However, Thomas Wolfe is still the most perennial, and D. H. Lawrence runs a close second. (But perhaps a romantic revival is on the way. Jean Stafford recently taught a course at Wesleyan, where she found many students' novels set in Scotland or in "the snowbound trackless wastes of Canada"; most were faithful to Hardy's vocabulary.) The reappearing American folk heroes are Swedish longshoremen who become good union organizers. Braver, more honest, and much sexier than their contemporaries, these Vikings often have wives who conveniently die in childbirth. American novels about India describe young men who leave their studies for women—with horrifying results.

Expatriate novels are usually the most incoherent. A startling number follow young executives sent by oil companies to the Middle East, where they are swiftly embroiled on the wrong side of local intrigues; a desert love scene is almost inevitable. Travelers' fantasies are common: "There was Rosa in Berlin, petite Julie in Copenhagen, frivolous Bernice in London, and haunting Sonya in Moscow . . ." Office life, whether seriously or comically intended, is a particularly pathetic subject. Baby-sitting is a favorite topic for humorous fiction. Then there are "voices of nature" novels, as well as lots of "fragments of reality," and many take the form of notebooks addressed by fathers to sons: "When you read this, I shall be long dead." Of course many are therapeutic: "He had a low opinion of women, starting with his mother, whoever she the slut may have been [sic]." (Mothers are usually monsters, but occasionally, there's a kind evocation, as when a man falls in love at first sight: "She made me think of wind; cold spray in an icy creek; lemonade in a wet glass; and, strangely, of my mother at home.") Sometimes, the orientation is appealing: "He sniffed the air in an excremental manner." Expositions are often confusing, especially since quite a few men choose to speak through a female narrator. But in one novel, the hero was identified in the first sentence: "As God looked down on Colorado that night, it must have looked to him as earth did in the beginning."

All in all, many contest candidates remind me of A. J. Liebling's description of being twenty-three in Paris during an irresolute period, when he felt that his life hinged on an impossible decision. His novel-in-progress analyzed a twenty-three-year-old in Paris, whose future hung upon an insoluble choice. When the character caught up with his own day-to-day life, he was unable to finish the book. His enormous laughter thirty years afterward should cheer those whose diaries have no conclusion.

Many prize novels are cooked by critics, especially when the ads proclaim a masterpiece. It's unfortunate when the victim is a good first novel—no less, no more. If only the writer might be given some money, without ruinous praise. But publishers would hardly comply, since the point is publicity for the firm. Perhaps the foundations could handle it all more gracefully. But to date, some of them still concentrate on trying to tempt writers outside their fields (such as persuading poets to write plays), or demand phoney projects, or send travel haters abroad. There are too few grants for novelists, although someone recently received a grant to study those who receive grants.

Meanwhile, unfamous writers of fiction are doing poorly enough without prizes. In *Further Experiences of an Irish RM,* the narrator's cook assured him that "Wild pigs in America wouldn't be treated worse than what Mrs. McRory treated her servants." Wild pigs—which did roam Manhattan's streets in the 1840s—couldn't have fared much worse than the authors of many first novels in the 1960s. Their books are often slotted farther and farther back in production schedules; on publication, promotion—hence reviews—will be next to nil. Nothing is really less welcome to many publishers than "untried" literary talent. The contests are actually a hangover from an earlier period; now, the fear of fiction is almost as acute as the fear of emphysema. It's true that most novels sell sadly in any form but mass-market paperback. On jacket photographs, among the torn T-shirts, the expectant typewriters, the garlands of smoke, the unbuckled buckles, almost every novelist's expression—alert, defiant, or hopefully oblique—seems like a wistful bid for readers.

Paperback Gothics October 1966

JANE AUSTEN needn't have apologized, in her "Advertisement" for *Northanger Abbey,* because "period, places, manners, books, and opinions" had changed thirteen years after the novel's publication. She was worried that her parody of the Gothic novel had dated. However, while the form has often been vaguely defined, it probably didn't improve until it was already dead—by about 1830. But it's reincarnated in almost every decade. Now, new Gothic novels are the most violent paperback success; outdistancing the recently popular nurse books.

One hundred fifty Gothics sold over 1.5 million copies a month last spring. Published primarily by Pyramid, Lancer, Ace, Bantam, and Paperback Library, last year's flock did so well that a Gothic soap opera has commenced on TV: *Dark Shadows.* It's set in modern Maine, complete with Down East accents, a bemused governess, a small boy of bad heredity, a ne'er-do-well brother who has just returned from a mysterious voyage, and an old retainer of paranoid loyalties (combining Mrs. Danvers in *Rebecca* with Joseph of *Wuthering Heights*). There's a door which mustn't be opened for months (the cast darkly suspects that the scriptwriters haven't yet chosen between a lost diary, a skeleton, a will, or a hidden passage), and a recurring line of dialogue: "Stay out of this basement." Meanwhile, Hollywood is considering some of the original Gothic paperbacks. All their covers depict a running girl in a raincoat or nightgown, shrinking from a vast castle or house which is just about to lunge at her. Jacket designs are so important that publishers have discovered that *one* lighted window in the mansion will increase.sales.

The audience is "older women," who sometimes purchase six at once. These Gothics are so faithful to *Jane Eyre* and Daphne du Maurier that one editor simply buys outlines and clothes them himself. Many of the authors are pseudonymous, lurking behind such titles as *The Mistress of Mellyn, Thunder Heights, Durrell Towers,* and *Flowers of Evil.* They can be set in the last or present century, in New England, or the Hudson River Valley, or the moldering South. But whereas Mrs. Radcliffe and Mary Stewart have sent their heroines to the Alps or the Mediterranean, American Gothics depend on England: a crazed little kingdom largely occupied by the state of Cornwall, where cliffs rise in the middle of new highways, and the weather is reliably vile. The peasants of Cornwall speak a foxy dialect: "Ee dun't knoow you, Miss." The English are given to spasmodic laughter, poisoning each other with herbal teas, stroking harps at midnight, and an occasional bruising kiss. Such Anglomania ("But how wonderful! Scones!") can furnish a villain with medieval ancestors, unobtainable in wildest Rhode Island.

Naturally, the vocabulary has been purged for the drugstore trade; the rain has ceased its "incessant crepitations" on the pane. Most of the heroines are indeed orphaned governesses ("since the auto accident took Mother and Dad"); they're sensible, but "not wise," as they keep confessing. Brisk and priggish, they consider themselves plain—only a lover can reveal their hidden beauty. Just as Elizabeth Bowen stressed in her Introduction to Lefanu's *Uncle Silas* (1864), these Gothics are sexless, and the women are triumphantly infantile. (At least there are two kinds of nurse novels: chaste and unchaste.) One New York Gothic editor says that he allows "a kiss at the end if the heroine's been a very good girl." The contemporary governess is a classical teacher: "There's one thing to learn before you begin to ride, and that is to love your horse." And she's far too literal-minded to write a sonnet like Emily's in *The Mysteries of Udolpho:* "Go, pencil! faithful to thy master's sighs . . ."

Heroes (true or sham widowers), owners of the Gothic-Doric-Tudor homes, where "things have changed since the mistress died," always appear at first as villains; their unfaithful wives were murdered (usually by other women). They make disturbing first impressions— "I thought him somewhat dissipated, with brown eyes that twinkled ironically"—and their initial treatment of the governess ("Dammit, call me Caleb!") is brusque and "mocking." However, none are ever so insulting as Mr. Rochester was when he called Jane Eyre cold, sick, and silly.

Plots haven't been so impudently prolonged since the search for the will in Wilkie Collins' *No Name.* After "the queer doings up at Greystones" have been established, there is normally only one murder in the past to be unraveled. The heroine stalks among cobwebs, crenelated towers, and headless gargoyles, wrestling with jammed drawers and self-extinguishing lamps. Meanwhile, the wind is accused of pronouncing more names than all the witnesses ever called before the House Committee on Un-American Activities. The supernatural suggestions and the "nameless terrors" of the 19th-century models have been eliminated; the shadow on the blind is revealed as a mad in-law, not a ghost. For a period when sadism is so fashionable, these Gothics are amazingly tame. (Also prosaic: "I have an upset stomach. I thought I'd better not exercise too much.") Hazlitt's condemnation of *The Castle of Otranto* as "dry, meagre, and without effect" is almost apt for these (largely architectural) productions. There are no extrasensory aids as in *The Moonstone,* and few such chilling lines as *Udolpho*'s: "You shall instantly be removed to the east turret." Corpses are rare: "the remains" may consist of an old brooch, or a couple of very clean bones. Publishers have found that predictability certifies success, and—since the covers are so similar—that eager readers may buy the same Gothic twice. Gothics may appeal—as stated in the anonymous "prefatory memoir" to Mrs. Radcliffe's works—at moments "when the whole head is sore, and the whole heart sick." But no one quite knows why this should be an acutely Gothic year; the luxury may be fear made comfortable, long-skirted—and remote.

Hindsight: The spectacular sales of the paperback Gothics dipped in the spring of '67. But they soon revived, and are selling well to date. However, the latest are somewhat more sophisticated: an editor said, "These girls now have feelings below the belt," and it's conceivable that the governess might go to bed with the master of the house. Also, the heroines travel farther: in one recent novel, the young English governess goes to Russia to work for a wealthy family —it's *Jane Eyre* and *The Cherry Orchard.* But the supernatural is still largely avoided in women's fiction (the occult is packaged more for campuses and for the young of both sexes).

Therefore, the wild success of *Dark Shadows* is intriguing because it appears to have captivated both housewives and their teen-age children. In '67, the show acquired a female Phoenix, an emissary of the Devil, and a vampire; later, there were witches, warlocks, and so many apparitions and ghosts that someone observed, "You can no longer tell the living from the dead on this show." The vampire, who was deluged with fan mail, came from the stop-me-before-I-kill school. He hated to bite, but had to do so for his own survival. Since so many people do things which they don't want to, the public seemed to identify with him. According to a colleague, his sad soulful eyes established him as "a reluctant vampire." There was also a repentant werewolf; in his human form, he used to chain himself to the radiator when the moon was full. His fiancée once gave him the last moon-poppy on earth to eat—to forestall his transformation. But it didn't work.

Dark Shadows people also switched identities—by inhabiting each other's bodies—and they made a humanoid of spare parts from the cemetery. (And when he needed a wife, they made him one.) There were 18th- and 19th-century flashbacks (to discover how certain persons became vampires or werewolves), and earlier incarnations of some characters. There was also "parallel time," in which one person could lead several lives at once, as though he were on a series of astral flights. Seances and sometimes the *I Ching* were used to transport everyone back and forth in time; once, they went up to 1995.

The time-traveling solved one of the oldest problems of the soap serial; normally, when a character gets repetitive or boring, he has to be killed off for good. But in *Dark Shadows,* he was just moved back a century or two, or else he was murdered, so that his spirit could roam. The cast was grateful for this steady employment; one actress said, "The only way we stayed on that show was to get killed off."

Dark Shadows died in '71—some think because it had grown too complex. If you missed one installment, you couldn't possibly understand the next one. But it's fondly remembered by many, and was famous for rousing the passions. In '69, a couple in Queens, who had been married for thirty years, fought bitterly because the wife demanded *Dark Shadows* while her husband was watching a very close baseball game: the Mets in the ninth inning against the Cubs, on Channel 9. When she flipped the switch, he killed her. When the producer of *Dark Shadows* heard about the murder, he said that he was grateful that it hadn't been the other way around.

GARBAGE AND RUBBISH
April 1966

GARBAGE DISPOSAL is a passionate subject in New York, even more so since the brief but pungent scandal over buildings owned by the father-in-law of Mayor Lindsay's buildings commissioner (Charles Moerdler), which were found to have ninety violations, including hallways cluttered with garbage, plus what the *Times* daintily calls "dirty conditions." But since the National Academy of Sciences reported that "the average person" throws out 4.5 pounds of garbage per day (increasing at 4 percent a year), and adds that "one person's trash basket is another's living space," there is intensified bickering about the ultimate responsibility for refuse. Some consider that the Sanitation Department, which has a budget of $130 million a year, and is distinguished for its musical band, is meagerly staffed with 14,000 men (10,000 in the "uniform force," which cleans 6,000 miles of New York streets, and removes 10,000 tons of garbage per day). Of course, they service neighborhoods with higher residential incomes far more carefully than they do the poorer districts. However, landlords and janitors must also be blamed for many trash vexations. Middle-income New Yorkers have few problems: rubbish disappears at dawn from outside their doors with a modicum of reproachful stamping and swearing. But a few of the rich and most of the poor have almost insoluble problems with litter.

A characteristic tenement experience concerns a writer who lives in a $50 railroad flat. His landlord provides no cans and no system of disposal (although there is "a real Pinter basement, for which everyone has enormous life-enforcement plans"). So he stuffs his refuse in the Sanitation Department's vast wire street baskets. Since this is illegal, he has been arrested three times. Summonses are served by a pleasant Irishman ("You're a nice man, but I've got something terrible for you"), and arrests are made by an Italian garbage detective. (The Sanitation Department is traditionally Italian.) The detective wears a Gay Nineties frock coat, and drives an elderly lemon-yellow Chevrolet. Grown cordial in their association, they recite some rondo dialogue: "There are no cans." "There got to be." Using someone else's can might be considered grounds for justifiable homicide in New York; also, it's rather pointless to buy one, since cans are constantly stolen, as are the department's baskets.

The writer next goes to what's locally known as garbage court, where his fines range from $3 to $7. Once, he dismantled a striped satin sofa and left the shards on Second Avenue, hoping that the professional rag pickers would remove it. They came at twilight, with their hooks and knives and baby carriages, and tenderly slashed the fabric from the corpse, but left the skeleton, which prompted another arrest. The criminal has tried to defend himself by protesting that the *New York Times* isn't garbage, and by demanding a definition of the legitimate refuse for which the baskets are intended. The answer was: "Anything you got in your hands on the street." He later found his detective crouched inside a huge cardboard box in a local delicatessen; he had a notebook of names and addresses, and appeared to be bookkeeping; the writer now suspects him of graft.

Actually, the Health Code defines garbage as "putrescible waste," i.e., "organic material which tends to decay," while rubbish means papers and bottles. The controversial baskets are strictly for pedestrians. Thus, the *Times* is rubbish when you transport it from your home, but not when an outraged, strolling reader wants to reject some editorial opinion along with his banana peel or gum wrapper. But there is no legal solution for slum residents whose landlords are above contact with trash.

The rich, who inhabit some of our badly designed new buildings, can sometimes regret the privilege. In one ten-room penthouse in the East Sixties, the private incinerator chute is too high (four feet) and too narrow (fifteen inches) to receive waste poured from the can. So the fastidious tenant must deposit his eggshells and coffee grounds by hand. On reopening the chute, which is built at the wrong angle, he finds his trash intact. He must therefore push each individual orange peel down the slant, until he is elbow deep in garbage. Immediately, disgusting smells and smoke rush into his face, soon filling the entire penthouse, which costs $700 a month. He is investigating the private "rubbish removal" companies, but has been unnerved by recent warnings on the radio that unregistered disposal trucks from New Jersey are scavenging Manhattan—possibly operated by the Mafia. Meanwhile, tenants on lower floors of luxury buildings complain of *hearing* all their neighbors' rubbish. Since the communal chutes are built into thin apartment walls, champagne bottles and beer cans hurtling down twenty flights can sound like an execution squad, and the explosion of gin bottles after a late Saturday night party evokes the end of the world.

Naturally, apartment incinerators and the municipal burning of garbage contribute generously to our famous air pollution. While scientists research the acknowledged impairment of "human thought processes" by polluted air, trash-in-orbit becomes a tempting fantasy for New Yorkers. Visions of old shower curtains wheeling through outer space, accompanied by tires, ruined mattresses, blobs of marmalade and everyone's Kleenex, seem preferable to the altercations with slumlords, or inhaling the wreckage from a meal eaten yesterday. Still, there's a mild comfort in remembering that much of New York was built on garbage—as was Venice.

BAD NEWS
Woes of the New York Press August 1966

"THE TOWN was crazy and wide open and full of scandal and uproar; there was no war, no bomb—just a perfectly wonderful murder now and then"—thus, a veteran New York reporter of the Twenties, when many journalists loved their jobs to a degree that is unimaginable now. Until the New Deal switched the national focus to Washington, local New York news "wore the big breeches," crime reporting was considered an art, and competitive papers gleefully published each other's errors—a system that made reporters wary of invention. (One famous lie of the Twenties concerned a giant floating speakeasy outside New York's twelve-mile limit, which was featured in the *Herald Tribune,* and turned out not to exist at all.) Survivors echo *The Front Page* imagery: "the average reporter had a bottle of gin in one pocket and a copy of *The American Mercury* in the other; we were full of booze and trying to think like Mencken."

Yet, surprisingly, some of them think that New York papers have improved. They say that the Twenties nourished too many "whimsy boys," who wrote with biblical simplicity—many of their sentences started with "And." Characteristic of the period was a reporter who wrote up the drowning of two nuns and a child from the point of view of the wave. Robert Benchley remarked that the *World* failed because so many stories began: "Up the dark staircase crept a lonely figure." Divorces got far more space than they do today; even the *Times* gave a lot of attention to the split between Peaches and Daddy Browning. (On their bridal night, Daddy brought along his African honking gander, and he spent most of the night sandpapering a shoetree.) Reporters I know over sixty now praise the number of specialists, especially science reporters; one remembers having to cover "the atrophy of the optic nerve" when his usual beat was Fifth Avenue parades.

Still, there are few other compliments for the New York press— although most experts disagree on the location and the dimensions of each tumor. Flatulence and giantism from the *Times;* noise and newslessness from the *News;* sentimental inaccuracies from the *Post*: our papers don't survive through excellence. The fine feature reporting in the *Wall Street Journal* is naturally limited by space. (I do confess a personal affection for the *Post*'s grab bag of liberal columnists, Earl Wilson, "Man In The Kitchen," Doctor Rose Franzblau, and Mary Worth, and the throaty emphasis on psychology. Of course the casual factual coverage closely repeats the *Times.*) George Lichtheim's meticulous *Commentary* article (September 1965) explored the *Times*'s unfortunate foreign reporting to an extent that has been confirmed by certain young correspondents, who say that they can often expect to be sent to the country about which they know the least.

Equally disturbing are the gaps in local news. Recently, when Democrat Frank O'Connor announced his candidacy for governor of New York, he downgraded Robert Kennedy's party influence while promoting Hubert Humphrey's—a surprising and important position for an ambitious Democrat. Yet, aside from one small reference in the *News,* no New York paper recorded his views—

although they were fully described in the *Los Angeles Times*. A few in the trade claim that news is intentionally suppressed; others cite recklessness and ignorance, also "censorship by omission," and what demoralized reporters call "editorial second-guessing." (There's also the mentality expressed by the new TV term, "produced reality"— which seems to mean a "realistic" approximation of what may have happened.) In the late 1890s, the *Times*'s daily slogan was "It Does Not Soil the Breakfast Cloth"—which still seems more appropriate than "All the News . . ."

As for dullness: when the *Times* ran a long profile of Lindsay's first budget director, Eugene Becker, who happens to be very intelligent and amusing, also a Whistler scholar and a former curator of the Frick Museum—the paper disdained all such material to report that "he stands 5 feet 11 inches tall and weighs 185 pounds," and "for lunch he sends out for a cream cheese and olive sandwich (which he won't eat if the white bread isn't fresh), milk and chocolate ice cream." His politics were totally neglected. Some journalists defensively insist that "colorful" writing is increasing, giving the example that campaign stories often start with a line like "The leaves were falling." Still, one did object: "But they've been falling for at least two thousand years."

While our papers claim to be "independent," it's easy to agree with the late A. J. Liebling that the press is "the weak slat under the bed of democracy." Earlier than some, Liebling analyzed the papers' desperate dependency on advertising. In 1964 he argued that if department stores withdrew their ads from the *Herald Tribune* (which, by its mere existence, did stimulate foreign coverage in the *Times*), that the *Tribune* would fold, and that the *Times* would reduce its foreign news without the *Tribune*'s competition; thus, "the country's present supply of foreign news . . . depends largely on how best a number of drygoods merchants in New York think they can sell underwear." But competition—which Liebling and so many others thought crucial to a healthy news service—is now considered pointless by some, who believe that monopoly ownership results in a "balanced" editorial page, which will include both left- and right-wing views.

Moreover, many young reporters deride the mere concept of competition. First, all New York newspaper publishers, except the *Post,* belong to the same association (the American Newspaper Publishers Association), which bargains as a unit with the unions. Hence all of our papers are economically bound together; they even map out areas of newsstand sales. During the current strike their mutual affection has gone to such lengths that the nonstriking *Times* has kept its distribution below the demand. Second—and perhaps most important—papers rely on public relations departments and press releases for so much of their information that individual reporters don't need to compete by digging for original stories. (Don Marquis complained that the processed handout originated during World War I.) Since the AP and UPI wire services provide so much eagerly repeated material, one expert says that newspapers are now so similar that comparing them "is like examining a warehouse full of anvils." Even stories delivered by the New York AP staff are simply rewritten by New York papers. Third, it's noticeable that curbstone interviews are increasingly conducted by TV (rather than newspaper) reporters: the NBC or CBS men may ask the majority of questions, while the journalists stand back and take notes. Many New York reporters share their beats (especially City Hall and the police department). Those from different papers often fill in for one another, or even wait to phone a story while a rival gets drunk or goes to the bathroom. Hence the diversity of earlier decades is nearly dead.

One former newspaper reporter, who has fled to TV, summed up the general disgust: "We judge newspapers as harshly as our dearest friends. We're fiercer about them than we would be about any other inanimate objects—except maybe cars. But we'd never be so hard on a refrigerator."

Since the Newspaper Guild struck on April 24—in theory, to protect a percentage of staff jobs on the merging *Herald Tribune, World-Telegram & Sun,* and the *Journal-American*—it appears that even more writers will be unemployed than was previously expected. Some are still loyal to the Guild, and most agree that the Guild was needed when Heywood Broun started it in 1933. (However, some reporters of the Twenties scorn the notion of "sending reporters home to their wives." Originally, they worked a six-day week, with no overtime pay. And no story was supposed to be abandoned: "If a ship was sinking, you didn't change your socks for a week." H. L. Mencken protested that "a forty-hour-a-week reporter is no more possible than a forty-hour archbishop.") Later, the Guild included clerks, elevator and phone operators, accountants, ad salesmen, and others, to the degree that its membership is now one-half to two-thirds "noneditorial." (Many of these have little interest in the quality of journalism, but merely in higher salaries.) Quite a few feel that the Guild is murdering the New York press even more swiftly than incompetent editors, wire services, the loss of advertising, and automation itself. Of course TV has the ads and the audience which stopped reading long ago.

Requiem for the World-Journal-Tribune May 1967

NO GRAVE could be deep enough to bury all the accusations for the death of the *World-Journal-Tribune.* Unions, labor disputes, insufficient circulation, diminished advertising, costs of all colors, plus stimulating (and unprintable) rumors of "internal" strife: all were blamed for transforming the starveling paper into a corpse. It will soon be hard to recall the character of a publication which lived for less than eight months.

Inappropriate to the sign of Virgo, the *WJT* emerged on September 12, 1966, as a species of desperation-sandwich. Visually, it most resembled the *World Telegram & The Sun;* the atmosphere was still mainly Hearst's *Journal-American*, while the flaws of the recent *Herald Tribune* were preserved—pseudo-sophistication and the attempt to sound serious while frivolously reporting on serious topics. Between the columnists (ranging from Evans and Novak to Walter Winchell) and feature writers, the thin, gray fact pieces offered little which hadn't appeared elsewhere in the New York press. Three thousand lost their jobs when the papers merged. Of the seventeen hundred remaining, some were forced to switch their fields, which may have accounted for the notable bleakness and insecurity in their writing.

In the paper's first three weeks, storms appeared as the most important world events: Hurricane Inez had the biggest headlines on October 1 and 2 (in smaller type: "Biggest Viet Clash Shaping

Up"; also, "Soviets Walk Out After Peking Blast"). Inez may have been an editorial favorite because her targets were Cuba and the Dominican Republic. But elsewhere, "Typhoon Disaster in Japan" and other storm songs established the *WJT*'s concern for meteorology; it also carried New York's most garrulous weather report. Otherwise, murders received the thickest page 1 headines: SEEK JEALOUS SUITOR OF SLAIN GO-GO GIRL (smaller type for "Hanoi Charges U.S. Plotting Biggest War") on September 30, when the *New York Times* featured the war's worst week for casualties in Vietnam. Previously, the Valerie Percy murder in Chicago had the *WJT*'s main headlines—even after the police had run short of clues. At that point, the headings grew quite desperate: EVERYONE SUSPECT IN PERCY MYSTERY, and there were subheads like A LOVED, FAMILIAR FACE—AND TEARS. Also page 1: IT LOOKS LIKE THE REAL THING (Lynda Bird and George Hamilton). These days, almost any woman called Candy gets a headline—thanks to the Candace Mossler trial as well as Terry Southern. Still, after the *WJT*'s first month, the headlines became slightly more international—perhaps because other papers carried some needling jokes on the subject.

Politically, the paper ranged from "conservative to reactionary," as Liebling wrote of the whole New York press. William Randolph Hearst, Jr., denounced U Thant on Vietnam: "worst of all was his disclosed willingness to accept a peace at any price." Bob Considine announced that "China was enticed—rather than bludgeoned—into trying communism." On the editorial page, only Art Buchwald, Joseph Alsop, and William Buckley continued to sound like themselves; the latter, on "LBJ and the intellectuals," mourned "the unfortunate coincidence between ultra-liberalism and ultra-articulateness. . . . If you can get, say, Richard Rovere, Arthur Schlesinger, Dwight MacDonald, James Reston, and Walter Lippmann to agree on something—and when can you not?—the reading public has just about had it. . . ." One editorial, "Love, the Miracle Drug, Will Lengthen Your Life," balanced nicely with a feature on "A Tasty Trick with Burgers" (olives, pickles, cheese). The *WJT* had no foreign news bureaus—only stringers' reports and wire services. On page 27 of the first issue, "Nuclear Power for Bonn a Delicate Subject in Europe" was a rare bulletin from outer space. As for the average level of Washington news: "Sad LBJ Yearns for Texas

Hills": ". . . the President is unhappy. The Vietnam war and its unwelcome handmaiden, inflation, overshadow all. . . . So, there is general restiveness."

The local New York reporting was frail; there was lots of space for "color," but little for fact. A characteristic shock headline, VIET-NAM WAR COMES TO NEW YORK, disguised a story concerning Congressman Leonard Farbstein's primary victory against Theodore Weiss—which some thought was due to Farbstein supporting the war, while Weiss opposed it (however, the vote was very close). This was by Jimmy Breslin, distinguished for winsome bearishness and first sentences like this: "A bald man was playing the piano loud and the numbers guy sat at a table and drank Remy Martin." Breslin's writing was never better, but readers were disturbed by the lapses of other reporters, who wrote well for the *Tribune,* but later seemed infected by the Hearst style. *Newsweek* noted that the average age of the sports writers was fifty-two.

Unheard stories were scarce, but a few appeared: "Communist Coed Romps At Berkeley" ("Hammer-and-sickle oriented Bettina Aptheker, 22, *is* far too busy being naughty to be nice.") There were occasional originals: "Why Tranquilizers Aren't Used in Riots" —because the dart guns used on animals might kill humans. Otherwise, "How Ginger Rogers Stays Young," or "Is Dreaming a Waste of Time?" kept the pages limp. Factual errors were noted throughout, but the best was the first day's page 1 announcement that Mayor Lindsay pushed the button to start the *WJT*'s presses—when he was actually barred from the pressroom by the Pressmen's Union's president; an unhappy glimpse of the mayor's relations with labor.

Otherwise, space was largely reserved for a sloppy though enjoyable Women's Section; seven gossip columnists (whose bent was hardly salacious: "The Whitneys are remarkable for their complete unstuffiness"); Bishop Sheen ("When a man loves a woman, then it follows that the nobler the woman, the nobler will be the love of a man. . . . The English novelist, John Osborne, says that America is a 'sexual nuthouse' "); *Dear Abby* ("Will a home for unmarried mothers take in a married woman?"); comics, and dozens of shattering jokes, especially from Bennet Cerf: "Q. What city in Kansas is loaded with Peeping Toms? A. Topeka." The Sunday edition had *Book Week,* which had steadily improved under a series of good editors; it was the only really valuable part of the *WJT*. There was also the Sunday *New York* magazine, which contained many excellent ideas for articles; the topics were admirably chosen. But many were kissed off quite superficially, and the style of frantic with-itry made Manhattan sound like a psychedelic toy department. The Sunday gardening section was promising, and had some of the *WJT*'s best headlines, such as "Time To Take Up Tender Bulbs."

In its first month, the *WJT* reported: "AMA Journal Asks Limit On Uniting Severed Limbs": ". . . too many surgeons have been sewing on severed limbs that are better left off. . If a patient has one good leg, the AMA said, the other should not be replanted." At the time, this sounded like wise advice for the three-legged paper. But the *Tribune's* best ligaments were not replanted, and the *Journal-American* remained the stoutest limb of all.

Hindsight: Of course my disdain for the established media is reserved for management; I have abundant respect for many individual reporters, and for the fine pieces which they manage to sneak through.

Magazines are naturally as manipulative of material as newspapers. In 1970, I attended a rebel meeting of some *Life* staffers. The tie clips and well-ironed creases I've always associated with *Time, Inc.* weren't there; amid the jeans and minis, a young man with yellow lace-up flies and Rapunzel hair told me, "Man, this fuckin' place is freakin' out!" (My father, who wrote editorials for *Life* in the mid-Fifties, howled with joy.) However, a mutinous writer later referred to *Life* as "a paramilitary organization." He said that the magazine—which was doing badly—was currently shy of "negative news," and that editors were demanding "cheerful stories about America." Cheer meant "either what the United States was like thirty years ago, or an example of somebody pulling pearls out of the shit." He added, "They want stories about the triumph of the human spirit. But they really mean the submission of the spirit—not beating the system, but finding a way for *Life* to announce that 'the system made this possible.' " Like so many others in the media, some I talked to at *Time, Inc.* felt that their own institution was responsible for acclimatizing millions to the continuation of the Vietnam war, to accepting disguised racism, or sexism—all shaded under the umbrella of liberalism. After all, you can add an upbeat ending to a massacre (how

GIs gave food to those they'd orphaned), or make black militants appear as clowns. Still, a magazine that commissions a feature on a topless anthropologist wouldn't call itself conservative.

In April of '72, *(MORE),* the New York journalism review, brought some three thousand reporters and press-minded persons together at their counter-convention, which was held while the American Newspaper Publishers Association was having their annual meeting, mainly to dissect financial matters. Aside from (*MORE*), there are now about a dozen journalism reviews; the first was the *Chicago Journalism Review,* which was founded after the Democratic Convention of '68, when Chicago reporters saw how inaccurately some of their own papers covered the event.

Although there were many objections to the panels arranged by *(MORE)*—black and women reporters were sparsely represented, and the Vietnam Veterans Against the War were indignant that there was no panel to discuss the coverage of Vietnam—and despite some inevitable guff, the counter-convention was a heartening occasion. It was the first time that so many of us had come together to chew on the problems that reporters have in common. The towering concern was with the mass media's talent for twisting the news, plus the humble allegiance to the views of owners or advertisers. (Incidentally, General Motors is the biggest newspaper advertiser in the country.) Some suggested that journalists should demand editorial control of their publications, as some have done in France and West Germany and England. Newspapers were constantly referred to as corporations which simply protect their own interests. Many spoke of the widening news blackout—the subjects which simply aren't covered—and also about reporters being subpoenaed for their confidential sources: which will make many sources unavailable in future. Some kept quoting A. J. Liebling's reflection that "freedom of the press is guaranteed only to those who own one."

We all ripped our own publications apart, as well as each other's, and the individual reporter's responsibility was underlined. At a panel on the new journalism, Tom Wolfe and Gail Sheehy took some wallops concerning inaccuracy and invention—which didn't seem to bother them. Calvin Trillin expressed some distress that it was no longer a serious criticism to say that a piece of journalism wasn't really true—and that errors which would embarrass a traditional reporter didn't seem to trouble some newer journalists. Pauline Kael objected to "all this personality guck" which is often used in covering political or public figures, and called it dangerous "because then people are judged totally on the basis of their style." Wolfe spoke of the immense amount of legwork that his writing requires. Renata Adler retorted that legwork was no defense: she cited all the hard work that Clifford Irving had put in on his Howard Hughes biography.

Throughout "The Wayward Press Bus," those who follow campaigns were intensely critical of their own work. Martin Nolan, of the *Boston Globe,* stressed that political reporters spend far too much time trying to project into the future, rather than thoroughly covering the immediate past. Jeff Greenfield asked, "Who decides the character of a crowd?" He referred to the press reports that the New Hampshire crowds listening to Muskie were "attentively silent"—before it was acknowledged that they were stupendously bored. Dan Rather of CBS mentioned the reporters who have a vested interest in seeing a candidate win. "A good candidate," who's likely to be elected, "puts *you* on the air a lot." He said that TV "needs a mad dog for every candidate. A reporter who doesn't like him. But the trend's in the opposite direction—reporters who play cosy with the candidate, write a speech for him, give him advice."

Later, Gore Vidal spoke of the *New York Times* as "ten bad newspapers rolled into one"—since so many others have folded. He stressed that "You can't change the press until you change society," and recalled the occasions when he'd been asked not to talk much about politics on TV—although he was perfectly welcome to describe a new book or play of his own. Abbie Hoffman unleashed a Yippie proverb: "Free speech is the right to shout 'Theater!' in a crowded fire."

Quite a few complained that the *(MORE)* gathering represented only privileged persons. A nice, very drunk young reporter told me rather aggressively that I was the first person he'd met who'd written for *Esquire.* I said he must be kidding. "But weren't you ever from the Middle West?" he wailed—a reminder to New York reporters that we take our turf for granted. "I may be drunk, but I'm not wrong!" he cried, and then detailed the curdling confinements of working for a suburban paper; "You think *you've* got problems!"

Again and again, journalists stated that their editors' pretense to neutrality was false: that altering a reporter's material to reflect editorial views was a more distortive act than allowing a reporter to express an opinion. Tom Wicker said, "What we have is the kind of journalism that accepts and projects the *status quo* and official policy," and he condemned "that spurious objectivity on which our editors insist." He struck a common nerve when he said, "We must insist that somehow we have got to be set free to do our best work."

Of course rebels know that they may get fired. In an informal meeting, some discussed the searing question: "How do you protest to your editor without getting on his shit list?" (Pronounced "shit-less," I noticed.) There were references to the punishment of being switched to trivial subjects, "or transferred from Paris to Queens." No one had an immediate solution. As for publishers killing stories due to pressures from the government, Sidney Zion said, "If Agnew kills a story, you go to Abe Rosenthal. If Rosenthal kills a story, you go to Sardi's." Later, reviewing the convention, *(MORE)*'s editor, Richard Pollak, wrote about all the intense bellyaching which is intrinsic to newspaper reporting: ". . . most of it is triggered by the nagging realization that right now, today, in the newsroom in which one is sitting, the talent and energy is available to make a journalism that might not drive one to the nearest saloon at the end of the day."

The great high for many of us was the presentation of *(MORE)*'s A. J. Liebling Award to I. F. Stone. Among his remarks on reporting was a warning not to "over-personify the evils of our time"—not to hang them on a few public figures, but to trace them to the institutions which are responsible. Also: "I think a journalist should be committed—to the big issues of his time. . . . Yet you have to stand slightly aloof—so you can always tell the whole story." Later, someone reversed Lincoln Steffens' phrase about seeing the future: "We've seen the past, and it doesn't work." Stone said, "Facts by themselves don't mean very much. . . . If people's concern for other people were greater, we'd have less of a job. What we're trying to do—part of our job—is to increase people's sympathy for each other."

"Far-*out!*": from an underground reporter behind me. And indeed, amid a crowd which included lots of cynics, sophisticates, infinite ambitions, punchdrunk frustrations, and many who detest each other's work, it was rather astounding that quite a few were there to talk about accountability in journalism.

LEAGUE FOR SPIRITUAL DISCOVERY
December 1966

HUNCHED IN white pyjamas on a low divan, caressing his bare feet to a background of plangent guitars, his hair tangled rather like a crown of thorns, Dr. Timothy Leary welcomed an audience of twenty-four hundred in a former Yiddish vaudeville theater in the East Village. "In the beginning, let us pray . . ." Then: "We know that you know that there is a hunger for more, for more . . ." Pigeon notes have already been detected in his voice; indeed, he sounds like a whole flock of something in St. Mark's Square. His six-week-old religion, sponsored by his League for Spiritual Discovery, is being advertised through a series of psychedelic celebrations, which he says re-create aspects of the LSD experience. Changing kaleidoscopic patterns from painted slides, film, collages, and mime on three layers of scrim accompany Leary's "gospel lectures." Ovarian shapes and visceral suggestions, fractured pinwheels, butterfly wings and ganglia, produce a very appealing brand of visual salad.

Leary's first service was "The Death of the Mind." Explaining that "you've got to die in order to live," he advised the overeducated person to "leave his mind behind," to stop being "caught in thought," and to enjoy the visions which "will come when the biochemistry of your body brings about a state of grace." The boy beside me wagged his head when Leary repeated, "The price of admission is your mind." An actor (who was also a doctor) behind the now scarlet screen mimed the sensation of traveling through his own arterial system— apparently a common LSD fantasy. At one point, he felt that he was drowning in his own blood, while Leary jovially remarked that doctors under acid are particularly prone to this "body trauma," and often think that they're bleeding to death. Cooing praise for "the lattice work of cellular wisdom" and "the chemical bibles of the nervous system," while his disciple was "tumbling down the capillary networks," Leary promised that "protein memory banks are waiting with a million file cards." A successive stage recalls "all the couplings . . . the endless dance of male and female." Twitching chalk buttocks filled the screen: it was strictly a male fantasy. The subject next imagined that he had murdered a girl, and was reproached by Leary in his role as guide: "Didn't I teach you the chess game of life? And how to make a baby smile?" (Earlier, he urged those over forty to look for their guides among their teen-age offspring. He's also prescribed LSD for seven-year-olds, because "children are less entrapped in their minds.") Guaranteeing that he can remove "the delicious pleasure of guilt," Leary showed his subject happily reborn, after "his heartbeat became the pulses of the universe."

Leary described his new League, which has four hundred and eleven initiates. They're trying to legalize acid—but only to be administered by spiritual guides like themselves, for whom "the temple is the body, while the shrine is the home." Admitting that "it's very easy to become a prophet," he explained turning on and tuning in and dropping out. Turning on means "contacting the energy within—turning off your mind—and you've *got* to do it biochemically." Tuning in: "You've got to become an active artist if you take LSD," and express your revelations. Dropping out: cultivate detachment, "get free of ambitions and jealousies." ("Yes, man, yes!" from some of the audience.) But, "These are *not* acts of rebellion—*please!*" My neighbor said, "Awww." Throughout, acid was recommended with almost no reservations; however, in passing, Leary did say that "For every ecstasy, there is terror and paranoia." Finally, soothing mandalas appeared on the screen; Leary advised the audience to remain for meditation—as "a preparation for reentry after rebirth" into the vulgar, commercial world. He then adjourned to the lobby, to autograph copies of his book which were on sale.

Leary made $1,000 at the box office in his first week; he plans that his new religion will be tax-free. "The Reincarnation of Jesus Christ," an "LSD Mass," was the second celebration. Here, the subject "drifted through his respiratory system," and also entered his own body through the center of his own eye. Leary didn't actually say that he was Christ, but parallels were permitted. Acid was called a sacrament, which should only be taken by those in a state of grace; an act of confession before turning on was recommended: "Review all your sins—whatever *you* think you *shouldn't* do—because they will expand under LSD." He paraphrased the Gospels ("I am here to lead the brokenhearted"), and used cinematic litany (repeated shots of Christ), emphasizing images of the Consecration, including the Elevation. His main source appeared to be the Apocrypha. There was a sham police raid in the middle, because Christ (like Leary) is in trouble with the law. A former Catholic, whom I dragged along for my own education, said that these parodies would probably not offend the church—except for the muddled thinking behind them.

Leary is devising fifty-two celebrations, one for worship each week of the year. He promised a Manhattan reading room and discussion center soon. His audience has an air of silent, gleeful confidence: they appear as more of a community than any gathering of reform Democrats. Leary welcomes "skeptics," and there are excellent seats for the press. He does seem like such a showman that it's hard to believe he's sincere. But he must be—to face the fines and jail sentences that are probably awaiting him.

Hindsight: I never had the guts to try acid, simply because I've seen so much suffering among those who've cracked up without drugs. And of course I thought that Leary was an ass. Yet I rather regretted my own fears of acid: I would have liked the rewards without the pain— which, as someone said, is rather like wanting to be Baudelaire without the syphilis. Still, I couldn't flow with the friend who said, "Oh, but the bad trips are the best ones"—meaning the most enlightening. All the agonies I heard about clenched my resistance against those heads who put so much pressure on the unconverted. In '66 and '67 I was also maddened by the political passivity that acid seemed to establish in some, plus all that "groovy revolution" talk which implied that a stoned America would automatically become a benevolent democracy—no more poverty or racism or war, not if we all stay high. (As '69 turned into '70, Leary was optimistically announcing that the revolution had already occurred, even though Washington hadn't yet realized it.) But even in '67, some had already called Leary a bad prophet.

And yet, as one who stops at grass, I've appreciated many of the changes that acid and other expanders have wrought in our culture. And I enjoyed living in the psychedelic society of '67, which affected so many who dwelled far outside it. I learned quite a lot from some who'd taken acid—I can say that their experiences have enriched mine. There's a nice speech from one character in Donald Newlove's novel, *The Painter Gabriel:* "The head culture is passing through the national body like waves of virus, shooting up everyone's imagination—even the imaginations of people who hate drugs. They can't stop its influence anymore than they can stop Coca-Cola ads . . . LSD and pot are . . . rippling over the continent, see, like the first effects of radio earlier in this century. Radio was a consciousness expander. Pretty awful, too!"

As for Leary, I did savor his remarks about "revolutionary chauvinism," after he and his wife had been put under house arrest by Eldridge Cleaver in Algiers, in January 1971. (Four months earlier, Leary had sought the Algerian Panthers' protection, after he'd escaped from jail in California with the aid of the Weather-persons.) As described by Michael Zwerin in the *Villiage Voice,* the Panthers' "revolutionary bust" occurred just before the Learys' first dinner party. Cleaver had decided that acid was destructive to revolution, that Leary's mind had been blown by drugs—"There seems to me to be something very wrong with Leary's brain"—and that both Learys were careless of security, in terms of the "uncool" people they saw and the guests they planned to entertain.

The Learys were guarded and held in custody for more than a week, while Cleaver and Leary exchanged mutual accusations but somehow sounded as though they still rather liked one another. Leary maintained his commitment to "internal revolution" as the precedent for any other revolution: ". . . external revolutions simply substitute armed dictators . . . A change of jailers. Politics really comes down to who controls the jail keys." Leary also told Zwerin: ". . . I've found there is revolutionary chauvinism. People say *my* revolution is the only one. You've got to give up your liberations until I get mine or you may never get yours because your liberation is really reactionary repression. . . ."

Despite the high comedy that Cleaver's arrest of Leary suggested from a distance, both their arguments were strong ones. I suspect that it would have been impossible to side with either exile.

COLLEGE FOR POLICEMEN*
March 1967

VISITING VARIOUS colleges this winter, I haven't yet found that the Berkeley Free Speech Movement has made a wide impact on the traditional eastern campuses; there's some pensive talk about student strikes, but nothing seems organized so far. However, the same old academic discontent seems to be thickening: furious or flatulent professors, students whose courses mean little to them, tired blood, hatred, jargon, and disgust. Many scholars still show the familiar reluctance to discuss their specialties—instead, some flee to ignorance or minutiae: mushroom culture or stamp collecting or vintage engines; it's now known as "the withholding trip." Hence it's rather astounding to discover an institution where a dedicated faculty repeats its praise for the students, while the students' eagerness and progress generates a contagion of cheer. But the John Jay College of Criminal Justice, for policemen, perpetuates a level of morale which some academics would envy.

The college, a senior college of the City University of New York, started in 1965. (Previously, the Baruch School of City College offered some higher education courses for policemen, but a much larger operation was needed.) This is the only college in America—perhaps in the world—devoted to the study and development of the criminal justice system in its entirety. However, the undergraduate program is about 80 percent liberal arts. Fewer police science courses are required than in any other police college in the country. The current degree is a BS; next fall, there will be a BA in criminal justice and an MPA in public administration. Currently, there are about 1,475 undergraduates; the majority are policemen, plus some correction officers and "uncommitted" high school graduates.

Entrance is optional. The students are undoubtedly the most ambitious—and some of the most intelligent—in their profession. At

---

* In the winter of '66 to '67, when policemen still objected to being called "cops," the John Jay College of Criminal Justice wasn't yet referred to by other New York students as "Pig U."

present, a degree doesn't mean promotion. Since all policemen must have high school degrees, any member of the force is eligible. The police are not given time off from their work to study, hence the four-year course takes approximately ten years to complete. (There are quite a few dropouts, but few failures.) Most will graduate at about forty; the average age of the students is about thirty-five to forty. (The professors have taught at Columbia, Princeton, Brooklyn College, City College, N.Y.U., Rutgers, and others. Most are now full-time at the college.) They compare their students to the veterans of World War II: adults whose drive to learn makes them a delight to teach. Also, these students are free from the wandering Socspeak or the garbled language heard so often at many other universities. A policeman will refer to "the whole fishbowl" when an Ivy Leaguer might speak of "a grouping of interrelationships." Speech at this college is notably graphic and lucid, and "dichotomy" or "charisma" are not there to wound the ear. Another scarce word is "cop," which was inspired by the copper shields which policemen used to wear, and also by "constable on patrol." The term is still considered insulting when used by those outside the force.

The college emphasizes education for its own sake, with a minimum of technical courses. President Leonard Reisman said that "the college stimulates the police to find a rationale behind their work." Dean Donald Riddle remarked that the police are a fairly isolated group, which needs to be related to the rest of the species. (Also, policemen who've been to college are found to be less authoritarian than those who haven't.) And, as everyone's noted, the modern policeman is asked to be a lawyer, a clergyman, a psychologist, a linguist, and a neighborhood uncle—a quite impartial soldier who's supposed to be able to act more quickly than the brain itself. Yet their teachers constantly remind them that it's not their role to interpret the law, but just to make arrests. The blend sounds like a recipe for schizophrenia.

While the New York force is still 50 to 60 percent Irish, Italians are plentiful. Hence Catholicism is still dominant. Before 1900, the department was primarily German. Jewish policemen increased right after the war, but there aren't many at present. Now, there's a general shortage of recruits, due to Vietnam. Though the height requirement was recently lowered for Puerto Ricans, few have joined. Black recruits are also sparse, partly because those who are qualified prefer to work in less controversial departments of city service, and especially because black neighborhoods still don't trust the police. I asked all the John Jay students I met why they became policemen, and the vast majority said that they'd had relatives in the profession.

Professor Robert Pinckert's lecture on *Lycidus* included an analysis of the pastoral conventions, Dr. Johnson's abhorrence of the pastoral form, Milton's technique of delaying the verb, the devices of hyperbole, metonymy, and oxymorons, "the visualist fallacy," the controversies about the "two-handed engine," onomatopoeia, and the alternation of pagan and Christian settings. Water imagery was detailed throughout. The professor continued to relate certain themes and facts to his students' experience and background. After asking why Milton invoked "Laurels" at the start—"Yet once more, O ye Laurels"—he said, "How many of you have cooked spaghetti sauce?" Many hands were raised. "What do you put in it?" Chorus: "Bay leaf." On learning that bay is laurel, one policeman said, "It stays green. So that symbolizes immortality?" The professor agreed, and remarked, "When you receive your baccalaureate, you too will be crowned with laurel." (Shy laughter.)

Stressing that everyone needs a fantasy life, such as the notion of the pastoral, Professor Pinckert added, "The American cowboy is to us what the shepherd was to Milton," and then compared Marie Antoinette to the U.S. cowboy—in light of her shepherdess games. Later, when he explained that Memory (Mnemosyne) was the mother of the Muses, he referred to the "Mnemonics" (police code) which all his pupils had studied. (One muttered "Bed pain that triggered first burglary"—a line of police code that sounds like Freudian poetry.)

There was much discussion of the Muses, as well as the concept of inspiration. The line "Return *Sicilian* Muse—" was interrupted: "Hey, they didn't have the Mafia then." During a discussion of river gods, the professor asked why rivers should be characterized as male. A policewoman laughed and said, "Because rivers are dirty!" (Groans from the class.) "And why should the sea be female?" First policeman: "Because it's just there." Second policeman: "Yep, and it's fickle. It keeps changing." The policewoman hissed mildly. Concerning "the mantle blue," the many Catholic students knew that blue is associated with purity and the Virgin. Professor Pinckert innocently added, "You men wear blue to signify your incorruptibility." (There were a few smiles, but not many.)

Literary judgments range from a strong identification with Coriolanus (who also seems like a heroic figure who was "shot down," like General MacArthur or Goldwater), and admiration for Dostoevsky, to a complex reaction to James Baldwin's *The Fire Next Time:* most didn't like it, yet they voted to retain it in the course. Some said that it had no literary merit. They were obviously suppressing their antagonism to the remarks about whites and about policemen. Freud was considered "too old hat"; aside from the familiarity of his sexual theories, his references to religion as an "infantile delusion" are offensive to the police. In examining Camus' *The Rebel,* they distinguished between crimes of passion (which they find more forgivable than others) and calculated or organized crime.

In the drama class there were lively disagreements about Hedda Gabler. One student said she was a sacrificial victim, while others felt that she was the instrument of sacrifice. One said, "Hedda is an unfriendly goddess inserted into a human situation. She holds herself aloof, but she controls and destroys." Another retorted, "Hedda Gabler is everybody's wife." The hair symbolism intrigued them: "Hedda thought she deserved a great bull-mop for herself." One student argued that the play is more of a farce than a tragedy, especially since Lovborg was shot in the bowels. Last year, the drama class performed the Gide-Barrault dramatization of Kafka's *The Trial,* and have been rehearsing Aristophanes' *The Birds* with gusto. (I saw one scene where a gigantic blond with a gun at his hip was declaiming: "Aha, you reckoned without the Muses! Fleet, fleet as twinkling horses' feet. . . . the airy, fairy rumor of the Muses sped to me . . .") In their written evaluations of the course, many policemen said that it helped them in the range of role-switching needed in their own jobs.

The music professor, Milton Schafer (who wrote the music for *Bravo, Giovanni!* and *Drat! the Cat!*), says that policemen are responsive to musical categories because they've already been trained to think in an orderly fashion. Most prefer programmatic music, like Tchaikovsky's *Romeo and Juliet,* but are friendly to Mozart and Haydn. Quite a few students have asked for a specialized course in contemporary music: "They hate it, but they want to know more about it." Still, one term paper compared the street noises of the New York '66 subway strike to "a traffic symphony." The student wrote, "The Rhythm (Flow) of thousands and thousands of cars, bumper to bumper, hour after hour, across the bridges and through the tunnels. The car horns begging the vehicles ahead to move, possessed Tone, the medium of music. Each had its own distinct Pitch, Intensity, Quality and Duration.

"And how was this music listened to? Passively by those in the buildings who were not caught up in its ordered confusion. Emotionally by those suffering through hours of driving. Perceptively by police officers, who knew every sound had a meaning and guided their actions accordingly."

One of the most animated courses is a colloquium; the reading list extends from Shakespeare to Orwell, and includes Bettelheim, Isherwood, and Hannah Arendt. Compared to the languid section meetings at many universities, the energy of these students' arguments was striking. A colloquium on *Catch-22* revealed their profound respect for authority. Many were indignant because the novel satirized a military organization. They felt that a similar burlesque on their department could be "corrupting" and very harmful: "Our uniform is covered with blood and guts and glory, and to mock it—that would be a sin." Only one of them felt that the army and the police force weren't comparable: "You need the absolutism of the military to make these situations valid, plus the jeopardy that the men were in. You need the pressure cooker of your own extinction."

Objection: "But the equivalent of death could be a ruined career, or losing your job in a big business corporation." There was an argument about the nature of satire—where "pure humor" was hotly defended against "the absurd."

"But a few of us could laugh at the military, or at a chaplain, couldn't we?"

"Not many of us."

"No."

Several were distressed by *Catch-22*'s distortion of fact—"Look, *how many* nuts do you meet in any organization?"—although the professor kept reminding them that it was fiction. Most of these men had fought in World War II, and gradually they began to agree that they'd known irresponsible officers. "I knew one who sent a man through enemy fire just to pick up a book he wanted to read."

"Well, what's wrong with that?"

"The book wasn't any good!"

Most policemen support the war in Vietnam. One said, *"Catch-22* is an antiwar polemic. It feeds the One-Worlders and the people who think that peace is the answer to everything." It bothered them that "the youth" like such a "subversive" book—"when they're already bombarded by the liberal influence." One teacher told them that William Buckley had deduced that because fourteen professors at Yale had voted for Harry Truman, education was controlled by liberals.

"Well, it *is* controlled by liberals."

"Why can't we have a book of Buckley's in this course?"

"Aw, we read him anyway."

There was a reference to Norman Mailer:

"Listen, didn't he stab his wife?"

"So that puts a dent in everything he writes?"

"Yeah."

"Listen, he was probably a pacifist when he did it."

In a discussion of responsibility, there was a prickly dialogue:

"Anything that causes death should be eliminated? How about cars?"

"Look, guns don't kill people. People kill people."

"Bombs kill people."

"Yes, but somebody had to drop the bombs."

A professor asked if any of them felt that they'd been subverted by *Catch-22.*

"No. But we're not typical students. The youth of today have such pliable minds."

"The youth of today are just going into a corner and fornicating."

"Well, the youth who aren't well educated won't read it. Even the vocabulary was selected for the intellectual."

"Yeah, those four-letter words are tough."

Finally, most did (reluctantly) agree that criticism of any organization is valid, although one man still held out: "This book undermines authority—it almost makes you feel that authority should be questioned!" In this class, as in others, the professors gently encouraged that idea. Other teachers later said that it's hard for most police-men to challenge their instructors, even when they violently disagree with them.

There are extensive courses in government and law, and everyone must take European history. After delivering a lecture on Louis XIV's centralization of the state, and his suppression of the Hugue-nots, a history professor said that his students are torn between their loyalty to the church and loyalty to the idea of religious toleration. While studying the Protestant Revolution, the police took serious issue with the idea of salvation through God's grace alone, without good works. (In the class I visited, most seemed ill at ease with the concepts of revolution.) The professor added that many policemen are now displaced because of the changes in the church, "and the discomfort shows in their faces when they discuss these subjects."

However, the philosophy professor said that none of the reactions were extreme—or even particularly Catholic—in his Comparative Religions course. When the police study Judaism, Christianity, Islam, Hinduism, Buddhism, Zen, Confucious, and Taoism, "their ability to analyze is more conspicuous than any parochial training." Among philosophers, they do prefer Aristotle to Plato, and many have said that they approve of Aristotle's Golden Mean. The professor re-marked that while his Princeton undergraduates are acquiring a frame of reference to apply to their future experiences, the police already have plenty of experience, but want the frame. Hence, he said, the exhilaration of teaching policemen: "They bring experience in search of interpretation."

Naturally, sociology and psychology are prominent fields at the college. A lecture on "Cognitive Dissonance," in the Social Psy-chology course, focused on persuading someone to change his mind. The greater the pressure, the greater the resistance: "You take a good Democrat, ask him to campaign for Lindsay, and offer him a hundred dollars. He might do it, and while he was repeating the arguments in the candidate's favor, he might come to think that Lindsay's a good guy." (Guffaws.) "But if you offer him a thousand dollars, he'll probably do it—for the money—but he won't revise his views. Excessive pressure—money *or* threats—means that a person is *less* likely to change his mind." The professor paid a joking tribute to the mayor, and a student said, *"You've* just gone down the drain."

Especially since the attempts at a Civilian Review Board, Lindsay is disliked by the police. Also, he recently made the diplomatic error of saying that sanitation is more "hazardous" than police work.

The professor explained ego-defenses and the rationalizing process which make "dissonance" more bearable, and dislikable situations easier to live with. For example, people may decide that something they don't like is good for them; they may reason that an unpleasant diet has lots of vitamins. He said that a person's attitude can be changed for a short period, but that it's very hard to change it permanently—and gave the example of racism. He distinguished between "compliance" (which is most common in a military organization, since rewards and punishments are controlled by an established figure), "identification" (which occurs when people want to be accepted members of a group), and "internalization" (a personal belief or one acquired from someone you trust and respect). An attitude altered by compliance won't last—as soon as the authority figure turns his back, the attitude disappears. Identification continues as long as there are good relations with the group. "Internalized" beliefs persist as long as they're relevant to situations. Naturally, all three states can coexist. This thesis led to a discussion of Catholicism and communism. The students agreed that very few Catholics "defect," but that many lapse, and they asked lots of questions about mind changing.

Few policemen liked the idea that people may reverse or modify an intense conviction. One asked rather wistfully, "Isn't there an absolute value system?" The professor's *"No"* was powerful. The students liked his example of the rationalizing process: "Say you've been in the precinct for a while, and then you're promoted to a seat in a radio car. Then you make a blooper, and you're sent back to the street. So you say, 'I was getting too fat, I'll lose some weight walking the beat.' " There was a lot of rueful laughter at that one.

A visitor to the college can momentarily forget that these students of polyphony or poetry work steadily among people who may kill them. While the police are ingesting liberal arts, they're studying their own craft. In a police science course called The Principles of Investigation, taught by an expert, a lecture on the subtleties of "interviewing" showed how very skilled a practitioner must be. The lecturer warned against calling witnesses "friendly" or "hostile";

"cooperative" or "uncooperative" are preferable psychologically. (The printed outline for this topic includes "The Jekyll-Hyde technique," which recommends using a mild approach before a harsh one. The latter "may alienate the subject permanently," or he may feel that it's synthetic.) Later: "Emphasize the impression that you are not concerned with conviction or punishment. It is your duty only to learn what happened." "Giving him rope" is considered the best technique: "If a story is sufficiently involved, it's probably impossible for him to keep it straight." *Outline:* "(a) Consider that it will be impossible for him to lie consistently. (b) If he tells a phony story, let him talk. (c) Subtly have him repeat the key lies. . . ."

A "standard problem" is the "code against informing." It was repeated again and again that the subject must never be threatened. People sometimes admit to something they didn't do, because it's easier—as in the case of traffic offenses. And there are numbers who are sufficiently disturbed to make false confessions. Another problem is the man who denies his guilt—when no one thought he was guilty. An irate citizen who makes "empty threats" at the police—"I'll have you transferred to Staten Island!"—may be showing symptoms of guilt rather than innocence.

In the "psychological battle" of confession, the detective may depend on a person's sense of guilt to make him feel uncomfortable: "A hardened criminal can have a keen sense of right and wrong." But he must be caught off guard. Moreover, "If we present ourselves as the forces of retribution, it won't work. You can't behave like Cotton Mather. Instead, present yourself as a bridge between him and society." Also: "You must have great self control not to express the revulsion that you feel towards certain criminals." And it's important to treat the wife and family well.

Timing is crucial: "When confronted with evidence, he'll often do the wrong thing. We want to capitalize on the fact that he'll be groping at straws." The "psychological stamina" of the professional criminal was acknowledged: he has been interviewed before, and he may feel quite confident of the detective's limitations. (The outline mentions "Friendly Forces Reduced," during the period when the suspect should be brought "to perceive confession as the path to freedom.") The danger of the whole process was automatically admitted; throughout the imaginary confession scenes, there was the possibility that the subject might pull a gun or attack. But the teacher renewed his warnings about the intricacies of assessing guilt. He stressed that innocence is often bewildered, rather than vociferous or righteously indignant.

The police are fiercely sensitive about their reputation. They feel quite persecuted, and want to talk about it. Some kept asking me, "Are you going to write about police brutality?" In an advanced speech course, a brisk student panel examined the new Supreme Court decision on confessions. Henceforth, the police must inform a suspect that he has the right to legal counsel before making any statement.) The panel echoed with the words "hampered" and "hindered." There were many respectful references to the original Constitution and "the intentions of the Founding Fathers." Some were perturbed by the idea of amendments: "I don't think our forefathers meant to make the kind of laws we have today." Their intense moralism—"It would really shock me if a criminal went free" —appeared as strongly in this class as it does in others. It was clear that these particular policemen really want the public to obey the laws.

However, the delicate question of confessions was freely sifted.

"Do you think we actually railroad a guy?"

"Well, we all know what methods we've employed. We do sometimes elicit enforced confession. I know that I wouldn't want it done to me—what we do to some guys. The Supreme Court decision hinders me as an officer, but I approve of it as a citizen."

There was angry talk about the policemen whose malpractices blacken the reputation of the whole Department: "Maybe some of us are slow to learn. But we all pay the price for officers who make mistakes."

A panelist elaborated: "We've been taught how to make a person break down psychologically. I'm a very strong person psychologically myself. But some people aren't. And we're trained to recognize mental defectives." He added, "The forced confession is the fruit of the poisoned tree."

Emphasizing that "our function is to detect crime and arrest it —*not* to prosecute," they concluded by approving the Supreme Court decision—with no enthusiasm whatsoever.

"Everyone loves a fireman—but they don't love us." Unpopularity was considered by another group. Some seemed unwilling to admit that racial hostilities are related to the reputation for brutality; however, there were unhappy remarks about being disliked in Harlem. (There's a powerful reluctance to discuss anything to do with race. One professor said that the police are controlling strong negative feelings—as they've been told to do.) Some thought that the automobile was "the greatest single reason for being disliked": due to parking tickets and arrests for traffic violations. They explained that everyone associates the police with punishment: "We're not condemning people personally, we're condemning their *acts*. But they do take it personally!" And: "Sure, nobody likes to be arrested. We're a public animal—we're supposed to keep traffic moving, catch criminals, and stop noise. But people want these things applied to others, not themselves. You don't want your son jailed, just someone else's."

Almost every man present had been bitten by a woman. Apparently, female assaults on policemen are the highest for any group. One officer added, "There was this five-foot-two, two-hundred-pound woman. I arrested her for stabbing her girl friend and also for biting me. You know, I had to have tetanus shots and blood tests for syphilis? But she only got charged for 'attempted disorderly conduct.'"

Asked to define a liberal, the class finally agreed on "obstructionist." "Someone who's more concerned with the rights of individuals. Whereas policemen are concerned with the rights of the group." "Yeah, a liberal tries to make your job harder, to erect roadblocks. He wants to make the laws more lenient." One said, "We *can't* be a semimilitary organization—that's like having a semi-leakproof pail." Yet self-criticism was constant. Several later said that they would like to work unarmed for certain assignments, and that they regretted having to carry guns off duty.

Due to President Johnson's crime commission—and many citizens' nervous systems—the pressure on policemen will be intensified, and the FBI has said that serious crime has increased by 11 percent in this last year. For these New York police students, it's obvious that the college expands their judgment; coincidentally, they're receiving a very fine education.

Hindsight: A month after I wrote this piece, I saw some of the John Jay students patrolling the huge antiwar march of April 1967.

Even a couple who'd made indignant remarks about "the youth" were beaming and nodding at the marchers, channeling them carefully through traffic and letting the crowd fan out where it wanted to. From seeing them in action, I felt that a lot had indeed been learned and taught at the college—even if these particular men were just controlling their feelings and putting on an amiable act.

Since then, since many of us have acquired a bitter mistrust of the police, one's more concerned than ever with the training that they're given. The intensely moralistic views which I heard from so many seem to make them oddly vulnerable in a period of changing values. Since the Knapp Commission has revealed such gigantic proportions of graft, I wondered if cynicism came most easily to former or knee-jerk authoritarians.

Small wonder that the police are confused, especially since some revolutionaries, who claimed to revere the working class, forgot that policemen are workers too. In January 1971 there was a six-day wildcat strike of twenty thousand policemen demanding better salaries. When police union leader Edward Kiernan urged them to return to work at a Patrolmen's Benevolent Association meeting, some young cops yelled "more gutter language than is heard at protests that cops are usually called on to maintain order at," according to the *Daily News*. We also saw photographs of young cops raising their fists and shouting slogans. A *News* editorial called the strike "an adventure in anarchy more fitted to radical riffraff than to men whose sworn duty it is to uphold the law." To the strikers' demands for amnesty, the *News* replied, "Amnesty, nothing."

In *Revolutionary Notes,* Julius Lester remarked that some apparent enemies must also be regarded as "victims" of the system. "All too often . . . we confuse the doer with the deed and think that they are one and the same. It is the deed we must hate, not the doer of the deed. The policeman acts like a beast, but to call him a beast, a 'pig,' is only to negate the potential of man that is within him. . . . To yell 'Fascist!' at a Wallace supporter is only to guarantee that that individual will be a fascist."

In May of '72 I went back to John Jay to ask Professor Robert Pinckert how the college had weathered the last five years. He spoke rather wistfully of '67—"It was an academic paradise then"

—and said that morale had held through '69, despite bomb scares and threats of disrupted classes, which came mainly from other students in the City University. Since then, morale had sagged.

In 1970 Open Admissions changed John Jay from a small criminal justice college to a senior college of CUNY—with a severe lack of space. Some felt that John Jay simply took on too many students. (From some 1,500 in '67, it rose to about 5,500 students, although it then decreased to 4,900.) The cops, who were once a 90 percent majority of the students, dwindled to 40 percent. The new young students hardly have the same frame of reference as the police, and some teachers find it hard to devise lectures or courses that can be understood by both groups. Professor Pinckert said, "No, I couldn't give the same lecture on *Lycidus* now." (However, he said that he uses New York as a frame of reference, and has related it to *The Inferno.*) Free debate has diminished: "In every class, there's a certain amount of brass—lieutenants, captains, inspectors—and that tends to stifle discussion."

While race is rarely mentioned, the bathrooms have flowered with graffiti, ranging from "Fuck you, Whitey"/"Same to Niggers," also "Black/White Power" (both crossed out), and more elaborate retorts: "Nixon Masturbates with a Paper Towel"/"Thank the Lord For Such A Good President." "Right On, Spiro!" is frequent.

Professor Pinckert said that the cops are no longer so moralistic in class. "They have their tails between their legs, but they still won't admit that cops can err. . . . But the moralism you heard five years ago was genuine, sincere. Now they're shakier, and resent it.

"Some cops are cynical after they've been on the force for a month. They're fed a lot of mickey mouse stuff in regular training —about how great it is to be a cop. The word corruption is *never* mentioned. Then they go to the precinct, and find that everyone's on the take. That's where the cynicism enters—and all that basic training goes out the window. The few who are still idealistic put up defenses. Graft is just denied. And if a man has a guilty conscience, he'll become more vehement in the pursuit of criminals."

There's a big waiting list of those who want to become policemen. Applications have soared in the last couple of years, especially from veterans returning from Vietnam. Many more blacks have applied, but Puerto Ricans are still very wary. White cops are now complaining about the number of blacks ones, and insisting that they're getting special treatment. Meanwhile, John Jay works no less than ever on humanizing the police, and their graduates are rising higher in the department; these are probably its future administrators.

Professor Pinckert reports that the policemen he knows so longer believe in Hell, though they're still 80 to 90 percent Catholic. However, there's still a vague belief in Heaven. During his class in *The Inferno,* the cops said that they were sorry to see homosexuals in Hell. Then several added that they wouldn't want to see Hitler there either. He asked if they believed in universal redemption, and most said no. He pressed them harder, and they expressed the hope that people "would somehow be cured"—and *then* "get to heaven." Professor Pinckert said, "The social sciences have won! Everyone's going to get cured." One wonders if his students could ever equate redeemed criminals and policemen involved in the traffic of heroin.

HARASSING TENANTS
July 1967

NAIVETÉ AND stoicism are not normally characteristics of New Yorkers, although fatalism may be. A recent page 1 story in the *New York Times,* recording the "harassment" of tenants, need not have been written in tones of wonder, since the violence detailed is a familiar pattern throughout the city. (It's true that real estate is a passionate subject here; visitors are often startled by the native compulsion to discuss it with emotions usually reserved for sexual excitement or frustration—or for war. In June, six hundred landlords rioted and threw rocks outside City Hall, protesting rent control.) The *Times* article described how tenants were driven out of some buildings on West 65th and 66th Streets, between Central Park West and Columbus Avenue—where property values naturally exceed the rents—through the talents of a possible "building breaker." One of the arts employed was introducing new residents:

drug addicts, homosexuals, prostitutes, and alcoholics, who entertained themselves by smashing windows and the contents of tenants' apartments. A community worker was severely thrashed and received a broken nose, a tenant's five-year-old daughter was told "You're real cute. How would you like it if I beat you up?," urine was poured through a ceiling, while most building services ceased. A dead dog was placed in an empty, doorless room, so that the stench was universal, and there were convenient fires in adjacent buildings.

A luxury apartment house, a school, and an office building are planned for this site. When tenants are so speedily expelled, money is saved on slow eviction and sums for relocation. The real estate agent, a vice-president of Pease & Elliman, one of Manhattan's most powerful firms, denies all connection with the former building manager whom the tenants blame for their experiences. The manager, who is finally being investigated by the city, feels that he's being persecuted: "I'm a pretty good guy. I got a lot of people out of that slum of an environment." He has also unleashed a cri de coeur appropriate to any antihero: "If there's anybody that's been grossly abused in this, it's been me. Everybody likes to look for the underdog. And then they step on him." The *Times* adds that "the city has not yet determined the validity of the tenants' complaints." Still, it's a rare feat to capture the interest of New York's Department of Buildings, which often responds to pleas for help with promises of forms to fill out, which don't arrive, and inspectors who never appear, courteous letters noting that "attention will be paid to your allegements," and phone calls which end gleefully: "That's not *my* department."

These West Side tenants had rent-controlled apartments; they were welfare clients, old and "Spanish-speaking" people. Their dilapidated dwellings seem to cost about $60 a month. But parallel experiences occur at all economic levels. Last year, a middle-income building on East 80th Street was sold to an executive from Lever Brothers, whom the tenants considered "respectable." He was persuaded to hire an "agent," who resembled a bantamweight boxer. Knobs vanished from the front door and lightbulbs disappeared from the bathrooms, and the toilets were blocked by rolls of toilet paper, the door lock was repeatedly jammed with a match stick. Mail was obstructed, and phone calls after one A.M. shattered tenants' sleep. Garbage cans remained in the halls in summer, with sickening results. A vacationing postal clerk returned to find his door battered down and all of his possessions in a city warehouse; another man's belongings were strewn down three flights of stairs. The janitress and her son used to wait with a chair leg and a baseball bat to confront the agent, who finally told the son, "I'm going to cut your guts out," and delivered a corkscrew punch that left a faceful of abrasions.

Meanwhile, the new owner professed distaste and dismay at such reports, and the city agreed that it was all deplorable. Eventually there was a hearing, at which the owner sighed and said, "I think our problems are all semantic. If only we can just get together, like ladies and gentlemen, and talk this thing out." Right after the (useless) hearing, the agent bored multiple holes in the roof during a torrential rainstorm, so that three apartments were flooded. Finally, the janitor's possessions were thrown into the street, and all the tenants departed. A resident writer, who kept a daily log of these events, said that the technique was to intensify the abuses so rapidly that all previous complaints became obsolete. The vacant building is now once again for sale; having declared "the intent to remodel," the owner can now resell most profitably without having made any renovations.

Friends sometimes urged me to seek psychiatric aid when I used to rave about my landlord. In fact, my landlord was a psychiatrist, who had worked at Bellevue. My former building, a charming carriagehouse on East 75th Street, used to be rent controlled. Early in '67 it entered the category of luxury housing: some of the 1½-room apartments went up to $250 a month. In the last five years, the doctor has harassed his tenants so imaginatively that neighbors call them "the inmates": their rolling, red-veined eyes, convulsive speech, and trembling limbs are cured only upon their release from the doctor's care. (We used to say, "If he does this to his *tenants*, what's he doing to his *patients?*") His specialties include forged leases (either to shorten a tenancy or in order to sue someone for rent who has never lived in his buildings), suing almost every tenant for imaginary damages (including three invisible rats, for which he wanted to fine the tenant $100 apiece), and making unwanted renovations or decorations while tenants are away on weekends—especially erecting wooden sleeping balconies which look like lions' cages at the zoo. (These necessitate crawling to bed on all fours, and cracking your head against the ceiling when sitting up.) It's a psychic shock to find such fire hazards constructed in your absence, with plaster smeared over everything you own, and then to be given a vast bill. But this has happened to many of the doctor's tenants.

He likes prowling through empty apartments, disarranging private papers, stealing vacuum cleaners, and gouging unexplained holes in the walls and floors. (In some cases, the holes had "something to do with insulation," or "trying to see if there's a chimney behind this wall.") As one tenant said, "He makes these insane raids on your home, and the nice middle-class suckers who live in these buildings can't believe it's happening." He has also permitted his friends to use several tenants' apartments for making love; scars of fornication greet the returning traveler. He frequently enters at midnight or at seven A.M., when residents are naked or asleep; the usual excuse is that he "has to measure": an operation which means extending his arms as though crucified and then slowly pacing sideways across the floor. He also rents apartments which aren't available; when the new tenant arrives with his furniture, he finds that the home for which he's paid some advance rent contains a previous resident with a substantial lease, who never planned to move. Money is not returned on these occasions.

Understandably, this landlord encourages a brisk change of tenants, since a higher rent can be charged every time. But a few apartments are still controlled, and others are much cheaper than the majority. Hence the acceleration of his onslaughts: sudden bellowings through the doors, threats of all colors, promises to "ruin" property. One woman (whose twenty-five-year tenancy infuriates him) has been assaulted: he banged her head against the wall, has waved his gun at her, and once fired shots in her presence. So far, his practices have failed to intrigue the city, even though most of his former tenants, like myself, have reported his actions again and again. While there's no law to protect you from psychotics, his (hardly legal) activities have been called "unclassifiable" by the Department of Buildings—especially since two of his buildings are decontrolled.

For a municipal government where officials are always available for press conferences, time is scarce when small groups ask for aid or protection. The lush vines of bureaucracy strangle many organized (or agonized) efforts to appeal to the city. Perhaps people are even more vulnerable in their housing situations than in their professions. The threat of being roofless, with possessions on the pavement, can reduce the most resilient persons to feeling like human debris. Admittedly, the mere concept of home is a perishable luxury in this city. It's said that rents have increased by 200 percent in the last ten years. Unable to find apartments that they can afford, many New Yorkers settle for dwellings they dislike, which quite a few can then expect to lose.

Hindsight: As of 1972, my former landlord is still thriving, even though many ex-tenants like myself have given evidence against him, and we've heard that there's a file on him in Mary Lindsay's office. (Some of us also used personal pull, through friends in the Lindsay Administration, but it had no effect.) He now owns at least eight buildings, from the Village to upper Yorkville, and is thought to own quite a few more. Indeed, he has become quite famous; strangers tend to shriek and jabber when they learn that they have him in common. Due to this landlord, some liberal tenants voted against Lindsay in '69, just because of the uselessness of the City's Housing and Development Administration.

This ballad would be incomplete without the voice of a landlord. What follows is one of my favorite New York documents: a 1970 letter from a landlord to a tenant who had organized his neighbors into signing a petition which detailed the deterioration of their building. They rather liked this landlord personally, and were merely concerned with the disintegration of a very fine old apartment house.

Dear Mr. X,
    Please be advised that anybody can make a petition, and the flock will follow to sign up.
    You seem to forget that we are under Rent Control and Rent Stabili-

zation. Under these statutes, a landlord is required to perform only essential services. I have always co-Operated with my tenants, but my tenants do not and never have co-Operated.

Trash cans and lids are provided on every floor. I have ordered my porters to make sure they will be there, but you must also remember that a lot of tenants live like pigs and throw the garbage out of the cans, thereby causing the garbage areas to be filthy at all times. We do not make the halls dirty, the tenants do.

When the weather is inclement, the streets are muddy. The tenants do not wipe their feet on the mats and bring the mud into the building. We cannot follow the tenants with a mop.

Hot water and heat are provided at all times, except when a boiler is out of order. A radiator that does not function properly is the fault of the tenant. It should never be turned off because when it is, the water condensates in it and makes it difficult for the heat to come into it.

We use the best exterminator in the city (Sameth Exterminating Co.). If we could get rid of the dirty and careless tenants, the roaches would go elsewhere.

Let me fill you in on a few of these objections. Under Rent Control, I cannot afford uniforms for our elevator men. Our men are as nice as you can find anywhere. They do their work properly. This building is too nice for many of the tenants that have signed this petition. I will point out some of these tenants to you.

[There follows a list of more than twenty tenants, listing their rents and some of their professions. The landlord rather bitterly notes that several "earn their living by teaching voice in their apartment," and he's outraged that some of them "signed the petition twice." Of one tenant, he wrote, "Did you ever notice the slop he brings into the building. Thank God he will be out by March 31."]

If these tenants lived in slum buildings in Harlem or Bedford Stuyvesant, they would pay more rent than they pay now. What have they got to complain about. This building has been upgraded many times in the last twenty years.

Let me sum up and give all my tenants a piece of my mind. If they force any of these issues, I will put in self-service elevators and really let the building go downhill and unattended. With a self-service, this building will have only a superintendent and a porter. At present, we have no superintendent, and are endeavering to get a good one. Forty per cent of the tenants are living practically rent free and should be happy to live there.

The Laundry room is too well equipped, and is running at a loss

on account of the carelessness of the tenants who can't get enough for
25¢ and overload the machines, thereby causing them to break down.
No building of this size has so many breakdowns. If the practice does
not stop immediately, we will dispense with this Laundry room.

Dogs and cats are permitted to mess the halls, lobby and entrance.
You can't blame the dogs, but put the blame on whom it belongs,
the filthy tenants.

Mr. X, you are the leader. As the leader, why don't you call a
meeting of all the tenants and put the responsibility where it belongs.
That is the only way to improve the building. We are doing more than
our share.

We cannot afford a supervisor. If all the tenants will co-operate,
no further supervision will be necessary.

Sincerely,

Z———

GO WITH THE FLOW
Diggers and Their Friends in New York July-August 1967

PINWHEELS ERUPT, mutate themselves, red blurts into blue: any
galaxy of psychedelic lights is a valid image for the new consciousness, which can't be captured by the panting media nor the earnest
sociologist. Still, among the oozing diversities of hippie phyla, pliant
as plastic foam, the Diggers emerge with some perceptible traits.
Named for the 17th-century common-land cultivators, they evolved
from the San Francisco Mime Troupe about two years ago; there's
now a New York chapter. Their philanthropies have caused comparisons to the Salvation Army—"But we don't make anyone sit
through religious services!" Their Free Store, crammed with books,
clothes, and furniture that's collected by "going garbaging" at night,
has only one rule: "You Can't Steal." Free stew is dispensed every
afternoon in Tompkins Square Park, and a Digger sweep-in cleaned
up a startled neighborhood. Diggers collected and distributed a
truckload of food after Newark's riots—noting that canned food
was preferable, since it could also be used as a weapon and thrown
at the police. However, the Diggers have quite amiable relations

with their local East Village precinct officer, Captain Fink. When he heard someone say "Fuck the cops," he asked if it meant loving the police.

Runaways in their early teens are now a national anxiety; the New York Youth Board suspects that there are usually about four thousand under eighteen in the city, perhaps half a million in the whole country. While there are rescue societies for lost dogs, there's no equivalent for humans. New York is absorbing in a dual sense: aside from its fascinations, it absorbs strays to a merciless vanishing point, rendering their afflictions and their very existence unknown —as though they had fallen through the cracks in the pavements. The youngest runaways are often sexually abused and exploited, made to hustle or turn tricks, as they grow more and more desperate for food and shelter.

One Digger, who said he'd found some four hundred runaways sleeping in Tompkins Square Park, formed the East Side Service Organization—motto: ESSO—IT's A GAS!—to take runaways off the streets and to find beds or jobs for them. The Diggers also ran an ad in their newspaper: "Buddy, Can You Spare a Bed?" There are rules—"No balling of chicks"—and selective screening to see who's capable of staying with strangers. Runaways spring from all economic contexts, many from homes so brutal that it would be futile to advise them to return—although the Diggers suggest sending postcards. They want to renovate an old hotel for a runaways' dormitory. The city hired—but then fired—some Diggers for this project, which they hope to continue on their own.

The Diggers agree that the East Village attracts many ravaged waifs, who want drugs but aren't "conscious hippies." So the Diggers have kept an eye on certain "transits' communes"—such as one recently abandoned by a head called Galahad, which became so famous for amphetamines and syphilis that the Diggers asked the Health Department to close it. They also urge the organization of workshops to educate parents about drugs, and are trying to establish a free medical clinic, plus free legal aid services, in their neighborhood. Free schools—bred of disgust with public education and the Digger practice of "pied pipering" (teaching children Digger values, telling them to reject straight jobs: "Don't do anything a machine can do")—are starting in many parts of the country.

Some thirty $1 bills floated down to the floor of the New York Stock Exchange, flung by Diggers who were miming "the death of money." Stockbrokers, clerks, and runners on the floor blew kisses and cheered, while others shouted angrily and shook their fists, until the dollar-deriders were hustled out. The point was to give the dealers "some real money," instead of coupons and stock certificates, and to ridicule the entire Western economy. Often, the Diggers hand out "free money" at their events. Well nourished in theatrical history, they've swiftly developed their concept of street theater. It's the recurrent tradition of dealing directly with the audience, with no division between actors and spectators, plus an opportunity for everyone to participate. Naturally, spontaneity is cherished, but each performance has a purpose that happenings lack. Some of their street scenes are an improvement on some of Off-Off-Broadway's random audience touching, and the tedium of many happenings—just as the best media mix is a huge advance beyond many scrambled but boring underground movies of the mid-Sixties.

The Diggers' games sprinkle absurdity over whatever they protest. Con Edison, distinguished for pollution, and constantly rebuked by City Hall, was recently deluged on Black Flower Day: the Diggers brandished a sign reading "Breathing Is Bad For Your Health," presented executives leaving their offices with begrimed daffodils, and then threw soot on their white summer suits. The Diggers next set off smoke flares which stained the building responsible for soiling so much of New York. Protesting the despotism of traffic, some of the same crowd blocked St. Mark's Place for about half an hour, chanted some Hare Krishnas, and then polished the windows of the waiting cars. Later, they planted a (quickly uprooted) tree, passed out five hundred free cups of strawberry yogurt, and had a street dance.

Admittedly, this society hardly comprehends its clowns, especially those who marry protest to fantasy or burlesque. "Unpredictability is beautiful!" But parodies aren't always understood.

The Diggers and their friends live in what they call "intentional communes" (as opposed to crash pads), where they share the rent from their earnings from part-time jobs or making beads or painting posters. One "closed" commune, called The Family, was supported by a long-haired computer analyst. Another is the Group

Image, which has an acid rock group which has made $2,000 per week in uptown discothèques. It has thirty or forty members; referring to Christ's robe, one said, "The Group Image is a seamless garment!" (In California, there's a legendary tribe of water sharers, inspired by Robert Heinlein's science fiction novel, *Stranger in a Strange Land*. Members share each other sexually, and jealousy and possessions are forbidden.)* In some communes, people choose the roles of mothers, fathers, or children. "Sure, there are some middle-class problems of authority—like who does the dishes. But you can't be rigid. People still need some privacy, need possessions —even like just a hairbrush." But of course the code is collectivism. "The idea of individuality is baloney. Collective energy is so much greater than any one person's, and even mediocre people can do more when they're together in a group." Solitary egos aren't admired; the goal is "collective ego." Since the waxing population forces everyone to live more closely together, the "Good Vibrations" that the Beach Boys sang about are considered more important than ever. (Also, when someone's very upset by a bad trip, his tribe may may start omming until he joins in, is forced to merge with the group, and is eventually made to feel better.) Diggers feel that people must take care of each other, particularly during spells of limbo, when someone "needs to be freaky." Of course the styles in intimacy have titillated the press. However: "So many people think we're acting out their fantasies! But lots of us are shy, or lonely, just needed to come together. . . . Some kids have to feel quite desperate in order to join us—desperate about all the lies in this country, the double standards. But dropping out is hard. You almost need a death wish to drop out."

In New York, there was a tribal council (now disbanded but quite likely to regroup), where leaders from many tribes sat in an Indian circle, each addressing himself to the center, debating such problems as what kind of school to form, and—most urgently— "How do you protect yourself from being seduced by uptown?" A young man pondered the difficulties of maintaining an avant-garde— since the media makes everything so public. "Now we're all acting

* *1972:* We heard quite a bit about them in New York, but no names were mentioned. Now I wonder if it was Charles Manson's tribe. Ed Sanders and others have documented the influence of Heinlein's book on Manson.

out the myth created by the media." Meanwhile, many musicians and painters have been scooped up by the commercial world which they thought they wanted to reject. Hence they've already dropped out of the new society which some have hoped to build.

However, despite the collective efforts, the Diggers insist that no one must impose his will on anyone else. The familiar dictum has been amended to: "Do your thing—until it encroaches on some-one else's thing." "See, you can't *make* a cop take your flower—you can't *force* it on him." In the inscape of Things, everyone has a talent, from painting to driving trucks or having babies—or just being.

It's cheerfully admitted that most flower persons came from middle-class families. (Voluntary poverty could hardly appeal to blacks, nor to anyone born too far outside the system to be able to reject it.) Quite a few who now live in the East Village are civil rights dropouts, especially those who were disillusioned about voter registration. You hear a lot of remarks like: "Marxism sounds like a groove, but Russia is just a drag." They dislike the Vietnam war, but don't want to talk about it. "We don't know what to do about Vietnam or Harlem. But people must be turned on to themselves. Politically, a be-in is more meaningful than picketing." Still, they're amused that a statement like "Fuck it, I just want to be beautiful" can alarm a politician.

In the communes, those "clusters against meaninglessness," acid has been called "a binding substance." One young man added, "The whole process of growing up here is desensitizing. You have to peel off layers, and the easiest and quickest way is drugs. Drugs are more easily assimilated by someone of fifteen than somebody twenty-five. But you don't *have* to take them." Many feel that acid makes them more patient and tolerant. "Oh, maybe you can call it a synthetic or artificial feeling of nonaggression. *After* acid, people can have that feeling naturally. Acid makes them *think* they have confidence. Acid can be the biggest copout *or* very help-ful." At any rate, the Diggers I encountered had such good manners that sulky waitresses in the restaurants where we met brightened up and gave us excellent service, even though one was freaked out by a Digger's complaint about the menu: "It's too linear."

I noticed that some who've dropped a lot of acid do speak very slowly indeed; also, although they were perfectly willing to talk to me, it took them a long time to decide where and when to meet: these decisions seemed immense. One initiate explained that the chief problem that arises under acid is choice: "It appears as though perception is a ladder." So, if a friend says, "It looks like a good day today," every factor must be considered before replying: is it *really* a good day? What's "good," anyway?

Also, this world mistrusts words. "Once you define things, they're meaningless. Truth is just fact, and fact doesn't mean anything. Hey, you wrote that down! See what I mean?" Incoherence is almost a virtue; one very intelligent Digger even apologized for being too articulate. It's felt that how people speak reveals far more than what they say, that eventually (say in the year 2000) vibrations might replace speech—that people won't need to talk, but will converse through all their senses. Gibberish is very popular, and there are fond references to Danny Kaye's old git-gat-gittle. Theater, movies, all visual experiences, and music are of course hugely preferred to books. Still, certain Eastern philosophers, Norman O. Brown, Alan Watts, and Buckminster Fuller, do have a small audience here, as does the *Wall Street Journal,* "the hippest paper in town." Fiction, the despair of publishers, is indeed ignored, with the rare exceptions of Thomas Pynchon, Heller, Ken Kesey, Richard Fariña, John Fowles, and Doris Lessing. These are enjoyed "because they don't preach, they're talking about personal experience." But, primarily, "music is the literature of this generation."

Grass was long ago pronounced middle class. There's a slight, new caution about acid, due to the recent reports about chromosome damage, but many shrug that off. The San Francisco Diggers encouraged people to exchange free LSD, and liked "bad-assing the illegal drug trade." The slogan was: Don't Deal. Make It—Grow It—Give It—Share It. They've had a group to bail acidheads out of jail, but they didn't aid those on speed, since they consider amphetamines so dangerous. In the last year, I've had the impression that many very ordinary people—especially those in jobs which bore them—were imbibing acid: insurance men and shoe salesmen as well as painters or students. One Digger said that *Time*'s modish cover story "gave us thousands of overnight pseudo hippies." Moreover, "We got some who only know what they *don't* want—they're full of screaming, aggressive, hostile love—*pushing* flowers at people. Some love." Now he wonders if a "post-drug" period may lie ahead, mainly for those with substantial drug experience—although the newest hippies, who've made no "deliberate choice," are still clamoring for drugs. But he added that "the automatic record changer is even more important than psychedelics"—as a wellspring for electronic culture.

The Diggers say that they do want to convert others, and they stress that the best way to destroy the middle class is to leave it. "Throughout history, Bohemia never created a subculture. Now we have the numbers to do it! But the country's making them into a criminal class." It's expected that America will become very ugly —as racism increases. Their answer is "not guerrilla warfare, but *monkey warfare* and *silly sabotage*"—such as chanting mantras around the Pentagon to exorcise the evil spirits within. While depressed liberals contemplate the notion of profound national lunacy, these jesters are a cheering presence in the landscape: few humanists have their humor, and humorists are rarely so humane.

Memories of the East Village April 1969

READ AMONG the brisk spring sounds of clubs on skulls, the shouts of pain, the explosions of small bombs in schools and libraries, and the hoarse faculty voices in debate, while the sun glints off policemen's plastic face visors and riot helmets, Tom Wolfe's *Electric Kool-Aid Acid Test* seems almost as remote as a Bloomsbury memoir. And the Beats seem nearly Victorian. In 1959 Herbert Gold wrote, "The hipster doesn't want to feel; he keeps cool. He has checked up on experience and found it wanting; he . . . doesn't dig overmuch. He carries books without reading them, drives cars without going anyplace, goes places without arriving anywhere. . . . He . . . is the delinquent with no zest, the gang follower with no love of the gang . . . the youngster with undescended passions, the organization man with sloanwilsonian gregorypeckerism in his cold, cold heart."

Who has lately seen such a creature? True, you meet a few

querulous relics in New York, but their fatigue is no longer distinguished: being tired and numb is no longer a style in sensitivity. Most of those I've encountered have complained about the noise, the heat, the cold, the food, the young, and the air conditioning; they said that everyone talks too quickly, and implied that anger and enthusiasm have "gone too far." Carping as creakily as suburban parents, few seem to have kept pace with Allen Ginsberg—a decade jumper who will probably bury us all.

As for what were called hippies: 1967 seems very long ago. Lots of love beads got broken and rolled into cracks too deep to reach; horoscopes went awry; the moon betrayed Virgo; murders and diseases and threatening pushers drove them from the neighborhoods they hoped were theirs. The Diggers' Free Store in New York was raided by toughs who beat them up several times—even though they kept no cash and boasted that nothing could be stolen because everything was free. Finally, they painted out "Love" on their window, painted in "Hate," and departed.

There are still urban hippies, of course. But they are mainly the instant variety who arrived yesterday from Westchester, and who are only concerned with style—or the more militant brand, who wage revolution by undressing during political speeches, or prevent speakers from finishing a sentence. Recently, Norman Mailer was stopped from describing his platform as a mayoral candidate by a few of the Crazies. (He'd come to a Panther dinner to ask the Panthers for their support, which he didn't get.) In passing, he remarked that he wouldn't call cops pigs, "because they've got balls." A Crazy yelled, "No, they haven't, Norman." "Yes they have." "Stop bullshitting!" "I'm not bullshitting!" "Yes you are." "He is!" "I'm not!" "You are!" "Shut *up*!" "*You* shut up!" "You shut up *too*!" The Panthers rebuked the Crazies: "Stop this frivolous, silly shit." But we were never allowed to hear Mailer's fantasies about uniting the left and the right.

At any rate, I miss the street gamesters of two summers past. The Beats were never funny—was that their tragedy?—but '67 gave us some nimble comedians. Endearingly uncool, beguiled and beguiling, they seemed ready to be zonked by the gritty world; acid detonated all those feelings which the hipsters shunned. Those I knew were delightful company: gentle and generous, sweet if sometimes slow. Hence some of the *Acid Test* makes me rather nostalgic —as for those brief, flowery fables about levitating the Pentagon. I was told that one of the levitators had visited a Pentagon official before the demonstration, who asked how high the building was going to be raised. "Oh, maybe ten feet." The official said that it couldn't be levitated without his permission, and that he would only allow it to go up to three or four feet. One boy told me later that the levitation had gone splendidly, but that the rest of us were too busy to notice it.

In '64 Ken Kesey, the gifted novelist, assembled his Merry Pranksters for a "group adventure." They toured the country in their psychedelic bus, inviting others to "Go with the flow." In their California commune, even the woods were wired for sound, and the trees were striped with orange and green Day-Glo paint. Acid was legal until October '66. Wolfe credits the Pranksters with the beginning of the whole Haight-Ashbury scene, the invention of mixed media, and even the style of psychedelic posters. Meanwhile, moments of horror tunnelled through the gaiety. Amid all the put-ons, the footloose clowning, and the snuggling atmosphere of group therapy (such excitement but so little apparent sex), there was the toppling paranoia that often accompanies LSD, plus the scenarios of madness for those who couldn't be reassembled. Naturally, Wolfe makes no comments; he simply unleashes the Prankster "allegory of life" in all its defiance, naiveté, and freaking charm. Parts of the book are as repetitious and exhausting as some acid trips must be. But it does take you "into the pudding," as they say: by bestowing the experience of "the Group Mind," where even reading or smoking are selfish acts, since they gratify only one person, and give nothing to the group. Those who can't read Wolfe's other books may well appreciate this one as the best account of tribal living that's yet appeared.

Throughout this celebration of technology, one irony nibbles at the unblown brain: the Pranksters and their heirs have been so dependent on *equipment*. Projectors, tapes, slides, cameras, loudspeakers, mikes, and amplifiers were essential to their spiritual or sensory liberation. Yet, last month, when the Living Theatre disrupted a symposium at New York's Theatre for Ideas, the uproar included screams of "Fuck technology!" Perhaps machinery is tolerable only when you play with it; for some, it may be a desperately necessary toy.

Thus, the *Acid Test* freezes and preserves the immediate past. And since history is hurtling, it's pleasing to remember that Emerson anticipated one maxim; in an 1841 essay, he wrote, "But do your thing and I shall know you."

Hindsight: Since I wrote the last two pieces, cool has returned with a vengeance. But it seemed very dated and remote in '67.

After Chicago '68 some of us grew impatient with Yiphood, because it confused many people politically. The problem with put-ons is that the straight world sometimes takes them seriously—just as the Chicago cops really believed that joke about putting acid in the city's reservoirs. But I still think that '67 was a rather innocent time, and part of the pleasure was parody.

A RIOT AVERTED
October 1967

REBELLIONS, REVOLUTIONS, altercations, and disorders: the vocabulary of "riots" is still scant on the words "incident" and "occasion." Many seem anxious to deny that diffuse anger and desperation need only a small event to build a revolt. The image of a fire hydrant extinguished on a hot day in the ghetto recedes in the search for nimble interstate inciters, ideally employed by some crimson network which is keen to disgrace us abroad. But while national figures sift the ashes and the shattered glass for evidence of conspiracies, and eighty bills concerning punishment for rioters now wait before the House, the "antiriot" panelists might profit by learning how a particular explosion was prevented: in 1966, in Brooklyn's East New York section.

A "bloodbath" was expected; there was only "an eruption." One of the key peacemakers was Albert Gallo, a minor leader in the Brooklyn Mafia. Although a racial battle on the scale of Watts or Newark was potential—yet was averted—New York showed its gratitude by reviling the members of the Youth Board who enlisted Gallo, while the police complained that their "morale" had been "sapped," and the press played tunes of scandal about "mobsters" and "the underworld."

It's true that Bobby Kennedy called Gallo and his two brothers—Larry and Crazy Joe—the "toughest witnesses" he had ever questioned; they were summoned to Washington in 1958 to testify on jukebox racketeering and extortion. Joe's first remark to Kennedy was: "Nice carpet you got here, kid. Be good for a crap game." Joe, who reportedly kept a lioness called Cleo in his basement to impress shakedown candidates, is now in jail for extortion. His small gang has been reproached for the barbershop murder of Albert Anastasia in the Hotel Park Sheraton in 1957, principally because Joe said, "From now on . . . you can just call . . . us the barbershop quintet." But the killing was never solved. The other brothers have been accused of irregularities in the pinball and vending machine trades, trot-race fixing, loan sharking, and muscling into legitimate business. None of this has been proven, although they've been jailed for contempt. The Gallos also rescued six Puerto Rican children from a fire, and raised funds for the family. Meanwhile, employing Albert Gallo showed an understanding of the power skeleton of a neighborhood—a brand of realism that's rather rare in city government.

The following account comes from my conversations with Mr. Frank Arricale, Rabbi Samuel Schrage, and others who were involved in the crisis in East New York.

The city has eleven other areas which share the characteristics of this slice of Brooklyn. It's not quite a ghetto; therefore, poverty programs and other forms of organized aid are scarce. The community, molded by hostilities long before black people moved in, was dominated by "the three I's": Italy, Ireland, and Israel. The Italian group—according to an Italian expert—is anarchistic, mainly because the only group is the family; there's no civic organization, and no corporate identification with the church. (Here, the Irish identify with the parish, but Italians don't.) For these Italians, the church means only the spiritual support of *la famiglia,* and provides no mechanism to cope with local problems. Gambling isn't considered illegal in this neighborhood. While Italians are the majority group in New York State, and the second largest group in New York City, they still feel like a minority and lack a political power base. Thus, organizations like the Cosa Nostra—and others which aren't entirely illegal—do flourish. The tradition derives from the period when Italy itself lacked a robust central government, and the vigilante groups emerged, outlived their function, and then became a threat when the government grew strong.

Coexisting, but not cordial, the neighborhood Irish are very reactionary and highly political—children of the organized labor movement. Their church, still sympathetic to Joe McCarthy and William Buckley, is a corporation, but it doesn't heal their severe family problems, which are especially acute between fathers and sons. The very authoritarian families are eventually attacked and rejected, in a way that the Italians can't understand, since the Italians rarely turn on their own families. Among the Irish, drinking is lavish. The pub is the social center; there are two or three per block. (Drink is the puberty initiation for the Irish boys, whereas sex initiates the Italians.) Both groups used to be anti-Semitic. At the same time, some of the neighborhood Jews mistrust the numbers of Orthodox and Hasidic Jews among them. Once, theirs was a successful ghetto —unlike the troubled Irish and Italian clusters. But the Jews who prospered moved to the suburbs, leaving behind those who had not done well, whose sons did not make it to City College. Among these, bitterness at their own professional failures, plus the strain of aborted ambitions, has resulted in many nervous breakdowns. This particular Jewish group is known for its poor mental health.

Many of the blacks who joined the community had just won free of the ghetto: they were civil servants and others who had earned enough to escape bottomless slums. For them, as a city official said, moving to East New York is "their first step out of the booby hatch." But this area is no tangible improvement. The pressures are as vicious as the ghetto's. City services, such as sanitation and housing are bad. Also, there are some other absolutely depressed black people, who don't even have a welfare client league. For them, this is worse than a slum. They're apt to be rejected by the advancing blacks, who feel that they're being dragged down. When the blacks first arrived, trying to live the myth of integration, the Italian, Irish, and Jewish groups were united for the first time—in the tradition of racism. This became the dynamic of the neighborhood.

In July 1966 these factors fell into fury. The area has a street corner society which ranges up to the age of thirty, and includes married men; adolescents join them. SPONGE (The Society for the Prevention of Negroes Getting Everything, a teen-age club) sent out pickets chanting "Two, Four, Six, Eight, We don't want to integrate." Groups of twenty-five to a hundred roamed the streets, while garbage cans, tire jacks, and bricks were flung about, and firebomb caches were found on roofs. At night, priests of all churches paced the blocks in their "clericals," risking their lives by walking alone, trying to calm people; their role has been compared to Christian witness. The police were in full force, yet attempting restraint. There were even bullhorns, announcing that "Things are under control." But they weren't.

Frank Arricale, who was then the director of the Youth Board (and is now the Commissioner of Relocation), had been working for months to forestall pandemonium. In February he'd predicted that "summer problems" were not going to be in the ghettos, but in areas like this one. Social and poverty workers, civil rights volunteers, city officials, the local black nationalists (whom Arricale found very helpful), and many other groups—all had been called in, and still the danger accelerated. An eleven-year-old black boy was killed by a sniper, and a black of seventeen was arrested (he was later released). The Youth Board learned that ample crowds (mainly Italian and black) were ready to bring their guns and rifles and join in from neighborhoods all over New York. (Many of the Irish were away, since their parochial schools give vacations that are different from the Italians'.) There might have been a traveling, city-wide siege which could have meant fiercer warfare than other cities have yet known. Whites began to invade East New York, and blacks were threatening to come. Since organized gangs are rare these days, it's difficult to know who to deal with, or who might be a leader in an unstructured, roving mass, where the affiliations are formed on violence.

Fearing a shooting war, Arricale accepted the suggestion of Rabbi Samuel Schrage, a Youth Board official, that Albert Gallo should be asked for aid. Gallo could command allegiance from many neighborhood Italians, and he was certain to know who the snipers were. (Neither the police nor the Youth Board could possibly identify the snipers.) Arricale and Rabbi Schrage visited a waterfront candy store, where Gallo and his friends often met to drink beer and talk baseball and politics. Gallo, who was stunningly dressed, sent his companions away, and offered them soda and cigarettes. Both were impressed by his immediate concern; he too felt that many people might be killed. He introduced them to his father, who said, "You do it, Al." He said that he was proud that his son should be consulted by the Youth Board. Admitting that he must first confer with his attorneys, Gallo agreed to help. One of his three lawyers was enthusiastic, but the others feared bad repercussions from much of the city administration and the press.

Gallo, who only went through sixth grade, "got on his own soapbox." He intently questioned Arricale and Rabbi Schrage about the Youth Board: "If you stop the fighting, it'll happen again next week. What are you going to do for an encore? What about education and jobs? They have no preparation. What are you do-gooders going to do about that?" He was insulted when Rabbi Schrage stressed that cooling the neighborhood must be done on "a social work basis," without threats or arm-twisting. Since his lawyers felt that the police might assume that Gallo was making trouble, the officials gave him a letter stating that he was "a member of an ad hoc intergroup relations committee, working to ease community tensions." (But Gallo was given no immunity, as the press implied.)

Frank Arricale said, "The Gallo name will become like the Rockefellers': they weren't so hot to begin with." Gallo replied: "From your lips to the ear of God"—a Yiddish saying. The press has wrongly reported that Larry Gallo worked with his brother; in fact, Larry, an opera lover who was nearly garotted to death by the Profaci mob, a rival faction, and still wears the rope burns on his neck, "didn't want to get involved."

Albert Gallo began by phoning all the potential fighters he knew, instructing them to stay out of the neighborhood, and telling whites to leave blacks alone. The orders spread quickly: there was simply to be no more fighting in East New York. He held meetings in cafés, bars, candy stores, luncheonettes, and private homes, conferred with parents and with groups of older men, and collected embattled boys. (The whites averaged about twenty-four years of age, while many of the blacks were in their late teens.)

Sitting at the head of a long table, he began his interracial parliamentary conferences by asking everyone to introduce himself. He opened by announcing: "The purpose of this meeting is to avert bloodshed. I expect you to feel the way I do. Anyone who doesn't, say so right now, and I'll pay for his psychiatric fees. . . ." Then: "I'm not here to listen to your problems or your grievances, and I know they are many. Tell the rabbi about them later. But it's too dangerous to take the time now. How are we going to stop people from killing? Any suggestions?" Complaints would usually follow, with each racial group eagerly blaming the other. The line heard oftenest was "*We're* not looking for trouble—it's the others." Gallo would answer, "Then what are you doing in East New York? Shut up and sit down." He lost his temper only once: a white boy said, "We don't want anything to do with those niggers." Gallo, who has many black friends, slapped his face and said, "Don't you ever use that word again, you Goddamned wop!"

Usually he lectured slowly and quietly: "We're not animals, we're human beings trying to live with one another. We don't really want to kill anybody. Now I've no business being here—I've got more interesting things to do. I even broke a date for this crap over here. But I felt that we could prevent killing. And we're going to. . . . You have families, how would you like to see your sister killed?" Once, he added, "If anyone has to be taken away from this world, let God do it." Eventually, there was no further disagreement, and the young men would ask what he wanted them to do. He replied that they were to keep everyone they knew out of East New York. Moreover, "I want you guys to stay home and watch a TV program, no matter how crummy it is. I want you to let the cops be—don't interfere."

In a few days, the neighborhood was quiet. Naturally, Gallo was not the sole engine of peace—he was one of dozens who tried to save lives. But, as part of the whole mosaic, Arricale and Rabbi Schrage say that his role was unique: in personally reaching the key troublemakers. They themselves were swiftly summoned before a Brooklyn grand jury, and numerous critics raised the rhubarb. Mayor Lindsay defended Arricale, while phrases like "civic disgrace" and "deplorable abdication of official responsibility" exploded instead of the Molotov cocktails which might have been hurled in East New York. Since Brooklyn is fiercely and provincially Democratic, and

consistently anti-Lindsay, it's probable that those officials who protested most against Gallo's participation were eager to malign the
mayor. They complained that Gallo had been given "prestige" through
the publicity. But it was they who made his efforts public, while
larding the term "Mafioso" into every reference. A man in Gallo's
position can hardly sue for libel. It would be foolish to endow him
with a halo. But, as he said to Rabbi Schrage, "I was never so
clobbered for doing a bad thing as for doing a decent thing."

Rabbi Schrage said that the "local subculture" in a given neighborhood often likes to be consulted and asked for help. (A colleague
of his has suggested that potential upheavals in Spanish Harlem might
be quenched if the city used the influence of the numbers runners,
who are so important there.) Last summer's emergency in Brooklyn
yields an example of the unconventional methods which are increasingly essential for coping with so many aspects of life in New York.
Following standard procedures rarely works; citing the law is often
as ineffective as flushing a broken toilet. Postponements, deadlocks,
paralysis—and in this case, murders—can result from resting on
traditional rungs. But New Yorkers, notorious for their collective
impatience, have hardly realized that they didn't have a riot to rival
the most savage in the country.

The last report on Albert Gallo was his arrest in October 1967,
for activities (including extortion and coercion) related to an in-
tricate ticket-cashing project at Roosevelt Raceway. He described
himself as an "unemployed dress manufacturer," and was released
on bail.

Hindsight: I finished typing up the preceding piece from '67 for this
book the night before Joe Gallo was gunned down in Umberto's Clam
House, on April 7, 1972, at 5:30 A.M. He was celebrating his forty-
third birthday. At first, the theory behind his execution was that some
of Joe Colombo's men held Gallo responsible for the June '71 shooting of Colombo. Since Gallo had made a number of black friends
while he was in jail, and had announced on his release that more
blacks must be hired in his own organization, he was suspected
primarily because Colombo's assailant was black.

But in May of '72, the New York police had a new idea about
the murder of Gallo: it was thought that he had "masterminded" the

$55,000 robbery of Ferrara's pastry shop in Little Italy, just south of Greenwich Village, which occurred just five days before his own death. Ferrara's, which opened in 1892, is one of the most sumptuous bakeries in New York, and it specializes in wedding cakes. Since Little Italy is considered off-limits for organized crime (and is consequently one of the safest neighborhoods in Manhattan), the underworld suspicion that Gallo had violated an unwritten rule may have shortened his life—even though he had claimed that he had retired from crime to write his autobiography. (He kept announcing, "I'm a writer.") Even so, the police were still convinced that some of Columbo's men had done the shooting.

Larry Gallo died of cancer in '68, and Albert Gallo succeeded him as the head of the family business. But soon there were complaints that Albert was an ineffectual leader. Some of his employees switched to working for Columbo, and his nickname—"Kid Blast" —gave way to "Kid Blister."

However, a few months after Joe was shot, Albert was thought to be gaining in stature, according to the police officials who kept an eye on him. (At that point, he claimed to support himself through investments in a furniture company.) They also said that he had been marked for assassination.

DEATH OF THE *REPORTER*
July 1968

THE LINEAR landscape is littered with the living dead of our magazines; there are few that one yearns to read or write for. Meanwhile, book editors are commissioning topical discussions or slabs of reporting which would once have appeared as tighter or sequential magazine articles. Between hard covers, these are often published too late and forgotten quite soon—they're dated because the issues have changed during the months required for book production. But, as the agonies accelerate, so does our need for weeklies. This is an excellent period for magazines—if only they could make the most of it. Thus, the death of the *Reporter*, in mid-June, was regretted by many who no longer followed it: another possibility was fused. It was hardly an organ of delight, but it had printed many fine pieces, by such authors as Alfred Kazin, Henry Steele Commager, Marya Mannes, Paul Jacobs, Robert Ardrey, Gore Vidal, Malcolm Cowley, Saul Bellow, F. W. Dupee, and others since it began in 1949.

The *Reporter*'s best territory was opposition. (What seems tame now appeared courageous about fifteen years ago.) It was one of the first to rebel against Joe McCarthy and the China Lobby, and in '58 the editorials suggested that atom tests should be suspended. Distinctly a creature of the Fifties, its success sprang from combating the brutalities of the anticommunist causes, while insisting on containment. As one former editor said, "The *Reporter* is the victim of the end of the cold war." For the magazine crystalized the contrast between the old left and the new: it seethed with a horror of communism which seems ridiculous to current members of the movement.

Since it has been called "the last of the one-man magazines," it's significant that the founder and editor, Max Ascoli, is an Italian political scientist of seventy, who had been jailed for his attacks on Mussolini and Fascism. He came to the U.S. in 1931, as a professor of jurisprudence, and he has always passionately identified with America—more so than some natives. His hatred of totalitarianism was reflected in his response to any dealings with Russia: he even objected to Khrushchev's 1959 visit. Throughout, he felt that the U.S. was threatened by "neutrality": ". . . if we say that the evil of Communist states is a myth, then so is freedom and so is America." Many of his editorials sounded like this one from June 1955: "Nobody knows whether the Communists are on the run, but certainly they are on the move, and we must see to it that the move is backward." "Peacemongers" incensed him as much as "Communist barbarism," although his argument was sometimes rather clotted: "We cannot have war with the Russians and we cannot have peace." There were no tangible solutions, except that "we must outlive Communism," and must maintain contact with those who live "under" it. Whatever liberalism means now, it streamed across the *Reporter*'s pages of the 1950s: progressive positions on domestic issues, such as housing and school integration, and the protection of civil liberties, plus a confidence that the American Way should be showered on other countries—for their salvation. These positions now appear like a tossed salad of gentility and paranoia; the approach seems humane yet often isolated—sometimes, merely furious.

In his editorials Dr. Ascoli continually announced that the magazine was "liberal." Yet his staff says that he detested the word, since it implied sogginess and bleeding hearts. The contradictions of Fifties' liberalism crackled more sharply when the magazine derided first Stevenson, then President Kennedy and his advisers, the UN, and the new nations—as though all partook of dangerous radicalism— and even stated that McCarthy, by "not producing a single live Communist, rendered a service to American Communism for which the country is still paying." Lyndon Johnson's action in the Dominican Republic was praised, and he was warmly supported on Vietnam. Despite railings against "dogma," politics appeared as a war between absolute good and raging evil.

Meanwhile, many contributors departed—not only because of the views unfurled, but because some of their pieces were rewritten past recognition. Although Ascoli deplored political tyranny, he was an authoritarian in the office. Finished essays were treated as "raw copy," in the words of one editor, and the staff pasted some of the employer's stylistic habits—such as inverted phrases and compulsive slang— into the prose that they were editing. (Perhaps lingo appealed because it seemed especially American; Ascoli is said to have repeated "Give them the old shampoo" to a mystified audience.) I wrote a few book reviews for the *Reporter*; once, a piece of mine was lengthened by some hundred inept words, and I learned from sheepish editors that most of the articles in that issue were fattened because an editorial had been canceled at the last moment. The staff, by its own admission, dwelled in chaos. Independents were apt to leave or get fired—mainly because internal criticism wasn't allowed. Commissions were flighty, since the subject once sought might later suddenly be spurned, or because two writers had accidentally been told to write on the same topic. But, despite the lunge toward group journalism, it would have been hard to imitate Ascoli's own style, as when he described the *Reporter*'s "angle of vision": "The processing of news in order to reach the facts, the dissection of opinion in order to reach ideas, the interplay, the grinding of facts and ideas—all this is not simply based on a denial of the notion according to which all news and all opinions are born free and equal, each one approximately as good as the other."

Percolating with praise for President Johnson, the pro-war editorials expelled numerous subscribers, particularly those who read the *New York Review of Books* or the *New Republic*. However, circulation didn't decline severely—presumably, the magazine found new readers, perhaps within business and management. Still, it would never have beguiled the devout right, since the domestic policies remained quite balanced. Advertising decreased, notably from publishers. However, the magazine wasn't financially distressed, since it was privately funded. Some of Ascoli's staff think that he killed the *Reporter* because of LBJ's withdrawal from the presidency. The once-loved figure, formerly called "quite a man," was finally denounced: ". . . we did not expect that the president would run out on his pledge to the people of South Vietnam, and at the same time run out on the American electorate by proclaiming himself a lame duck." The last issue did support Humphrey. But, all in all, Ascoli seemed to imply that the public and the president had failed him.

Recently, the *Saturday Evening Post* peeled down its subscriptions to a readership that supposedly buys the products it advertises: the cars, TV sets, hard and soft drinks, and the shimmering plastics which prop up its pages. Perhaps the *Reporter* should have done the same: by limiting its readers to those who could afford to buy a fuller war.

Hindsight: The *Reporter*'s final years are interesting in light of the confusions of old-style liberalism. In the Fifties I was an apolitical student, an English major hiding in the past; when I occasionally paid attention to the present, I was perplexed because liberals and conservatives sounded so much alike. In mildly liberal circles, people knocked McCarthy and "the anticommunists" *and* communism. (I remember the term "noncommunist" being used to praise a moderate liberal.) Reading through stacks of old *Reporter*s makes a useful review of the overlappings that occurred; also, when the editorials chided JFK for *his* "liberalism," it's one of many reminders that a cold warrior who was extremely recalcitrant about civil rights was actually considered a progressive.

I should add that there were some very nice people at the *Reporter,* among them, my nameless sources for this piece. While they agreed on its ailments, and on the great difficulties of working there, some were fond of Ascoli, and they were genuinely sad that the magazine could not be rescued.

In the winter of '71 and '72 I started hearing about "anti-Americanism" again. The *Reporter* reflected some of the themes that we see in *Commentary* now, especially the idea that if you really like America, you won't criticize it loudly. Attacks on institutions or individuals or groups are fine, but our society at large is the best in the world, and you ought to be more grateful to be a part of it.

NEW YORKERS AND GEORGE WALLACE
October 1968

A SNOWBALL: vanilla hairy with coconut shreds, overwhelmed with dark chocolate sauce. It wasn't an emblem of white purity drowning in Black Power, but it was dessert for Wallace: at a dinner in the Hotel Americana at $25 a head. Next to me, a sad middle-aged nurse said that she'd been jobless since January, and explained that thousands of Filipinos had infiltrated the New York hospital system, depriving her of work. "Everyone knows that the Philippine Islands have been communist for years, and our communist State Department is *hustling* them into our country." She said that two Filipinos and two blacks had mugged her recently—"They work together, you know"—and urged me to join her local Birch Society: "You can't know until you've *studied,* and read, and heard what's being planned against us now." She added that it had been so hard to choose a dress for this evening; she wanted to look her best, but had so few things to wear.

She and the others at my table—carefully groomed family clusters —were indeed "The Folks," as Wallace calls them: "the forgotten." Clenched in a tax bracket which paralyzes them, their vulnerability is valid, and so are some of their fuzzy fears. Some observers think that the terror of nuclear death has gone underground: that the cries for law and order, and the spasms about communists and rioters, are partial, indirect expressions of the fright instilled by the lavish H-bomb testing of the early Sixties. Shelters, air-raid drills, children taught to hide under their school desks, and all the lunacies of "protection" accelerated—until civil defense became an acknowledged farce. But the fear stayed.

The treadmarks of fatigue and anxiety dent many pro-Wallace faces—which bloomed with delight when he appeared. (Earlier, Norman Mailer had strolled in, looking self-conscious, but in that crowd he wasn't recognized.) Wallace said very little; he just hurled a few unfinished slogans into the air. But his dexterity seemed confusing for this audience. They hardly knew when to hiss—though many booed when he mentioned "the newsboys" at the *New York Times*. Often, he cleverly leaves sentences incomplete: "Now I'm not talking about race . . ."—which drew applause. They cheered at "I believe that God made all of us, regardless of race, creed, or color," were uneasily silent when he mentioned the number of black voters in Alabama, but clapped when he said that his wife had received "a large Negro vote." Whoops rose when he shouted "Your family cannot go out on the streets at night!" heightened when he described how one of his followers had socked a heckler "for obscenity," and diminished when he chided, "I'm not recommending that you hit anyone . . ." Beside me, a man said, "Safety's all we want." Wallace then challenged Nixon and Humphrey to a debate, inviting them to "Come down out of that antiseptic, touch-me-not bubble. . . ."

Later, penetrating the necklace of cops around Madison Square Garden, a friend of mine was given a free ticket by a benign officer— which seemed to confirm the rumor that some in the force were dispensing tickets. At the rally of sixteen thousand, many brutal faces split with yells, and folding chairs crashed like cannonry. Wallace posters read: STAND UP FOR AMERICA, suggesting an erection policy that increases virility—as when he told a Texan crowd that a vote for him means that "You've asserted your manhood." Other banners proclaimed: IT TAKES COURAGE! WALLACE HAS IT! DO YOU? (The anti-Wallace signs also showed sexual inspiration: "GEORGIE IS THE ILLEGITIMATE SISTER OF LBJ" and "WALLACE WAS BREAST-FED BY AUNT JEMIMA.") Some Wallace supporters joyfully waved a picture of a pregnant black, holding her belly with a cryptic, downward glance, wearing a button that announces "Nixon's The One." This is a favorite poster of the left, sold in hip shops. But it enchants the far right, thus yielding another (recurrent) example of how the trappings of dissent can be tools for the dissenters' opponents. There's an innocence on both sides: the Wallaceites kept giving the peace sign and the raised fist. Clearly, they think these gestures mean victory— without realizing that both belong to radicals.

Wallace's running mate, retired General Curtis LeMay, was cheered when he unleashed one of his best lines: "I've never been a politician and I don't profess to be one now." As fights flared across the floor, he said that Wallace will "restore our reason," while several blacks, who were accompanying a pastor from Harlem, were attacked and thrashed, and hundreds of men shrieked "Niggers, niggers!" "Throw them out!" "Kill them!" "Get him!" The police quenched the fights quickly, and rushed the warriors out. Although so many policemen support Wallace, they were very restrained within the hall, although some blew their cool on the streets.

During the twenty-minute ovation for Wallace, the screaming crowd bounced up and down under red, pink, and yellow balloons— surely a guileless choice of colors. Later, many literally leaped with glee when he mentioned communism. His speech was the familiar one which he has recited before: in favor of states' rights; against "kowtowing to an*arch*ists," "the domestic mess," open housing, "the sick Supreme Court," "pseudo-intellectuals," "students who collect money and blood for the enemy"—"and there are two four-letter words they don't know: W-O-R-K and S-O-A-P," and "professors calling for communist victory." On foreign policy: "We must always be superior. When you are superior, you can always go to the conference table. . . . We should never have gone to Vietnam by ourselves"—instead, we should have appealed to the Allies, and told them to join us or to repay all foreign aid.

Wallace is said to welcome hecklers; he also offered to "autograph their sandals." Certainly, their presence intensified the crowd's frenzied response to him. As a turmoil of toughs howled for Law 'n' Order, noise seemed like an overkill weapon. Yet, despite Wallace's lack of programs, one of his main strengths may be enabling people to express themselves. After an evening among the faces gashed with fury, you realize how thoroughly anger has changed to hate. Today, there's a crackling nervous contagion that rebounds from walls and buildings and hurtles into open windows: into anybody's home. You can feel it even at the deli and the drugstore. People are frightened of so many things that it distills a mutual fear —of one another. It's beginning to seem almost impossible for various groups in this country to merely continue to live with each other. Squatting in the mud in a Harlem park last week, at a Panther rally, hearing a speaker say, "We should give the man a deadline for stopping that war, or we start a second front here," and then eating with the Wallaceites, who shout for their own protection, makes it hard to imagine how these passions can coexist for many years. A weary ironist said, "If Wallace is elected, we can get the revolution over by Christmas."

Hindsight: Things seemed much simpler in '68, when Wallace ran a mainly racist campaign. In '72, Dan Rather of CBS referred to a poll which asked voters whether Wallace was moderate, liberal, or conservative. He came out equally in each category, but some said that he was all three. It's the old reminder that a politician is defined more by what people think he represents, rather than by what he actually says or does. But by early '72, Wallace had become harder to classify. He had already built new state medical schools, junior colleges, and trade schools in Alabama; he had also substantially raised the rate of unemployment and workmens' compensation benefits. And he even took to finishing his sentences. At the Democratic convention in Miami Beach, he fully completed his statement against "the senseless, asinine busin' of school children." The ambiguities had dwindled. So, despite all the confusions about "real" or "phony" populism—despite the bullet in his spine and the pain in his face— his long-term supporters heard more from him about specific issues than they had in '68.

It took the professional pols and the press until about the end of September 1969 to really discover Wallace's constituency. Aside from the Nixon-Agnew silent majority speeches, I think that the mayoral candidacy of Mario Procaccino in New York had a lot to do with that enlightenment—mainly because working class voters had so greatly preferred Procaccino to his rivals in the primaries, including former Mayor Robert Wagner. Suddenly there was a rush of cover stories about the working/forgotten/average man. There was a huge, crude astonishment on finding that working people couldn't afford more than a sparse existence—and that they didn't want to lose what they had. John Lindsay's campaign for his second term as mayor reflected the same last-minute discovery, when his staff realized that Lindsay had been neglectful of the Bronx, Queens, and Brooklyn. And the response to Wallace did educate us about those who are taxed for a larger percentage of their income than the very richest persons in this society.

Whenever I saw a Wallace button in New York, I recalled the botched attempts on the left to reach these people. A group of young revolutionaries, who were trying to organize the impoverished whites of my neighborhood in Yorkville, had concentrated on housing. It was a good idea, since many tenements were being demolished to make way for luxury apartment buildings. When they called a meeting to oppose some local landlords, a large number of worried tenants—many of them elderly—showed up. But when a speaker lectured them about "fucking bourgeois pigs," they didn't linger.

Of course anyone can stop a bullet in this country. But Wallace's mere presence did seem to bring out violence in others, or to appeal to what was frantic in them. I'm accustomed to wild audiences and fierce speeches, but the crowd which had screamed for Wallace in Madison Square Garden in '68 was the only one I've ever found frightening. Hence there was no surprise when he was shot.

On the first day of his trial, Arthur Bremer had three times as many guards as Wallace did on the day of the Maryland shooting. Bremer's diary informed us that he had switched his assassin's focus from Nixon to Wallace while he was seeing *A Clockwork Orange*. However, Bremer wasn't sure that killing Wallace would really make him famous. "I would have done better for myself to kill the old G-man Hoover," he wrote. "In death, he lays with Presidents."

HARLEM ON MANY MINDS
February 1969

White Man's
  DREAM!
    of
White Being
Supreme!
Has Turned to
Sour Cream

THUS A sign in Harlem, '64, next to a poster urging "Buy Where Black Santa Claus Is"—reminding Christmas shoppers to patronize black stores. Caught in one of the many superb photographs in the Metropolitan Museum's well-intended show, "Harlem on My Mind," which has been used as a racial spittoon, this little rhyme recalls Malcolm X's remark about enjoying cream: "Coffee is the only thing I like integrated." Cream gone wrong is an ironic emblem for this show, which offers a wealth of magnificent lore, and yet fails as a whole. The failure hurts some, enrages others, and it has probably made history. Meanwhile, the exhibition has had the largest attendance of any in the museum's existence, and more black viewers have come than ever before.

Many single pictures make it worth seeing the entire display: two black grandmothers of 1900, arm in arm, their faces puckered with pain as they simply gaze into space; Ethel Waters in 1919, a slim, pensive waif; two very young bridesmaids of 1926, with flat chests and celestial smiles, their excitement radiating from beneath enormous hats; a 1931 line of unemployment registration, where men's bodies are squeezed together behind a prohibitive rope; the 1943 riot, where chests burst with blood, while three teen-age boys pose in looted tail-coats and silk hats far too big for them, and are later trapped by cops who are also too big for them; Helen Levitt's 1945 *Graffiti,* where someone has chalked a small circle on a crumbling stone wall, and written "Button to Secret Passage—Press"—a fantasy of escape from the ghetto? There's a 1948 billboard on which a pretty Wasp boy weeps "I am *so* an American!", followed by YOU BET, Sonny . . . No Matter What Your Race or Religion! FIGHT Racial and Religious HATE; in front of the clean board, a couple of hunched black figures stroll—the cherubic boy etches an insult in claiming to speak for them. In 1954 fatigued young men sit on garbage cans; obviously, there are few alternatives before them. In a '68 street demonstration, hundreds of sober faces fill a wide block with the suspense of waiting.

Adam Clayton Powell praised the exhibit, but many other black people have denounced it; some, because it includes no painting or sculpture by contemporary black artists; others, because they feel it distorts their history, and that it's an insult. Pickets outside the museum passed out leaflets: "Soul's Been Sold Again!" Unfortunately, these critics are right. Though much of the staff was black, it was assembled by Allon Schoener, a white—and his show is naively patronizing. There are far too many happy laughing faces—even in the sections on the Depression and the Sixties—and there's an excess of pictures of show business figures, athletes, dressy Twenties' weddings, beauty parlors, and nightclubs. The old phrase *"clever as monkeys"* seems to caper through these rooms. A quote from the 1930 *Herald Tribune,* conscientiously displayed, characterizes much of the show: "The attitude of the average white New Yorker to Harlem is one of tolerant amusement. He thinks of . . . prosperous nightclubs; of happy-go-lucky Negroes dancing all night to jazz music. . . ." Later, in the same article, it's noted that "90% of the nightclubs in Harlem are owned by" whites.

In fact, the total effect of the show is rather like going slumming for pleasure—as so many whites did in the Twenties. Poverty isn't carried up to the present; there's almost an implication that the poor belong to the past, and one set of Sixties slides flashes color shots of corn on the cob, clothing stores, and Afro-American groceries— as though plenty were the just reward for lots of dazzling grins. Many of the Twenties' and other period pictures stress black prosperity, which is exaggerated by this show. Throughout the past, the non-famous black faces turned to the camera look timid or defiant. Many who posed seemed to be asking for tolerance; surely an all-black staff would have chosen a fuller variety of expressions. Yet the seeds of protest and militancy lie much farther back in history than many whites realize—although few of the circumstances are explained. Of course the show couldn't (and shouldn't) have been merely a record of suffering. But it's amazingly jolly—in terms of what anyone's heard about the black experience.

Gurgling tapes, buzzing sound domes, slides, lights and voices which collide only to negate each other: the use of mixed media deprives the show of dignity, and makes it seem all the more merry— and terribly difficult to unravel. In his foreword to the catalogue, Schoener states: "We don't respond, as we once did, to an orderly progression of facts thrust at us in a fixed order." Thus, "No attempt has been made to describe the sixty-eight-year history of Harlem as a continuing sequence of events." Hence most ideas and many facts are omitted. What can a photograph of Marcus Garvey tell us about his views? Flashing slides that give figures of black unemployment pass too rapidly to make any point. And how does a record label of "Paradise Wobble—Stomp" instruct the spectator? The trouble is that mixed media can't think, and that the sum of racial culture and racial agony is just too serious for a twinkling discothèque style. Sensitivity slid out of sight when this choice was made. Of course, it's always sad when experimentation is a mistake. But a traditional show could have taught us much that's still unknown about Harlem.

The museum withdrew its catalogue because Mayor Lindsay frantically proclaimed that its introduction (written by a black student as a term paper when she was sixteen) was "racist"—during a week when anti-Lindsay feeling was most acute among some of New York's Jewish groups. When the "anti-Semitic" sentences are read in context, they don't sound racist; they merely reflect the strains which the U.S. has long stimulated among the poor of many races. However, Allon Schoener, who is Jewish, revealed that the particular "offensive" remarks were actually paraphrases of *Beyond the Melting Pot* by Daniel Patrick Moynihan and Nathan Glazer (the latter is also Jewish). Schoener unwisely told the adolescent author to drop her quotes and footnotes, which cited the book, and to translate all source material into her own words. Therefore, Moynihan and Glazer's observation that "subconsciously" blacks may find that "a bit of anti-Jewish feeling helps them feel more completely American, a part of the majority group," became ". . . psychologically, blacks may find that anti-Jewish sentiments place them, for once, within a majority. Thus, our contempt for the Jew makes us feel more completely American in sharing a national prejudice." Indeed, editing has always been a perilous trade, awash with unsound advice. In this case, where the editor is forty-three and the author is now seventeen, one wishes that she'd been old enough to ignore him. (The *Times* thoughtfully noted that *Beyond the Melting Pot* "was not attacked as being anti-Semitic when it was published in 1963.") But amid all the furor, Congressman Edward Koch had one of the few sensible reactions: "I feel that the . . . museum was not endorsing anti-Semitism any more than it was endorsing slavery when it included a photograph of a slave ship in the Harlem show."

The show and the teachers' strike, aided by hysteria from the press and the mayor, have congealed many natives' notions about hatred between blacks and Jews. The only valid sources now are one's black and Jewish friends—who are pleading for sanity. Certainly, some mutual dislike has existed—depending on the nature of particular ghettos. And some black militants' remarks about "kosher nationalism" haven't helped. (In '67, James Baldwin wrote that the Jew "is singled out by Negroes not because he acts differently from other white men, but because he doesn't.") But anti-Semitism was hardly invented by blacks—as some pundits seem to imply—and infinite Jews have fought for blacks' rights. Five years ago, a Jewish writer most unhappily told me, "Don't forget that the Negro is the Jew's Jew"—and proceeded to deplore his lifelong feelings, his admitted preference for segregated schools. A black writer said recently, "Of course I don't blame my Jewish editor for what our landlord did in Harlem. But I was very wary of him at first." Currently, one has the bleak suspicion that the theme of black anti-Semitism is being magnified as an excuse for whites to put down blacks. By inflating the idea that blacks and Jews are steeped in enmity, the media is nourishing conflicts which could later be used as ammunition against both groups.

CHRISTMAS CRISES IN MANHATTAN
Children's Toys December 1965

DETOXIFIED ALCOHOLICS in Santa Claus suits collect money in their wooden chimneys outside New York's department stores; their intake aids the Volunteers of America, which operates a men's shelter in the Bowery, as well as helping prisoners' wives and children. The Santas are instructed to keep their breath pure, and not to promise to deliver the presents that children demand. Within the toy departments, it's crucial to remember that children are far more resilient and less morbid than adults. Amid the debris there are cloth-bodied Van Gogh dolls with one ear apiece, next to some martyred-looking Einsteins, also "Marybel—the Doll Who Gets Well," whose kit provides crutches, arm splints, and pastable spots for chicken pox and measles. Games include "The Big Funeral"—the winner get▸

the most expensive rites, and the losers become zombies who aren't buried at all; "Live A Little," in which you murder the other players in order to collect their insurance; and "Administration," which is won by contriving to pay the government the smallest amount of taxes. Nearby is the "Witch Doctor's Head Shrinkers' Kit," which "actually shrinks your favorite monster before your eyes," with two captivating incantations: "Powdered Flesh Feels Like Skin Mysterious," and "Turns Bonelike As It Shrinks Unbelievable."

All these seem far less sinister than a well-intended educational toy: two three-dimensional mannequins, "The Visible Man and Woman," complete with "all vital organs." In childhood I inherited two thoroughly honest Victorian cardboard mannequins, which revealed every property of the inner man. But the modern equivalent is unnecessarily ugly. The pink plastic pancreas is so unattractive that it makes you dislike your own. By disfiguring the body, the toy seems like a stimulus for future hypochondriacs.

Meanwhile, the famous polygamous dolls (Barbie, Ken, and Midge), who are packaged three in a box, have just been joined by "Ken's buddy, Allan." Allan deceives no one, despite the claim that he escorts Midge "when Ken and Barbie double-date"; he has the face of a surburban wife trader. Midge's expression has grown slyer since she was a bridesmaid at Ken and Barbie's wedding; she seems more in character when she's sold as a detachable head for wigs and hair dyes. Subscribing to the quartet's wardrobe can cost about $150, a sum probably emulated by GI Joe, the first doll for boys to succeed in many years. He has over a hundred accessories, including costumes for jungle warfare and the ski troops. Although his face (with one small scar) is a compilation of twenty winners of the Congressional Medal of Honor, GI Joe is considered morally odious by the many pacifist groups who would like to end his existence. All in all, the toy stores offer little to ignite Christmas morning's usual exhibition of lust, greed, and envy, except for a charming set of finger puppets: five realistic fur mice ranging through brown, white, and gray, which can move delightfully on one hand. Still, it was unsettling to hear someone call them "very sexual."

Adult Games December 1968

ALTHOUGH THE chairman of Tiffany's observes that "diamonds remain an important staple for the holiday," games for adults are lavish among the trembling tiers of gifts in elegant stores. Dr. Eric Berne noted that games are an escape from the boredom of pastimes as well as from the "dangers of intimacy." Hence, perhaps, the waxing popularity of adult games, bought hip-to-hip, elbow-to-rib, and jaw-to-shoulder by throngs of (bored) shoppers, all too intimate in elevators and crowds. Christmas *cafard* has two conspicuous sources: the neuroses imposed on most large cities, where traffic and flesh-packs swell until communal claustrophobia incites a passionate crossness, plus the mass dread of spending the day with lots of relatives one rarely sees. Decades of unforgivable Christmas scenes will be recalled. The horrors of family intimacy bristle in anticipatory nerves—they befrenzy our already electric air. (Affectionate families, like mine, sometimes agree to pass the day apart—instead, we have it with friends. This helps us to sustain our liking for presents, food, songs, wrappings, and each other.) Meanwhile, no one has quite explained why children cry so much on Christmas day—disappointment in their gifts? Or too many presents? At any rate, adults can sympathize. Many, yearning to yell or weep themselves, may flee to games.

This year, many adult games flatteringly insist on the intelligence of the players; these promise to "stimulate," "challenge," and even "ignite" the intellect. "Sophistication" is underlined, while "Games for Thinkers" are often "scientific." Stock market games, like Acquire and High Bid, abound, along with Student Survival. Some have frightening names, like Agitation or Jeopardy—where the players are given the answers and asked to supply the questions.

Many are hooked on Diplomacy, which was invented by an MIT professor in 1959; it's been played with passion for years in Cambridge, Massachusetts. The board is a map of Europe, circa 1901; there are seven countries for seven players, who try to capture each other's countries. Each has two armies and a navy; every time you seize a city, you acquire an extra army. Moves are made at fifteen-minute intervals; in between, you confer with others and make alliances. (Some favor conferences in the bathroom, with all the taps turned on.) But there's no obligation to make any move you've promised. France may be in league with Germany against Italy, but Italy may at the same time ally with Germany against France. "The essential beauty," said an addict, "is that you're supposed to lie *all the time*. It combines the tactical skills of chess with all the arts of cajolery, deceit and intimidation. Threats are vital." "It turns people into monsters," said a detractor. Apparently alliances can lead to adultery, while those who've betrayed each other often explode with every other hostility that plagues their private lives. Diplomacy can be played for days, and has been called "the game that breaks up more families than Monopoly."

Others are less cerebral. There's the "Executive Mental Block: The *Infuriating* Three-dimensional Jigsaw Puzzle—How to Drive Him Out of His Mind in ALL Three Dimensions." There's also a rash of new ESP games; the instructions and equipment are so complex that they would surely fuse anyone's psychic flow. Plastic phosphorescent ouija boards are everywhere. As a devout ouijaphile since childhood, I've discovered that it should be used mainly with strangers, and is perilous among partners: JACK LOVES LINDA is ominous news, when Linda is after all married to Tim—and the board says that Tim hates Jack. YOUR ROOF NEEDS REPAIRING can tempt a marital homicide as easily as JOANNE WISHES AAGGHH THAT RODNEY WERE DEADXHMPH.

For more amicable evenings, Bar-Spreezy requires that you sip a drink for every point won; you skip sips by drawing "Intoxicards" or landing "On the Bowery." The literature encourages you to "Take Your Friends 'On the Town' in Your Own Living Room!" where "All Sorts of Crazy Things Can Happen to You!" Surely the sequel is "Mate-Match," the "Computerized Compatibility Fun Game for 2 to 50 People," which will determine if "Your Mate Is a Real Swinger." There are also lots of "body contact games," devised for teen-agers, but flourishing in the adults' departments. These involve getting looped together, scooping or dropping plastic cubes from or into a bucket tied to your opponent's waist, or, as in "The Game of Love," smacking down your hands, knees, and other extremities all over the playing board. Oddly, there are also many solitary games: for those who detest the party? Or for those alone with a broken TV set.

One of the best games I've seen is "50 Easy Steps to the White House," created by Godfrey Cambridge. While the board's addressed to blacks, it's offered for "discriminating people of all races." You start at Watts, Harlem, Mississippi, and Newark; at thirteen, you become a moderate or a militant. A moderate "seen lunching with Stokely" goes to jail; a militant loses two turns for "pasting black power posters in the White House john," also if his son "intermarries, goes to Africa in search of roots." For straightening your hair, you go back to Gary, Indiana. Later, "You run for mayor and win assuring people that you will not be a 'Negro' mayor. Roll again." It's selling very well, although many stores were wary of carrying it. The manufacturers were questioned by the Secret Service, which had feared that the game promises to "overtake" the White House, and that it showed a map of that citadel.

Scrabble repels those who find pushing little squares of cardboard around a depressing substitute for talking. If "interpersonal relationships" are too intolerable at social gatherings, charades still seem the best escape. At least people must leave the room to dress up, rehearse, find props—and no one is a victim. An adolescent favorite of mine was extension: eggs—stench—shun, which gave a hilarious opportunity for hen-like misbehavior, a wonderful passage of gagging and retching, and the necessity of snubbing everyone on hand. Hopefully, charades are not yet marketed: unlike Christmas, they come free.

REELS OF CALIFORNIA: A NEW YORKER'S VIEW
1969-72

THE EXTREME East (Manhattan) and the acute West (all California) each maintain the same myth about the other: that the opposite coast is where everything happens first. Both New Yorkers and Californians suspect that their politics and clothes and horoscopes and language are being predetermined across the country by slap-happy or formidable strangers, who sculpt the future with all the carelessness of media freaks. I've had seven Californian trips in the last three years; as a New Yorker, I do feel that the left and the right are farthest along in California, though the natives tell me that New York is the capital of radicalism. Landing in Santa Barbara or Berkeley, I lunge toward locals with urgent questions, which they interrupt to demand tidings of New York. We each think that the other's drug culture is more lavish than our own, along with the span between magic and mantras, self-destruction, revelation, revolution, celebration, or beads. (Still, some Californians have said that their head scene may be more frenzied than ours.) So I can only record what delights or alarms a New Yorker in a state which seems more foreign than any European country I've known. Meanwhile, California ignores Europe and most of the globe—a fact which sets an easterner adrift.

Throughout, the sheerly physical exhilaration—simply expanding into space—seems to triple the energy that can be curtailed by canyons. Bombing down those great silky highways in a souped-up Mustang, with electronic rock ribboning out of the radio, made three adults feel about twelve years old. We were impatient when the music broke for bulletins on the first moon walk. (As the spacemen were put in quarantine, the back seat asked, "If the astronauts are contaminated, do we send them back?" The perils of exposure to moon dust make the old songs about stardust sound quite sinister now.) The excitement of California driving overwhelmed our normally vast appetites for news, although we were desperate for newspapers that reported more than an outbreak of mumps in Santa Ana or San Luis Obispo as soon as we climbed out of the car. California makes you feel your own contradictions. We complained about the provincialism but sometimes found it infectious: when you feel so extravagantly healthy, your own body seems more important than many world events. (I could never feel that elsewhere. But one's own ethics back up the spout in California.) Hence the surfers on the beaches that we passed seemed justified in their isolation, their ignorance of everything but the next wave.

Yet other forms of ignorance were infuriating. Political misinformation spat through the air like birdshot. (In '69 I was told that Mayor Lindsay would soon be exposed as a tool of the CIA.)

Denials were shrugged away. The car also taught us that many San Franciscans don't know where they live. We gave lifts to white radicals after some evenings at a Panther conference: most weren't able to guide us to their own addresses, and we drove in giant ovals until two or three A.M. while they explained that they'd moved to California forever—six days ago. (Yes, the frontier mentality still lingers: the West still seems to promise to enlighten or enrich you.) One boy nearly lost us for a lifetime with his street directions: "Right on" meant straight ahead (*not right*); "Ray-Gun (argot for Ronald Reagan) meant turn to the right; for making a left, he murmured, "Socialism, man." Wondering if we'd still be on the streets at dawn, I remembered driving in Santa Monica on Labor Day some years ago: the radio was regularly announcing state-to-state car crashes as though they were football scores: "Massachusetts, 12; New York, 17; and *California* is *still leading* with 24 road deaths!"

The car makes it easy to see life as a movie: watching your own footage, which draws in others or is rewritten by them. It's the state of mind that was developed by the acid converts of the early Sixties, and the sensation seems especially Californian. Still, John Barth nailed it nicely in *End of the Road* in 1958: "we are all casting directors a great deal of the time." Later in the novel, a character remarks that "A man's integrity consists in being faithful to the script he's written for himself." Quite a few in California seem to have lost or betrayed their own scripts, while others hunt for them.

□

People often argue that New York gives you too much reality, while California yields an overdose of fantasy. It sounds too simple, but I can't reject it. Riding the New York subway or just trying to phone the Health Department because you've had no heat for a week seem to have no parallels to being stoned in the sun, staying warm, getting tanned. Watts was full of red flowers beneath a blue sky: someone kept repeating that it didn't look as harsh as Harlem.

□

Walking down a Santa Barbara street at dusk: some feet ahead of me, a young man draped in quivering buckskin fringes strolls and punctually yells, "I'm going to die!" Not frantic: he's just telling the world. He's probably descending from acid, or just rising, as the sunset ebbs and chills. Meanwhile, house owners emerge and stand on their porches, each gripping a huge flashlight as though it were a gun. Beefy men in bright shirts watch silently until he shouts himself out of sight—the street is lined with grizzled householders protecting their own steps, their electric weapons ready. Self-defense takes on a new tang: they do look ready to attack. "I'm going to die!" And they probably wish he would—it's a collision of cultures that just can't live together. Ironically, the paranoia that often springs from acid or speed seems contagious for them. So they're afraid of losing what they have; he fears he's already lost it. His drugs, their homes and flashlights, his noise, their ominous quiet: the threat is mutual, as unforgivable as death.

☐

In the windows of shops on Telegraph Avenue in Berkeley, groups of people lie jiggling on waterbeds which are covered with patterned rugs; they read and chat and exchange the day's news, heaped casually together. Here, I'm pleased to learn that "fucking your Ma" means nothing Oedipal—just living free at home, if you're a student.

☐

Some California deaths are hard to miss. The *Los Angeles Times* reported that a young man in Hollywood was found frozen stiff inside his own refrigerator. His hands clutched a rope which kept the door closed.

His neighbors said that he lived on a diet of Cutty Sark and Hostess Twinkies, and that he was obsessed with fighting crime. He had a homemade, life-size robot to "sniff out illicit drugs," and he alternated between wearing his police costume and a Superman suit, in which he used to jump on roofs at night. The cops heard complaints that someone dressed as Superman had startled pedestrians by springing at them from phone booths. But no action was taken against him, because he had no record. His landlord said that the young man had tried very hard to make adult friends, but most of his conversation was about comic books.

□

Legendary Hollywood is scarce; since most of the big studios are sagging, and more than half of the usual number of studio staffers are out of work, the industry and its survivors are on the defensive. Still, those I saw were friendly because my father wrote the movie of *Gunga Din*. But they and the younger scriptwriters I met clearly suffered from the same affliction that was famous in the Thirties: so much commissioned work unused, so many scripts and projects scrapped, all that rewriting and polishing for nothing. Paid for, of course, but it still feels rotten. And some of the abandoned movies sounded as though they might have been good.

Looking for lore, I was finally rewarded by a seasoned publicist who described working for a producer of costume serials, B-Westerns, and jungle pictures of the Forties. He explained the problem of dealing with chimpanzees: "After seven years, you can't work with any chimp: their brains get bigger and start pressing against their craniums, and they get very mean. When that happened with Tomba —she was our best chimp, we'd used her for years—my boss thought he'd simply get rid of her. I told him, 'Sam, you just can't drop a chimp like that.' I insisted that she be retired. I made up a lovely little story: that Tomba had been having dizzy spells, and one day she finally passed out during a scene with Johnny Weissmuller. I said she got knocked up by a chimp named Hooligan, who went off with a traveling circus. So we showed pictures of her knitting booties, there were pieces in *Variety* and everywhere about her long career. . . . So when it comes to Sayonara, there's no need to be a schmuck— you don't have to break a broom handle off in anybody's fanny."

Someone said later that Tomba's retirement could yield a lesson in humanity for all of Hollywood: "Mostly you just get the foot. Then blam. You're over."

□

"No lice in my wigs!"

Sitting in a motel lobby, famished for world news—forgetting how the car had made me indifferent—the only factual report I could find on TV was an interview with a pet-shop owner in Long Beach, whose piranha fish had been stomped to death by the local police. There was some question about the legality of breeding such deadly fish in California. But the distraught fish-loser exhibited his empty aquariums hung with little black drapes and signs reading "Police Brutality"; he was vowing to sue the state.

Meanwhile, I was aware of shouting near me: "My wigs are pure!" a salesman wailed into a public phone, his voice trembling with the threat of tears. I gathered that he was talking to an assistant DA. He said that $10,000 worth of his merchandise had been seized without a warrant—here his voice broke—because a female competitor had bought a wig and then claimed that it was crawling with lice. "She did that because my wigs are *cheaper* than hers. And now they're sitting in that bastard's office—collecting dust and crap and for all I know people are *walking* on them—and my sale's supposed to start tomorrow!"

The desk clerk looked miserable; his gaze cringed around the lobby in fear that the motel would be accused of sheltering parasites. "And you know," the salesman screamed, "lice couldn't live in wigs. They need *warm-blooded* animals. They depend on a bloodstream. . . ."

On TV, photos were shown of the dead piranhas, while their owner elaborated on their wholesale and retail prices. Momentarily, all California seemed insecure: so easy to lose your fish or your wigs to ruthless servants of the law—to be stripped of your marketable property. "How's a man to make a living!" the salesman howled. Writers of junked scripts would have understood him.

Indeed, despite all of California's coastal splendors, you're less aware of the rich there than of the many who haven't made it. You meet the rich in their own homes, which are often tastefully remote from town centers or main streets, lapped in shielding shrubbery. The very poor are usually in isolated ghettos—you don't see them daily, as you do in New York. But the strugglers swarm through motels and drive-ins and Pizzaburgers, clanking with failure: the boom state withholds its promise from them, and the Gold Rush seems like the remains of a real estate flack's lies. . . . So it's eerie to remember that I got my name from the Gold Rush: my grandmother's uncle was a Forty-Niner, searching for nuggets in Sonora, California. She was named for the town in hopes that it would reward him, but he struck no gold at all. Still, I regret that the name was shortened by the time it came to me—I'd like to feel a closer kinship to all that elation and certainty, when the West spelled a guarantee.

☐

Two friends of mine were refused a room at a San Diego hotel on their wedding night, because the management was convinced that they were brother and sister. (They did look rather alike, until the husband grew a beard.) But it shows you what a local hotel manager has trained himself to expect in California.

☐

Charles Manson told *Rolling Stone* that "Death is psychosomatic."

Musing on Manson as part of an American ballad, or as one of our handiest myths, I can see why he has something for everyone. Not young himself, yet he gives some people the excuse they've been waiting for to simply hate the young—to hate all of them. After Manson's conviction, one of the jurors said: "I hope this verdict will be a lesson to the young people of this country—that you can't just go into a person's house and butcher them up. . . ." And Manson was as satisfactory for Weatherman as he was for their conservative elders; the Liberation News Service reported this slogan: MANSON POWER—THE YEAR OF THE FORK!

Manson did understand that he was a symbol. "Anything you see in me is you. If you want to see me as a vicious killer, that's who you'll see, do you understand that? If you see me as your brother, that's what I'll be . . . I am you, and when you can admit that, you will be free. I am just a mirror."

One of the women in his tribe explained, "Charlie taught us that instead of dying slowly and treacherously—aging—you can speed up the process and do it in your mind. Because you're right at the point of life and death all the time. Every time you're totally willing to die, it brings you right back into living. The point of death is rebirth."

Dear old death and rebirth: these days, it almost sounds like grilled cheese and bacon. However, while people are on death trips all over the country—nowhere do I feel it so strongly as in California. It's said to have the highest suicide rate of any state.

In 1972, the director of the Los Angeles Suicide Prevention Center told a convention on "Suicidology" that more young people were killing themselves than in the past. He said, "I've never known a generation as interested in death as an experience, something you can pass through."

□

In December 1970, those who stayed on after the permit for the Laguna Beach rock festival had expired were roused or awakened by lines of cops singing "Here comes Santy Claus" as they prodded dozens of sleeping bags with their sticks and feet.

□

From L.A. to San Francisco, you meet the beached remnants of 1967: the searchers who haven't yet fled to rural communes—gentle freaks and strung-out waifs who may still learn self-protection. California seems to display even more casualties than New York—perhaps because the brilliant skyscapes and delectable styles of living make the battered or vulnerable faces more conspicuous. There, you're more conscious than ever that many have lost the courage or the mere enjoyment of language, that words have yielded to vibes. . . . At the Esalen Institute I sat reading in a parked car for several hours, while a friend had interviews inside (fairly enough, the directors didn't want a reporter wandering about and collecting haphazard impressions). Still, the inmates were hospitable: a few fed me chocolate bars through the car window, and one said, "If you want to . . . you know, um, you know . . . if you want to . . . *you* know . . . it's over there." I thanked him, hoping that the very expensive Esalen treatment would eventually strengthen his confidence in being able to name the bathroom.

□

After all the enchantments of driving down the Pacific coast, envying the lushness of anybody's garden (a New Yorker hardly sees a weed these days), reveling in the spaces and breezes, astonished by the cordiality of strangers and the sweetness of abalone steaks, still riveted by the crusts of Hollywood and the density of the occult, I returned each time to the East convinced that New York is the most peaceful and rational of communities, soothing in its stability after all the conflicts of California. Snuggling into the Manhattan ooze, savoring a reflection from Donald Barthelme—"this muck heaves and palpitates. It is multi-directional and has a mayor"—a native yields to New York chauvinism: California is stunning, but . . . all that freedom seems illusory whenever Ronald Reagan blows his nose.

PART IV:
THEATER
AND MOVIES

Starting in about '66 the theater began to echo the political and social themes of the period (as well as the sexual malaise). So many plays were nagging at America, reflecting or rejecting what we lived with.

OFF-OFF-BROADWAY
June 1967

INTOLERABLY WHITE lights glare off tinfoil walls, while two voiceless giant dolls with vacant faces tear up books, sheets, and curtains, smash pictures, write and draw obscenities on the walls, dance, and goose one another. Throughout the defilement, the vast gray motelkeeper obliviously drones her praise of the room: "All modern here, but . . . with a tang of home. . . . The toilet flushes of its own accord. . . . Oh, it's quite a room." Her monologue is an advertisement—a style that's currently exploited onstage. A siren howls while the dolls rip the walls apart and then wreck the motelkeeper's body; they then strut proudly down the aisles. *Motel,* one of Jean-Claude van Itallie's

329

three plays in *America Hurrah,* superbly directed by Jacques Levy, distills the most crucial ingredients of the new theater which resides in lofts, cafés, and churches, drawn from a wellspring of workshops.

Triumphantly visual, unverbal, concerned with images rather than characterization, the movement is wary of content. (Naturally, no one from Off-Off-Broadway quotes Henry James, but if they did, he'd come in handy: "The subject doesn't matter; it's the treatment, the treatment!") Consequently, some of the plays' problems are rarified, such as how to build a bookcase, or persuading a dead cat to drink milk, or living with varicose veins. Still, certain themes are discernible: destruction (as in *Motel*); hoaxes (from government to art, especially as expressed in the style of the TV commercial); quandaries of sexual identity; the panics instilled by forms to fill out, hating one's job, trying to learn the time, or even obtaining street directions; growing old; Vietnam. Simultaneous effects—noises, lights, dialogues in unison, yells, gunshots—collide to make the audience feel that everything is happening at once—as it does in a war, or during the familiar (and total) confusion that can assail you while watching TV. (Jacques Levy stresses that TV provides a state of consciousness wherein the attention is free-floating and unfocused.) When this style is at its peak, as in *America Hurrah,* the spectator can feel that he's having a private hallucination.

On the savage ending of *Motel,* Levy wants the audience to ponder two different kinds of killing—or ruin. He said, "How do you feel about someone who takes an axe and kills his wife's lover in a fit of jealousy? Now compare him to a doctor in a concentration camp who experiments coldly with the threshold of pain. You're *not* sorry for that doctor. He must be from another planet—but he looks more like you, like us, than some wild nut." Levy explains his concept of the doll-monsters by contrasting the old film personifications of Frankenstein (pitiable, even sympathetic, with no control of his emotions) and Dracula (motiveless malignity, "unshakable cool"). The *Motel* monsters are Dracula's descendants: uninvolved by reason or emotions, Levy says "they're just doing their thing." However, part of the calculated shock is their human appearance; their masks are chill but cheerful Pop cartoon faces: clean-cut, not grotesque. Neither an orgy nor a purge, *Motel* succeeds as an image of senseless destruction where many (naive) antiwar plays have failed.

Off-Off-Broadway is more than an incubator; not only has it hatched some of New York's best productions, but its virtue is that it can afford to fail—financially as well as artistically. A few years ago, as Broadway and Off-Broadway died from expense like mastodons sheeted in ice, New Yorkers who love live acting despaired of having any kind of theater. (At present, there are fewer commercial plays running than there were during the Depression.) While it's true that most of the professional offerings are feeble, dim overnight critics who can close a play after one performance have empowered economics to kill the existing theater. (Usually, only a eulogy in the *New York Times* can preserve a "serious" play.) But in a loft, a production can cost under $200; a three-week run—with or without critics—can often be guaranteed. Naturally, many groups hope for subsidies or grants, and almost everyone involved must earn his living elsewhere. But the movement cheats two near-impossibilities in modern Manhattan; first, the product isn't controlled by money or publicity, and second—in a period when the newest and the latest are hourly proclaimed, and then followed by some ancient familiarity —something we haven't seen before is actually occurring.

Definitions would cause most of the new playmakers to choke. Still, since so many have worked together at the Café La Mama, the Judson Memorial Church, the Caffe Cino, The Open Theater, and many others, they share certain stylistic preoccupations. The workshops sometimes enlarge the actors' conceptual role to the extent that, when the plays develop out of classes, the dramatist becomes more of an editor than a writer. Occasionally, the actors may have so much power that they can refuse to deliver lines they don't believe in. Many actors and directors say that they must agree with a play's statement if they're to perform it—or at least believe in its "antidote." As a result of the workshop evolution, most of the new plays are so "visible" as to be unreadable; it's difficult to judge them outside production. So far, most of the experiments have produced more fine actors than playwrights, opportunities for brilliant acting rather than durable plays.

Denial of language is sometimes an obsession. (However, since the movement is intentionally antiliterary, readable drama is no criterion.) Improvisation, which is sometimes related to the spontaneity of happenings, and to the notion that all of life is art, can yield some toxifying boredoms which make you wish that the author had had more control. However, the opportunity for production—which was previously so rare—is far more important than the frequency of stillbirths. In particular, Ellen Stewart, the founder of La Mama, has managed to stage plays against odds which would have capsized the most resilient producers.

It seems unlikely that most of the productions could be transferred to larger theaters, or to film. Physical proximity is essential to the style. When an actress two feet away screams directly into your face while gazing into your eyes, it's hard to feel detached from her pain or ecstasy. *Futz,* a recent award-winner by Rochelle Owens, which concerns an amiable man who humps his pig so enthusiastically that his enraged neighbors kill him, depended almost completely on the smallness—hence the intimacy—of La Mama. The play (which proves that nonconformists tend to suffer) is negligible, despite a few appealing lines, such as "Hell has no fury like a woman scorned by a man—for a pig." (There's another nice moment when Futz, worried about her frustrations, croons to the pig he loves: "Piglets I can't give you, even though I am a healthy man." However, most of the sparse humor is lost when he dies in the posture of the Crucifixion.) But if you accept the dictum that content isn't important, experiencing the excitement of the production is tremendously rewarding. Baked in brick walls, in body heat, the tiny café throbs to zither notes while a young man makes rhythmic farting sounds into the neck of a jug; a girl blows the recorder while hanging from her knees around his neck. The chorus orchestrates a murder confession with gasps and wheezes, grunts magnificently while the invisible pig enjoys her human lover, and springs head over heels in exuberant body celebrations which only a born paralytic could reject. Delight of the limbs is made contagious—especially since the actors are nearly in your lap.

Here, an already mossy conflict must be acknowledged. Most of the directors shun naturalism. The voices of off-off-Broadway insist that the audience must remember that it's in the theater, must be constantly reminded that the stage action isn't life, and should never be lulled into "taking anything for real." (For this reason, Lanford Wilson's *Balm in Gilead* rapidly repeats a murder scene.) In light of keeping realism at bay, Jacques Levy said, "Pop has more balls than Camp. Pop has a cool that I love—it has a way of discussing subjects at a distance." There is also the physical assault by actors: you get touched, stroked, and patted while performers run through the audience, shouting accusations or endearments. The aisle is full of noises. You're hugged while bombs explode. (Before some audience-participation shows, the spectators eye each other nervously—as though wondering what they'll have to do to each other later.) Obviously, the technique works in some plays and not in others. John Lahr, the drama critic for *Manhattan East,* has objected to "the tyranny of the actor" on the grounds that no artifice is attempted—that the directors are really resorting to the naturalism which they claim to have eliminated. Again, the suggestion that there's no distinction between art and life. Currently, there's a happening in the Village where you can pay 50 cents to watch a family that simply lives on stage.

In this same context, there have been objections to the extremely convincing sacrifice of two chickens in Sam Shepard's *La Turista* (also directed by Levy). This furious yet impersonal play shows two young American tourists stricken with savage diarrhea in Mexico; they're serviced by witch doctors who fail to cure them. (The travelers' disease is locally called *la turista.*) The Americans, both named for cigarette brands, seem to personify the collapse of "the Greatest Society"; their sterility is itself a disease which can't survive the dirt of poverty. The production aimed at making the audience feel uncomfortable and very out of place—like tourists. The famous chickens were condemned by some as a naturalistic device—especially since Levy originally wanted to use live fouls. (He has retorted that there's no difference between eating a real or sham apple on stage, and refers the debate to the end of *Motel:* when the dolls demolish the motelkeeper's body, it's a valid shock to learn it's an empty figure, with a recorded voice—that "nobody's there.") The arguments will of course continue, and some spectators may follow John Lahr's rebellious advice by leaping onstage, or flinging the actress who fondles them to the floor in a passionate embrace.

The influence of movies—from parodies of old Westerns to reincarnations of Laurel and Hardy—is conspicuous, as is the employment of film techniques. The use of sudden stills recurs, as in van Itallie's *Interview* (directed by Joseph Chaikin), where the actors' faces are frozen in silent screams while a governor says that he can't give a statement on Vietnam. (In classes, Levy also works on "mesmerization"—suddenly going dead—as television watchers sometimes do.) Sharp transitions—or often, the absence of transitions—can resemble fast film cutting; sometimes montage is used. The spectators are asked to make the connections for themselves. Using filmic devices is another antinaturalistic effort—to make what's seen "less real." (While using the theater for "live movies," Levy took one straight three-act play, cut and changed the sequence, and produced three plays all occurring at the same time—as a way of combining past and present.)

Since character logic is no longer sought, swift transformations of character are common: an actor may spring into a new role, or abruptly demonstrate a contradictory force within the persona. Motives are considered far less important than the way people affect one another; their styles of behavior and mutual response take precedence over their conscious intentions. Much of the new theater shows how everyone plays games, detailing the degree of seriousness or viciousness through actions rather than words. Van Itallie's *TV* is shot with the game of humiliation: a man gagging on a sandwich crawls choking on his hands and knees while his colleagues quarrel about whether to give him bread or water. Motives are related to perpetual game playing.

Games of course rouse the question of Camp—we can't yet abandon this tiresome discussion, and many of the new plays keep it plodding. A recent success, *Gorilla Queen* by Ronald Tavel (directed by Lawrence Kornfield), dredges the jungle flicks of the 1940s to deify a winsome Queen Kong: God is a homosexual gorilla, complete with sequinned nipples. Mens' crotches are caressed beneath grass skirts, male spectators' ears are licked by a chuckling, red-bearded "Brute," a transvestite's false breasts are squeezed, removed, and restored, while a huge lesbian named Paulet Coldbare is nearly burnt as a sacrifice until it's realized that she will increase "smut-pollution." It might be amusing if it were truly outrageous. But most of the jokes are desperate—"I now pronounce you man and wife, or man and man"—as are the lyrics: "Dip your tricky dicky/In the sticky soft spot."

It's been said that the intended dreadfulness makes *Gorilla Queen* and other products of the Theatre of the Ridiculous impossible to criticize. But it still seems worth protesting the boredom of these romps—even if Andy Warhol has said that he loves to be bored. A good recent essay by Jacob Brackman in the *New Yorker,* described the put-on as "a basically hostile means of expression," enabling an artist to be "hostile to his materials, his audience, and his own talent." Many who've seen *Gorilla Queen* are timid of admitting that such hostility leaks all over the stage. Camp theater may continue to thrive simply because the terrors of squaredom can keep most audiences humble.

Infantilism, willful obscurity, ghetto club-forming, the conviction that anyone's an artist if he says he is—none of these irritations invalidate the finest 5 percent of Off-Off-Broadway. Initially, some saw it as a halfway house to the professional theater. Now, many call it a distinct alternative, since failure and dullness compound the sludge of Broadway and the Lincoln Center. Producing plays on minimal money has been a stimulus for certain imaginations. And some say that the pressure to make a lot of cash forces artists to repeat themselves—to throttle experimentation. But it's ridiculous to deduce that the theater flourishes on austerity. Still, there's a pleasing irony: at a moment when culture is furiously fashionable, some gifted practitioners have made a mockery of publicity and economics.

FURTHER OFF BROADWAY*
March 1968

LATELY, THE Off-Off-Broadway actors' involvement with the spectators has so intensified that you fully expect to get laid during the next evening at the theater. The performers are sometimes so close that you smell their sweat before it's shaken onto you. Actors

---

* I wrote this piece at the beginning of March 1968, but by chance it happened to be published on the day that Martin Luther King was murdered. In that early winter, just a few weeks before Mylai, we saw some of the most devastating photographs yet released of the dying Vietnamese. At home we were still getting used to our own atmosphere of random death, which became the groundnote of '68.

sprinkled throughout the audience heckle those on stage, yell advice or derision, correct their lines, throw sugar at them. Meanwhile, hisses, grunts, and squeals accelerate to replace language; gibberish is refined; respiratory noises have been perfected as exclamations of horror. Some directors insist that "content isn't important," that style's far more significant than any subject. However, between an expert grope-in at the Open Theater (where a church meeting flowered into a vast bisexual feel-up), the wistful put-ons of certain hopeless hippie musicals, and some inept, despairing charades about Vietnam, racial themes recur with the relentlessness of the unfashionable. Although racism isn't the central subject of these plays, they're directed to force the audience to think about it: the topic that so many would love to shelve or shun, since it's more tangible than "peace."

Perpetual game playing is still an obsessive style. Games of hostility and destruction stress the helplessness of mutual aggressors, as well as their ignorance of their own motives, their unconscious need to assault. A fury of whiteness focuses the ferocity of Sam Shepard's *Melodrama Play* at the Café La Mama, where the whole cast wears white military suits against a glaring white vinyl setting. When it's time for killing, there is even a white pistol. A menacing guard tyrannizes a flighty songwriter. Threatening his victim with immediate death, the guard alternates his murderous impulses with childish insecurity: "What do you think of me as a person?" The murderer is desperate to be liked, while the thrashed suppliant writhes with the terror of being killed at any moment. At the end, although his life is finally preserved, he continues to crawl on hands and knees in a slow, small circle, wheezing out his agony, moaning, howling, retching. Reduced to a crying animal, he can't yet—if ever—recover his human posture. Finally, all the actors bow while blood trickles from their mouths onto their white jackets.

The tyrant's role was written without racial specification; in Europe, it was played by a white—in New York, by a black man. Thus, the character can personify police brutality and/or sudden black aggression; his personal fear of being disliked embodies both the very American neurosis of yearning to be loved by everyone, and the black's natural anguish at being scorned. Literally bringing a person to his knees is what whites do to blacks; it's also a black's fantasy of what he might do to whites. It yields a searing image for the current atmosphere of the country; beating your random opponent into submission, battering him into mindlessness. Meanwhile, the phrase "psychological victory" comes dribbling out of Washington to describe recent events in Vietnam.

Aside from the excruciating finale, Shepard's play is a dispassionate metaphor. Earlier, three people are killed onstage, and—despite the dramatic shock—one doesn't care, because they haven't been characterized. As allegorical figures, they impart no sense of loss when they fall dead. But, during Israel Horovitz's *The Indian Wants the Bronx,* the intimacies of torture are so intolerable that some spectators have admitted that they wanted to jump on the stage and stop the action. The torment springs from magnificent characterization. Two street boys—high-strung, humorous sadists who are not dislikable—attack a meek East Indian on an isolated bus stop. He has just arrived in New York, needs directions to find a relative in the Bronx, but knows too little English to learn his way. The polite, turbaned foreigner is at first merely puzzled by the twitching boys. He smiles hopefully as they dance on the edge of hysteria, drum their heels against ashcans, and mock their social worker, "Pussy-face," a lady who gave them knives as presents, and who has urged them to "play games" to release their energies. The Indian becomes their game—just because he's there. The sport evolves as their moods flicker, change, and flare. They pantomime burning him at the stake, suddenly knock him to the ground—apologize frantically to him: "Everyone gets crazy sometimes, don't they?"—and finally pummel him into such a frenzy that he wails to an empty telephone booth for rescue. They cut the wires. The play ends with the dead phone ringing while the terrorized Indian screams into a severed receiver: "Please! . . . Thank you! . . . *Thank* . . .you": the only English words he has.

Since nursery school, we've been told that we're a violent people. Early in life, the notion of native savagery becomes a cliché—almost as hackneyed as a radio commercial. But it has a new meaning now. Since Jack Kennedy's assassination, the climb of crime, and—despite their validity—the nationwide riots, the possibility of being suddenly maimed by a stranger is unsurprising. (Murder—as opposed to mutilation—still occurs oftener among friends and relatives than strangers.) Stray madness or "things that just happen" or being in the wrong place at the wrong time, are chances that we all have to live with, without indulging in irrational fear. There's a sense of haphazard execution in our gritty air: a barber has been killed by a customer who didn't like his haircut; recently, four were shot in a luncheonette because the waiter was slow in serving the soup; a woman stabbed a cab-driver in the face and shoulder when he said that he was off duty and on his way to breakfast. Also, we have a new term: "involuntary manslaughter," an act which was committed by parents who told their daughter to kill her dog; instead, she killed herself. In the pressure chamber that we now inhabit, Israel Horovitz has expressed what everyone knows, and very few writers have achieved.

Of course no subject should be shielded from humor; no one has been funnier about racism than the black militants I met in Watts. But Bruce Jay Friedman's *Scuba Duba* is repellent in its effort to squeeze a merry evening's entertainment out of racial hatred. It's particularly depressing from this author, whose superb novel, *Stern,* was a comedy of humiliation about a Jew who fed his own fears of anti-Semitism until he gave himself a nervous breakdown. The distinctions between racism and personal neurosis, sympathy and ridicule, were flawless. Now, in his new play, the hero is meant to personify the dishonesty of the white liberal—who is really encancered with prejudice. An amiable, infantile man, who once thought himself enlightened, loses his wife to two black lovers. Hence he spews forth the loathing that's supposed to lurk in us all: "coon," "shine," "goddam spade," "chocolate shit-head," "fucking Mau-Mau"—until the blacks politely tell him, "You're far from a credit to your race." As a "one-handed" lover, his sexual jealousy peaks at paranoia, which he tries to dilute by clowning: his own game. After abusing one of the black men, he says, "Just overlook the racial stuff." The play is clearly intended as a shower of honesty about bigotry, but—since the humor is so heavy and naive—the result is a deluge of hate. Also, the two blacks are insulting caricatures: a sleek, impudent monster of bullying sexuality, and an overeducated Uncle Tom.

The well-dressed audience laughs cozily at the very simple one-line jokes about hominy grits and *Ebony* and Freedom Marches, which clank like spare parts from the old-fashioned Broadway situation comedies that have benumbed the commercial theater. Ticket buyers can go home feeling comfortable after a pseudo-contemporary snigger. But what passes for probity is a very native flight to an easy psychological excuse: if a black maid punished you as a child, you have a reason for the racism that embarrasses you as an adult. *Scuba Duba* is a feverish success. Soon, there may be a new folk-rock refrain: "Black is black and what is white?" Self-laceration is becoming another white luxury: a way of petting and forgiving oneself.

HOWLING FOR HELP
July 1968

VARIOUS ENCOUNTER groups have been very rewarding for some I know, and maddening for others. Certain rebels report that they resent learning what all small children know: that a group can make one person cry. However, you're constantly reminded that an outsider can't presume to judge an experience that enriches others.*

Still, despite the threat of losing the empathy race, it's painfully easy to judge *The Concept*—as theater. This bath of actuality has been improvised and acted by former drug addicts from Daytop, the rehabilitation center which is run by ex-addicts. (As the playwright's role dwindles on Off-Broadway, while the actors' and the directors' power swells, *The Concept* is the last possible refinement: it eliminates the author altogether.) Hailed for its humanity, the play has been nuzzled by some of the most loving reviews in New York. Punctuated by yells, screams, mutual accusations, enough hostility to win a war, and sufficient tenderness to sink a whale, *The Concept* congeals the process of a marathon T-group which can last from thirty to forty hours. A "new brother" is made to plead for admission to Daytop, until he gags, "Huhhhh . . . lllp!"; then, *"Help?"* After he's carried out shrieking, it's explained that "Your investment for getting in . . . is howling for help."

---

* In the late Sixties, quite a few of the groups I heard about sounded rather sadistic or authoritarian. Now, the theme of humiliation for your own good seems to have abated; instead, some groups sound much more supportive.

Inhibition appears as the fiercest problem of 1968. An actor said in an interview that it's essential "to relate from your feelings instead of from your image. You have to blow your image"—as though it were your nose. Onstage, the group keeps bullying a member because his "image gets in the way." Yielding the self to a group becomes a higher morality: "You're part of something bigger than yourself, which everyone is building." Privacy or loneliness or independence are made to seem equally destructive—a theme of the tribal Sixties. "I saw something last night that really flipped my guts— a new brother, sitting alone." Groans and moans reply, as though the notion were the worst one in the world. Amorphous guilt seeps through those who are too uptight to unzip fully in public. In this symbiosis, no experience seems to exist until it's shared, while the fractions seek their identities from one another. Some T-groups have been rebuked for developing such meshed dependence that members seem lost without each other. Sometimes, neurosis seems to bind these relationships as egg-yolk binds a sauce, while confessional horror can range from the revelation of a cigarette left burning in a linen closet—"I did it! I did it!"—to lying.

The evening improves when each person admits his most "embarrassing moment," from being caught "cattle-rustling in New York" (stealing steaks from a supermarket) to: "I'm really making love to this chick, and her teeth come out"—also, she turns out to be a man. The rather muted humor is welcome, as when a boy describes being discovered while swiping a TV set, by a huge man who hisses, "What's the matter, sweetie, don't you want to watch TV with me?" The boy adds that he stayed and earned fifty dollars.

Education through suffering—that cherished American tradition— is hymned as pain is propelled; perhaps pain is needed as a proof of feeling anything at all in this cool age. At the end, the performers demand of each other: "Will you love me?" A girl cries when she's made to beg for love; finally, a man onstage hugs her. The actors then dispense free hugs to the audience. (I remained unembraced only by scowling furiously into space. However, due to the intimacy of the small theater, I wrote some of my notes on a surface which suddenly turned out to be a stranger's thigh.) The ending recalls a line which bedecked many Broadway plays of ten years ago: "Why don't we touch any more?" This favorite seems ripe for a revival.

One can't deride the success of a program that aids addicts—nor mock their belief in it. But the grizzling tedium of a T-group is dulled by the demon of "honesty": verbally, this is a true group-grope, since rambling incoherence and repetition are preserved for probity. Some insist that boredom is justified because therapy itself is boring. Since the acting's indifferent, you're urged to remember that these are *real* addicts—like the real blind children who were used in *The Miracle Worker* some years ago. Yet reality on stage seems a pathetic argument for fine theater: it's like praising a company for hiring real black actors instead of smearing on the shoe-polish.

Actually, watching a T-group seems about as rewarding as taking someone else's pill prescription. Yet numerous observers respond as though the therapy includes them. Some in the front row even swung their legs in rhythm with the discussion. (I did have a moment's temptation to react to the No Smoking sign by proclaiming my own addiction: to shout that—deprived of Viceroys—I was at the end of my tether.) Actors have been plunging into the audience for several years; now—as in some recent productions—the spectators have started to surge onto the stage.

BLACK THEATER
July 1968

GLEAMING LIKE a vast, unwinking mirror, the black experience reflects our white society; Negro art not only helps black Americans to define themselves, but it also forces the white audience to face its own world. While it's not news that much of the system is splintering, liberal whites may wring their withers over the prickling doomsday sensation, but few blacks seem surprised. The ardent white self-flagellation that Leroi Jones' work encourages isn't needed to nail the point. Every clear black voice echoes our condiiton as well as theirs, from James Baldwin's remark that *"Whoever debases others is debasing himself,"* to Eldridge Cleaver's insights as an "Ofay-watcher": "When I see the whites of *their* eyes, instead of saying 'devil' or 'beast,' I say 'imperialist' or 'colonialist,' and everyone seems happier. In silence, we have spent our years watching the ofays, on the principle that you have a better chance of coping with the known than the unknown."

The current productions are not furious. The superb Negro Ensemble Company chooses plays which express suppression of any stripe. (They've said that they might even include Sean O'Casey on the Easter Rebellion.) Peter Weiss's *Song of the Lusitanian Bogey* details Portugal's savage domination of Angola. The theme is liberal hypocrisy: "the exploitation of the people for their own good." Whites say that they have tried to "raise" the blacks, but the blacks have "failed." Members of the all-black cast—ranging from jet to some who look mildly tanned—alternate in playing cruel whites with gusto, with the authority of those who know cruelty from the receiving end. A black actor shoves out his chin in a succinct imitation of an Irish cop; actresses purr like benevolent liberal ladies, or lift a pearly nostril in disdain. The bogey is a junk deity: its metal jaws clang open to disgorge a series of raging authoritarians. Straining and stamping in a circle with outstretched arms, trotting helplessly in unison, the players sing and dance out their anguish. A man stands on two kneeling bodies, which crawl to support him—later, they form a human chair; a ballet of brutality rounds up beaten workers; enslaved women's slippers soundlessly paw the floor. Families are torn apart and shattered, and a pregnant girl gets kicked by a cop in the stomach—until she isn't pregnant anymore. The final wild wrecking and looting of the bogey leaves the stage full of debris and gasps of exhaustion. Ironic, snowy-toothed smiles stab the audience during a song that guarantees that "The white visitor meets only friendly and grateful faces." The play is muddled and weak, because there's so much factual and economic information to be dispensed, which is clotted by the neo-Brechtian form. But the stunning performance compels a witness to writhe with black oppression throughout the world. What we learn from our own ghettos becomes international fact.

The NEC has also revived *Daddy Goodness,* which was written in 1958 by Richard Wright and Louis Sapin. A nearly buried corpse rolls out of a wheelbarrow, yelling "God *damn!*" Although he wasn't dead—merely dead drunk—his friends believe that Daddy Goodness (nicknamed for his foul character) has been resurrected as "the

Lord." They promptly build a new cash-happy religion around him. (Obviously, the play was inspired by Father Divine.) Coincidental "miracles" propel a feverish adoration of the randy old whiskey-head. At first, he protests his apotheosis; then he comes to believe it. Promising joy and instant paradise on earth, he also asks people to "forgive themselves," rather than to ask for forgiveness, and emphasizes that sin does not exist. He opens workshops and soup kitchens for the poor, but entreats society to do away with money. However, the hysterical religion becomes a corrupt business corporation, and soon "the New Faith" is as fraudulent as the Great Society. A con-manager shouts, "This Heaven's lousy with Revolution!" Someone tries to shoot the wretched Daddy Goodness, who finally drinks himself to death. The play is flawed with rambling repetitions, but it was extremely worth producing for its contemporary themes: guru-making and the search for magic, lying institutions, a hippyish love cult, poverty, "violent demonstrations" by the unemployed, and assassination. "The Lord's" final bewilderment is agonizing to watch: the bemused, hesitant, tormented face of an old bruiser, contorted with the pain of being rejected by those who also demand his help.

Much of the performance maintains the NEC's impeccable standards. However, slabs of it slide into a style that's amazingly recurrent in black companies: the same shuffling, head-scratching, Stepin Fetchit routines for which black groups have rebuked Hollywood and the commercial theater. (Lawrence Olivier's strutting Aunt Jemina act in *Othello,* in which he seemed perpetually eager to serve flapjacks, was almost a parody of the old-fashioned movie Negro.) Since black troupes are formed to stamp out these very clichés, a white spectator gapes at the deep knee-bends, rolling eyes and pouting lips, the ultra-drawling accents, the sniggering exaggeration of black women's sexuality, and the overstatement of black "simplicity": "Mmmmmm*huh.*" Meanwhile, the black audience—which is often at least two-thirds of the house—laughs freely. At first, you wonder if it's all a defiant put-on. But it seems too broad—and too familiar— to be a subtle form of black camping. Many whites share a puzzled reaction, and cannot guess why pioneering black companies should dish up a hominy-grits Tom-style that degrades black people. Again, James Baldwin offers a clue: "People are not . . . terribly anxious to be equal . . . but they love the idea of being superior." Naturally, he was writing about whites. But perhaps middle-class black laughter at foolish black behavior betrays a whiff of superiority.

An identical perplexity is triggered by *The Believers:* a dazzling review of "the black experience in song," performed by The Voices, who can sing screams without feathering a crescendo, or fall to a whisper on the same note. In 1965, Ronald Bryden asked in the *New Statesman,* "Is it still permissible to say they dance brilliantly?" It is, and The Voices do. Shyness about praising black rhythms could date from the 1850s, when Frederick Douglass, the escaped slave who became a black leader, grimly observed that "slaves are generally expected to sing as well as to work." But black culture now celebrates the pulse that was once patronized. As *The Believers'* program notes, the American black "has expressed his lot in song," from 17th-century slavery to the Sixties civil rights marches. (At times, music must have been the only safe release.) The show opens with leaping, drumming African incantations, kidnaping blacks for slavery, and proceeds to the plantations, the freeing of slaves, a Gospel meeting which jumps into jazz, and a blues scene among the jobless in Harlem. Between the voluptuous dances and songs, black actors once more caricature themselves with a fish-fry winsomeness —as though they couldn't speak without squealing or cackling. As in *Daddy Goodness,* the black male is often a baggy figure sloshing whiskey into a tipped-back head, or a naughty twinkling child. The players finally achieve the dignity they've been denied in a joyful militant finale, where the dancers flash glistening posters of Malcolm X and Martin Luther King, while the African drum throbs.

At a symposium afterward, The Voices asked the (mainly black) audience for its opinions. Since no one could fail to respond to that music or those bodies, all were enthusiastic. The Tomming wasn't mentioned. One young Afro said, "Millions of black people didn't accept the term 'Black Power' until lots of whites did—very recently." He stressed that the same applied to black music, from spirituals to jazz and soul: "We are just starting to accept what we ourselves produce." So a white leaves the theater humbled by realizing (all over again) how triumphant suppression has been—and confident that the sound of shuffling won't last long.

BLACKER THEATER
January 1969

LOVE-BATHS IN the theater are subsiding. Now, instead of shouting "How I love you!" or—like the Living Theatre—stroking spectators while murmuring "Holy skin, holy hair, holy sleeve, holy wool," the actors are beginning to declare their hostility. While the grope-ins were mainly farcical, the new form of audience involvement is not: because the actors are black. At last there's a searing validity in participation—since we're all in the racial situation. (As Malcolm X said, "the Negro problem" should be renamed "the white man's problem.") But many—especially the critics—seem astonished that blacks are angry at whites, and chide them for rebellion.

There's a curious contrast with England in the Fifties: when *Look Back in Anger* and kindred works lashed the issue of class in Britain, much of the public was acutely interested; as the denunciations of the system grew more furious, the audience seemed increasingly fascinated and concerned. But here, where black revolt and even indignation have been slow to surge, a racist society is startled by reproach. The playwrights have been accused of "going too far," "losing perspective," "expressing their own point of view." The sound of shuffling has dissolved—completely. Black theater has developed so swiftly in the last few months that members of many cultures can be envious: at the potent evolution of a style that swells and celebrates and stings.

In the Wine Time by Ed Bullins, author of *The Electronic Nigger,* unskins the exhaustion and hopelessness of the ghetto without any references to whites or to white racism—which are unnecessary. A simmering August night: on a worn wooden porch, a family marinates in cheap port, while a strolling cop swats his club against a wire fence, neighborhood voices yell down the block, their words entangling many lives, and people mutter through screen doors. A husband bickers with his pregnant wife. She berates him for being jobless while *she* goes out to work: again and again, she says that he's not a man. At first, he parries her nagging with mocking affection, calling her his "Hottentot queen." She asks if he couldn't call her "something more northern . . . Ethiopian?" He teases her about a Ubangi great-grandfather and the Irishman who seduced her grandmother. Finally, she cries, "I'm the one who made a man out of you—when your mother and the whole United States Navy failed!" After he slugs her, he adds ruefully, "Ahhhh honey, I'll forget about it if you do." Their teen-age nephew watches queasily, later to be rebuked for a small independent gesture by his aunt: "You gettin' kind of *mannish* around here." It's the recurrent theme of poverty: that women have the authority (which they also resent) because more jobs are open to them, and because whites have crippled the black male. At the same time, more and more black women are rebelling against this role casting—and against the accusations made against them by black men.

As the gentle, uncertain boy tries harder to seem like a man, he appears even more childlike. After some bawdy chat with his uncle, he admits that he's never slept with his girl: "We just look at each other and smile." The uncle is horrified—and the Harlem audience whoops. Neighbors join the querulous porch life. People swear at each other for swearing, fight without meaning to, remark grimly on the numbing repetitions in their lives. Ed Bullins has distilled the language and the experience of the ghetto so magnificently that we learn more from this one mood play than from scores of sociological studies about growing up in the black slums, where the fatigue that oozes out of the suppression seems even stronger than despair. While the play has a limp, sudden ending—the drunken boy kills a man who stole his girl, and the uncle pretends to be the murderer—the last ironic crunch is almost unbearable. The man says to his violently trembling nephew, "It's your world, go down there and claim it, boy." Shaking from foot to skull, he stands there peering at a world which will discard him.

Harlem's New Lafayette Theatre, where Bullins is resident playwright, belongs devoutly to its neighborhood. There are very few whites in the audience—which often joins in the play as you would in the life of your own street. They may shout encouragement— "Give it to her!"—or applaud what's most familiar: like the community drunk, whom everybody knows. Fingers snap in the darkness as cool, prickling jazz precedes an act. But (unlike many Broadway audiences) they were not taken in by a forced conclusion: they laughed at the contrivance. It's a theatrical education to see a play among those who respond only to its most honest moments—which were abundant in this production.

KNOW WHO'S BLACK: a sign on the stage of *Big Time Buck White* brandishes the quest for selfhood like the clenched-fist power salute. This gritty satire, by the white writer Joseph Dolan Tuotti, ripened out of the Watts Writers Workshop, and had a three-year success in California. In the office of BAD (Beautiful Alleluiah Days), a "poverty gig," black men battle over funds and the power they'd like to wrench from one another. Feverish insults fuse their collaboration: *"Superspook,"* "Who you callin' nigger, nigger?" "You mahogany Eskimo!" punctuated by the slow, mutinous hiss of "Shhhhhhiitt." They repeat, "Why do we have to fight all the time?" (At a black rally in Harlem, last October, a militant said, "Blacks are the most *un*together people. . . . We spend more time fighting ourselves than fighting the enemy—which suits him. We've got to get our shit *together*.") Later, an Afro-style leader takes over, and the blacks batter whites instead of one another. The (mainly white) audience is invited to ask questions, most of which spur savage or scornful replies, such as: "Yes, the white man's got ɑ conscience. Enslaving a human being is against his feelings—so he has to think of blacks as animals." A white inquires if white help can still be accepted? "Yes, you can help *after* you've cleaned up your own neighborhood. Go home and clean up your mother's mind." (Malcolm X: "Let sincere whites go and teach nonviolence to white people!")

Buck White has been criticized as an indulgence for white masochists—which is a silly complaint. In fact, it's a partial T-group, spliced with wry put-ons, which succeeds as an experiment. It's flawed by clichés of black characterization—a glossy, threatening street hood, thumbs hooked in his back pockets, and a strutting, huffy bantam—and by the fact that some of the questions are asked by actors who are planted throughout the audience. But whites can only profit by hearing directly how blacks feel: for once, the moldy term "dialogue" is valid. The director says that on some nights, "people forget it's a play. Birchers and Panthers get up and start shouting at each other across the room. For blacks, it's a celebration of the black spirit, and for whites it's an opportunity to become involved in the black experience. . . ." *Buck White* helps to destroy the silence which has become dangerous for us all.

The linguistic brilliance of Ed Bullins and the free-fall exchanges of *Buck White* are complemented by the nonverbal *Riot*—a slice of the new gut-theater, which involves the audience physically, so that shocked senses may later ventilate the mind. *Riot,* from Boston's OM Theatre Workshop, was conceived and directed by Julie Portman during the summer of 1967, in "response to what was happening in the street." In a church basement, a panel of liberal and conservative whites, and moderate and militant blacks, churn helplessly in a racial debate—until they yell with fury at each other. The discussion alternates with bursts of revolt: real bayonets are thrust within one inch of the spectators' chests in the front row, and karate teams drill: "Kill!" Under frantically flickering lights, the actors' faces freeze in tableaus of agony—which were culled from the news coverage of the Newark riots, when many were photographed at the very moment of being shot, screaming, shooting, fleeing, dodging or dying. There's a terrifying silent pause in the dark, when you don't know what will happen—and dread what will. The players drag chairs across the floor until that metallic whine becomes a shriek that's more sickening than a siren or a human howl. Then, amidst the peppery stink of burning, the space erupts: beer cans and bodies hurtle through the air, people fall dead at your feet, shots and explosions heighten the gasps of anguish, groans wrench the ribs of writhing figures which can't get up.

You keep telling yourself that you're in the theater, that you must be safe, while knowing that accidents can happen—as in any riot. Or theater. (Actually, one critic's hand was nicked by a bayonet, and another's ankle was bruised by a beer can. As a coward, I cringed in the third row.) Finally, the basement is still: every single body lies crumpled on the floor. The stunned audience rises slowly. No one claps. And no one gibbers about "artifice": *Riot* has all the reality that anyone can bear. The play embodies what James Baldwin wrote in 1962: "The Negroes of this country may never be able to rise to power, but they are very well placed indeed to precipitate chaos and ring down the curtain on the American dream." One can hardly ask more of the theater than words made flesh.

349 THEATER AND MOVIES

RAPTURE UNWRAPPED
August 1969

RITUAL AND ecstasy are becoming rather like ham on rye: available at any drugstore, unreliable in quality, sometimes fuzzy on the tongue, a quick bite in a hurry. (There's a Harvard cafeteria, where, if you order poached eggs, the waitress howls "*Drop* two on *toast!*" to the kitchen, and couples often flinch. It's the problem of the new theater: should you take it personally?) However, although some producers of the theater of liberation do resemble short-order cooks, certain moments at the steam table are still worthwhile. *Dionysus in 69,* a hashed-up serving of *The Bacchae,* validates the use of nudity —as some other fleshpacks have not.

The Performance Group, directed by Richard Schechner, plays all over a room tiered with wooden jungle-gyms. Oozing throughout the audience, the actors climb in and out of their shorts and T-shirts, proclaiming their mythic characters in some lines, rejecting them in others—announcing their own names, or the fact that they come from New Jersey. (Perhaps falling in and out of roles is even more popular than falling in and out of bed.) One slumps when they talk about "making this room a community," and starts to attention at the percussive splat of people slapping their own bare flanks in relentless rhythm. There's the pleasure of watching good acrobats: a slow headroll or a backward rotation shows the flutter and ripple of muscles beneath tight skin, the exhilaration of elasticity in control. Three passages (quite amazingly) succeed: the birth of Dionysus, who writhes through the spread legs of several girls who straddle him (inspired by an Asmat Indian birth ritual); the pursuit of Pentheus by the Bacchae—his panting nakedness is intensely vulnerable as he runs and leaps to escape the thud of their brutes' heels; and the triumphant bloodbath at the end, in which red paint unspills a shock when it's smeared over jerking bare bodies. Then the ceremony sags, as Dionysus hoarsely begins to parody a modern radio announcer: "There's only one ritual in the country now—it's killing." Thanks, but we understood. It's the familiar flaw in the (best) nonverbal theater: as soon as the words return, they're apt to be mediocre. When the bodies are so articulate, the fudging of language betrays the fine use of arms and legs as well.

The performance changes constantly. When I saw *Dionysus,* the experience was abstract though intriguing; one reviewer called it "the funniest Greek tragedy I ever saw"; another remarked that "it's impossible to really dislike or be disturbed by it"; several of the most critical minds I know said that they were painfully involved and moved. On certain nights, the impulse to rescue Pentheus has driven some spectators to hide him or hold onto him. Naturally, the seduction of "participatory games" rides on the strength of the production: while an actor whispered deep in my ear that "Dionysus cannot bear a mocker or a scoffer," I managed to keep a straight face, but he didn't—an unwilling snort burst out of him. I decided that was his problem and not mine.

Schechner uses group therapy (known to a friend of mine as weepstakes) in his actors' workshop, and has declared that ". . . life style and performing style are not separable. You simply cannot be a great performer and a lousy human being." Lousiness means failing to understand yourself and the world, not being "whole." But, despite all the cheese in *that* conviction, and the chunks of clumsiness and naiveté in *Dionysus,* this particular group-groping toward a fresh style is riveting—when it isn't hilarious. Also, relevant to the textual (not sexual) revolution that's current in the theater, Schechner has one robust point: that the "traditional" theater in America treats the playwright with as much contempt as the new experimenters do.

If only *Oh! Calcutta!* had indeed delivered "elegant erotica," celebration, "fun." There's a rather lovely dance in the buff for two, with the women bicycling slowly in the air on the man's back, and some lyric capering, plus a few engagingly caustic lines, mainly between a querulous couple in bed: " 'Move this way—that way'—you're like a goddamn *traffic* cop," and "Come on, it's role-reversal time!" Otherwise, one suspects that any virgins who see the show may cling to their condition. (At the performance I saw, many of the people in the audience were terribly and pathetically unattractive, ranging from obese to crippled. So I couldn't help wondering if *Oh! Calcutta!* was being used as an alternative to sex—by some who were deprived of it.) Since the authors were asked to contribute their sexual fantasies, or "observations," it's startling that almost all of them stress the difficulties or the miseries of trying to score.

The nimblest skit (*Dick and Jane* by Jules Feiffer) details exhaustion and raging tension between two people who can hardly stand each other; the coital cries are all out of sync. Finally, the man introduces a wheelbarrow, a basketball, spray paint, and so much other paraphernalia, that—after shouting how good it was (for once) —he discovers that the woman herself wasn't even there. So he's upset when his speech to his wife turns out to be a soliloquy: Don't you feel good, Jane? I feel good. Don't you feel loose, like your limbs are floating in air? Don't you, Jane? The best I have had it . . . Janie, honey, come lie in my arms for a minute. (*He lights a match.*) Jane. Where are you? . . . (*Dick rummages through the debris, calling out for his wife.*) Jane! Hey, Jane. Hey, weren't you here? Don't tell me you missed it. Jane! Jane!"

Sexual substitutes occur in other charades: "fucking an aardvark in a parking lot," desperate wife-swapping in hopes of juicing up a flabby marriage, references to girls who "like a finger" as much as the act itself, plus a frantically grim sketch about men who masturbate before a "telepathic thought-transmitter"—their visions of vast breasts appear on a screen, rekindling one another, until they're all switched off by one man's appetite for the Lone Ranger. Throughout, frenzied crotch-grabbing and gagging orgasmic groans remain unsensual. In a heavy spoof of sex research, a man plugged full of wires finds it dreadfully hard to perform. An atrociously winsome house-playing scene, where the man and woman are dressed as children and drooling with babytalk, ends in botched rape. As in so many contemporary movies and novels, bad sex gets all the publicity (it's funny how pleasure tends to be private). Moreover, *Oh! Calcutta!* actually denies the delights of bawdy, and, as many have agreed, the total effect is desexing. It also reminds you that various forces seem to be unsexing many urban societies: fatigue, office strain, money grubbing, fear of failure between the sheets.

Some clammy considerations about nudity. . . . If you're fond of the human body, parts of *Dionysus* and *Oh! Calcutta!* are beguiling. There's a special charm in seeing some variety: such very different shapes are handsomely sculpted—there's no longer a classical norm. But all the bodies have to be (very) good ones. When buttocks (the main feature of *Oh! Calcutta!*) clench and unclench, some sag and others grow mottled; the haunches pleat unbeautifully at certain moments; sharp ribs don't enhance a pot belly. All in all, it's hard to forgive the imperfections in a body you don't know personally. Self-dislike promptly follows: how unfair to be critical of a body. Soon, the spectacle makes you clinical—and that's not likable either. To see so many random genitals at once, when none of them bears any relation to your own body, is disturbing simply *because* it isn't exciting. As Benedict Nightingale wrote in a review of *Antony and Cleopatra* for the *New Statesman,* "The more sex, the less passion; or, rather, the more thoroughly we contemplate sex, the less we seem to believe in its power . . . many [theatergoers would be] distressed, indeed appalled by the suggestion that sex could matter, deeply, to its practitioners. . . . We just don't believe nowadays that people could kill themselves or each other for love or lust. . . . We can't take 'passion' seriously."

However, if one were impassioned by slabs of nakedness, one would have to cope with all the codes of cool that are now imposed upon us. So many experiences are "not supposed to matter": "freedom" demands the discipline of not allowing oneself to feel very much. The new puritanism is emotional, not physical, and it certainly has a repressive effect on comedy. Jokes wither in this chilly air. It's odd that the word "screwing" is still so frequent, at least in New York—surely the term is derogatory. After all, if you say that you were screwed at the laundry, you mean that they mangled half of your drygoods, lost the others, and overcharged you. Unfortunately, the image serves for *Oh! Calcutta!*

KNOCKING THE NATION
October 1969

HISTORY AS a hanger, a coat hook, a contemporary hang-up: the theater can (and often does) do worse. Arthur Kopit's *Indians* is the most robust play on Broadway, granted a fragile competition. Buffalo Bill is characterized as the wrongheaded modern liberal who helps to destroy what he claims to save, patronizes those whom he pretends to champion, sells out the constituents who have been derailed by his false promises. His self-delusions are so lavish that he doesn't perceive that he's lying, while—drunk on public relations—he reels away from facts. He unfurls the currently fashionable political excuse (a great favorite of Mayor Lindsay's): lack of information at the time. Hence he kills thousands of buffalo without realizing that he's depriving the Indians of their food; he later says that he didn't know that buffalo reproduced so slowly. The savaging of the Indians naturally suggests the persecution of blacks and the killing of the Vietnamese. But the parallel isn't slammed into our skulls—it doesn't need to be. A few cold-water radicals have complained because Stacy Keach, the rousing young actor who had the lead in *MacBird!*, resists the wheezy temptation to mime LBJ again. But that benevolent drawl grinds loud enough in anyone's short memory, and Buffalo Bill's lines sound very much like Washington in the late Sixties: "There's always someone who'll call an overwhelming victory a massacre."

Virility: rawhide: old Westerns: power notched by the number of scalps swinging from the belt. It was an excellent idea, and we do need some red studies. But *Indians* is no mere text: there are flashes of fine theater. Bill lollops up to the footlights on a wonderfully nervous (wooden) horse; as the jouncing, rearing, sidling animal fights against its rider, it's impossible to believe that the actor's own body bestows all life to this prop. Under flickering silent-movie lights, drums throb and threaten, flutes squeal, and there's an actual stink of sulphur from the effects. In a delightful scene in which Bill presents a self-justifying skit at the White House, Italian and German actors take the Indian parts, snorting through their accents to play primitive: "Ze white man izz grrreat, ze Indian —nothink!" Later, the ghost of Sitting Bull details the humiliation of "imitating our own glory" when the conquered Indians perform in Bill's Wild West shows. During a massacre, when the dying Indians drop to a stylized white sheet of snow, some frozen arms stick rigidly upright; the tableau recalls many news photos we've seen from Vietnam. However, the strongest line is narrated, not shown: when Sitting Bull was shot, his horse began to dance—because a gunshot was its cue to perform in the rodeo.

Bill isn't presented as a slavering villain: the treatment is sympathetic when he learns that his promises to the Indians are being betrayed by the government. Like a Sixties politican, he protests, "Things are just getting beyond me." At the end, he still clings to the shafts of self-defense: "Anybody here who thinks that we have done something wrong, is wrong." He pathetically entreats the audience to buy some feathered headdresses, postcards, and Navaho dolls. He says that the sale of these trinkets will help the Indians "to know themselves, and raise their spirits." It sounds quite like the rhetoric about self-determination which used to spurt out of the poverty program.

The themes are what we live with now: property and ownership, treating people like objects or animals, genocide. The play hurts when you think about it later—more so than when you watch it. It's far stronger as a metaphor than as a full dramatic experience, partly because the lines have a definitive flatness which makes them awkward for spoken delivery. And there are swatches of boredom, when the Indians talk slowly, proclaiming their own nobility. *Indians* has been called "sick at heart" and "a guilt glut." Those who think it exaggerates a native ruthlessness must have very snug lives indeed, bereft of even audiovisual aids. Or perhaps conscience has become a sagging trampoline: numb flab that's been jumped on too often.

Jumping all over the U.S. now means deploring or condemning policies and history; in the Fifties, it merely meant mocking social behavior and the clichés of pop psychology. (Perhaps only Jules Feiffer has managed to do both.) Elaine May's play *Adaptation* is a gentle skit which seems at least ten years old, safe in its references to all the hang-ups that we know and love. A few fingers are waved at the new left and the CIA, but the context is prepot, prerevolution. The jokes of the Silent Generation weren't deadly or daring; there was thumb-sucking (as in this play) but no clenched fists. Deriding the sorrows of suburbia predated black satire from the ghetto. The comedy of love gone wrong was hung on alienation rather than sexual discord; many plays unveiled characters who "just couldn't get through to each other."

Still, Miss May's mild play does bristle with her marvelous deadpan use of platitudes, recalling the devastatingly straight lines which she and Mike Nichols used to fling at one another, often tinged with the triumph of discovery. A girl explains: "I have this problem. I can give but I can't take"; a psychiatrist reveals that "We can't change the world until we change ourselves." Another girl says, "I believe that we've got to try to be good instead of bad. I suppose you think I'm crazy for having ideas like this?" (She has just given her boy friend a copy of Kahlil Gibran's *The Prophet:* "This book is an outcry, Phil.") The child of Wasp liberal parents asks his mother what sex is; she replies, "Sex is a term." However, when he asks what a Negro is, she evokes birds and bees, light and dark flowers, adding sweetly, "You must think of the Negro as something very, very beautiful that God gave white people to enjoy." Winning maturity points for guilt and dissembling, he becomes a prosperous hotel manager, complete with home and debts, plus two doubting women; both his wife and his mistress ask, "Where are we going, Phil?" After the '68 Democratic Convention in the Chicago Hilton, he's depressed because so many sheets and towels are missing. Dying of a coronary, he lists his unfulfilled ambitions, such as sending his son to a college where he could make good business contacts, and being able to "eat out without fear." His wife tells him that he aimed too high.

As the poet of cliché, Elaine May has directed her cast to uphold a bright, brisk, nose-to-nose delivery: they are meant to be unconscious of their own acute self-consciousness. And the audience laughs faithfully, on cue. But, at $10 a ticket, most of the cozy, fur-backed spectators personify the very American failings that Kopit and May have decried. The happy banalities she parodies fill the lobby after her play; a man said, "Oh God, it's all so *true*"—and referred to his suburban neighbors. Ladies near me at *Indians* kept saying what fun it was, with all the horses and the costumes. . . . Perhaps merely sitting in the theater bestows a sense of safety, laughing at or censuring those who aren't there, or at the amusing-awful creatures on the stage. Last year, after a preview of *The Great White Hope,* the elegant audience gave the sweating James Earl Jones a standing ovation. He deserved it. But self-congratulation sparkled in the air: they seemed to be applauding their own liberalism.

NEW STYLES IN MUSICALS
November 1969

CONSIDER THE dressing table. Whoever thought of putting skirts on kidneys must have had something awfully wrong with him. But perhaps he was straining for a new approach, and was beguiled by incongruities. A similar desperation shapes and swathes our latest musicals, distinctly a rum lot. Discrepancies—the loopiest matings of topics and music—dominate the form. Fresh and tired styles are struggling to be born or re-created; few of the angles seem to fit, although conventions still breathe heavily in the wings. At least one requirement is noticeable: contemporary musicals have to be against something. It's not sufficient to merely provide a villain (pore Judd), nor to blame society (*West Side Story*), nor to have a hateful mother (*Gypsy*). Currently, rebellion and dissent are being packaged as quickly as those cosmetics which are hyped as "revolutionary." Yet three new musicals' targets seem tame enough: the church, the rich, and the British.

Draped with awards, *1776* is an amiable puzzler. It disturbs no one *because* the subject is revolution: our first one. Still glorious, pure and plucky, unsullied by self-interest, it yields a safe libretto in 1969. "Cruel oppression" from England finally forced the squabbling congressmen to unite against "the enemy . . . out there." The entire dramatic action details the writing and signing of the Declaration of Independence, railroaded by testy John Adams, randy Thomas Jefferson, and lovable Ben Franklin. Jefferson can't write the document until he's spent some time between the sheets with his new wife. She gratefully belts out a song that likens his sexual talents to his ability with the violin: "My strings are unstrung, I'm always undone." (Later, love again inspirits politics after Adams sings a duet with his absent wife: "Yours, Yours, Yours." The Adams' songs are mainly about recipes for saltpeter and the trials of abstinence.) There's one good, sleek, chilly number: a silent minuet danced by "Cool, Cool Conservative Men" who oppose Independence—while a dispatch is read that announces the arrival of British troops. And there's a bitter neo-Brechtian aria from a proslavery South Carolina congressman about the hypocrisy of the abolitionist North, which still sends its ships to gather slaves. Otherwise, chatty *My Fair Lady* songs are employed for this hardly musical subject: "We're waiting for the chirp, chirp, chirp" of "a new nation." In great gaps between the songs, the authors have tried to construct a serious play about the vulnerability and the humanity of these historical figures. (Also, it's conscientiously recorded that two southern congressmen refused to sign until the antislave clause was removed.) But the treatment is too naive, and few of the singers are actors. The forced, wide smiles which they must maintain throughout each other's solos look fairly hysterical on 18th-century politicians. Dances are confined to heel kicking and a subdued reel or two. You can't dislike *1776,* but it hardly quickens the pulse. *The Versailles Treaty!* might have been easier to adapt.

Another bewildering success, *Promenade,* is expected to influence future musicals by and for sophisticates: the taste-rakers are astir. It's difficult to guess what the tremendously talented Al Carmines —who has scored Gertrude Stein's *In Circles, The Sayings of Mao,* and Aristophanes' *Peace*—intended in this melodious hash-up. Usually, his strength is satire: musical jokes which extend or mock the lines, ironies of a gay tune to underline a harsh point, or to puncture a pomposity. Here, an earnest morality skit which pits the natural goodness of the poor against the insensitivity of the rich is coated with the most extreme musical camp that may yet have been produced. It takes thirty-four songs to state that money makes you dumb and mean, and that poverty keeps you charming. The rich sing proudly about their possessions: "Things, things, things, things," while the poor dispense wisps of folk wisdom: "A poor man doesn't know what his pain comes from," and, "You have to live with your own truth." The styles mingle silent-movie music with Kurt Weill, Noel Coward, a few Benjamin Britten recitatives, Victor Herbert, lashings of Gershwin and Puccini, foxtrots and tangos, Mark Blitzstein, echoes of *Sous Les Toits de Paris,* Sandy Richardson, *Irma La Douce,* and Gilbert and Sullivan. A tough-girl Forties' song switches halfway through to a heavy-sweet Thirties' aria. A grim, slow barroom dirge by a mother looking for her lost children manages to be soppy yet sardonic. But far too many numbers recall those passages in the Marx Brothers' movies when the young lovers were allowed their one lush operatic duet, and also the collaborations of Jeanette MacDonald and Nelson Eddy. And there are infinite reminders of *The Chocolate Soldier*—especially "Come! Come! I Love You Only!" This is parody stretched so far that much of it sounds merely derivative. The show succumbs to reproducing what it meant to ridicule. Therefore, the oversimple social theme weighs like asbestos. There's one very appealing song addressed as a complaint to a railroad about bad hamburgers, and a genuinely distressing number in which the rich use the bandaged heads of two soldiers as a maypole, unwinding the bloody linen and dancing in a circle, while the wounded clutch their damaged skulls. But most of the camping cancels out comedy *or* affliction. After all, the rich have the best costumes and the best songs.

Hair will keep sprouting for years, of course; its most recent outgrowth, *Salvation,* lacks all the gumption and the sorcery of the original, but has been richly applauded for its nowness. Against a scrambled light show, where yellow amoebas try to divide and unite —a failure of fission and fusion—a frenzied cast derides religion and celebrates sex, which the church doesn't seem to sanction. Several sing confessions which are really hymns of praise: to whatever their sins are supposed to be. There are songs about masturbation ("I don't want hair in the palms of my hands . . . Lord, I'll never do it again"), pregnancy testing and dirty-minded doctors, and the cozily desexing effect of drugs: "Let's make love and maybe tomorrow/If we feel the same way/We can do it again." Sunday is a good day for hitting the sack—surely not a new idea. At times, there are difficulties: "Open Up, Open Up, Open Up, Receive Me," and there's a pantomime of buggery behind silk screens. Hand mikes are used alternatively as wagging phalluses and lickable ice cream cones: the innocence of freedom and the freedom of innocence should enthrall any child of twenty-nine.

Dancing merely means bouncing up and down in place to rock that sounds pre-Presley, circa Alligator-time. The church seems a mild adversary for a pop musical, which ends with some obligatory oriental chanting. There was one lavishly tolerant line: "Even God has His ups and downs." At any rate, He was exorcized by sex and drugs in this show, which I'm tempted to dedicate to Malcolm

Muggeridge. Admittedly, this musical evokes Saint Bernard's remark about fantastical animal carvings: "Great God, if they do not feel shame at the nonsense they produce, why don't they at least shun the expense!" Most of the spectators looked about fifty years old, probably due to the cost of the tickets. They seemed nervous, as though faced with an injection or assault. But *Salvation* doesn't even offend, and isn't ravishing.

HEAD PICS
February 1970

NEW YORK film critics—envisioned in Hollywood as eyeless parasites besotted with power—haven't deterred vast audiences from crowding into Antonioni's *Zabriskie Point,* just as bad reviews failed to dent the voluptuous success of Kubrick's *2001.* The now audience doesn't lie down with the *New York Times* or wake up with *Newsweek* or *Time*—a fact which ought to soothe Spiro Agnew about the influence of the media. While the critics were (extremely) accurate about the absurdity of Antonioni's America, the Department of Justice betrayed an unnecessary panic when it summoned eleven people from the film's staff before a California grand jury to testify about the movie's anti-Americanism. Actually, the film won't pollute any patriots; instead, the U.S. seems to have corrupted Antonioni. Although he has leaned heavily on the trappings of capitalism— evil billboards, the wicked slogans of ads—he himself appears to have been seduced by a brand of commercialism: the old, souped-up Hollywood love formula, which has sold infallibly for fifty years. The boy on the run from a crime he didn't commit and the girl who's seeking "a fantastic place for meditation" unite to synthesize one of our most marketable products.

Even the industry's creakiest dialogue has been trotted out:
"Would you like to go with me?"
"Where?"
"Wherever I'm going."
The conversation between these two switched-off waifs recalls

the remark of an old film publicist about sugary movies: "If you had diabetes, you'd die in the front row." (Wisely, MGM cut the line which made preview audiences howl: "I always knew it would be like this"—an afterglow reflection in Death Valley.) Between the speaking glances and glancing speeches which are routine in Antonioni's movies, there's only one exchange which we've never heard before: after the first kiss, the girl jerks her head toward the desert, saying, "That gypsum?"

"Well, it ain't table salt."

When the Open Theater does its familiar grope-in—embodying the girl's fantasies after smoking a single joint—you can recognize the ancient Hollywood tradition of lovers merging with the whole creation, when all of nature tends to sing along with them. Children of the elements, they also mingle with the earth to the extent that it's hard to imagine them ever making it again without lots of dust or talcum powder. The sex isn't exciting; the girl does most of the work, while the boy is passive, becalmed. The two amateur actors (Daria Halprin and Mark Frechette) seem stunned by their own lack of skill. She alternates between a brow-puckering stare and ticklish laughter; he, who looks quite like Hedy Lamarr, relies on parted-lip reaction shots. Antonioni has also succumbed to another native fallacy: that society's victims need only return to childhood, that lost innocence can be recaptured by playing games outdoors. All in all, this love story clatters like an overworked machine—which it always was.

Still, the movie would be inoffensive if Antonioni hadn't messed up several crucial themes, such as violence, death, and revolution, as well as the native cruelty which taints or derails us all. His early campus revolution sequence can only inflate the public's confusion on this subject, since he presents no tangible issues behind the confrontation. He had muddled Fifties' alienation with the politics of the Sixties, and has failed to detect the difference between life styles and commitment. (By making the youngest generation seem so stupid, he will unwittingly satisfy those who condemn them and their freedoms.) When the boy is killed by the police, after returning a stolen plane, Antonioni's image of radicalization is a long shot of the girl swaying within a cactus grove, conveniently dressed in cactus green. Just as his critique of materialism is weakened by banality, he has even made death dull. In interviews, he's given to dropping such profundities as: "In life, the only certainty is death." That may be news in Italy, but we've already noticed it here.

However, none of the nonsense prevents long young lines from forming at the box office. Much of the movie is so visually delightful that you can easily enjoy it by ignoring Antonioni's ideas as much as he ignores ours. As the girl's car bowls between the squatting haunches of bleached hills, or a red sweatshirt flung from a plane floats down through blue air, there's an immense privilege in sharing the director's eyesight. And of course the optic experience is the main interest of many audiences now. There's also the question of whether *Zabriskie Point* qualifies as what *Variety* calls a head pic: a movie for those who are already turned on. Actually, the style is far from psychedelic, although some might be able to trip to the mass feel-in scene, or through the final recurrent shots of an exploding house, where tables, TV sets, cloths and clothing, books and fluttering papers, drift quite beautifully in space.

Meanwhile people have been expanding with grass and pills at movies for some years now. During pictures like *The Yellow Submarine* and *Monterey Pop,* the smoking sections of many theaters almost bestow a free high, and usually smell like the back of a Morocco bus. Acid converts have told me that they "always" go to *2001* at intermission, so that their trips will last throughout the psychedelic passages. On a recent visit to Hollywood, I found that quite a few youngish actors automatically assumed that anyone who liked their favorite movies must also drop acid. For them, taste is predetermined by the acid plunge.

During one California conversation about science fiction films, a man referred to his own plane. Someone eagerly asked, "Do you fly high?"

"Yes, always. It's the only way."

"Wow! What's it like?"

A five-minute misunderstanding unleashed some lovely dialogue, until the flyer mentioned the advantages of altitude. He cautioned that flying on acid is bad for landings, "because you just wouldn't care."

At any rate, we can soon expect some movies which truly advertise the drug experience, since Hollywood is able to exploit it more quickly than the cigarette companies which may be considering the styles of ads for rival brands of grass—in the event of its legalization. Movies do, of course, cleave to some compulsory suffering, such as Peter Fonda's in *The Trip,* or the random sobs of hallucinators in *Easy Rider.* But it's easy to foresee drug imagery being used as a pacifier as well as a celebration—as well as a commercial enterprise. Also, one can't help suspecting that some officials in this country would rather see the young absorbed by (soft) drugs and drug culture rather than by radical politics. Some of the "tolerant" responses to Woodstock showed a wistful desire to believe that the Chicago demonstrators of '68 were tranquilized by pot and pills and music in '69. Actually, I doubt that more than a few of those at Woodstock were in Chicago—the individuals in those two crowds had very little in common. Besides, many radicals are against drugs; on the left, the movement against them is widening.

Meanwhile, the ultimate trip movie of early 1970 is *Fantasia,* which lost Disney so much money in 1940. Currently, its New York revival is jammed with heads and hippies: the ticket queue previews all the underground fashions for the year. It's astonishing to see how contemporary *Fantasia* is now. (It's also far less sadistic than Disney's other pictures.) Kitsch and Camp collide with spurts of Op and some exhilarating graphics; his most abstract work was always his best. It's all curves: there's hardly a straight line throughout. During Bach's *Toccata and Fugue* (hideously hoked up by Leopold Stokowski), suggestions of violin bows chase each other like comets amid all the blinks and blurts of light, and great striped waves of magenta and purple devour one another. Stravinsky's *Rite of Spring* holds up well, as the dinosaurs march like a dying army, or the pounce of a predatory creature leaves a few floating feathers behind. Moussorgsky's *Night on Bald Mountain* casts some hallucinatory spells: Satan's colossal hands trickle down a mountainside, their shadows blackening a town, while ghosts drift upwards from their graves. *Ava Maria* is sung to an almost black screen: what seems to be a church spire finally penetrates it, and then turns out to be a chink in a glimpse through a forest. Throughout, Disney's gift for making you feel that you're in motion surpasses the effects that Timothy Leary used in his League for Spiritual Discovery celebrations of 1967. Disney causes you to swim in space, glide, and definitely fly, while shapes and objects dissolve and merge into each other, sensually satisfying in their mutations. While you don't quite "tumble through the capillary networks"—as Leary used to say— parts of *Fantasia* yield a heightened sensitivity, plus the pleasure of basking in yourself.

However, other sections of the movie underline the hypocrisy of censorship in this country, from the Forties to the present. Those who worry about obscenity on the screen could treat themselves to a fit at *Fantasia*. Here, sex is prettified and distorted for children—transferred to animals, which makes it safe. As some have noted, the Disney creatures have a bewildering sexuality, and they switch roles with all the deftness of a mod bisexual. (*The Realist* published a cartoon of the Disney animals "doing all the things they couldn't do while Disney was alive, like balling each other," and those familiar faces look very natural in flagrante delicto.) In *Fantasia,* you can't miss the genital obsessions: even a shot of a hippo's uvula manages to be phallic, as are the dancing thistles, Mickey Mouse rising in a cone-shaped sorcerer's hat, the brontosaurus's long wavy necks, the unicorns' horns, and even a take of Stokowski's silhouette on his conductor's platform. In *The Nutcracker Suite,* a dance of some macho mushrooms is followed by flowers opening and turning inside out in a cleverly vaginal passage. Crotches are rather neglected, but buttocks are stressed, whether huge and baggy (on elephants), heart-shaped (cupids), or coyly exaggerated (on elongated fairies). Bosoms are eliminated—although the female centaurs in Beethoven's *Pastoral Symphony* wear ghastly flower bras—but the animals behave as though they had marvelous cleavage, and keep posturing in the pinup poses of the Forties. Their enormous eyes and mouths are especially provocative, as when a frilly fish with lanquid lids and mammoth bee-stung lips trails her see-through fins like a stripper's veils.

Even evolution is sexy: orgasmic volcanos yield to microscopic organisms teasing one another, and fission is perhaps the most erotic act of all: there's a happy little shudder when a round shape elongates and divides. There's also a birth trauma, when Mickey Mouse— bereft of his salacious grin—shoots on tidal waves through hallways and tunnels until he's sucked into a whirlpool. The castration sequences provoked roars of adult laughter, especially when a big female hippo flattened a sword-shaped male alligator, who later almost deprived a unisex elephant of its trunk and tail. Struggling with revulsion at some of this guile, I couldn't fight off a strong spasm of awe: Disney must have known exactly what he was doing, and *Fantasia* is the only pornographic movie I've ever seen. Still, it might have startled the old animator had he known that his inventions would one day be absorbed by the drug culture, and that his own fantasies would be reshaped by uppers and downers, grass, and the insight of acid.

DEATH ON AND OFF BROADWAY*
May 1970

How nice—to feel nothing, and still get full credit for being alive.
> —*Vonnegut, Slaughterhouse-Five*

Now THEY say that you can get cancer from swilling low-cal drinks in front of your color TV set. Are artificial sweeteners going to croak you? Much of New York's recent theater has been stiff with artificial sweeteners and spiritual cyclamates, and some critics talk about dying of boredom. Hence it's an appropriate irony for 1970 that the Open Theater is one of the few groups which now gives our theater life; its theme is death.

It's probably hard for foreigners or visitors to realize the degree of death-in that we're feeling here: from the ghetto and Cambodia to the campus, across the hall or upstairs or after lunch or on the way home. Nothing new, of course. It's just that we feel it more than ever. The Open Theater has mimed the anguish as it mounts each year. Their "ceremonies" are intentionally fragmented—like most native emotions now. In '68, their nonverbal war games ranged two lines of actors toe-to-toe, making friendly and hostile sounds—squealing and then retching at each other, building to swamp-at-night noises. Then hatred hissed. Moans and mutual comforting followed, plus

---

* I wrote this a few weeks after Kent State and Jackson State.

some happy howling which diminished to whispering and suspicious shrinking apart. Enmity was senseless, but it couldn't be turned off.

In '69 they uncoiled Jean-Claude van Itallie's *The Serpent,* in which assassinations were played back at us, repeated (as they are on TV and with old random film clips), and then reversed—as by a movie camera run backwards. The actors functioned as parts of computers, chanting "I-am-not-involved . . . I stay alive." Later, in a charade of Eve's temptation, they played with apples and weavingly writhed like a whole treeful of snakes with flickering tongues. Soon the apples splashed and split against the floor, and Cain killed Abel while the chorus stressed that Cain *wanted* to kill his brother, but had failed to realize that killing Abel would actually cause his death. (Chop-logic is daily food: one of the FBI's motives for investigating the Kent State killings was to determine "whether the civil rights of the students who were shot had been violated.") During the murder, some actors became perfect sheep, baaing on all fours, quietly nibbling grass as Abel died. "Did you know that you could go into eternity screaming with pain?" Haphazard voices punctuated the action: "A field of dead men is very loud! Teeth clack! Bones snap! . . . the last sound is the trumpet of escaping wind." But it all ended blithely with the old song, "We Were Sailing Along on Moonlight Bay": the artificial sweetener once again.

The whole company compiled its newest work—*Terminal*—which begins with the blank-faced incantation, "We come among the living to call upon the dead." With their "Dance on the Graves of the Dead," introduced by listless harmonies on wavery mouth organs, they remind us that there are bones beneath the floor of the church they act in, that everyone living is dying gradually now. They evoke an institute where the not-quite-dead are made up for their appearance after death, while they're cheerfully instructed about embalming: "We stitch the lips together for a more attractive expression. . . . Of course we prefer to work on faces which are already well-preserved." A tall man becomes a jerking, dancing puppet, grinning while he gibbers about the sufferings of his people; his dance grows more frenzied as he assumes a monkey-see-monkey-do accent, parodying a funny dusky native or one of the Vietnamese. The voices of futility build: "Pa, why don't you do something?" "Oh, but I do . . . I train people and they train people. I have children and they have children." There are ghastly bulge-eyed impersonations of death; an embalmed corpse wails on a table; bodies hang by their knees and elbows from a coat rack, wasted and unimportant among old clothes. "I was walking down the street—buildings topple—what have I done? I saw a woman chewing at the pavement, she had no teeth—forty-one dead—what have I done?" "What was given me was impossible to work with." Then some are bound and gagged (at that image from the Chicago courtroom, the audience murmured "Bobby Seale"). The dying crawl, arms clutching each other's thighs. At the end, they gaze sardonically at the audience while it claps. . . . The Open Theater has distilled much of the death that's coming down, plus the numbness which seeps through a society which also worships guilt.

Living deadness is also the motif of *Company,* the Broadway hit musical with (excellent) lyrics and (forgettable) music by Stephen Sondheim, who wrote the songs and words for *A Funny Thing . . . ,* and was the lyricist for *West Side Story* and *Gypsy. Company* crumbles the tradition of musicals about New York. Unlike *On the Town, Wonderful Town,* and *West Side Story,* it's triumphantly unromantic, undramatic—urban fatigue has replaced excitement and even pain. It's also the first musical I've ever seen that's focused on the love life of a man: a wan bachelor of thirty-five who recoils from his rich friends' compulsion to marry him off. (Their dinner invitations aren't hospitable, but are demands for diversion from couples who don't want to be alone with one another.) They sing naggingly at him from terraces and platforms and fire-escapes on an elegant abstract set laced with elevator shafts, in which he rises and sinks in isolation from all the couples who drive each other bananas. Thus, a marital chorus: "It's the little things you do together . . . Children you destroy together . . . Becoming a cliché together,/Growing old and gray together/Withering away together/That make marriage a joy." Husbands sadly sing, "You don't live for her/You do live with her/You're scared she's started to drift away/And scared she'll stay . . ." Spouses plant their fantasy lives on him ("Have I Got A Girl For You") and itch to hear what the chicks are like in bed; "Marriage may be where it's been/But it's not where it's at." A couple announces their divorce with bashful dimplings—as though it were an engagement—in keeping with what my parents' generation called "divorced in name only." The hero's three girl friends address a boop-a-doop song to him full of arpeggios that sound like little screams: "You impersonate a crazy person/Better than a zombie could." There's a frightened song about city crowding and the difficulty of merely arranging a meeting, which ends in a desperate prolonged wail: "Look, I'll call you in the morning or my service will explain . . ./And another hundred people just got off the traaaa-aaaiiinnn." On a wedding day, a bride sings of her terror, while the groom—hunting for his pants—punctuates her horrified aria with "Today Is Forever."

Company drops home truths that any native can savor: "You know what the pulse of this city is?" "A busy signal?" The friends who scare the hero off marriage croon to him, "Poor baby, all alone/ Throw a dog a bone and it is still a bone." But he finally climaxes with a dead finale about "Being Alive," entreating "someone" to be a burden, to simply make him feel something: "Someone to hold you too close/Someone to hurt you too deep/Someone to need you too much/Someone to know you too well." While the rational fear of marriage—inspired by the experiences of others—is expertly detailed, it's noticeable that all the women in the show are dumb or drunk or threatening or frantic: "too busy to know that they're fools." The men are just tired or brittle.

As a New York operetta, *Company* is fascinating and irritating; the calculated aridity is valid, but it's hard to bleed over the problems and the weaknesses of the rich. After all, chic is neither our prime crime nor the main source of city suffering. Society may be empty but the subway isn't. And Sondheim's dancing pantsuits and tunics who flavor the coffee with cinnamon and complain about soot on their terraces and envy those who don't diet are not the ultimate New Yorkers. However, this hymn to unfeeling has a harsh, sour strength that underlines the Seventies' sense of helplessness and the dread of (half-desired) change. As in *Terminal,* the characters protest against being stuck with their lives, against accountability, and the cast of *Company* looks almost as dead as *Terminal's* at the final curtain. It's not an accident.

NOSTALGING ON BROADWAY
December 1971

FLEEING THE present: nuzzling at what you've never known. While teen-agers are reviving the pop culture of the Fifties—pony tails and Howdy Doody, old Elvis ducktails and slow, wailing songs about loving forever and ever, really and truly—some of us who were students in the Fifties have to remember that we ourselves shunned the period. As apolitical aesthetes, we escaped into history and English literature, snugging into earlier centuries while turning off the tube. We blocked out most of McCarthy and Eisenhower, groggily aware that they were bad. But the past was superior to the present—just as Europe was superior to America, or art to politics.

Hence it's rum for the Silent Generation to get such a dose of the Fifties now. While the cultural landscape is smeared with revivals, plus reincarnations of old material, it's astounding to realize that the new nostalgia is only about fourteen months old. It ballooned soon after the emotional exhaustion following Kent State, the blast that killed a researcher at the University of Wisconsin, the feelings of futility and fatigue about nonviolence *and* violence, the final inability to respect professional politicians, or to expect much of the immediate future. So—we've been blanketed by the immediate past. But the presentation isn't joyfully escapist: instead, there's a theme of self-flagellation, which is even reflected in two tremendous hits on Broadway.

Under murky mauve lights, beneath a tattered, spleen-colored map of the U.S., *Lenny* spills out images and facts from the life of the satirist Lenny Bruce, who died of drugs in 1966. The show starts in '51. The play's based on Bruce's own routines, and Cliff Gorman is brilliantly hysterical as a comic falling apart during his own act. The message is that Bruce was "a*hedo*viz time," as my neighbors kept remarking loudly. Bruce's trials for obscenity and narcotics, his marriage to a druggy stripper, his sputtering, frenzied gags about rebellious prisoners whom the warden orders shot, North Korea, contraceptives as blown-up balloons, his wife as "the heroine of his nocturnal emissions," homosexuals, the 1958 recession, the Lone Ranger, lesbians ("It's hard to spot dykes, because sometimes we're married to them"), nice Jewish boys from Brooklyn, exhibitionists, Orphan Annie, niggers, spics, and greaseballs, how President Kennedy "jacked off during the Cuban missile crisis," sex with a chicken, "Grandma Moses' tits and Norman Rockwell's ass," and a song about "coming too quickly or not at all"—all evoke the man who loathed racial and sexual hypocrisy, especially the self-deceptions of the "liberal-schmiberal." In the Fifties and early Sixties the style was ponderously analyzed as sick humor. Now, since four-letter words have so little impact, and fuck practically means hello, Bruce's personal desperation emerges much more strongly than his social rage— which isn't the dead man's fault.

There's a nice moment with Nixon as a drunken dummy sitting on Ike's knee, discussing the 1958 headline "Nixon Stoned in Caracas", and a lively scene where Christ and Moses return nakedly to earth, while the pope and a cardinal panic over the reception committee and call each other schmucks, and lepers play trombones. I love dirty jokes and also very bad ones. But here, many of the old boffolas shriek with the strain of trying to be startling: the boy killed by Leopold and Loeb "was a snotty kid anyway;" or, "Ya can't stop masturbating gradually, ya gotta do it cold jerky." For those of us who never saw Bruce, it seems unfair that he should be allowed to appear forlornly unfunny—although I'm willing to take his comic genius on faith, and delighted to agree that the Fifties were hideously stuffy.

Hair's director, Tom O'Horgan, and the author, Julian Barry, have celebrated Bruce's private anguish but confused it with his fierce protests against society. Backed by vast Mount Rushmore-like heads of Nixon, LBJ, and Kennedy, Bruce's final bankrupt misery—as he thrashes on the floor with his own tapes, unleashing great animal retches and then cackling like a tape recorder run backward—is as devastating as it should be. But then the director can't resist showbiz: Nixon's huge papier-mâché face opens to reveal Bruce nude and dead over a toilet bowl. Lights blink inside Nixon's skull as Bruce's corpse is photographed, flutes peep sadly, and it's easy to imagine that Bruce would have sneered at such a chic image for any death, including his own. Still, the audience adored it. So the old device of turning a hearse into a bandwagon still seems foolproof. The play certainly insisted that Bruce took all our sins upon him—and that reminds me how our quality lit. courses of the Fifties taught us to look for scapegoats (as well as waning moons), and that redemption through suffering was a favorite literary theme. Is packaged guilt a new commodity? Perhaps—as long as it's limited to a few hours, or set safely in the past.

Follies, in which aging stars reunite at a last party for a Ziegfeldish theater that's about to be demolished, is an impressive piece of musical history. Stephen Sondheim has written songs of the Twenties, Thirties, and Forties, which define the styles of each period; Alexis Smith, Dorothy Collins, Yvonne DeCarlo, and Fifi D'Orsay leap about as living memories. The middle-aged hoof their old routines, while the ghosts of their young selves, sheathed in fantastic blacks and whites, mimic their movements behind them. Old troopers reassure each other that they haven't changed—"You look as cute as ever"—as they glide down steps with hands on hips or arms extended in pinup gestures of the Forties. A fat woman does high kicks; a bald man turns a somersault; as shapeless bodies dance with grace and gusto, you start to dislike yourself for being depressed by their looks. *Follies* uses old people well, yet it also uses them cruelly: by making them act winsome or downright pert. It rather recalls the occasion when Anthony West, who was researching old age homes, saw one institution where a great iron grill divided the two sexes. The director said, "Well, you wouldn't want them *breeding,* would you?"

Amid the rhymes of "eerie" and "dreary," two former showgirls and their jaded husbands reveal that their marriages are lousy, and rather frantically try to relive their youth. A raucously romantic little woman grabs uselessly at an old boy friend, even though she has clung to her husband: "On his shoulder/I won't get older," while he sings, "The girls I'll never know I'm too tired for." The need for illusion fights with the sense of self-disgust—"I just wanted her. Until I had her;" "I thought you needed me." "For *what?*"— and no one gets what he wants, including rejection: "As long as you ignore me/You're the only thing that matters." A man yawns while he tells his wife how terrific she used to be in bed. There's some deliberately tired wisecracking: "I love the way you hate it when I'm happy and you're not," and: "If I knew what was the matter, I'd get it fixed." At the end, the spouses plod off together, resolving to start afresh, which is impossible.

The prize-winning *Follies* has a weary fascination, especially when the vitality of old numbers is pitched against the characters' own numbness. And the theme of show folk trying and failing to live out the fantasies of stage life is a rich one. But the academic virtuosity of its range is really weakened by the fidelity to period styles —despite the top hats and feathers and bugle beads and marvelous tap dancing, many of the songs are simply soupy or boring. We've had bitter musicals for over ten years now; *Follies* merely carries self-dislike further than Sondheim's own *Company*. Maybe nostalgia isn't what it used to be.

PART V: CONTRADICTING THE CONVENTIONS

THE DEMOCRATS
July 1972

THE LAOCOÖN: outside the Eden Roc Hotel, statues of the Winged Victory, the Apollo Belvedere, and an unidentified goddess were momentarily looped together in a snarl of TV cables. Well before the convention began, they were released. But the brief alliance of those snowy stone figures stays with me as an image for some of the coalitions formed around McGovern's nomination: a simultaneous struggling that might not last. To some of us, much that happened in Miami Beach appeared to be very fragile, and many collaborations seemed temporary.

Infinite commentators told you that those who fought in the Chicago streets of '68 were inside the Convention Hall in '72, that this was the youngest, blackest, most female etcetera. On the floor, it seemed much less so; one most powerfully felt the presence of the old pols, the hacks, and the establishment. Yet it was hard to find the edge of some people's cynicism; for many—except for the youngest McGovern delegates—cynicism overlapped with hope: some cautious hope. While those who've campaigned for months usually end by believing all the puff they've been putting out, some of McGovern's supporters seemed to believe less of it than they had in the spring of '72. But when McGovern was nominated, others behaved as though they'd already won the November election. The evidence of both mentalities swelled the doubts of yet other participants.

Amid all the frenzy, after some 18 months of uphill work, what seemed to be lacking was almost any sense of consequence—the idea that we would really have to live with whatever happened within that Hall for the next four years. Here were thousands of people jellied in the aspic of fatigue: a stiff but transparent wall which had thickened between them and the issues. Some seemed dulled to what McGovern was supposed to represent, such as the rights of blacks or women or the poor; they could think only of gaining delegates. And in some cases, certain McGovern aides seemed immune to anything but scoring small points for their own power.

From the first night, at that moment when the backs of our hands were stamped with invisible ink, while the band played, "What The World Needs Now Is Love, Sweet Love"—I kept peering at my paw to see if some stigmata would surface, wondering if I'd wear it all my life—to each evening's battle for a floor pass, and then diving into that sea of bodies with the credentials slung around one's neck like a life-preserver, or watching others emerge from the floor looking half-drowned, one saw the waves of collective numbness spreading. After three days, some of us felt that we lived at the Hall, that we would return each night for years to come. But no wonder that security was tight—since it was quite easy to break. On the last night, I saw dozens from Flamingo Park, draped with passes, also someone who'd been rumored to have been blown up in the Eleventh Street townhouse occupied by Weatherpeople in 1970. (I managed to gasp, "I thought you were . . . in Europe.")

You don't have to be dead to be a ghost, I realized. Until Teddy Kennedy appeared on the final night, igniting the kind of excitement which might be provoked by the Resurrection, he seemed almost as ghostly as his brothers. Even news photos of his portly figure racing his small son on a Squaw Island beach seemed to recall Chappaquiddick.

Despite one low-keyed rendition of "Hello, Lyndon"—which nearly gave me a hallucination of that jovial face swimming up on the huge projection screen—LBJ was hardly mentioned. Kennedy did say ". . . and Lyndon B. Johnson promised us that we shall overcome, and with George McGovern we shall." There were cheers —but not so loud as those for the lettuce boycott. Indeed, Johnson is like the living dead, and almost no one wanted to raise him.

In Miami Beach, where the average age is 65.2, I was told that a number of vehicles which collect the dead or the dying are made to look as though they belong to the Fire Department; no one wants to see so many ambulances. Bunched and pleated brown flesh, withered feet in sandals: somehow, the elderly look much older when they're deeply tanned and wearing orange or purple playclothes. Hence the irony of many skin-flick marquees, which are labeled "Adults Only."

Nowhere else but Miami have I seen such a number of white-haired couples holding hands. At a large rally for Senior Citizens, where the White House was accused of neglecting the old, I even saw a few freckled fists raised. A speaker announced that four years of Nixon was enough; "*Dig* it!" said the bald head beside me. When McGovern promised to improve the lot of those over sixty, a skeptical grandmother kept repeating, "Beautiful *words*." Some young people held up signs: "Long Hairs and White Hairs/Struggle— Unite" and "We Are The Senior Citizens Of Tomorrow." The elderly made a rather unruly audience: they pushed and shoved more than many crowds I've known, and wouldn't stop talking during the speeches, not even when their juniors tried to shush them. *The Miami Herald* had a nervous headline: "Heart-Pill Culture Feels Strange Surge of Youth."

One of the more political events during the convention was the Wedding of the Generations. Allen Ginsberg and others had decided that it was time to end "youth chauvinism." At Lummus Park, close to lots of retirement hotels, Ginsberg and his friends decorated a lamppost like a maypole, banked an alter with vast bunches of flowers, and handed out chrysanthemums. First, a rabbi performed a symbolic wedding between two old people. (The groom said, "She's my wife for tonight.") The rabbi told the spectators to sit down "on Mother Earth," and then compared marriage to wine: "The older it is, the better it gets." Next, Ginsberg, in a yarmulka led the crowd in a slow, winding circle, while he played on his harmonium and sang: "The younger generation is living in a Marx Brothers movie . . ./Do you remember the Marx Brothers movies when you were young/And everyone was happy and Harpo Marx did not have a tongue?" He sang to the ring of seated white heads: "The younger generation—because it felt all alone/Married the entire world/So that it would not turn to stone . . ./If everyone over seventy would take us by the hand"—which they did—". . . Everybody in Miami Beach is married to you and to me." Meanwhile, Revy Wikler, the author of *Sex and the Senior Citizen,* gave out copies of her book, which were flourished aloft while Ginsberg intoned: "The generation war is at an end."

Abbie Hoffman, in a shirt sprinkled with pineapples, climbed onto a stepladder and read a statement in Yiddish. Some clucked when they heard his accent: "It's not good, but he tries, he tries." He yielded his perch to an old lady who read a poem she'd written:

> Today is a joyous wedding,
> A wedding of young and old . . .
> Our bride is three-score and ten,
> Our groom just out of his teens . . .
> She glows with an inner beauty
> Which transcends the wrinkles of age.
> Our groom with his vim and vigor
> Is entranced by his radiant bride . . .
> To harmony and understanding they have found a key . . .
> They wish for peace in this world,
> Wars ended, peace banners unfurled . . .

There were loud cheers. Ed Sanders, former Fug and Manson biographer, read a salute to his grandmother, who made it with her future husband in 1888.

> We are here on a tropical
> beach to tell you that we love
> you. . . .
> And we have changed
> the mode of love
> > & we have
> > changed the mode of our will
> > & we have changed
> > into true-tempered humans of peace. . . .

Everyone took a glass of orange juice, and Ginsberg sang "Shalom" again and again, accompanied by Peter Orlovsky in a patchwork vest and pigtails, while flowers were thrown over the ecstatic crowd. A photographer exclaimed, "This beats all the Bar Mitzvahs I've ever shot!" and the TV cameramen looked ready to faint in a body. Several old women told me that they were "charter members of the Yippies." Then the young and the old seized hands and danced the hora and sang "Sholom Aleichem" and "Hava Nagilah." One young woman said, "Let's do Mayim;" an old woman shouted, "You good Jewish girl!" and embraced her. Ginsberg jumped off the ladder to join the dancing and several grandmothers cried in protest, "You'll break your foot!" He sang an impromptu hymn, and everyone repeated his lines:

McGovern will win this year
The war will be over this year
The old will have peace this year
The young will find the old dear.
To the Vietcong I give a big cheer.
The old in Vietnam need a cheer . . .
The old folks in Vietnam are here . . .
The old in Miami don't fear . . .
The young and the old are all here
The young grow older each year
The old and the young are more near.

An old woman in a wheelchair kept time with a chrysanthemum. Then she hollered, "The hell with Nixon!" and the crowd whooped. Commanding, "Harmonize, Allen!" she and Ginsberg sang "An Old-Fashioned Girl," "I Wonder Who's Kissing Her Now," and "Once I Met A Blue-Eyed Sailor." He began "Last Night the Nightingale Woke Me," but was interrupted by old women crowding up to hug him. One said, "Allen, I've been reading about your trials and tribulations and your miseries." He answered that he wasn't miserable now. She replied that she could see that, and went on to praise his poem, "Kaddish," which details the mental illness of his dead mother. She added, "Your mother was one of us gals, Allen."

Several old people told me how much they'd feared the kids before they arrived—had dreaded muggings and purse-snatchings by dopefiends. An old man added, "Now I've got three sleeping in my house."

At sunset, we were back singing around Ginsberg on his stepladder by the sea: "We've had a mystic marriage here." As the TV crew packed up: "And now the eye of the world departs from us/We hope the cameraman will give us his blessing."

Finally:

Behold the common family
Extends from here to Saigon over the sea.
We hope the elders of Hanoi
Participate in Miami Beach's joy.
We hope the people far and near
Are able to dispel the words of fear.
We hope the myth that we're at war
Is ended here for evermore.

The next morning, I heard Kirk Douglas and Dinah Shore soberly discussing the generations on TV. They decided that there should be "more reaching out."

When some Yips came to Miami Beach weeks before the convention, they stayed in cheap hotels—where they encountered the elderly. They began to focus on what the old and the young have in common in a society which mistrusts both. They visited Senior Citizens' groups, shared meals, and tried to diminish the community's alarms about invasion. They also gave out balloons reading, "We're your friends." One woman told her neighbors, "You won't like the way the kids look, but they're fine inside." For some evening meetings, the young brought guitars and their seniors had mandolins; they taught each other their instruments and exchanged songs.

A very young girl told me, "We've got to revive respect. So many of them have a history of picket lines—they kept fighting, the way their middle-aged children never did." Meanwhile, the elders of Miami Beach have their own divisions. Some are left of center, with a lot of early union experience; others are far to the right. Those I met said that they had been for Humphrey, because of his initial efforts on civil rights and Medicare, but that they would vote for McGovern.

Among the 87,000 year-round residents of Miami Beach, some 55,000 receive some form of Social Security. There were many complaints that the old were under-represented at the Democratic Convention. With the Yips, some picketed the La Gorce country club, for discrimination against Jews. One old woman said that perhaps her contemporaries in Miami Beach were some of the most independent in their generation—because they lived there on their own, rather than with their younger relatives. Almost every Miami Beach native I talked with came from New York or New Jersey.

Throughout, I heard many old people praising the young visitors. It was repeated that grandparents and grandchildren often get on better than parents and children. A woman of seventy-eight said, "The forgotten people are the young and the old. Lots of us are broke, and they can't get decent jobs." She added that she came from a very strict family, which "didn't approve of" her: "That comes back to me when I see the kids now." While she and her friends were dubious about grass, and also about mothers holding jobs—"You cook, you bake, you sew, you bring your children up. *Then* you go out to work. Not before"—they were also very tolerant about new ways of life which they would never share.

Some of the elderly took food to the young campers in Flamingo Park. One woman, horrified to see them eating peanut butter, asked how it could give them strength for demonstrations. She returned with knishes and matzohs; others brought lots of bagels and cream cheese, and gallons of turkey soup. One leaflet suggested:

A LITTLE CHICKEN SOUP NEVER HURT ANYONE
    SO MAKE A MITZVAH IN THE PARK
There is a pipeline between the Senior Citizens and the kids
    Which you can fill with Love
    and a little chicken soup
    or a kugel or a kigel
    or a few cookies
    or whatever
What could be bad . . . ? ? ?

What to do?	COOK AND BRING
Where?	Flamingo Park, of course
Who do we give to?	Anybody and everyone
	(Who wouldn't like your cooking?)
What do I get?	**Naches
	**Love
	**Lots of smiles and thanks and whatever else they have to share with you
	**And a little more understanding on the chicken soup pipeline

What could it hurt???

Some of us wondered if the concern for old people would continue after the conventions. Still, it had given many of them a very enjoyable lift.

In Flamingo Park, I felt rather as though I was back in the Sixties; especially since so much was going on at once, it seemed like the old mixed media. Frisbees sailed past my nose while about forty marchers took off under SDS banners for the Playboy Club—"We-don't-want-your-fucking-war" was hastily changed to "racist war" after two old people said "Oh"—while a few Jews for Jesus sang about rocking in Abraham's bosom, others in sweatshirts stenciled SCIENCE NOT POLITICS preached "cybercultural revolution power"; an evangelist yelled, "De*struc*tion is coming *soooon!*" and some wistful young Bible readers crooned about Jacob and Esau to indifferent ears, while the bodies of those on a smoke-in dangled from the branches of a giant banyan tree, or lay coiled among its roots. There, I heard a heated argument about whether coffee is really a drug: "Not if you don't *abuse* it." I've never seen so much grass in public, and the police didn't interfere. But I saw none on bad trips or heavily stoned. There was some worried discussion about catching "the mad shitter" who had been fouling the pool where some swam naked at night. A twilight feast was designed to dishonor Nixon, whose face was outlined in pieces of watermelon lying on the ground; a sign said, "Nixon Is A *Seedy* Character—Eat Nixon Tonight." Many did, while a stern young black with a bullhorn warned them to "*deal* with your rinds," and not leave them lying about. At night, the park became a world of split screens: a movie of the bombing of a Vietnamese hospital was projected on a white wall, while, about thirty feet away, an outdoor color TV set showed cops fiercely chasing robbers to those who lay upon the ground.

The mood was mainly mellow, but some of the Jesus people produced tensions. Their attitudes towards dope and women angered some, and, although one old woman urged tolerance over a bullhorn—"It's just their trip"—which brought applause and shouts of "Grandma Power!" some began to bait a grizzled hysteric who screamed, "You've *got* to come to Jesus!" They circled round him laughing, while he ordered them to "throw away crutches like sex," and denounced marijuana because it wasn't "a seed-bearing plant." (He got a lot of corrections on that one.) He also outraged a group of gay men by insisting that they were dirty sinners. While some feminists sang, "We no longer will be prisoners in the same old gilded cage,/That's why we're marching on," another religioso shouted that they were "sexual devils." A young man in overalls growled at him, "Quiet, *garbage-mouth.*"

Stew Albert of YIP addressed the crowd as the irritations accelerated. He said, "We're not against Christianity," but that many of the Jesus persons were using their religion to build a right-wing movement. (Of course some also claim that Jesus was a radical. But few of that viewpoint were present.) Albert said that it troubled him to hear the Jesus people "using our language and our culture:" calling themselves freaks or speaking of liberation. However: "We have no right to put them down—because parts of our own movement have been really fucked up, really ugly. So some of our people went into bad drugs—and then off them into the Jesus movement. It's *our* fault . . . We have to be self-critical now . . . Why has our movement become a tourist attraction nightmare?" He urged his contemporaries to rebuild their programs—"We need to be so that McGovern will listen to us"—and to recognize the Jesus people as a by-product of the drug culture. He got some sturdy applause. And I thought of his speech that night when I passed the old man in the neck-and-chest brace outside the Convention Hall, where he sat in a buggy drawn by a small burro labelled, I'M PULLING FOR WALLACE, with a tiny burro reading, ME TOO. The owner said that his burros were descended from the one which Jesus rode into Jerusalem.

On the first night of the convention, as Ralph Abernathy and a black saxophonist led a march of the National Welfare Rights Organization and others, I again flashed on the Sixties when Abernathy included the verse about "Black and white together" in "We Shall Overcome." I hadn't heard that line for several years. Old people smiled and waved from their balconies, but I doubt if they heard a few Zippies shouting, "Free Arthur Bremer! Give him a second chance!" Outside the Convention Hall's $75,000 hibiscus-covered chain-link fence, where you could see guards with legs akimbo through the flowers, there was a rally which stressed that the Democrats—"who are *supposed* to be the party of the poor"—had turned their backs on poor people's issues. Speakers repeated their demands for a $6,500 yearly income for a family of four. (This is the minimum needed according to surveys by the U.S. Department of Labor, Bureau of Labor Statistics.) After the rally, Abernathy's group and some Vietnam vets pleaded with the crowd to disperse. (The theme throughout the convention was "Don't mess it up for McGovern.") But some of those who remained stormed the hibiscus fence and brought a part of it down. Injuries were slight, clubs and gas weren't used, but there was a little Mace.

The small SDS meetings I attended seemed like parodies of the Sixties. As was evident on campuses in the spring of '72, they now have a gift for picking the wrong issues, or for confusing the public about their main concerns. I suspected that the extremely young SDSers I saw had joined very recently, probably well after the organization had divided into warring factions in '69. They seemed to know nothing about the best years of SDS, and appeared to be trying to catch up with the experiences of their elder siblings. Hence they sounded like an anachronism—even on the issues which still absorb us all.

Outside Flamingo Park, an ice cream vendor aroused their wrath because he had raised the price of banana splits from 50 cents to 90 cents. The filthy capitalist was denounced with all the passion once reserved for LBJ; a young man urged others to link arms around the ice cream truck to prevent people from buying. A Vietnam vet rather wearily said that the guy wasn't a capitalist, that he probably just broke even. But few even wanted to boycott him. By the time that SDS and others confronted McGovern in the lobby of the Doral Hotel, many of his delegates were just as disturbed as they by his statement about keeping residual troops in Thailand. (Later, he said that any such troops would be withdrawn after he'd had ninety days in office.) But SDS and some Zippies made it seem as though the legalization of marijuana was just as important as the war. Again, they lost the support they might have had.

One of SDS's major targets was a fashion show sponsored by Mrs. Reuben Askew, in honor of the candidates' wives. About twenty-five demonstrators marched around the circular marble lobby of the Americana Hotel—the circles made me think of Ginsberg's ceremony, and the spheroid nature of this convention—shouting, "The rich get fat! The poor are starving! A thousand dollars a dress!" And: "More jobs, higher welfare, no-more-fashion-shows!" They jigged off, yelling in a crescendo, "Attica means! Fight back! Welfare mothers! Fight back! The Vietnamese! Fight back! SDS! Fights-back-fights-back-fights-back!"

Inside, where a large gathering of middle-aged women—many wearing little plastic oranges in their hair—clapped timidly when told, "Today we want you to meet the women behind the men behind the wheels of Florida," three young women from SDS began to stage a "poor women's fashion show," showing the jeans and T-shirts that could be bought on welfare. "Notice the worn-out heels—" They were very roughly ejected. A grey-haired woman in a long printed gown came up to tell them, "A lot of us are with you," but they shrieked, "Wait till the revolution!" The display of clothes from Saks that followed almost made me feel that the fashion copy had been written by or for SDS. As the models pranced in to wavering organ music, we heard "It's cotton canvas that's *in* this year," and "The American closet is red, white and blue, and it's *you!*" Silk moiré pajamas by Mollie Parnis appeared to the tune of "The Caissons Go Rolling Along," and a white jersey caftan flowed by to "The Stars and Stripes Forever." Different regions were symbolized by colors— "For the East, it's soft gray interpretations" (flannel)—but my favorite was Chicago: "A city of contrasting power: vibrant in coral or restrained in beige and camel." Chicago means baby-blue for policemen's helmets to me.

Throughout the convention, YIP (which now wants to be called the Youth International Party, not Yippies) was assailed by the Zippies. There aren't many of the latter; they're led by garbage-analyst A. J. Weberman and Tom Forcade, director of the Underground Press Syndicate, who had claimed that Abbie Hoffman had ripped him off for editorial work on *Steal This Book*. Hoffman said that Forcade didn't contribute. The facts are uncertain.) The Zippies also said that Rubin and Hoffman were elitists who had sold out the revolution—mainly by urging people to vote for McGovern. The Zips threw pies and water in hotels—frightening the old people there—and then said that YIP had done it. The Zippies also announced that they would have a Che Guevara Appreciation Day, which would have infuriated the large conservative population of Cuban refugees in Miami. Fortunately, it was called off.

Several old people told me that they thought Forcade was a cop and that the Zips were paid provocateurs. One elderly woman said, "*Plants. I think I'm seeing plants. To discredit the youth movement."* Meanwhile, the Yips, who were trying to establish themselves as a community organization, also had some fond words for Martha Mitchell: "She's really one of us. And she's being treated like one of those Russian writers who gets called crazy." A few discussed the notion of forming Martha Mitchell Brigades for the Republican Convention.

I spent the last afternoon of the convention with Tom Michaud, a deserter from the Marines who planned to give himself up on the floor of the Hall that night. He was a very quiet Connecticut Yankee, from a French Catholic family, who had spent some eleven years in an orphanage in Lowell, Mass.—"Hell's Angels territory, you know." He had enlisted at seventeen "for general patriotic reasons," and the need of a job. He'd volunteered for six months' service in Vietnam, where he served in the 3rd Marine Division, 3rd Reconnaissance Battalion, at Quang Tri. There, he'd turned against the war and the military after a few months. "When you're in the bush, and you get fired on, you just turn around and pull the trigger. You don't even know who you're firing at." After three years' service, he split from Camp Lejeune, N.C. He then spent three years underground, mainly in New England, where he'd worked as a maintenance man in big hotels in Boston, in a hunter's camp in Vermont, on a compost project in New Hampshire. He described life on the run: "For the first six months, I was looking over my shoulder, looking in post offices to see if they had my picture on the wall . . . Then I got used to it. But I couldn't use my own name, or make any long-range plans—I'd like to buy land and build my own house—and I couldn't be open with people: that felt bad. I was tired of having to hide something." At moments, his manner was withdrawn—as he had trained himself to be; at others, he talked rapidly with the relief of one who has been silent for too long. He'd decided to surrender himself to the Democratic Party because amnesty—which McGovern had mentioned so often in his campaign—had become a muted issue at the convention. Michaud felt that he represented another 100,000 deserters, some of whom might be likelier to surface after a test-case like his own.

On turning himself in, he might get a dishonorable discharge—or a maximum sentence of five years' hard labor. "I'm not nervous about it now. But when I hear the helicopters here all night—it sounds like being back in the Nam." We stared out the window: high up in a Miami Beach hotel, with blue skies reflected in the pool, it hardly felt like being underground. But he was a country-dweller, to whom simple freedoms meant a great deal, and I didn't like the thought of him in jail.

That night, Michaud revealed himself by talking to TV interviewers on the floor, near the California delegation. Meanwhile, dozens of flags massed and paraded down the aisles to a military march tune; we were fenced in by flags while the audience pledged allegiance and stood through the national anthem. Michaud and his lawyer, Tod Ensign of the Safe Return Committee, which works with "self-retired veterans," spoke quietly about the war, while TV reporters grew cynical: "How do we *know* you're a deserter, or that you were ever in the Marines?" The crowd thickened around them, while (by coincidence) a Gold Star Mother gave a strong antiwar speech from the platform, and then a Vietnam vet from Alabama praised the war and attacked amnesty. At this point, frantically upset security men rushed Michaud off the floor, enraged to find a visitor without credentials. Soon, the FBI hustled him away in an avocado green car. He was later delivered to the Marines, who removed him to his original point of departure: Camp Lejeune.*

I'd never thought it would be possible to feel sorry for Hubert Humphrey. The memories of his pro-war speeches are still so powerful—well before that stunner of '67, when he referred to Vietnam as "our greatest adventure, and a wonderful one it is." Sitting in the Convention Hall in '72, there was the ashiness of reading his booklet —headed, "Tomorrow is the first day of the rest of our lives," a line borrowed from the rock musical, *Salvation*—after he had withdrawn. His positions on tax reform ("Our tax system is rigged against the working family") and Vietnam ("Our prisoners home, our involvement ended within ninety days") had the tired desperation of some-

---

* On September 20th, Michaud, who had pleaded guilty to "unauthorized absence," was sentenced to a year's hard labor, forfeiture of all pay and allowances and a dishonorable discharge. His military counsel, protesting the harshness of the sentence, argued that he felt that the court was influenced by President Nixon's acceptance speech at the Republican Convention, in which Nixon had opposed amnesty.

one who knew that he was already defeated. Many of us felt a new surge of anger when he tried to stop McGovern by such tactics as making him appear like an abortion-freak, as he did in the Catholic neighborhoods of Omaha. But, as many noted, Humphrey's earlier liberal history was permanently cancelled before Chicago, and he probably knew now that he had been beaten for '72 in '68.

Quite a few of McGovern's supporters left Miami Beach feeling that they knew less about what their candidate represented than they had before the convention. I heard some repeating Jane Fonda's sentence, which was quoted in the *Washington Post:* "I think he would wage wars with a heavy heart." They'd been warned by many—even by Abbie Hoffman—that McGovern would move to the middle as he drew closer to the nomination. People kept saying "But we want to elect him" to those who were demoralized by seeing so many of the minority planks voted down, including those on tax reform, frozen rents for the poor, civil rights for homosexuals, and government-subsidized housing.

Perhaps one of the most crucial (and often neglected) aspects of political campaigns is not so much what a candidate represents—but what voters *think* he represents. Some of McGovern's young troops— as well as some of the opposition—*thought* that he would be friendly to abortion or to a more substantial guaranteed income for the poor. Yet McGovern's own radical following was asked to vote against the very issues which mattered most to them. The fact that these planks were defeated may not be clear to some who deplore McGovern: I'm willing to wager that some still believe that he upholds abortion on demand and "free money." *(The Miami Herald* continued to trot out nice headlines: "Antiwar Issue Plagues McGovern On Eve Of Success;" ". . . And An Unkooky Platform.") But some of the young went home uncertain whether they would continue to work for him. Angered on learning that "the open convention" was slickly and thoroughly controlled by a new machine, they were also chewing on the old discovery that you can change the person but not the system. When Abbie Hoffman pretended that his credentials were from *Popular Mechanics,* that magazine's name seemed like a reminder of the compromises which professional politicians make. Some older radicals considered the disillusionment to be educational· "There's nothing like a toe in your ass to raise your consciousness.'

But McGovern had acquired one of the mustiest of politicians' problems: risking some of his earlier constituents in the efforts to gain others.

Staring at the screaming crowd on the floor on the final night, a 21-year-old delegate said to me, "I guess the grown-ups need a freak-out now and then."

The women's feelings were among the most diverse. Some were immensely heartened by the number of women delegates (38 percent as opposed to 13 percent in '68), and by the solid women's rights plank which was rammed through. (There wasn't a word about women's rights in the '68 platform.) After Mayor Daley and 58 of his delegates were thrown out and replaced by more women and more blacks, under the party's new rules, I heard a few young black women shouting happily, "Shaft the Shamrock!" But it was steadily repeated that too few women were included in policy-making.

Many were extremely bitter about the defeat of the abortion plank—while others insisted that its passage would have sealed McGovern's defeat in November. Some considered abortion "the one non-negotiable demand." (The repetition of "DNC" did make the Democratic National Committee sound rather like dilation and curetage.) An audience of women who had hugely cheered McGovern became suddenly indignant when he dodged a question about abortion by cutting his speech short and promptly leaving; the chant of "We want McGovern" was almost drowned out by those who changed to "We want abortions!" Many were disgusted when he said on another occasion that "the abortion question . . . must be resolved at the state level." Some McGovern aides later admitted that the plank—which also included sterilization and birth control—would have passed had they not worked against it. The actual wording read: "In matters relating to human reproduction, each person's right to privacy, freedom of choice and individual conscience should be fully respected, consistent with relevant Supreme Court decisions." To those who said that abortions would be legal throughout the country "some day," many replied that it's hard to ask anyone to wait for an abortion.

Some women were also very disturbed by the manipulations of the McGovern team concerning the South Carolina delegation, which had only 28 percent women—when the state contains 51 percent.

The National Women's Political Caucus tried to replace nine men with nine women. McGovern had promised his full support on this challenge. However, fearing that winning the credentials on South Carolina would risk losing the credentials on California (due to some parliamentary fudge), the McGovern aides arranged some nimble vote-switching, so that the challenge was defeated. Some felt that McGovern's staff had overridden his wishes on this matter; others thought he simply hadn't understood it. For certain women, South Carolina was very important as a symbol; for others, it wasn't crucial when the California delegates might be at stake. But throughout this convention, symbols were considered a test of McGovern's sincerity.

Moreover, many were appalled by the TV coverage of women's issues or representatives. Cissy Farenthold finished second behind Eagleton in the balloting, but her actual nomination by Fanny Lou Hamer hadn't been shown—it was time for everyone's commercial. Walter Cronkite joked about "a lady named Farenthold," but failed to realize that her nomination was serious, or that it also signified a rebellion by the women who had been promised backing on abortions and on South Carolina. There were also many grim remarks about the "white-out" of Shirley Chisholm: "As far as the media is concerned, Shirley's name is 'others.' They just talked about the big candidates 'and others.' " And of course the ridicule of women—and the habit of judging them by their faces—was a familiar groundnote throughout the convention. I heard a cameraman grumbling that there weren't "enough pretty ones." When Chisholm arose to speak, the man behind me laughed and said, "If only she could fix her buck-teeth!"

However, Florynce Kennedy, the black lawyer and founder of the Feminist Party, said that she felt that women hadn't yet worked hard enough, and that some were still relying on men's efforts. She urged women to elect local pro-abortion candidates, and to "put the foetus-fetishists out of office." She added, "But it's a sad sack scene: how little people work. We still want the husband to provide; we say: come on *George,* bring home the *bacon,* bring us an abortion plank. As though we expected him to bring it to us from the store on the way home. We're too busy saying he's backsliding, asking: Georrrge, did you bring the *wine?"*

As Ms. Kennedy packed her bags in her hotel, while talking with a few friends, those who spoke of their disappointment in the media were chided for their expectations: "Look, telling people that Muskie was a front-runner is like telling you that Arrid Extra-Dry will get you a husband." She was also eloquent on the subject of "loserism," especially among black people and women. "It's neurotic to want something and then to talk in a way that's likely to prevent it happening. Liberals stand in the way of what they want—maybe because they didn't get what they wanted in childhood. It's pathological to put McGovern down when you want Nixon out . . . When you were a child, in the family car, you misbehaved and your parents said: *Wait till I get you home.* I feel the same: we should put McGovern in the White House and *then* make fire under his ass." She slammed the lid of a bulging suitcase. "But people who've been oppressed don't trust their leaders or themselves: they nearly elect someone and then they kick over the milkpail . . . It's part of fear. Success imposes a tremendous burden on you. Failure leaves you free—to whine and wail. Agonizing instead of organizing is typical of all oppressed people."

At this point, someone looked out the window and reported that the hotel staff was trying to clean a large swimming pool with one small can of Ajax. Laughter exploded when it was called a metaphor for the women's movement.

Flo Kennedy gave us some cold fried chicken and we gnawed away as she continued: "Once McGovern had a clear path to the nomination, everyone pounced on him and did a piranha bit. They tore off his flesh. The bones were just about to go when he lost the California delegates—then they could tolerate him again. But only just . . . I'm telling students to work for McGovern; they've got nothing else to do between jerking off and going to the laundromat. Not that he's great. But we gotta get rid of Nixon. You see, we never really recovered from the victory of getting Johnson out. So we weren't angry enough at Nixon. And we get a function-lock on our ass when we get what you call success. Then we go into a catatonic seizure for three or four years."

The analysts and the delegates and the press and the very young drifted away from Miami Beach, still arguing that *something* had happened, or that little had, that the "difference from Chicago" was highly significant or unimportant. He's not a radical: older liberals told each other happily, while some of the young shared that revelation—glumly. There were those who said that they'd "give the system one last chance," others who talked of regrouping for '76, some who felt wiped out and said they might not vote, and a few optimists. Most agreed that the disregard for working people was probably disasterous. But there were almost some flights to magic: did merely criticizing McGovern cast a bad spell, ensuring Nixon's re-election? Many seemed quite superstitious, but few seemed really sure of their own feelings.

Hindsight: The local astrologers had been pessimistic all along: well before Miami Beach, they'd warned that the eclipse of the sun on the first night of the Democratic Convention was going to be destructive to McGovern. After the Eagleton uproar was under-way, people kept speaking of "accidents" that would influence the presidential election: Wallace's paralysis, Chappaquiddick, Muskie's televised tears from New Hampshire, or Eagleton's reticence about his health. Perhaps some were trying to cheer themselves about bad luck. But, when McGovern delayed on dumping his running-mate, some of his former fans began to mention Adlai Stevenson's vacilla-tions. As Mary McGrory wrote, McGovern's keenest supporters did "not applaud his loyalty to a man who had duped him." And, as Mc-Govern himself admitted, the whole crisis obscured the issues of the war and the economy.

Others were disturbed afresh that McGovern still wanted that pinnacle of stability, Teddy Kennedy. Indeed, Eagleton's suppression of facts reminded some of Kennedy's first responses to Chappaquid-dick. We bleakly remembered that the Democrats' vice presidential candidate was supposed to show up the irrationalities of Agnew. Rep. Ronald Dellums of California said, "Senator Eagleton on the couch is a thousand times better for this country in these times than Vice President Agnew standing up." But Eagleton's murky record gave Nixon the opportunity to speak of Agnew as "a man of poise, calm, and judgment." When Barry Goldwater praised Eagleton and said that his medical history was not important, it showed what a gift he was to those opposing McGovern.

As many agreed, 1972 was not a year for charisma. Some voters seemed almost relieved by their own lack of interest in the person-alities of Nixon or McGovern. But, for a couple of weeks, Eagle-ton's was the dominant personality in the election year.

Toward the end of Eagleton's eighteen-day candidacy, there was a grim fascination in studying the man who almost seemed to per-sonify a Democratic death-wish. That desperate presence on TV, the head pitched slightly forward, the eyes sunk deeper and deeper into a forlorn and defiant face, his speech speeding up while he pantomimed phone calls with McGovern, holding an imaginary phone while gesturing with the other hand or tapping his temple with a rigid finger—all this did rouse some sympathy for his past depressions, along with a distrust of whatever he might say now or in the future. I was intrigued by his habit of referring to him-self in the third person: "What's a skeleton to Eagleton?"; ". . . you have to put yourself in Tom Eagleton's shoes. Imagine that you're Tom Eagleton . . ."; "This is definitely not my last press conference and Tom Eagleton is going to be around for a long, long time." Some of us will long remember him signing his letter of resignation with several pens—as presidents do when they sign certain bills. He gave the pens to his staff as souvenirs of his candidacy.

Perhaps the most absorbing detail was his response to Frank Mankiewicz's question: "Tom, do you have any old skeletons rat-tling around in your closet?" Eagleton's answer of "No" rested on his concept of a skeleton—which almost became a Rorshach test among some New York Democrats. ("What's a skeleton? Cheating in school?" "No, making it with your dog in front of your children." "Christ, that's much worse than a *skeleton*." "Maybe a sticky di-vorce?") To some, the image is a weak one, suggesting a cardboard figure for Hallowe'en, or a joke in a horror picture; medical draw-ings and cartoons have purged it of troubling associations. The closeted skeleton is even less concrete, and it sounds Victorian, like a "youthful indiscretion." But to Eagleton, "A skeleton is some-thing that's dirty, filthy, corrupt, illegal, sinister. There's nothing about having been fatigued and exhausted that I found sinister, dirty, or ugly." Few would disagree with the last sentence. But Eagleton's dishonesty showed that he truly feared to reveal his past. Also: "Skeletons are things where you have committed a crime or violated legal ethics or something sinister like that." As he continued to discuss his skeleton-hang-up—"I was not concealing anything. I was consciously hiding nothing—" it began to appear that McGovern's staff should have asked him about an albatross.

By the time that Sargent Shriver was secured, as McGovern's seventh choice for the candidacy, many Democrats were even more bewildered by McGovern than they had been in Miami Beach. Selecting a Kennedy stand-in with some cold war taint upon him, a man known as a clumsy administrator, married to an impassioned enemy of abortion, hardly smacked of the new politics. While the press referred to "Camelot"—an evocation that's been scarce of late—the pundits conveniently forgot that the Peace Corps was discredited among many of the young, who had come to see it as a form of imperialism, and that much of OEO had been a mishmash which had increased the mistrust of black communities. Also, McGovern's messy tactics for getting rid of Eagleton—such as instructing Jean Westwood, the party chairperson, to say on TV that Eagleton should resign, or making ambiguous remarks to the press, in hopes that Eagleton would get the message—decreased the confidence that McGovern could be straightforward. Thus, the "1000 percent" support of Eagleton made some Democrats very dubious about McGovern's pledges of support for other issues in the future.

THE REPUBLICANS
August 1972

The handwriting on the wall may be a forgery.
              —Ralph Hodgson

MAGNIFICENT COLESLAW: perhaps the best I've ever had. It's crisp, the vinegar rests lightly on the sour cream, the shreds of carrot are firm and fresh. At most conventions, there's no time for meals: you live on stand-up hot dogs and pockets full of chocolate, and—if you're in Miami Beach—quarts of Kool-Aid mixed in a garbage can in Flamingo Park. But during the early sessions of the Republican convention, there were opportunities to sit down at Wolfie's 24-hour delicatessen restaurant for platters of fine tunafish and salmon. However, the convention wasn't boring, as some observers claimed. In fact, it was an education for anyone who wasn't voting for Nixon. And there were many lessons for students of recent history—especially about the pliability of history.

I heard more references to John Kennedy at this convention than I had among the Democrats. Apparently, JFK (who had been brotherless—no one mentioned Bobby or Ted) was a Republican, and had embodied the traditions of the GOP. His "spirit" was cordially evoked, and it was evident that Nixon's molders hoped that some voters' nostalgia for Kennedy might turn into affection for Nixon. One of the films of Nixon showed the President walking by the waves on a beach in a shot which almost parodied those of JFK ten years ago. However, Nixon was dressed for the office and had his shoes on—black Oxfords that shone in the sand.

Of course we now know that the difference between Nixon and Kennedy was slender. Yet it was startling to hear Goldwater quoting "Ask not what your country can do for you, ask what you can do for your country" on the first night. I remembered that a middle-class black community organizer had said to me a few years ago, "Did you realize, that was a totalitarian statement!" The sentence has since been called "Stalinoid" by some young radicals: "Man, that's the *old* party line. Strictly *old* Moscow." So it was intriguing to hear it springing from the lips of Goldwater, the demon conservative of the early Sixties (who now seems rather moderate), who was featured to reassure the Republicans who think that Nixon is too liberal. (Later, at two different caucuses, I heard the "Ask not" line directly attributed to Nixon; soon, it may appear embroidered on GOP samplers.) Naturally, much of the Kennedy-clutching was intended to make bruised Democrats feels welcome. A feast of sympathy was offered to those whose party had been "seized" by McGovern. And some reporters felt rather wistful when the Republicans made McGovern sound like the radical he wasn't.

In an effort to make the President appear warm and accessible, as well as commanding, the convention movies showed Nixon being funny about Duke Ellington's birthday, strolling through a tomato field, "bringing order to the chaos he inherited," being bussed (not bused) by his wife, trying to lower the property tax—"He's always working, he thrives on work"—pronounced shy and sensitive by his daughters. All in all, "a man of vision born out of his own trials." He looked rigid throughout. A rather frightening zoom-shot of his mother suggested that the tension might be hereditary. But the film-maker (David Wolper) was determined to make him seem lovable—a project which had earlier been abandoned by some of his staff.

During the convention, it was especially instructive to study the treatment of particular groups which were thought to be partial to the Democrats. One black caucus, sponsored by the Committee to Re-Elect the President, was visited by Julie Nixon Eisenhower, who was introduced as "our friend." She began, "I am one of a small band—but a growing band—who believe that the government will do more for black folks." She explained that the White House had done its best for "the black man in this country," but that busing "would never include all the children we needed to reach." However, "the Nixon administration really cares about your children," and will "put more money in schools." A man behind me said, "Why, she's gonna give us two million peanuts! Like feedin' the monkeys." Later, a young alternate delegate wrote in the Miami *Herald* that she had made the very same speech to a Spanish delegate caucus.

Indeed, I heard scant enthusiasm for Nixon or the Republican party at this gathering, where most were middle-aged but many called each other "brother." A Miami delegate announced that the Republicans in Dade County had spent "lots of dollars" on attracting Cuban votes, but none on black voters. While it was repeated that Nixon had done little for black Americans, there was lavish disgust with the Democrats, who were mainly evoked as Wallaceites or the false-promisers of Lyndon Johnson's administration, especially those in OEO. Also, it was stressed that "We are tired of federal money going through Democrats"—specifically, white mayors. There was a great deal of bitterness against the Democrats in Congress, who were considered reluctant to pass appropriations bills which would aid black people. While tensions rose within the caucus—seemingly, less from disagreement than from a general nervousness about the future —Floyd McKissick was the only one I heard use the word "racist." (He said that they must watch for "racist flaws" in the wording of official documents.) McKissick, once of CORE, had received a pledge of fourteen million dollars for his Soul City in North Carolina, but he said that his support of Nixon had no connection with that grant. Another man said, "The Republicans don't care. But I don't want to knock the brothers who are part of the administration—I think they've done a helluva job considering the circumstances."

An elderly man sprang to his feet: *"Why are we here?* I'm *sick* of white reporters calling me Uncle Tom because I'm here. Things are still bad for blacks despite all the work. We're *here* to get some power for black people . . ." Someone else replied, "We're not being candid. We can't get much from the administration until we deliver the votes to them." Throughout, "Representation in *both* parties" was a recurrent phrase. The only reference to black militants that I heard came later, from a black woman from Michigan: *"They* don't represent the poor. Look at Bobby Seale's $650-a-month penthouse." (It seemed irrelevant to say that the penthouse was Huey Newton's.) Among the black Republicans I met, one rather quiet groundnote did emerge: that at least Nixon didn't *promise* anything; hence some respect him more than those Democrats who had guaranteed wall-to-wall advancement for many black people.

Later, I heard one (very light-skinned) black for George Wallace expounding for a radio station. He was asked, "What message do you have for do-gooder whites?" He replied, "The only ones who want to integrate are teachers and sociologists and preachers. *They* ain't got a nickel. The ones I want to integrate with is DuPont."

Some five hundred Vietnam veterans for Nixon were promised, but only about fifty showed up. They denounced amnesty as though McGovern had already granted it to every deserter, suggested that the antiwar vets had never been in the military at all, and referred to those who had "died" in Vietnam—as though they hadn't been killed.

Women were told that they were going to "come of age through the Republican party"—which did sound rather like aging. At the "Women of Achievement Brunch," featuring a low cholesterol lunch with margarine and yeast by Fleischmann, and a slide-show plus living models of such achievers as Dolly Madison, Amelia Bloomer, Mamie Eisenhower and Clare Booth Luce, we heard that "Martha Washington was no Women's Libber." The narration, by Altivose Davis (wife of Sammy), Pat Boone ("who represents the qualities we admire most in this country"), and Sammy Davis, Jr., included "all men and women were created equal." Boone racily replied, "But that was before Raquel Welch."

It was said that "the sewing machine and the typewriter gave women their freedom." Soon, the earliest feminists "were dabbling in civil disobedience" (refusing to pay taxes because they had no vote). Sammy Davis said that women "like the political kitchen as well as the real one." He also confessed that "the first thing about being a Republican is stepping in when you're needed." (Davis was later extolled by Nixon, who said, "We both came from rather poor families, we both have done rather well." Davis spent much of the convention denying that he had insisted that the Republicans provide him with a $4000 privately chartered jet-ride to Miami, as some Nixon staffers had complained.) At the end of the brunch, co-chairperson Anne Armstrong told Davis, "We're awfully glad that your ancestors decided to leave that old country"—meaning that she was grateful that blacks had chosen to come from Africa so that their descendants could enrich our culture.

While many women at the Democratic convention had left depressed, feeling that they had been put down by their party, the most serious of the Republican women seemed very pleased to have been allowed to participate in their own convention. They had pushed through a strong child-care program for the party's platform, although there was a "loophole" sentence which worried a few: "We oppose ill-considered proposals, incapable of being administered effectively, which would heavily engage the federal government in this area." (In December '71, Nixon had vetoed the child-care development bill on the grounds that it was too expensive, administratively impractical, and threatening to the family unit.)

At a woman's caucus I realized that environment and consumerism were considered the safest subjects for women. We learned that there was a controversy about a Senate bill on "zero discharge of pollutants." A male speaker said, "We're opposing that. Some say that the administration's bill is weaker. But it's impossible to have *no* pollutants. Why set that kind of standard when everyone knows it can't be achieved? This is a problem in America today: the *other party* has made impossible promises. Republicans must tell people not only what the government will do—but what it *can't* do." Again, I appreciated the intelligence of a tactic which had drawn some to the GOP and helped to define their anger against the Democrats.

Details on clean water, "fossil fuel," the removal of sulphur oxide, and the urgency of buying low lead gasoline (which sounded like an ad for Lead-Free Amoco), made many droop with boredom. (Afterwards, one woman murmured, "Why should our issues be so dull?") Then we swung into packaging: "We *must* buy returnable bottles." Also, it's time for citizens to rebel: a woman launched into a saga about Philadelphia Cream Cheese, which used to be simply wrapped in silver foil. Now, it has a box around it. "But we can protest! Against that box." Everyone was urged to start a recycling center in her community. A discreet discussion of child-care was interrupted by Betty Friedan, who spoke for abortion. Flurries of alarm rippled through the room. Natalie Moorman, a black physicist, gestured at Friedan: "This lady and I are both *past the point* where this is a pressing issue for us!" The questions of reproduction were hastily shelved, and many applauded when Friedan was made to stop speaking. A small group joined her in the hall to discuss abortion, and soon drugs were denounced, mainly in terms of how much they cost the country. However, it was said that drug addiction has decreased under the Republicans. But no form of drugs should be legalized, and "heroin is different from Methadone."

For the women's lunches and meetings, I wore a linen office dress from 1966; it shields the knees. Most of the women I met were both shy and friendly; few seemed accustomed to talking to groups of strangers of their own sex, and the conversations tended to range from diets to sunburn. A number asked me the same question: did I get my credentials due to being a delegate's wife? It was another lesson: I've rarely been in those realms where a woman would not be expected to function on her own. "Womanpower" (a recurrent phrase) clearly meant influencing your husband.

The Republicans' efforts to manipulate the young betrayed a certain contempt. Throughout, it was assumed that fledglings are always guided by their elders; Goldwater said that even the young who have "a distorted view of America" have been steered wrong by adults— they would never come to such ideas on their own. Later, the demonstrators who hassled delegates were repeatedly called, "those McGovern protesters outside." It was reasoned that they were *for* McGovern, rather than against Nixon or the war.

Some of the young Republican delegates I talked to firmly supported abortion and the legalization of marijuana. But the Young

Voters for the President with their "ELEPHANTS LIKE LETTUCE" buttons, were something else. Like their seniors, they assumed that everyone in Flamingo Park was part of one vast network: they saw no distinctions between the Vietnam vets, the Jesus people, SDS, the visiting American Nazis, YIP, the feminists, the gay activists, or the Zippies. Of the antiwar demonstrators, a YVP said, "Oooo, I could just kill them. Just let me punch their face." She and her friends then excitedly discussed the question of whether Pat Boone had *really* said that if the Communists took over America, he would shoot all five of his daughters. (He did make that statement, at a Goldwater rally in the Hollywood Bowl.)

Nixon's buttery tributes to the young—"you have inspired us with your enthusiasm, with your intelligence, with your dedication"—were all the funnier because we knew that the YVPs' "spontaneous demonstration" had been programmed and directed with a paramilitary precision. Their supervisors had insisted for days that their frenzied outbursts were fired only by their passion for Nixon and his views. Therefore, many spectators were amused when the Nixon staff unintentionally distributed some copies of the extremely detailed YVP script to several news outlets, including the BBC; CBS promptly put it on the screen.

I was on the floor when Nixon was renominated. A screeching conga-line of YVPs, bearing long olive green garbage bags filled with inflated balloons—air within air—thundered down the aisles. The balloons burst like gunshots, sticks from wildly thrashing flags imperiled one's eyes, people jumped on your feet, you couldn't budge, the elbows jammed against your ribs weren't yours. *"Four* more *years!* Four MORE years!" In that suffocation, the crushed crowd began to run in place, jerking their knees up and down. It was my idea of an urban riot: people trapped and screaming, frantic to breathe or move. Meanwhile, older delegates smiled indulgently at the ecstasies of the young. As the howls subsided, a YVP laid his hand on the floor-pass over my wishbone: "It says 'Press.' Can I press now?"

Reeling off the floor, I remembered that these teen-agers weren't born until after the Checkers speech, that they were seven or six or less in 1960, that they knew only the newest of Nixons. (They shrieked, "Hey, hey, whaddaya say, Nixon, Nixon, all the way!", having probably been too young or too sheltered in '67 or '68 to have heard the identical rhythm and phrasing of "Hey, hey, LBJ, How many kids did you kill today?") The extreme tightness with which they'd been disciplined during the convention may also have prompted their violence when they were told to bust loose.

None of the Republican blacks or women I met acknowledged that perhaps they were showcase tokens for the Nixon administration. But that did occur to some of the very young. Later, some YVPs said that they had been excluded from most of the functions which they'd expected to attend, had been kept in isolation, were "herded around like cattle," pressured to buy souvenirs, such as expensive gold cuff links engraved with Nixon's face, and merely used as stage props. "It was a . . . bummer," said a YVP from Ohio, rather as though the word was new to her. "When I get home, I'm not working for Nixon, and neither is my friend Debbie." Would she still vote? "Ummmm—probably."

☐

"You don't want to use those ice cubes—they're old," the bellboy told me. I thought of haunted ice cubes, or old ones—whose had they been? Frozen for what purpose . . . I thanked him, but used them anyway. He was fairly old himself.

In Miami Beach, I stayed in cheap hotels with cigarette burns on bedspreads, purple TV (the color so stricken that all politicians looked very ill), faucets that screamed thinly when you touched them, a few sluggish roaches. In this neighborhood, you could have your blood pressure taken for $1 at Woolworth's. "Pullmanettes" are advertised outside some retirement homes—they sound even smaller than the efficiencies. Is a Pullmanette a shelf for the body to lie on? Tired electric fans hardly cut the sweat in these realms. Hence the shock of the frosty plunge into the huge, chandeliered uptown hotels, where the bands played rumbas, and a few couples did the Lindy Hop. Some lined up to buy ballpoint pens in the shape of Nixon. The rich weren't much in evidence—I felt that they had been shooed away to their yachts or parties in villas, since this was meant to be the year for mid-America.

Within that setting, certain phrases and concepts reappeared rather punctually: "Better Americans," who were often evoked but never defined—except that they were better than those who burned their draft cards; "bricks and mortar" (what we need more of); and—to my mild surprise—"self-defense." I heard one alternate delegate argue that "If you had gun control laws, then only the criminals would have guns." (The platform did agree to "safeguard the right of responsible citizens to collect, own, and use firearms for legitimate purposes, including hunting, target shooting, and self-defense." Citing the national murder rate, the *New York Times* called the statement "shameful.") It was steadily said "other countries" want Nixon re-elected, also that the Democrats have become isolationists. I heard that McGovern was "very unstable" and that he has "a terrible temper." Those who had favored abortion were sometimes rather innocently called "abortionists"—as though they performed the operation itself. There were a lot of awkward jokes—"A good speech is like a bikini: brief, provocative, and revealing"—but the mood was certainly confident and expansive: people agreed that the last four years were "something to be proud of," a fine time for us all. Thus, it was odd to recall that Nixon had been called a possible "one-term President" in 1970, when some even thought that he might not choose to run again.

After a certain amount of folk wisdom, it was a relief to head for Flamingo Park. But much of what occurred there during this convention was rather sad. Some different groups got on very badly, while brain-frying heat and fatigue heightened the mutual hostilities. Quite a few had to be restrained from throwing punches at the Jesus people. (The latter made a stunned audience for the Hare Krishna dancers: they gaped at the orange whirlers as though they'd never seen them before.) The gay men and the feminists were needled and sometimes attacked by visiting local thugs. Tom Forcade and a larger band of Zippies than had been at the Democratic convention drowned out other speakers with their rock band. Forcade seemed loathed by almost every group, and some—including the Vietnam vets —said that he had physically threatened them. He earned quite a few comparisons to Charles Manson.

Medics told me that there were a lot of bad downers and speed on hand, also some heroin; they were constantly called to cope with sufferers. (They said they'd had no similar cases during the last convention.) Rocky Pomerance, the benign Police Chief of Miami Beach, had told the campers that they must police themselves. And so they tried: everyone dealing "death drugs" or "harassing" others was meant to be ejected from the park. The approved technique was to surround the culprit and walk—so that he was simply walked out of the park. I saw that well-done several times, especially by the vets. But, as they themselves said, they hadn't come to Miami Beach to be cops, and they didn't relish the role. Moreover, they had to fight hard to expel some twenty "Nazis" who invaded the park, made anti-Semitic remarks, and seized the platform. The vets also turned a man over to the police and destroyed the wrist-rockets and two fused Molotov cocktails which they said they had found on him. As far as the general public was concerned, the vets' silent marches—led by three crippled men in wheelchairs—and also their sober speeches, were obscured by the street games of the Zippies.

There were meetings every morning so that different groups could work out some means of coexistence on "the land," as the park was called, or create their own laws. But these debates often became battles about the use of the communal sound system. (Eventually, rock music was vetoed.) Meanwhile, dealers kept returning and the women were pawed so often that they put up a fence around their tent. Unhappily, that just seemed to provoke more attacks—it was tempting to those outside it, rather like the rope around the Pentagon in '67. But I also heard some rather touching male consciousness raising going on just outside the women's fence: "Would you like to get up on a stage in just a jockstrap?" "Christ, no."

Tripping over tent pegs in the darkness of early night, exploring the picture exhibits of maimed Vietnamese children and charred flesh, or xeroxes of "Ripped Off FBI Files," listening to wistful voices: "We must show Richard Nixon that the movement is stronger than ever," watching an incredibly thin boy dancing alone, fluid despite a bandaged rib cage, reading the hand-outs—a Jesus paper which praised Governor Reuben Askew as "a heavy brother on the Lord," but regretted that Julian Bond had said that he wasn't "very big on Christ or Christianity personally," or a recipe for steamed placenta, to be sautéed with onion and served with crackers, or warning information on ingredients used in some ice creams, such as pipernal, a chemical used to kill lice—declining to buy a sweatshirt stencilled, "Bernardine Is Hiding In Our Hearts," hearing a speaker say, "We're ready now! All we need is the projector and the slides and some electricity," glancing at placards for PIMP (People's Independent Military Party) while angry voices rose when a gay man was accused of grabbing a woman's breasts, and a singer taught others a new up-lift song to the tune of the Coke ads: "I'd like to see/The vic-tor-ee/ Of every people's war . . . It's the re-heel thing, re-vo-lu-hu-shon," and others spoke kindly of "Crazy Tom" (Eagleton), and the tiny communist cadre from Tampa closed their tent to a couple of squealing Zippies, I watched recurring lightning flashes without thunder. It suited this atmosphere of dry heaves.

All the tension that mounts before a major demonstration . . . Some discussed conspiracies: the CIA had John Kennedy assassinated because he was definitely going to pull out of Vietnam; the CIA was distributing the pills (especially Quaaludes) which had flooded the park, so that the protesters would be "all tranked up" and wouldn't want to march. Peering up at the night sky, someone said: "Stars that move—they must be helicopters." They were. And the dry heaves rolled through the park again: was Nixon plotting a violent final night, would he want to show his strength by the numbers of cracked heads? In contrast to '68 and '69, I heard no one saying that Nixon's presidency was a fine thing; he's no longer considered a tool for revolution, as he was a few years ago.

A young woman said to me, "There are lots of people here who aren't political, and it's troubling." Quite a few Miami teen-agers had simply come to the park in search of dope. But most of the others I met were also under twenty-one. For many, this was the very first form of protest; perhaps it would be their only one. Movement people from the Sixties and the early Seventies were conspicuously absent. Public figures like Rennie Davis and Bobby Seale made scheduled speeches at rallies, but you didn't see them mingling with the very young. (At the Democratic convention, a speaker had asked for Davis and David Dellinger to come to the platform and identify themselves. Few of these new troops knew the movement veterans by sight.) But without a number of the steady dissenters from the past, the beginners could have no sense of continuity, no indication that opposing the policies of the government was a long-term project. (There were old FREE ANGELA posters—but Angela was already free.) One 17-year-old told me, "I have no history to bounce this off of." He added, "I don't know anything about '68." He was against the war, he thought that racism was expanding. But he felt that the park was fairly isolated from these issues—he doubted that he was "doing anything" by being there. Since the movement has always insisted that it's leaderless, the field was left to Tom Forcade.

Almost no political education took place in Flamingo Park during the Republican convention. Some fine speeches given by three Vietnamese students—who referred in detail to Vietnamese politics, the Thieu regime, and also American strategy—puzzled much of this crowd. The listeners seemed especially bewildered when one speaker suggested that demonstrators should cease to display the NLF flag, which "belongs to the Vietnamese and shouldn't be used here by those who make it an object of hate to the American people." The audience chanted "Ho-ho-ho" at certain moments, and raised their fists, but some clapped when Forcade complained over the mike that these talks by the Vietnamese had delayed the performance of a rock opera.

□

"Did you hear? That bastard has ended the ground war": thus, I first learned from a friend on August 12th that the combat troops were departing from Vietnam. But it seemed to have little impact as an election strategy. The *Daily News'* big headline that night was "CLERK CHARGED IN 1M-PLUS GYP/Banker, Clergy Are Pigeons"; below, there was a much smaller heading: "The Field Is Theirs—Not Ours." The next morning, the *Times's* lead editorial was "Vietnam Mirage," and it emphasized that "aerial firepower" would continue.

Meanwhile, memories came in little gusts: Walter Lippmann recommending "A Vote For Nixon" in his column in '68, hoping that Nixon would end the war in his first term. (However, Lippmann's main reason for backing this candidate was that "the country may demand and necessity may dictate the repression of uncontrollable violence." Humphrey would hate to face this. Therefore, "It is better that Nixon should have the full authority if the repression should become necessary in order to restore peace and tranquility in the land.") Since Nixon's visits to China and Russia, I've been asked to admire his foreign policy "if you'll just overlook Vietnam." If you mentioned backing Pakistan's dictatorship against India, you were told, "That was a *mistake*," also that "people here don't care about those countries."

In '72 when we read about the methodical destruction of Quang Tri, it seemed a long time since we'd heard about "winning back the hearts and minds of the Vietnamese people." The President had sought to end the antiwar movement more systematically than he had tried to end the war. (Yet if he had achieved peace in '72, some would have credited McGovern's candidacy for pressuring him into it.) But in Miami Beach in August, the war was hardly allowed into the Convention Hall. When Nixon said, "And we shall never stain the honor of the United States of America," it sounded rather as though he was hoarding a piece of Kotex. Senator Edward Brooke of Massachusetts, a keynote speaker who had authored the last antiwar resolution to pass the Senate, skidded over it all rather tastefully: "Vietnam—well, we all have our differences . . ."

During the convention, there was a variety of interesting reversals, such as Agnew condemning those who "fasten group labels on people, and in the process . . . turn American against American . . ." He deplored "the practice of pitting the most publicized minorities against the least publicized minorities," a tactic which "will most assuredly push America backwards . . ." And the platform mourned that "the isolation of the People's Republic of China . . . went endlessly on" until Nixon's trip—as though he and his party had not upheld that isolation, had not even opposed negotiation with China.

As we skated around between the decades, I realized that an old Fifties phenomenon was surfacing: speakers were strumming on the idea of individuality in the midst of conformity. (Those two words used to go together.) Every five or ten years, we're reminded that individualism is the property of conservatives, as was revealed when Goldwater tried to swing—when he said that the young wanted "to do their thing," and praised them for their sense of personal freedom —and later, at a Jewish seminar, when an ex-Democrat said, "Nixon stands for achievement. So do we . . . And the highest form of Mitzvah is to help a man to become independent and self-sufficient, to be an individual. That's why very orthodox people are drawn to the Republicans." Throughout, liberty was fiercely protected by the GOP—especially against the tyrannous socialism of McGovern.

□

The demonstrators' "Street Without Joy" (named for Highway One in Vietnam) brought Nixon's coffin, a baby elephant, coolie hats, hands and faces dripping with red paint, and many white-masked women dressed like peasants, with dead-baby bundles in their arms, to the Convention Hall. A few spectators gasped at the starkness of that silent throng. But when the guerrilla theater began —as about a hundred acted out the death of Vietnamese peasants, screaming and falling down while papier-mâché bombers were rushed over their heads, and smoke bombs exploded—much of the audience began to chuckle, as did the large Cuban family who invited me to watch from their porch. Few of the delegates saw the show, since the marchers had been given the street, and those entering the Hall were rerouted. As the Cubans laughed and the kids playing peasants wailed, I realized that guerrilla theater probably moves only those who already agree with what it states—unless it's very, very good. (Or funny: like the Diggers throwing money on the floor of the New York Stock Exchange in '67. Perhaps comedy is mainly what succeeds.) My Cuban hosts nudged me as a mock B-52 bomber and the coffin were set on fire and flung over the fence surrounding the Hall, where they sizzled quietly in a light rain.

On that night, and on the one that followed—when my local horoscope read, "Pay attention to the young today. They will surprise you!"—the tactical script drawn up by the Miami Conventions Coalition was abruptly abandoned. The script—which had been shared weeks in advance with the police—called for "militant non-violence," pledged "non-disruption of the senior citizens' community," and warned against "attacking or provoking" police, the National Guard, or GIs. In a speech on the night before, Rennie Davis revived the old righteous style of the late Sixties: "We will seal off this convention with a people's quarantine . . . We'll resist, they'll have to drag us into the paddy wagons tomorrow . . ." Also, "we won't trash small businessmen, but the Lincoln Mall shops can be regarded as symbols of this convention or the administration." However, "We won't be violent with individual delegates."

But SDS and the Zippies had refused all along to cooperate with the MCC (which had served as an umbrella group for most of the organizations that were there). SDS said that it was all right to "trash imperialists." Thus, no scenario could have worked on the final night, especially since so many in the park had already clashed with one another, and also because a number of unaffiliated outsiders were on hand. No movement spokesman had any authority to tell others what to do—or not to do. Moreover, the Hall was finally barricaded with derelict buses, which prevented the mass sit-ins leading to arrests which so many had planned on. So some freaked out in the streets, while a small group of vets picked up the benches which others had overturned, and the Miami Beach police—who had been very restrained, on Rocky Pomerance's orders —grew rougher.

Until the last day and a half, the cops had frustrated some by their reluctance to make arrests—in fact, the police were practicing peaceful resistance. A few had even wheeled the crippled vets up the steps of the Fontainebleau Hotel for an antiwar protest. I saw one arrest (for "impeding traffic") of five young men which might have been choreographed by Balanchine. One pair of handcuffs called out, "Our enemies are not the police, the enemy is Nixon," and pronounced his arrest "orderly." As I talked with those in the paddy wagon, a state trooper shoved me back: "Look out, they'll spit on you!" "No, they won't." "They *will*." He glowered at the spitless young men. Shouts of farewell from the wagon: "Goodbye, take it easy!" Elsewhere, I saw some state highway patrolmen throttling demonstrators with sticks held across their throats; Pomerance's instructions were forgotten by some as the night deepened. Later, we heard that three marchers had been run down by vehicles on separate occasions. Some random cars and buses were damaged, and there were brisk bouts of tire-slashing and trashing.

As gas billowed down the avenue, and cries rose from blocks away, two Nixonettes reproached a black press photographer for dropping his popsicle wrapper on the ground: "Ooo, you just littered." "Murderers! *Murderers!*" the crowd yelled at delegates, who shouted back, "Nixon *now!*" I went into the Hall to hear the "Salute to Working Youth." A young man was saying that "youth" would be misrepresented if "people like us weren't heard from." A young woman spoke after him: "President Nixon has listened and understood the speech of the people . . . we young people." Outside once more, I was in time to see a sun-shelter burst into flames on the nearby golf course. The shelter had a thatched roof, and some exultant photographers exclaimed that it looked like Vietnam: "A beautiful shot!" Huge vans crammed with those who'd been arrested emitted muffled cries: "Power to the people!" The police then set off more gas than might be needed to subdue half of Cuba, and I dashed inside to hear Agnew. He seemed to be talking about "justice in the raw"—did gas effect one's ears? (It was actually "justice under law," unlike the lawless justice that we're used to.) A delegate jabbered, "My eyes are burning, those kids are crazy, the gas is their fault, they threw potatoes with razor blades in them, they threw decayed meat with soup-bones in it!" I doubted the deadly potatoes; a young woman reporter laughed. He said indignantly, "Listen, soup-bones hurt."

This time, the whole world wasn't watching—little news from the street was shown on TV. The actions, which had been intended to delay this session of the convention and to knock Nixon off prime time, had postponed the whole program by exactly seven minutes. In the press lounge, I saw Jerry Rubin looking bashful—moments earlier, a Southern delegate had inaccurately denounced him on the screen for "leading everything" in Miami Beach. But he and Hoffman were almost invisible at this convention.

All in all, the protests merely involved the participants—not the delegates who observed them, whose minds were hardly changed by what they saw. It was all too far removed from the war, and no political point was made. In Chicago, so many had been outraged by Mayor Daley and his troops, but the mayor of Miami Beach and his police chief had truly tried to save heads. So the delegates recoiled in horror from the demonstrators—just as we had responded in '68 to the Chicago police. (A young man said rather wistfully to me, "LBJ was such a good enemy. But Nixon doesn't *personify* his own policies, the way Johnson did. Somehow, it's harder to hold Nixon responsible for what he does.") And in '68, the issues had been out front. But, in Miami Beach, many were too inexperienced to know how to make a statement about the country or the war.

However, those days among the Republicans taught some of us more about the mood of '72 than infinite skirmishes in the streets. Throughout that whole shower of joy—the celebration of a happy and healthy America—one marvelled at the ability of many people to screen out or deny the facts that litter the sidewalk or hang from the walls of anybody's home. Most of those present truly seemed to believe what Nixon and the Republicans told them: "your dollar buys more," crime is dwindling, peace is nearly sewed up in Vietnam, women are more equal than ever. The platform stated, "We have brought about a rapid rise in both employment and in real income." (But the unemployment rate, which was 3.2 percent in '69, had risen steadily; it was just under 6 percent before the Convention of '72.) Inflation—which wasn't really a part of the last few years —is also receding into history. (The next morning, the layout of the *New York Times*'s front page made a deadpan reply: right beneath NIXON IS RENOMINATED . . . the headline read,

> "Prices Rise 0.4%
> Increase Biggest
> In Last 5 Months.") Goldwater announced

that we have "come closer to solving the problem of poverty than any nation in the history of the world." (There were cheers for that.) He also said that "we have a free press"—while some of us fingered our credentials, which read LIMITED ACCESS, perhaps the surliest welcome we've had in years. (For the Democrats, our tags simply said MEDIA.)

We're all accustomed to politicians' guff, and to audiences of any faith which enjoy being deceived. But, coming from a realm of skeptics, I was rather staggered to learn that those I met at lunches and caucuses really accepted what they'd heard. It was clear that the Republicans had persuaded many to ignore or mistrust their own experience. You can look in your wallet, or check out the price of spinach, or discover that the muggings have accelerated on your block—and then you're asked to erase the evidence of daily life: as though it came from outer space, or belonged to science fiction. Coming on the heels of the Johnson administration, these tactics are bold ones—when you remember a theme from the late Sixties: that the public could no longer stand being lied to, that "credibility" was dead, that few seemed able to trust politicians of either party . . .

Another device conspicuous in this campaign was giving people false alternatives, such as insisting that there has to be a choice between good education and busing. Some of the other distortions rely on non-sequiturs. A letter sent to voters from the Finance Committee to Re-Elect the President, signed by Maurice Stans, asked, "Do you agree with the Democrats that inflation (caused by uncontrolled government spending) is a good thing . . . or do you favor President Nixon's drive for a return to law and order?" (The dots are his. There you can see the hook-up between inflation and crime.) Other mistruths depend on subtle implications: for example, some "special Americans" (read blacks) have been rather pampered; now, their privileges must be extended to "all Americans."

Indeed, Nixon has deeply flummoxed his followers by mingling liberal and right-wing policies until people no longer know what he really represents. (At other moments, he masks reactionary ideas in progressive language.) Lowering the voting age of course pleased liberals of both parties; promising to make the Supreme Court even more conservative satisfied their opponents. But what of the rather moderate Republicans whom I met in Miami Beach—who seemed fairly dazed as well as seduced by what they were told? Peter Schrag, who wrote *The Decline of the Wasp*, remarked that Nixon had "liberated them from their principles." And one certainly felt that in the air. In the past, many had been hardline anti-Communists, like Nixon himself; their ideas of right and wrong were as sharply defined as the President's when, in 1970, he praised Westerns like John Wayne's because "the good guys come out ahead in the Westerns, and the bad ones lose." Since his visits to China and Russia —which were applauded rather cautiously when convention speakers mentioned them—many long-time Republicans no longer seem to know what they believe, or what to believe. Hence, I think, the malleability, the uncertainty about what is actually going on around them.

After hearing the negotiations with Peking and Moscow repeatedly hailed, many swallowed their lifelong convictions. They may also have been confused when Nixon evoked Roosevelt, Truman, Kennedy and Johnson as beacons of foreign policy. And they had good reason to be perplexed about some of his other positions. In 1969, it appeared that the President sanctioned some form of guaranteed annual income for the poor—an idea that was hard for many Republicans to accept. Later, this was translated into the Family Assistance Plan, which turned out to be far from liberal. In '72, the platform gave some muted support to Nixon's "welfare reform" plan, but stated, "We flatly oppose programs or policies which embrace the principle of a government-guaranteed income" —which was still supposed to be the aim of Nixon's plan. Thus, his most loyal constituents continued to struggle with the switches that he had pulled on them—all couched in extremely moral terms. Many of us who were grateful for the beginnings of diplomatic contact with China and Russia still thought it premature to regard these prefaces as complete chapters. But loyal Republicans might later be told that the communists had regained their evil, or that they were not worthy of our trust.

CS gas combined with Mace makes some people vomit. And, as the delegates came hawking and retching into the Hall, many had been frightened by the demonstrators, demoralized by the pain in their own throats. Yet, during the final session, what was happening in the streets was hardly acknowledged. Nixon and Agnew had campaigned on domestic "chaos" during the Congressional elections of 1970. In that fall—when campuses were quiet—Agnew had talked as though a nationwide bloodbath were underway. But at the Miami Beach convention, it was implied that the antiwar protests were part of the past, like the war itself, and both belonged to the Democrats who had ignited them. Inside the Hall, there were the realities of the Seventies, which culminated in a warmth-binge: Nixon shaking hands with a rapturous line-up, while the lights gleamed on Agnew's forehead. What went on outside was back in the Sixties: a suppressed memory of bad days that were over.